Martina Cole is the acknow
most recent novel, *The Life*,
and paperback and is one in
phenomenally successful no

Several of Martina's novels have been adapted for the screen, most recently *The Take* and *The Runaway* which were shown on Sky One to remarkable reviews. In addition, *Two Women* and *The Graft* have been adapted for the stage; both were highly acclaimed when performed at the Theatre Royal Stratford East, which also staged *Dangerous Lady* in 2012, celebrating twenty years since Martina's debut novel was published.

Martina Cole is a phenomenon. She continues to smash sales records with each of her books, which have sold in excess of eleven million copies in total. In 2011 Martina surpassed the £50 million sales mark since records began and was the first British female novelist for adult audiences to achieve this.

Martina's hard-hitting, uncompromising and haunting writing is in a genre all its own – no one writes like Martina. 2013 sees the publication of her twentieth novel, *Revenge* – read a special preview at the end of this book.

Praise for Martina Cole's bestsellers:

'A blinding good read' Ray Winstone

'All the favourite hallmarks – gritty dialogue, shocking violence and a gripping storyline' *Daily Express*

'The stuff of legend . . . It's vicious, nasty and utterly compelling' *Mirror*

'A gritty tale that will keep you hooked' *Sun*

'A rough, tough tale . . . Cole is one of the most popular novelists of our time' *Literary Review*

By Martina Cole and available from Headline

Dangerous Lady
The Ladykiller
Goodnight Lady
The Jump
The Runaway
Two Women
Broken
Faceless
Maura's Game
The Know
The Graft
The Take
Close
Faces
The Business
Hard Girls
The Family
The Faithless
The Life
Revenge

MARTINA COLE

DANGEROUS LADY

headline

First published in 1992
by HEADLINE BOOK PUBLISHING

First published in paperback in 1992
by HEADLINE BOOK PUBLISHING

This edition published in paperback in 2013
by HEADLINE PUBLISHING GROUP

1

Cataloguing in Publication Data is available from the British Library

ISBN 978 0 7553 7406 9

Typeset in Galliard by Avon DataSet Ltd,
Bidford-on-Avon, Warwickshire

Printed in the UK by CPI Group (UK) Ltd, Croydon, CR0 4YY

Headline's policy is to use papers that are natural, renewable and recyclable products and made from wood grown in sustainable forests. The logging and manufacturing processes are expected to conform to the environmental regulations of the country of origin.

HEADLINE PUBLISHING GROUP
An Hachette UK Company
338 Euston Road
London NW1 3BH

www.headline.co.uk
www.hachette.co.uk

To my parents

Book One

LONDON, NOTTING HILL

If possible honestly, if not,
somehow,
make money

– Horace, 65–8 BC

Am I my brother's keeper?

– Genesis, 4:9

Chapter One

1950

'You took your bloody time!'

Dr Martin O'Reilly stared down into the child's face and sighed.

'I had to see another patient. Now where's your ma?'

'In bed, of course.'

The little boy went back to sit on the stairs with his seven brothers. They ranged in age from three to fourteen. The doctor lit a cigar. He stood in the hallway puffing on it for a few seconds to make sure it was fully alight. The smell of the Ryans en masse was enough to turn the strongest of stomachs, though the slum stench was in his blood now, he reckoned. It permeated his clothes and skin. He started to pick his way up the stairs, careful not to tread on any little fingers. The children shuffled left and right on their bottoms to let him pass. He was also careful not to touch the wall. The smell he could combat with his cigar, but the roaches – he would never get used to them.

How the buggers ran up the walls he would never know. They defied gravity.

On the landing he pushed open the first bedroom door, and there in front of him was Sarah Ryan. She was lying on a large double bed, her belly huge and swollen. He smiled at her, his heart breaking. Sarah Ryan was thirty-four years old. Her faded blond hair was scraped back from her face into a bun, her skin was pale and dry. If her eyes had not been so bright and alert, she could have been mistaken for a corpse. He could remember coming to this house fifteen years earlier to deliver her first child. A fine-looking woman she had been then. Now her body was fat and scarred from constant childbearing, and her face wrinkled prematurely from habitual frowning.

'It's well on then?' His voice was gentle.

Sarah tried to hitch herself up in the bed. The old newspapers that had been placed underneath her crackled at the movement. 'Yeah. It's good of you to come, Martin. I told the little sods to get their dad, but as usual he ain't nowhere to be seen.'

She gripped her belly as another pain shot through her. 'Oh, it's dying to be born this one.' She smiled faintly. Then her eyes stretched wide as she saw the doctor take a syringe out of his bag.

'You ain't sticking that thing in me! We had all this out the last time. I ain't having any bloody injections. This is me thirteenth child and I never had one with any of them. Not even the stillborns. I ain't starting now.'

'Come on, Sarah. This will ease you.'

She put up her hand to stem his protests. 'I'm sorry but them things hurt like hell, whereas giving birth . . . it's nothing. Nothing . . .'

Martin put the needle on the small bedside table and,

sighing heavily, pulled back the blankets covering her legs. His expert hands felt around her sides and then he slipped two fingers inside her vagina. When he had finished he pulled the blankets back over her.

'I think this one's breech.'

Sarah shrugged.

'First one if it is. I ain't done so bad. Ben was saying the other day that soon they would drop out as I walked down to the shops!'

She laughed and the doctor laughed with her.

'That would do me out of a job. Now you relax for a minute, I won't be long. I want one of the boys to run an errand for me.' He left the room, shutting the door quietly behind him.

'She had it then?' This from eight-year-old Leslie who had let him in earlier.

'No, she hasn't had it yet. Be patient, you young bugger.'

The doctor turned to the eldest boy, Michael. At nearly fifteen he was already over six feet tall and towered over the little Irish doctor in front of him.

'Michael, go and get old Mother Jenkins. I'm going to need help with this one.'

The boy stared down at the doctor for a few seconds. 'Me muvver's gonna be all right, ain't she?' His voice was deep and concerned.

The doctor nodded. 'Of course.'

The boy still did not move.

'She's never had old Mother Jenkins before.'

The doctor stared up at the boy impatiently. 'Look, Michael, I can't stand around here all day talking to you. Your ma's bad, but if we can get this baby born she'll be all right. The sooner you get Mrs Jenkins the better. Time's short.'

Michael turned slowly away from the doctor and placing one hand on the banister and the other on the wall he slid down, jumping over the younger boys' heads. As he landed heavily on the linoleum, the doctor called to him: 'Tell her I'll be paying the ten shillings or she won't come.'

Michael waved to let the doctor know he had heard, then, opening the front door, he rushed out.

The doctor looked down on to the younger children's heads and his teeth clamped down even harder on his cigar. Michael's foray down the stairs had caused the cockroaches to fall from the walls. The youngest child, Benny, not only had them crawling in his clothes, but one adventurous roach was slowly making its way across his face. Martin watched the child flick it gently away and made a mental note to see the landlord about getting the house stoved. It would never get rid of the damned things permanently but at least it would give the Ryans a breathing space.

'Now then, I want a couple of you to go and find your father.' Geoffrey, Anthony and Leslie all stood up. The doctor pointed at them in turn. 'You, Geoffrey, try the Latimer Arms. You, Anthony, go up the Roundhouse. And you . . .'

Leslie nodded, his eyes fixed on the floor.

'. . . go to the Kensington Park Hotel. If you can't find him in any of those places then try the Bramley Arms. If by any chance you do find your da, tell him that he is needed at home. Can you all remember that?'

The three heads nodded and they went on their way. Martin went back into the bedroom with Sarah.

'Sure they're good boys you've got there.'

Her voice sounded sceptical. 'I don't know about that, Doctor. They're a bit wild at times. It's the old man. He takes the belt to them for nicking one minute, and then the next he's sending them out to do it. The poor little sods can't win.'

She doubled up as another pain hit her.

'Relax now, Sarah.' He pushed a few stray hairs from her face. It was getting dark so he pulled the curtains and put on the overhead light. He lit himself another cigar from the butt of the previous one. Then, with it firmly clamped between his teeth, he examined her again. When he had finished he had a worried look on his face. He visibly relaxed as he heard a voice in the hallway. A few seconds later Matilda Jenkins had pushed open the bedroom door. She stood at the end of Sarah's bed, all eighteen stone of her.

'All right, Doctor?' This was a form of address, not a question.

'All right, Sarah? The bloody stairs knacker me these days. But them boys!' She flapped her hand at Sarah. 'Talk about scatter them. One look at me coming up 'em and they run like mad!' Her deep booming laugh reverberated around the bedroom. The doctor was paying her the ten shillings, she could afford to be friendly.

'It's a big woman you are, Matilda, to be sure. Now get yourself back down the stairs and heat me up lots of water. I want to sterilise me things. This little fellow's breech.'

Matilda nodded her head vigorously.

'Righto, Doc. I'll send around the neighbours, get them to put their kettles on. We might even get a cuppa out of them!'

As she stamped from the room, Sarah glared at the doctor.

'What's she doing here? I ain't got ten shillings, and if I did have I'd give it to the kids. They ain't eaten since yesterday, and until that man of mine comes home, they won't eat at all! Knowing him, he's shacked up with some old sort somewhere and won't be home till the morning!'

She was near to tears.

'Calm down now, Sarah. I'm paying her.' He grasped one of her hands. 'Now be quiet, woman. I can't cope with this on me own. So you whisht now, and save your strength.'

Sarah lay back against the pillows, her face drenched with sweat. Her lips were cracked and dry. Turning awkwardly towards the bedside table, she picked up a glass of water and sipped the warm liquid gratefully. A little later Matilda brought up a bucket of steaming water. The doctor set about sterilising his things, including a large pair of scissors.

By nine in the evening Sarah was in great distress, as was the child within her. Twice the doctor had tried to push his arm inside her to turn the child and each time he had failed. He wiped his hands on a towel he had brought with him.

This child had to be born, and soon, or he would lose the pair of them. Blast Benjamin Ryan! It was always the same. He gave her a child every year, but was never there when it came into the world.

The little boys kept their vigil on the stairs. All were tired and hungry. Michael, waiting at the top, was silently cursing his father as he looked at his younger brothers' little faces. Benny was sucking the arm of his jumper.

Suddenly there was a loud banging on the front door. Six-year-old Garry answered it, only to be knocked flying as two policemen came crashing in. Michael took one look at them and, swearing under his breath, ran into his mother's bedroom. Cries could be heard from the stairs as the policemen tried to make their way up to the landing, the remaining boys making it as difficult as possible for them in the hope that their brother would get away.

Michael had opened the bedroom window and was half in and half out as the policemen burst into the room.

Then the lights went out.

'Who turned off the lights, you little bastards?'

'No one turned off the bleeding lights. The electric's gone.' Sarah's voice was faint. The policemen turned on their torches.

'Bring those over here. This woman is in danger of her life.' The urgency in the doctor's voice brought both men to the bed. The boy was long gone, they both knew that. Sarah was writhing in agony, tears on her cheeks.

'You lot want slaughtering. My boy ain't done nothing.'

Matilda Jenkins broke in, 'Look, has anyone got a shilling for the meter?'

'I have.' The smaller of the two policemen fished some change out of his pocket. Leaving his colleague to help the doctor, he walked from the room and carefully made his way down the stairs. Stepping through the children as gently as he could, he went to the cupboard under the stairs and, locating the meter, put a shilling in. He put in another, and turned off his torch as he stepped out of the cupboard. Seven pairs of eyes were looking at him with open hostility, even the youngest's who was not yet four. The man looked at the boys as if seeing them for the first time. At the heads close-cropped to combat the lice and the holey jumpers with elbows poking through. He stood for a while staring at them. He felt for the first time in his life what it must be like to be one of them and was overwhelmed with a feeling of sadness and futility. Taking out his wallet, he pulled out a ten-shilling note and offered it to Geoffrey, the second eldest.

'Get yourself over the Messer's and get some fish and chips.'

'We don't want old Bill's money!'

'Hark at the hard man! Well, clever clogs, your little brothers are starving, so go and do what I tell you.'

He pushed the money into Geoffrey's hands. All the boy's instincts told him to throw the money back at the policeman, their natural enemy, but his little brothers' faces changed his mind. They had not eaten for nearly two days. Sullenly, he pushed past the man, who held on to his arm.

'Tell that brother of yours that we'll catch him in the end so he might as well give himself up.'

Geoffrey pulled his arm roughly away. Then, looking at the man as if he was so much dirt, he let himself out of the front door. The constable walked back up the stairs, shaking his head.

In the bedroom, Sarah was fighting to get the child born. The other policeman was holding her down, while the doctor was cutting her down below. As he cut she gave an almighty push and ripped open to her behind. The child slipped into the world, still in its birth sac. The doctor punched this open and looked at the little blue face inside. He cleaned its nose and gently blew into its mouth while he pressed tenderly on its tiny ribcage. The baby coughed and gave a little cry. Then, taking a deep breath, began to bawl its head off. Quick as a flash the doctor had cut the cord, passed the child to Matilda Jenkins, and was stitching away at Sarah as if his own life depended on it.

She lay against the pillows, her whole body numb. She swore to herself that this was going to be the last child.

'Your first girl, Sarah.' Matilda's voice was kind.

She sat up in the bed, dumbstruck, her face aglow as if lit from the inside. She grinned, showing all her large yellowing teeth.

'You're joking! I thought it was another boy! A girl! It is really a girl?'

Even the policemen smiled at her. She was genuinely amazed.

'Oh, let me have her. Let me hold her! A daughter at last, thank Gawd!'

Matilda placed the child in her arms. The baby was now cleaned up and Sarah looked down into the bluest eyes she had ever seen.

'She's a beauty, Sarah.'

She stared down at her daughter in wonderment. This was her thirteenth child, but her first girl. All tiredness was forgotten as she gazed at her daughter. Then she looked around her at the other smiling faces, and remembered why the policemen were there. The elder of the two had been coming to the house for nigh on fifteen years. Ben had even been at it all through the war.

'What's my Mickey supposed to have done now?' Her voice was flat.

'He's been running for a bookie again, Sarah. I've warned him twice now. This time I'm going to nick him. So you tell him to come and see me.'

She looked back at her daughter. The doctor had finished, and, after removing the old newspapers from under Sarah, covered her up. She looked back at the policeman.

'I'll tell him, Frank, but he's like the old man. He goes his own way.' Her voice was low.

Matilda Jenkins opened the bedroom door and called

the rest of the boys in. They all trooped in, eating their fish and chips, and clustered around the bed. Benny could not see anything so pulled on the doctor's coat.

'What do you want, child?'

Benny looked up with his little monkey face. His mouth was full of food.

'Is it Hovis, then?'

'Hovis? The doctor's voice was puzzled. 'What are you on about, boy?'

'Hovis . . . you know, brown bread. Well, is it?'

The doctor looked around him for enlightenment.

'Brown bread? Are you delirious, child?'

'He means is it dead? Brown bread . . . dead. Get it?'

This was spoken by Anthony, and his tone indicated that if anyone was stupid it was not his little brother.

'Brown bread, bejasus! No, it's not. It's very much alive. Now eat your chips, you little heathen. Brown bread indeed!'

The policemen laughed.

'How long you been in London, Doc?' the elder asked. 'Twenty years? And you still don't know the lingo.' They thought this highly amusing. 'We'd better be off, Sar. Don't forget to tell Michael when he gets in.'

'I won't forget, Frank. I'll tell him, but he won't come. You know that.'

'Well, try and persuade him. Good luck with the new arrival. See you all.' The two men left.

Sarah looked at her sons' faces and smiled.

'It's a girl!'

All the boys grinned at her.

'A daughter for me old age.' She hugged the child to her. 'I'm going to call her Maura. Maura Ryan. I like that.'

'Shall I go and get Mickey, Mum? I saved him some chips.'

'Yeah, Geoff. Tell him the coast is clear.'

The doctor stopped packing away his instruments and looked at Sarah sternly.

'You knew where he was all along?'

She grinned at him. 'Course I did. He's in the Anderson shelter at number 119. He always hides there.'

Seeing the funny side of what Sarah said, Martin O'Reilly threw back his head and laughed out loud. Seven mouths stopped chewing as the boys stared at him.

'What a night! Your little girl certainly picked her time to arrive. She saved young Michael's bacon tonight, that's a fact.'

Sarah chuckled with him. 'She did that all right!'

Pat Johnstone, Sarah's best friend and next-door neighbour, came into the bedroom with a tray of tea. She ushered all the boys out and poured Sarah a strong cup.

'Here you are, girl. Get your laughing gear around that. What about you, Doc? Fancy a cuppa?'

'That would be grand. I'm parched.'

Pat poured the doctor out a cup of tea and placed it on the bedside table. Then she sat on the bed next to Sarah. She looked at the baby and gasped with surprise.

'Oh, my Gawd! She's a cracker, ain't she?' Her naturally loud voice seemed to bounce off the walls. 'Gis' a little hold, Sar.'

Sarah passed the child to her and took a deep drink of her tea. 'This is just what I needed, Pat.'

'Is that right the Filth came in looking for your Mickey and the electric went? I nearly wet meself laughing when Mrs Jenkins told me, I thought it was so funny.'

Sarah rolled her eyes to the ceiling. 'Oh, please, Pat. Don't remind me!'

The doctor finished putting his things away and drank

his tea. 'That was lovely. It just hit the right spot. Now I'll be off, Sarah. Don't get out of bed until I tell you that it's safe. I've had to put in a lot of stitches. If you start to bleed, send one of the lads around for me, OK?'

'I will, Martin. And thanks for everything.'

'That's all right. I'll see you in the morning. 'Bye now.'

He went out of the bedroom and down the stairs to the hallway where Matilda Jenkins was waiting for him with her hand out. He slipped a ten-shilling note into her palm.

'Thanks, Matilda. 'Bye.'

' 'Bye, Doctor O'Reilly.'

She closed the front door behind him. He walked down the flight of stairs that led to the road and looked at his car, a Rover 90. It was his pride and joy. There was not a windscreen wiper to be seen. He should have known this would happen in Lancaster Road.

'Little buggers!'

He got into his car and drove off. On 2 May 1950 he had brought Maura Ryan into the world.

Chapter Two

1953

Sarah Ryan glanced around her kitchen. A feeling of satisfaction swept over her. It looked beautiful. Taking a deep breath she sighed with contentment. She had not felt this happy for years. The table was laden with food. Turkey, ham, a large joint of beef, all carefully prepared and waiting to go into the oven. The kitchen was filled with the aroma of mince pies and sausage rolls cooking to a golden crispness in the oven.

She was startled out of her reverie by a loud crash from above. Her mouth set in a grim line, she went to the kitchen door. Opening it wide, she shouted as loud as she could: 'I'm warning you lot, one more noise and I'll come up there and scalp the arses off yer!'

She stood listening for a few minutes, trying not to smile. Then, assured that the children were all in their beds, she went back to her preparations, humming a little tune. Her last task was to lay thick strips of bacon across the turkey. Finally she stepped back from the table to admire her handiwork. Then, picking up the poker from the hearth, she banged it three times against the back of the fireplace. A few seconds later the banging was answered by two sharp thuds. Going to the sink she filled the kettle with water and placed it on the gas. As the kettle came to the boil she heard the back door open and popped her head into the scullery to see her friend Pat Johnstone kicking snow off her shoes.

'Get yourself in, Pat, I've got the kettle on.'

'Oh, Sar, it's brass monkey weather out there tonight!'

Coming into the kitchen, Pat dropped into an easy chair by the fire. She looked around the kitchen, impressed.

'By Christ, you're well set up this year.'

Her voice held a hint of jealousy. Sarah poured the steaming water into the tea pot and smiled at her friend.

'Michael brought the lot in this morning. I couldn't believe it meself when I saw it! There's sweets and biscuits as well as nuts and fruit. He's a good boy.'

Pat nodded her head, reckoning up the cost of everything in her mind. She realised that what was being said about Michael must be true. You couldn't buy all this working at Lyons bakery or the Black Cat factory. Crime certainly did pay by the looks of it.

'And there's presents for all the kids,' Sarah chatted on happily, unaware of the animosity she was creating. Pouring the tea into two thick white mugs, she gave one to her friend. With a tea cloth around her hand she opened up the oven and took out the mince pies and sausage rolls, placing them on the top of the stove to cool as she put the turkey in to cook. Her movements were quick and confident. She straightened up, wiping her forehead with the bottom of her apron, and then went to the dresser to open the drawer. Taking out a package, she passed it to Pat.

'I nearly forgot! Happy Christmas.'

Pat Johnstone took the package and placed it on her lap. She looked at Sarah's face with troubled eyes.

'I didn't get you nothing, Sar . . . I ain't got the money.'

Sarah dismissed this. 'Oh, shut your face and open it.'

Slowly Pat tore the brown paper apart. Then her hand went to her mouth. Her voice shook as she tried to speak.

'Oh Sar! Oh, it's lovely . . .'

Sarah patted her friend's shoulder gently.

'I knew you'd like it!'

Pat pulled the white blouse out of the wrapper and held it to her cheek, rubbing the soft material against her skin.

'It feels like silk!'

'It *is* silk. As soon as I saw it, I knew it was for you.'

All the terrible things she had thought earlier rose up in Pat's mind. Jealousy of her friend had been steadily mounting in the last few months. It had started the day three months previously when Michael paid to have the house stoved. Sulphur candles had been burning for days, leaving the house free of vermin, then the whole place had been painted from top to bottom. Like most of the women in the street, Pat Johnstone had been angered by it all. By Lancaster Road standards, the Ryans had gone too far up in the world, making them aliens. If it wasn't for the fact that Michael Ryan was now a force to be reckoned with, the other families would have tried to force them out.

All this flickered through her mind in a split second and she felt ashamed. She had gone to school with Sarah, and they had helped one another over the years. Now

Sarah was remembering her friend and Pat felt she didn't deserve it.

'It's absolutely gorgeous, Sar.'

Satisfied that her friend was happy, Sarah sat opposite her and took a quarter bottle of Black and White whisky from the mantelpiece. She poured two generous measures into their cups of tea.

'This'll keep the cold out, Pat. God himself knows we need it in this weather.'

Picking up her mug, Pat toasted her friend. 'Merry Christmas to you, Sarah . . . and many more.'

Settling themselves into their chairs, warmed by the whisky, the two women began the serious business of the day: gossiping.

Michael Ryan walked down the Bayswater Road. He walked, as always, as if he owned it – head held high, even in the driving snow. At eighteen, Michael was magnificent. Over six foot two, he was built like an athlete, his dark brown overcoat emphasising the spread of his shoulders. He still had thick black unruly hair, which he now wore cut in a DA. His eyes, deep-set and a striking blue, seemed to drink in everything around him. The only softness about his rugged face was in his lips. They were full and sensuous like a woman's, though at times they gave him a hint of cruelty. Women and men were drawn to Michael Ryan, and he knew it. He used it to his advantage as he used everything.

Now he watched the women lounging against the railings of Hyde Park. Even in the snow on Christmas Eve the streetwalkers were out.

A few of the younger girls, new to their beat, looked at him with interest. One opened her coat to reveal a scantily clad body. Michael looked her up and down, his lips curling with contempt. He wouldn't touch a tom with a barge pole. An older woman, seeing the exchange, laughed out loud.

'Cover yourself up, girl. Before you get frostbite of the fanny!'

The other women laughed, glad of some light relief. Michael carried on walking. He didn't really mind the prostitutes. In fact, he admired them. To his mind theirs was a business, like any other. Supply and demand. What he didn't like was the way some of them looked at him as a potential John. He liked to think that people put him above that kind of thing. He crossed the road, dodging the traffic skilfully. The snow was easing up and last-minute shoppers were everywhere. The Portobello Road had been packed.

He walked into the warmth of the Bramley Arms. Pushing his way among the men he went to the bar, nodding a greeting here and there. Over the last year he had worked hard to create an image for himself and it was paying off. People were deferential towards him. He snapped his fingers at the barmaid and ordered a brandy. He didn't particularly like brandy, but it was part of his image. It set him above other people. The men at the bar moved to give him room.

He sipped his drink. Ranging around the crowded bar, his eyes settled on a group by the window. He picked up his drink and made his way over to them. One of the men glanced at him, giving a double take as he realised who it was.

Tommy Blue felt a knot of fear somewhere in his bowels. The four other men at the table with him sensed his panic and stopped talking to look at the newcomer.

Seeing Michael Ryan smiling at them, they seemed to crowd together, hunching in their seats. Enjoying the terror he was creating, Michael drank his brandy in one gulp. Then, wiping his hand across his mouth, he placed his glass gently on the table.

'I've been looking for you, Tommy.'

His voice was quiet.

Tommy Blue felt his heart sinking. He tried to smile, his lips trembling.

'I think me and you had better have a little walk.'

Looking around the table at the other men, Michael pointed at Tommy.

'I'll be waiting outside for you.'

Turning, he pushed his way to the door. Outside he leant against the wall of the pub. He bit on his lip, the feeling of excitement in his breast causing his heartbeat to pound in his ears.

A group of Salvation Army singers were making their way along the road. Pulling a pack of Strands from his pocket, Michael lit one. The strains of 'Onward Christian Soldiers' gradually grew closer. He pulled hard on the cigarette. He would give Tommy Blue five minutes before going in after him.

Inside the Bramley Arms, Tommy was rooted to his seat.

'How much do you owe, Tom?' This from Dustbin Daley, a totter from Shepherd's Bush.

'Forty-five quid.' Tommy's voice was low.

One of his companions whistled.

'I'd better get out there . . . otherwise he'll come in after me.' Getting up unsteadily, Tommy made his way to the door.

Dustbin Daley shook his head. 'He must be bloody mad.'

The others agreed with him. Their earlier high spirits were gone now, out of the door with Tommy Blue.

Tommy shivered as the cold hit him. He was wearing a thin jacket, torn in places, and a thick multi-coloured scarf.

Michael threw his cigarette on the slush-filled pavement and ground it out with his boot. Pushing himself from the wall he grabbed Tommy's jacket and pulled him along the road. The Salvationists were alongside them. A young girl pushed a tin in their direction. She smiled at Michael as she rattled it.

'Merry Christmas, sir.' Her eyes held open admiration.

Pulling his coat open, he pushed his hand into his trouser pocket, and taking out two half crowns dropped them into the tin. The girl flushed with pleasure.

'Thank you, sir. Merry Christmas.'

Nodding at her, Michael resumed piloting Tommy Blue along the pavement. The tambourines and the singing faded into the distance. The two men walked in silence for five minutes. Tommy Blue could not feel the cold now. He couldn't feel anything. Fear had completely taken over. Tommy Blue was on automatic pilot. All he could do was wait. The beer he had been drinking steadily all day was now weighing heavily on his stomach.

Michael slowed down in Treadgold Street. The laundry here was known affectionately as the bagwash. Michael himself had brought his mother's laundry here on many occasions. Now it was deserted, shut up for the Christmas holidays. Taking a key from inside his coat Michael opened the double doors of the building and pushed Tommy inside. Pulling the doors shut behind him, he turned on the lights. Tommy stood immobile.

Taking out his pack of Strands, Michael lit one slowly.

He pulled deeply on the cigarette and blew the smoke into Tommy's face.

'You've made me very cross.' As usual Michael's voice was quiet.

Tommy's face seemed to come to life. He blinked his eyes rapidly.

'Look, Mickey, I . . . I tried to get the money. I swear it!'

'Shut up, Tommy. You're beginning to annoy me.'

Dropping the cigarette he grabbed Tommy's scarf, forcing him backwards until he was against one of the huge machines. Bringing his right fist back over his shoulder he punched Tommy in the face with considerable force. Tommy's nose seemed to collapse underneath the blow. Michael let him drop on the filthy floor. Groaning, Tommy curled himself up into a ball, his hands covering his head. Michael kicked him in the back, the force of the blow sending Tommy across the dirt-strewn floor. Picking up one of the large wooden podgers the women used to push down the bagwashes, Michael prodded Tommy on the shoulder.

'Hold out your arm.' Michael's voice held no emotion whatsoever. Tommy was blubbering.

'Please . . . please, Mickey, I'm begging you.' He looked up at Michael, his face bloody and awash with tears. 'Don't do this . . . I swear I'll ge-get the money somehow.'

Kicking him in the legs, Michael brought the podger down on Tommy's shoulders.

'If you don't put your arm out, I'll break your bastard back for you. Now put your arm out!'

Michael's voice echoed around the laundry. Slowly Tommy placed his arm on the floor, his whole body jerking with fear. Twice the 'podger' smashed down on his elbow, shattering the bone. Tommy screamed with pain. He was struggling to keep conscious as red-hot waves of nausea washed over him. He threw up on the floor, beer mixed with bile steaming in the cold.

'Get up, Tommy.' Michael's voice was quiet again.

Slowly he dragged himself to his feet, his arm hanging awkwardly against his side, the sleeve of his jacket gradually staining crimson. Droplets of blood ran over his fingers and dripped on to the floor. He leant against the machine, crying quietly.

'You've got seven days, Tommy, that's all, to find the money. Now piss off.'

Michael watched Tommy stagger from the laundry. He checked himself over to make sure there was no blood on his clothes. Then, whistling to himself, he washed the podger clean and put it back where he'd found it, against the far wall. Then, still whistling, he turned off the lights and locked up.

Joe the Fish listened avidly to everything Michael said to him, nodding his head now and again and every so often muttering, 'Good . . . good.' When Michael had finished, Joe smiled at him. 'The arm was good and broken?'

'Yeah. Smashed to smithereens!'

Joe the Fish sighed. He had a distaste for violence, but in his business it was a necessity. He looked at Michael Ryan sitting opposite him. He liked the boy, could see himself in Michael. The boy had the same urge to better himself. That had been Joe's ambition as a young man. Like Michael he had started out as a 'breaker' – a heavy – until he had built up his own business. Now he was a respected member of the community. He owned shops, clubs and market stalls, from Petticoat Lane to the

Portobello Road. His most lucrative business, though, was the bets. Joe had been a bookie for over twenty years, gradually moving into loan sharking. He had realised as soon as he had employed Michael that he had found himself a kindred spirit. Michael was innately honest. If he said the punter had paid him fifty quid, Joe knew that was what had been paid. Most of the breakers kept a portion for themselves, knowing that the unlucky punter would eventually pay that portion once again. Michael Ryan, though, had his own set of principles. He might beat a man up so badly he needed hospital treatment, yet Joe knew that in Michael's mind, keeping any money back would be tantamount to stealing. Joe liked him. He liked the way Michael looked at his home. He liked the respect that Michael afforded him.

He coughed and spat some phlegm into the fire, hearing it sizzle as it hit the coals.

'From January I want you to take over the "breaking" side of the business. I'll inform all the men that they're to take their orders from you.'

Michael stared at Joe. Then a wide grin broke out across his face and he shook his head in amazement.

'Thanks, Joe! Bloody hell!'

Joe, like most people, felt happy to see Michael grin. It was as if a blinding sun had emerged from behind a black cloud. Michael had the gift of making people *want* to please him, as if by giving him pleasure they were somehow indebted to him. Joe felt a rush of warmth go through him. He would enjoy working with this boy, teaching him the ropes. He let his eyes travel over Michael's body. He certainly was a fine-looking boy.

Michael watched Joe's eyes and a thrill of anticipation went through him. Joe the Fish was fifty years old. He had never married or had an association with any woman as far as Michael knew. What he did know was that Joe liked to be surrounded by young men. In the last few months he had consciously ingratiated himself with Joe, flattered him, let Joe think that he was grateful to him for giving him the breaker's job. He stared into Joe's face and smiled at him, his deep blue eyes seemingly full of gratitude and admiration. He watched Joe heave his bulk out of the chair. A flicker of repugnance crossed Michael's features, to be quickly replaced by the dazzling smile he knew caused Joe so much happiness.

Opening one of the drawers in his desk, Joe took out a small box. He walked around the desk and gave it to Michael.

'Just a little token of my appreciation.' Joe's voice was low and husky. Leaning against the desk he watched Michael's face as he opened the box. When he heard the deep intake of breath, Joe relaxed. He would not rush the boy, he had to let him come to him.

Michael stared at the tie pin glinting up from the red velvet lining. It was gold, in the shape of a large M, encrusted with diamonds. Looking up into Joe's face, Michael felt a moment of terror at what he had to do. Then, seeing the softness in Joe's eyes, he swallowed heavily. It was now or never.

Placing his hand on the top of Joe's thigh, he gently brushed his knuckles against the man's groin. Joe stared down at the large, rough hand gently rubbing against him. Closing his eyes momentarily, he felt a rush of ecstasy pulsing through his body. He opened his eyes and stared down into Michael's face. In the firelight, he looked like a dark angel. His blue eyes held an amber glow that caused Joe's heart to somersault inside his breast.

Dropping heavily on to his knees, he placed his hands on Michael's thighs, rubbing and kneading them, his breath coming heavily. Watching him, Michael smiled to himself. He thought Joe looked ridiculous, and noticed that he had a film of sweat above his lips which he licked at nervously.

As he felt Joe begin fumbling with his trousers Michael stifled an urge to slam his fist into Joe's head. He couldn't go back now, not after all the planning and scheming of the last few months. Joe was his ticket out of Notting Hill, his passport into the world of real villainy. Gritting his teeth he lay back in the chair and forced himself to relax. Outside, in the muffled stillness of the snow, Michael heard a lone voice singing 'Silent Night'. Looking down at the top of Joe's balding pate, Michael listened to the haunting childish voice and could have cried.

Sarah was basting the turkey when she heard Benjamin come in. The front door was slammed as loudly as possible, causing Sarah to wince. Putting the turkey back into the oven, she sat back in her chair. Benjamin stumbled into the kitchen, his hair and clothes still laden with snow. He grinned his wide toothless grin at her and made his way unsteadily across the room to her side.

'Hello, Sarah, my darling!'

As usual when drunk, he spoke to her as if she was at the other end of the street.

'Will you keep your voice down! You'll have all the bloody kids up!'

Benjamin stared down at his wife, blinking his eyes as he swayed unsteadily before her. The more he tried to concentrate, the more blurred she seemed to become. Finally seeing two Sarahs, he staggered into the seat vacated by Pat Johnstone not an hour ago. Lifting up one of his legs he broke wind loudly, causing Sarah to purse her lips. He sat in the chair smiling amiably at her, his clothes beginning to steam with the heat of the fire.

Wordlessly she pulled herself from her chair and swiftly began making him some ham sandwiches. She looked at the clock and noticed it was twenty-past one – everyone was in now except Michael. Placing the sandwiches on a plate, she gave them to her husband. She was bone tired. She had been working since seven in the morning.

Going through the scullery she pulled on an old coat and went out into the tiny back garden. Squatting down, she took a plate from the top of a large glass bowl. The snow had drifted up the sides and on to the plate. Carefully she wiped it clean. Then, touching the green mass inside the bowl softly, she smiled. The younger children loved jelly. That was one good thing about the snow, it kept everything nice and fresh. Replacing the plate, she stood up and went back inside the house, banging her slippers on the step to get rid of the snow.

Back inside the kitchen she heard her husband snoring loudly. He was sprawled in his chair, his long legs outstretched, his hand holding the plate of sandwiches away from his body. Taking the plate gently from him she placed it in the sink, then checked the turkey one last time, turned the gas down as low as it would go and made her way up to bed.

As she undressed in the bedroom she saw her daughter had climbed into their big double bed. This was Maura's first real Christmas. Slipping into the bed Sarah looked down on the white-blond head and felt the familiar tightening in her guts. The child stirred and burrowed deeper into the bed. Placing her thumb in her mouth, she sucked on it furiously for a few seconds before settling down once more into a deep sleep. If Benjamin had given her nothing else in their life together he had given her this child, and for that Sarah would forgive him anything.

Michael woke up and glanced at his watch. It was three-fifteen. Shaking his head to clear the fustiness he noticed a fat arm around his waist. In the dying firelight he looked down on the sleeping face of Joe the Fish. Somewhere inside himself he felt disgust at the events of the previous few hours. He was acutely aware of everything that had gone on in front of the then roaring fire. Mixed with his revulsion was also a tiny feeling of excitement. He now had Joe the Fish in his grasp, as he had sworn to himself that he would. A cruel smile played at the corners of his mouth. He would play Joe like a musical instrument. He would slowly become the focal point of his life. Then, when Joe had served his purpose, he would dispose of him. Michael knew what he had to do. He had been planning it long enough.

Gently, he brought his face down on to Joe's and kissed him on his lips. Joe's watery eyes opened and he smiled, displaying discoloured teeth.

'I've got to get going, Joe.'

Yawning lazily, the older man stretched his plump arms above his head.

'All right, Michael love. Try and get around tomorrow. I'm always alone on Christmas Day.' His voice sounded sad.

'I will. Don't worry.'

Joe watched Michael dressing in the firelight, his heart bursting in his breast. In his mind's eye he relived their love-making of a few hours before and the picture of

Michael lying underneath him as he penetrated him rose in his mind. He couldn't quite believe he had found himself such a beautiful animal. As Michael slipped on his overcoat Joe felt a wave of loneliness wash over him.

'See you tomorrow then.' Michael's voice was gentle and caressing. He favoured Joe with one of his blinding grins. Pulling himself up from the floor he stood before the dying fire, his short fat legs and large stomach making Michael feel sick inside.

'Haven't you forgotten something?' Joe's voice sounded like a young girl's – high and breathless with anticipation. Michael frowned at him, bewildered. Then seeing Joe's lips pucker, he walked over to the fireplace and embraced him. Joe pushed his tongue into Michael's mouth, kissing him with an energy that startled him. Breaking away gently, Michael smiled at him and quietly left the room.

The picture of Joe's doughy white body seemed to be imprinted on his mind. As he walked out into the silent white world Michael was glad of the freezing cold that seemed to cut down into his lungs. A light snow was falling and he raised his face to allow the soft flakes to fall on his skin, willing it to wash away the disgust he felt inside.

The streetlights gave the pavements a glittering glow as if thousands of diamonds were lining his path. Picking up speed, Michael began to smile. He shook his head and shrugged in the stillness of the night. The worst was over now. He knew what he had let himself in for and he was glad. Let the fat old queen use his body. It had put food on his mother's table. It had brought the kids clothes. It would eventually bring him untold riches. Never would he allow himself to feel bad about it again.

He looked up into the black sky and waved his fist at the stars. This was a new beginning for the Ryans. He was going to pick them up out of the gutter and establish them in the monied world where he knew they belonged. Shoving his hands into the pockets of his overcoat he felt the little box that contained the tie pin. He grinned. As soon as the shops opened after the holidays he was going to go out and buy himself a tie!

When Michael saw the happy faces on Christmas Day, the food that seemed inexhaustible and the merriment his gifts had brought, he finally came to terms with himself. Anything, however bad, was worth all this. After a large, noisy Christmas dinner, Michael sat with his sister Maura asleep on his lap. As he looked down at her sleeping face, sucking contentedly on her thumb, he swore that he would commit murder if it kept his family as happy as they were now.

It was a promise he was to keep many times.

Chapter Three

1955

Garry and Benny Ryan were playing on the bombsite that was once Testerton Street. The day before they had noticed while coming home from school that an enormous mound of sand had been left there. That meant one of two things – the remaining houses were either being patched up or demolished to make way for pre-fabs. Either way they knew that their playground was going to disappear. Both boys had been up and out by six-thirty. If they timed it just right they could scavenge for a few hours before going to the Royalty in Ladbroke Grove for the Saturday morning minors.

They had played in the mound of sand for over an hour. Benny, at nine, was already a true Ryan. Big for his age, he towered over Garry who was eleven. Garry had a long thin body, giving him a waif-like appearance. He was the only Ryan to wear glasses, which he was forever pushing higher on his nose, the thick lenses giving him an owlish appearance. Where Benny was dark-haired with the characteristic

Ryan dark blue eyes and full-lipped mouth, Garry was the opposite. He had light brown hair and a feral quality about him that made people do what he wanted. Garry was the acknowledged genius of the family, forever reading. His room was strewn with books and papers. He also fancied himself as an inventor – a pastime that had his mother caught between maternal pride and an almost uncontrollable urge to murder him.

The June sunshine gave their play an added vigour. All around them the world had come to life. The hum of the traffic was getting louder and every so often the rattling of a train set the dirt trembling. To the right of the mound of sand stood what remained of the houses in Testerton Street. The bomb had been a direct hit and only the last few dwellings had still been standing afterwards. These had no fronts left. Their rooms were great gaping caverns that miraculously still had wallpaper and broken furniture inside.

The two boys knew every inch of these houses. From the roof rafter of the most stable hung their 'bundle' swing. Now summer was here the swing would become a focal point for the children around and about. Boys would come from as far away as Shepherd's Bush and Bayswater to play on it between fighting rival gangs. Providing the work didn't start too soon, it would be a good summer.

Scrambling down from the mound of sand, Garry began walking towards the houses, his hands and knees stained orange. Seeing his brother walking away Benny followed hastily, rubbing off the damp sand from his hands on his shorts. He caught up with Garry, puffing for breath.

'What we gonna do then?' As always he waited for Garry to decide what games were to be played.

Garry looked up at his brother, his thin face already grimy. 'We's gonna look for bombs and things. Lee's hid some gunpowder he swiped from under the Arches and I'm gonna pinch it off him.'

Benny looked worried for a second. Lee at thirteen was already as big as Roy, who was seventeen, nearly six feet tall, and was also bad-tempered.

'Lee'll smash us up!'

Garry smiled and pushed his glasses higher up his nose. 'He's got to catch us first!'

Benny laughed nervously. Lee would catch them, he always did, but he kept his own counsel because when Garry got mad he sent him home. Then he'd have to play with his sister! He followed Garry into the end house. The stairs were still sound and both boys made their way up to the top floor. Standing dangerously close to the crumbling edge, the two looked out across London. Over the last few years the landscape had changed. From their vantage point they could see the whole of their world. In the distance Garry saw that the fairground had arrived at Wormwood Scrubs Park. He poked Benny in the ribs and pointed to it, a thrill of expectation going through them both.

'I'm gonna get Mickey to give us some money! We'll go there later and see what rides they've got!'

In his excitement Benny jumped backwards and tripped over a lump of wood. As he landed on the floor boards he gasped, 'Here, Gal, look at this lot!'

Garry was already staring at what lay beneath his brother's large feet.

'Where'd you reckon they come from?'

Garry shook his head. Kneeling down on the floor, he picked up an empty cartridge case. There were over a dozen in all.

'I reckon someone nicked them and then left them here!'

Pushing his glasses up on to the bridge of his nose, Garry snapped: 'Trust you to state the bloody obvious. These have been hidden here by a little firm, and I think I know whose it was!'

Benny pulled himself up from the floor with difficulty. Both his hands were stinging where he'd skinned them.

'Who d'you reckon hid them then?'

'I bet it was that gang from Elgin Avenue.' Garry's voice was triumphant.

'Come on, let's nick them quick. Before anyone comes.'

Both boys began stuffing the empty cases down their shirts. Then they ran down the stairs as fast as they could. As they ran out of the house into the sunshine they both skidded to a halt. Lee, Leslie and Roy were walking towards them. Garry looked at Benny, his face troubled.

'Whatever you do, don't tell them about this lot.' He patted his shirt. Benny's hands were smarting and he rubbed them gently on his shirt. Tears were already forming in his eyes.

Roy noticed the boys and called to them. 'What you two standing there for? What you done?'

Garry as usual did the talking. 'We ain't done nothing. We thought you was looking for us, that's all.'

'What would we want with you two?' Roy's voice sounded incredulous. 'We get enough of you at home. Now sod off, the pair of you.'

Neither boy needed to be told twice. They ran off as fast as their legs would carry them. When they reached the safety of the pile of sand they sat on top of it and watched their brothers. The three older boys stood by the opening of the houses. They were all smoking.

'Did you smell them? I reckons they've been to the baths in Silchester Road. They've all got that smelly stuff on their hair.' Benny's voice was disgusted. In his mind anyone who could have a bath without being told to needed treatment. He himself had a bath every fortnight, a sixpenny one with soap and towels supplied. He hated it. If his mother didn't stand outside waiting for him he'd spend the money on something important, like caps for his gun and comics.

A little while later three girls arrived on the scene, two blondes and a redhead. Garry laughed.

'Dirty bleeders! That's why they've been to the baths. They're going snogging!'

They watched the three girls pair off with their brothers and go off in different directions. Even more disgusted, Benny stood up.

'Come on, let's go home. I'm hungry.'

Silently the two boys made their way home.

It was three in the afternoon when Roy brought Janine into his house. It was the first time he had brought a girl home and both he and Janine were nervous. Grasping her hand in the hallway, he smiled at her.

'Everything's gonna be all right.'

He looked down into her green eyes and as always had the urge to kiss her. She had milk-white skin and long thick red hair. To Roy's mind Janine was class. She was also very tall – five feet eight inches. In a way he was glad that she was 'in trouble'. It would give them the push they needed to come out into the open.

He led her by the hand into his mother's kitchen. As usual Sarah was cooking. Even on days like this with the sun cracking the pavements Sarah still cooked. With nine children to feed, preparing a meal was a major event. She looked at Roy and Janine, her surprise showing on her face. Roy stood awkwardly in the kitchen and, still grasping Janine's hand, smiled at his mother.

'Mum, I'd like you to meet Janine . . . Janine Grierson.'

The girl stretched out her free hand and nodded her head. 'Pleased to meet you, I'm sure.'

Her voice was very low and refined. Wiping her hand on her apron, Sarah took the girl's hand and shook it gently.

'And you, love. Well, sit yourselves down. I've made some ginger beer. Would you like a glass?'

Without waiting for an answer, she went to the scullery and took the large jug from the table out there. She needed time to think. Grierson? Grierson? Where did she know that name from? She carried the jug back into the kitchen. Roy had sat Janine at the kitchen table and was standing beside her. Then, like a bolt out of the blue, it came to Sarah. This was Janine Grierson. Her heart sank in her chest. Her father owned the butcher's in the Portobello Road. He had also owned the house next door to Christie's round in Rillington Place. What on earth was Janine doing with her Roy? Not that she didn't think her son was good enough for her, oh no! But Eliza Grierson had great plans for her only daughter, Sarah knew that much.

Forcing a smile on to her face she poured out two glasses of ginger beer. As she placed them on the table, Roy spoke up. 'Janine's pregnant, Mum. And I'm the father.'

Outside in the garden, Maura was watching Garry and Benny working. Benny was holding the cartridges steady while Garry filled them with the gunpowder. After watching a particularly thrilling Lone Ranger at the

Saturday morning minors, Garry had experienced a renewed interest in the making of bombs. He pushed the wadding carefully into the cartridge before taking it from Benny and placing it on the garden wall. He stepped back to admire his handiwork. That was the last one.

Maura sat on the wooden crate. Her long blond hair seemed to come alive in the sunlight which gave it golden highlights. Her aquamarine eyes carefully watched every movement her brothers made. At five, Maura knew that if she wanted to be a part of their games she had to sit and watch quietly, otherwise they would sneak out of the garden leaving her alone.

She saw Garry give Benny a large hammer. Then Garry carefully took one of the filled cartridges and placed it on the grass. He had to press it down a couple of times to stop it falling over. Then he nodded at Benny who took the hammer and brought it back over his head, ready to smash it down on to the cartridge at a sign from his brother. Garry pushed his glasses higher on his nose and raising his hand as if he was starting a race, brought it down heavily to his side . . .

Inside the house Janine was crying quietly as Sarah spoke. 'It's nothing against you, lass, but think of your father. He'll go stark staring mad when he hears. Baby or no baby, there's no way he'll allow you to marry Roy. I know it.' Her voice had a finality about it that made Roy's blood run cold in his veins. He opened his mouth to answer. Both women were looking at him expectantly. They saw his eyes open wide until they seemed about to start from his head.

'Benny! Benny . . . don't you bloody dare!' His voice was so loud both women jumped in their seats. A split second later an almighty bang erupted from the garden, followed by Maura's frenzied screaming. The three adults seemed to be catapulted from their seats as they ran out into the back yard.

Maura had seen the hammer descend on to the cartridge just as she heard Roy's voice from the house. The impact of the hammer hitting the brass casing of the cartridge had caused a flash of blue light followed by an enormous bang. As if in slow motion she had seen Benny travel backwards through the air, landing heavily on his back among the rubbish that littered the end of the garden. That's when she started to scream. Through her tears she saw Garry scaling the wall as he made a run for it.

Roy ran to where Benny was lying, his heart pounding in his ears. This time Garry had really done it. He had finally killed somebody. Picking Benny up gently he cradled his head in his lap, conscious of his mother standing in the garden, her hand over her mouth as if terrified of what she might find. Benny was soot-blackened all over. The smell of burnt powder seemed to hang around him in a cloud. Looking down into his brother's face, Roy felt the tears come into his eyes.

'Benny . . . Benny!' Roy's anguished voice carried up into the pale blue sky. Janine, stunned, had gone to the little girl sitting on the crate. Instinctively she pulled the child to her breast, stroking the long blond hair.

Roy clutched Benny to him, cuddling the dirty head to his breast. Opening his eyes Benny looked up into his brother's tearstained face.

'What happened?' His childish voice broke into everyone's shocked thoughts. 'One minute I was hammerin'. The next I was blown up!'

Benny looked around him, a bewildered expression on his face. 'Where's Garry gone?'

Picking him up, Roy felt the terror slowly leave his own body. 'When that little bastard gets home, I'm gonna murder him. If it's the last thing I do in this life . . .'

Maura clung to Janine, enjoying the flowery smell of her. Her cries had subsided to little hiccups. Sarah let Roy carry Benny into the house, and as she looked at Janine comforting her only daughter, the ice in her heart melted. Going to the girl, she put her arm around her shoulders.

'That Garry will be the death of me. Well, if you think you could stand the strain of being part of this family, you're welcome.'

Janine's white face made Sarah's natural good nature come to the fore. Pushing the girl's heavy red hair back from her face, she said, 'I'm warning you, though . . . excitement like this is an everyday occurrence!'

'Oh, Mrs Ryan, my father is going to go mad.'

Sarah waved her hand at the girl, her voice sounding more confident than she actually felt.

'He'll get over it, love. He'll get over it.'

James Grierson was stalking around his house in a fit of temper so acute he could almost taste it. Unlike his wife, who had taken herself off to bed like one of the heroines in the penny dramas, he, James Grierson, was going to *do* something. What exactly he wasn't sure, but he would think of something. Stamping up the stairs he went into the bedroom he shared with Eliza.

'How could a daughter of mine take up with that bloody scum? A filthy, stinking Ryan!' He clenched his fists and raised them to the ceiling. 'I could throttle the bitch. My God, my mother used to say: "Show me the company you keep and I'll tell you what you are." Never was a truer word said!'

Eliza closed her eyes and groaned. Since Janine had told them that morning that she was pregnant, her whole world had fallen apart. Only a week ago, she had stood in their butcher's shop and completely demolished the reputation of young Carrie Davidson for the same thing: having to get married. She could hear herself talking to anyone who would listen about the shameless hussy. Now it had happened to her daughter and she didn't like it, she didn't like it one bit. Eliza Grierson was known as a gossip of Olympian standards. She prided herself on her ability to sift through the most innocent conversations and turn them into major scandals. She knew that this trouble with her daughter would be all the more enjoyed because it was a reflection on herself. She groaned again and pushed a pillow over her head. If it had been anyone but a Ryan . . . She felt tears of frustration stinging her eyes. She could cheerfully throttle Janine herself!

A loud banging at the front door stopped both of them in their tracks. Pulling back the curtain, James Grierson looked down into his garden and groaned. It was not a very good day today, and he had a terrible feeling that it was going to get worse.

Michael and Geoffrey stood in the Griersons' front garden. Like everything of Eliza Grierson's, the garden was what she described as 'classy'. It was also immaculate, as were the curtains at the windows and the shiny brass knocker on the door. This was opened by a rather subdued James who said gruffly: 'You'd better come in.'

Michael and Geoffrey walked into the spacious hallway as if they owned the house. Opening the parlour door, James ushered them inside.

Michael sat himself down in an armchair and looked around the room slowly. Geoffrey sat on the rather hard horsehair settee.

Taking a packet of Strands from his pocket Michael gave one to Geoffrey and after offering the pack to James, who refused, laboriously set about lighting the cigarettes. He knew that his slowness was annoying James Grierson. It was a calculated move. Drawing the smoke into his lungs he put his head back against the chair and blew two large smoke rings. Then, looking at James, he smiled.

'I understand, Mr Grierson, that my brother Roy has been shunting your daughter.'

Geoffrey watched the red flush creep up James Grierson's neck and continue until it reached his receding hairline. Stamping across the room, the man made as if to grab Michael's shirt. Grabbing Grierson's hand in a vice-like grip, Michael laughed.

'Naughty, naughty.'

Then pushing the older man from him, he sat forward in the chair. James was sent sprawling across his own parlour carpet, a blinding anger building inside him.

Michael pointed at him, the cigarette smoke curling around his finger.

'In three weeks' time, Mr Grierson, my brother is gonna marry your daughter, with or without your permission. Personally I would advise you to give them your blessing, what with the baby and all. A new little Ryan . . . a Ryan that your daughter is carrying inside her.'

Slowly James Grierson pulled himself up from the floor. Geoffrey put out his hand to help but was ignored. Waving his hand away, the older man slumped down on the chair opposite Michael.

Staring at him, Michael underwent one of his lightning

changes of mood. From anger and animosity he turned in a split second to a benevolent caring brother only here to see justice done. His rugged face softened. All irritation seemingly forgotten, he leant forward in his chair and smiled at James Grierson – one of his most stunning smiles that seemed to wipe the cruelty from his face at a stroke. He began to speak in a man to man voice.

'Listen, James . . . may I call you James?' The man nodded, not at all happy with this bewildering change in his antagonist.

'The way I see it is this. Your daughter has been made pregnant by my brother.' He opened his arms out wide in a gesture of helplessness. 'They love one another, they want to marry. It's not as if Roy's had it on his toes, is it? He's quite willing to do the right thing by the girl. I know you've had a shock. No man likes to think of his daughter . . . well, you know what I mean. But, the only thing left to do is to get them married. I hope you will change your attitude, soften towards them?' His voice was now redolent with an underlying threat that was not wasted on James Grierson. Michael Ryan was offering him a face saver and he knew it. He was being told in no uncertain terms that he could come out of all this as the loving, caring father who would do anything to keep his daughter's reputation; who welcomed her choice of husband with open arms; who would not bow down in the face of adversity, but would rise up and conquer it.

For the first time in his life James Grierson felt a grudging respect for a Ryan. He knew he was being manipulated but, he asked himself, what was the alternative? He had heard stories about Michael Ryan. That he was as queer as a nine-bob note. That he had taken over Joe the Fish's businesses and made a name for himself among the villains.

At nineteen Michael Ryan was already becoming a neighbourhood legend. 'Cruel but fair' was the local opinion. Could he really let his only child become a part of this family? Even as the question formed in his mind he knew it was useless. If he went against this young man sitting opposite him, he would in effect dig his own grave. The course was already set. Janine was marrying Roy Ryan whether James liked it or not. What he had to do now was stretch out and take the hand of friendship being offered to him. He sighed heavily and his voice came out in a nervous croak.

'You're right, of course. If they really care for one another . . .'

He swallowed deeply as Michael Ryan took his hand and shook it, the animal strength of the handshake reminding him acutely of exactly what he had done. His lovely Janine had brought him this low, had brought Michael Ryan into his home. He could have wept.

Three weeks later, on the first Saturday of July, James Grierson gave away his only daughter to Roy Ryan. It wasn't until after the reception, once home in his bed, that he finally gave way to the tears that had been building up inside him since Michael's visit. He felt he had taken his only child like a lamb to the slaughter.

It would be twenty years before he discovered how right he had been.

Chapter Four

1957

Michael was fuming, his blue eyes dark with anger. He rubbed one hand across his face and stared stonily at Joe.

'Look, Michael, you had no right to borrow any money behind my back. This is *my* business.' Joe the Fish pushed a pudgy finger into his chest.

Making a fist Michael smashed it down on the desk in front of him, causing their empty coffee cups to rattle in their saucers.

'So it's your business now, is it?' Michael's voice was bitter. 'I suppose this is *your* office as well? Don't let's worry about the money *I've* brought in . . .'

Joe sighed loudly. He interrupted Michael as if he was talking to a little child.

'Oh, for Christ's sake, Michael. No one's disputing that you've done well. What's annoyed me is the fact that you borrowed out five grand without even bothering to mention it to me.' Joe's voice was cajoling. In his heart he was frightened of Michael, frightened of his phenomenal temper. 'Come on, son . . . try and see it from my point of view.'

Michael picked up his pack of Strands from the desk and lit one. He sat at the desk, his head hanging forward on his chest, taking quick drags on his cigarette. Joe was conscious that Michael's hands were shaking. He knew he was trying to calm himself down.

Joe sat in the chair opposite and placed his elbows on the desk. Michael was such a difficult boy. He gravitated from extreme happiness to a difficult and dangerous depression in the space of seconds.

Normally Joe would have let Michael have his head, he was a good businessman, but this latest flouting of the rules had angered him. He had loaned five thousand pounds to Phillip Wreck, one of the most notorious villains in Paddington, and in Joe's mind Michael had more chance of getting the Pope's inside leg measurement than he had of getting that money back.

Michael stubbed out his cigarette, grinding it into the ashtray with such force Joe thought it would surely break. Snapping his head up he looked at Joe, his mouth clamped closed. In the quiet room Joe could hear his laboured breathing.

'I'm warning you, Joe . . . I'm warning you now . . . don't fight me on this. I know exactly what I'm doing. I'll get that money back. I'll get it and the interest on it, you just wait and see.'

There were tears in Michael's eyes. He's just like a child, Joe thought, it's as if I've taken his toys away from him. The difference being that when Michael was like this he was liable to explode into a raging temper at any moment.

Joe felt the familiar fingers of fear touching him. It was

Michael's very unpredictability that drew Joe to him. Twice Michael had lashed out at him and hurt him, only to be contrite and loving in the next breath. Although Joe had never tried to analyse their relationship, inside himself he knew that it was the boy's vicious streak that attracted him.

'All right, Michael, I'll let it go this time. But in future, you come to me.'

Michael's face broke into one of his winning smiles and Joe felt himself relax.

As Michael looked at the man sitting opposite, his fat ugly face grinning like a Cheshire cat's, he felt an impulse to smash his fist into his teeth. Instead he carried on smiling. Joe didn't know it but his days were numbered. Soon he would be out of the way and he, Michael, could get on with his life.

Joe got out of his chair and walked around the desk. Standing behind Michael he began rubbing his taut muscular shoulders. Feeling the solid flesh beneath his fingers he felt himself harden, completely unaware that Michael was planning his demise.

Roy was in the butcher's shop in the Portobello Road. His father-in-law had given up trying to explain to him the different cuts of meat. Roy had been working for him since three weeks after his wedding, and he hated it. He felt like a kept man. He couldn't do the job, he knew it and his father-in-law knew it, but it was all part of the grand master plan: How To Keep Your Daughter At Home. They lived with Mr and Mrs Grierson. They ate with Mr and Mrs Grierson. And they watched from the sidelines as Mr and Mrs Grierson between them brought up the baby, Carla. It had been a few months before Roy realised he had married what his mother would have called 'a lazy bitch'. Janine was quite content to let her mother take over the baby, the cooking, everything. That left her free to play at being married which consisted of getting herself done up to the nines and visiting her friends all day, now and again taking the baby, all nice and clean, out in her pram. Playing at being mother of the year.

Roy winced as he thought of her. What had happened to the girl he had fallen in love with? The spirited young woman who had been as eager for life as he was? Admittedly they were only nineteen, but surely, he reasoned, there must be more to married life than this? If he mentioned moving out of her parents' house, she dissolved into tears. Last night had been the last straw. He had told her there was a flat going in Westbourne Park and she had had hysterics.

'How am I gonna cope with a baby on me own?'

That's when he had lost his temper. 'Well, we won't find that out until you try, will we? God Almighty, Janine, you've never once looked after the bloody kid for a whole day since it was born!'

After that her mother, Eliza, had come into the bedroom and led Janine out, taking her into her own bedroom. Then this morning she had told him that Janine was 'delicate' and needed her mother to look after her. He was frankly bewildered by it all. He wanted them to have their own little place, where Janine looked after the baby all day and cooked his meal in the evening. What he had was a pampered, spoilt brat whose only interest in life was lipstick and what was on at the pictures. She never looked at the child unless she had to. Even his mother had noticed it. She had asked him a few Saturdays ago if everything was all right between them. He had felt like telling her everything but just couldn't. He wouldn't even know where to begin.

'Hello, Bruv.' Roy was brought out of his reverie by Michael's voice.

'Hello, Mickey!' He hadn't been so pleased to see someone in all his life.

'Fancy skiving off for a few hours? I've got a bit of business I want to talk to you about.'

Roy wiped his bloody hands on his apron. 'I'll be with you in a tick.' He walked through to the back of the shop and called out to his father-in-law. James Grierson came down the stairs that led to the flat above the shop.

'What's all this row about?' His voice was loud and agitated. 'Can't you even look after the bloody shop? Want me to hold your hand now, I suppose.' Roy was conscious that Michael could hear every word and groaned inside.

'I've got to shoot off for a couple of hours.'

'You what!' Grierson's voice was incredulous. 'This is a bloody business here, not a bloody knocking shop where you pick your own hours . . .'

His voice faltered as he saw Michael slip through the doorway. Grierson paled.

'Who do you think you're talking to?' Michael's voice was icy. He pointed at Grierson. 'I'm talking to you. You had enough bunny just now . . . so answer me. Who d'you think you're talking to?'

As Michael stepped towards him, Grierson stepped backwards, his hands coming up to defend himself if the visitor lashed out.

Michael snapped at Roy: 'Get your coat.' Then walking to where Grierson was cowering against the wall, he grabbed him around the throat. 'Now, I don't know what's going down here, but I know this much – if you *ever* talk to my brother like that again, I'll rip your nuts off and ram them down your throat. Do you understand what I'm saying?'

Grierson was nodding his head furiously when Roy came back with his coat. Pulling Mickey away gently, he led him through the front of the shop and out into the street. He was ashamed that Michael had heard his father-in-law speak to him like that. He was ashamed that he himself let him.

'Come on, Roy, we're going to the KPH. I think we'd better have a talk.'

They walked in silence. The bright October day belied the cold wind. Roy noticed that everywhere they walked people acknowledged Michael. It was as if he was their sovereign and they his subjects. Depending on how influential people were, Mickey either nodded at them or gave them a hearty greeting. Roy was impressed. Michael's name was becoming synonymous with those of the Krays and the Richardsons, two of the most influential young gangs of that time. Roy knew that Michael kept up a friendship with them. An uneasy alliance. It seemed that once people met him they decided they were better off having him as a friend than an enemy.

They walked into the red warmth of the Kensington Park Hotel. Michael ordered them both hot whiskies and they settled down in the lounge bar.

Michael took his cigarettes from his overcoat pocket, and then slipped the coat from his shoulders. Folding it up carefully, he laid it across a chair. All his movements were performed with a natural grace. Roy shrugged off his own coat while still sitting, letting it fall over the back of his chair. Adjusting his trouser crease fastidiously Michael sat down again, settling himself into the over-upholstered chair. Then, pulling a large white ashtray towards him so it would be within easy reach, he lit a cigarette. Throwing the packet across the table at Roy, he finally spoke.

'How long has he been talking to you like that?' His voice was quiet.

Roy hung his head. 'I know it sounds bad, Mickey, but he is my father-in-law . . .'

'I couldn't give a fuck if he was the Immaculate Conception! There's something wrong, ain't there? The Roy I knew would never take that from anyone, not in a million years.' He lowered his voice. 'Come on, Bruv. What's the SP?'

The barman brought over their hot toddies and Roy was glad of the few seconds' reprieve. He could feel Michael's eyes boring into him. When they were settled again, Roy spoke.

'I don't know, Mickey. Since Carla was born it's as if I don't exist any more. Janine and her mum and dad act like she never got married. I feel like a lodger in the house. I eat their food, I sleep in their bed, I shag their daughter now and again.' All the bitterness of the last two years seemed to boil over and come tumbling out. 'And I mean, now and again. Every three weeks when they go and visit her bloody granny in Bethnal Green. She says she can't do it while Mummy's in the house. Then old man Grierson treats me like the village idiot. I'm not a butcher, Mickey. I hate looking at the meat, I hate touching it . . .' His voice trailed off.

'So what are you gonna do?'

Roy shrugged and took a gulp of his drink. 'I dunno.'

'You don't know? So that's it then, is it?' Michael was getting annoyed. 'Why don't you give her a right-hander? Show her who's boss. Tell her old man to go and stuff his bloody butcher's shop up his Jacksey. I knew she spelt trouble . . . I bloody knew it!'

'All right . . . All right, Mickey. Keep your hair on.'

'Why don't you come and work for me? That's what I wanted to talk to you about.' He saw a gleam of hope appear in Roy's eyes.

'I'd jump at the chance, you know that.'

Michael laughed. Roy was like a bloody kid at times. He looked at his brother's open face, and made a mental note to tell his mother what was going down with him. He knew that she was worried.

'That's settled then.' He looked at his watch. 'From two-twenty-five today you are a working member of the Ryan dynasty.' They both laughed. Anthony and Geoffrey worked for Michael already. Now he had Roy.

'What's the pay, Mickey?' Roy sounded uncertain.

'Bloody good, that's what.'

'I wouldn't ask, but what with the baby and everything . . .'

'No worries, I'll start you on thirty quid a week. That's a bit more than the others, so keep stumm about it.' Michael tapped his nose with his forefinger.

Roy was amazed. He was going to go and get Janine and the baby and if necessary drag her to the flat in Westbourne Park. This was gonna be a new start. Mickey was right. Maybe she needed a right-hander. And if his father-in-law stuck his oar in, he would get one and all!

He drank his whisky down and felt the warm glow through his body. It was partly the alcohol and partly the knowledge that he was finally going to do something about his life. The worry he had been feeling about Janine was replaced by elation. He would take a leaf out of Mickey's book. Hit first, ask questions later.

Michael watched his brother's face and guessed immediately what was going through his mind. He motioned to the barman to refill their glasses, a feeling of satisfaction running through him. He had a soft spot for Roy, the same as he did for Benny. They were both too nice for their own good. He was going to toughen Roy up. Make him into someone. Then, when Joe the Fish was out of the way, the businesses would be run exclusively by Ryans. He raised up his steaming glass to his brother.

'To the Ryans!'

'The Ryans!'

Geoffrey and Anthony were sitting at the end of Penzance Gardens, where it met Princedale Road. It was nearly two-fifteen in the morning. They sat in a black Humber Snipe. Both were freezing and both were nervous, especially Geoffrey. At twenty-one he was two years older than Anthony. They were identical to look at. Both had the Ryan dark hair and firm chin. Anthony had more of Michael's ruggedness whereas Geoffrey had softer features, almost effeminate.

Anthony spoke. His voice in the darkness caused Geoffrey to jump. 'How much longer have we got to wait?'

'How the hell do I know? What do you think I am? The Oracle or something?'

'Very funny. You get on my wick, do you know that?' Anthony's usual animosity was coming to the fore. Anthony Ryan was known in his family as able to pick a fight with his own fingernails. The only person he was even remotely respectful to was Mickey. 'You think because you've read a few crappy books you know it all.'

Geoffrey rolled his eyes up towards the roof of the car.

'Do me a favour, Ant . . . Save all your hag for what we've got to do tonight. I ain't in the mood.'

They were silent again. Anthony was frustrated because he wasn't as quick-brained as Geoffrey so always came off worse in an argument. It didn't deter him though. He tried a different tack.

'I saw that sort you've been knocking about with last night. I'd give her one meself.' Knowing that it would annoy Geoffrey, Anthony braced himself for the ensuing argument. Instead, Geoffrey put his hand over his brother's mouth. They listened. Footsteps were approaching the car. They sat tense and nervous. Anthony's hard features looked as if they had been carved from stone. His fists were clenched tight on the steering wheel.

The man who was walking towards them stepped into the light of a streetlamp. It was Joe the Fish. He was walking unsteadily along the road, obviously the worse for drink. Geoffrey nodded and Anthony started the car. He did not put on the headlights. Reversing back a little, they waited until Joe began crossing the intersection between Penzance Gardens and Princedale Road. Pushing his foot down on the accelerator, Anthony thrust the car forward.

Hearing a loud noise through his drunken haze, Joe turned in time to see the car coming at him. He raised his arm as if to protect himself as the car hit him full on. His body flew into the air and landed on the bonnet. His head crashed against the windscreen. Anthony slammed his foot on the brake. As the car screeched to a halt, Joe's body slid from the bonnet on to the road. Anthony ran the car over him one more time before speeding off. The whole operation had taken less than three minutes. A woman who had been up getting herself a glass of water heard the commotion and ran out into the street. She took one look at Joe's face and began to scream. Lights began to go on all over Princedale Road.

Anthony and Geoffrey drove the car from Holland Park to Moscow Road in Bayswater. The streets were deserted. Parking the car they left it there and walked around to Porchester Terrace, throwing the keys to the Humber Snipe down a drainhole. In Porchester Terrace they picked up a blue Mark I Zephyr and drove sedately home to Lancaster Road. It was just three o'clock.

Inside a private house in Beauchamp Place, Knightsbridge, Michael picked up his cards and studied them carefully. He was on a winning streak tonight. He had three aces and two kings. Joe had left an hour earlier. He had been given a lift to the Bayswater Road by a mutual friend, Derek O'Connor. If everything had gone according to plan then Joe was well and truly out of the picture, and he, Michael, had the perfect alibi. He smiled smugly to himself as he raised the bet by fifty pounds. If Geoffrey and Anthony had bungled the job tonight, he would personally batter their brains out.

Sarah heard a loud banging on her front door. She glanced at the clock on the bedside table. It was five o'clock in the morning. Sleepily she dragged herself out of bed. Benjamin was snoring his head off as usual, so it wasn't the police after him – that would make a change. She yawned, went down the stairs and opened the front door. Two men stood there and she recognised at once that they were CID.

'Is Michael at home, love?'

Blinking her eyes rapidly to try and clear her head, Sarah said, 'Come inside and I'll go and look.'

The two men walked into the hallway.

She went upstairs and looked into Michael's room. The bed hadn't been slept in. As she walked back on to the landing, Geoffrey came out of his room.

'Who's that downstairs, Mum?'

'The old Bill. They're looking for Michael. What's going on?'

She knew her sons and would bet her last pound that Geoffrey had been awake waiting for something like this.

'You go back to bed, Mum. I'll sort out the Filth.'

Both turned as they heard a door opening. Maura Ryan came out of her room, clutching a raggy doll. Sarah went to her, picking her up in her arms. Geoffrey went down the stairs.

'Mickey ain't in.'

'Well, where is he then?' This from the older of the policemen.

'He's up West. At a house in Knightsbridge. What do you want him for?' Geoffrey yawned in their faces, scratching his belly lazily. The younger policeman noticed that his pyjamas were hardly creased. Geoffrey Ryan hadn't been in bed. The trouble would be proving it.

'Somebody tried to murder Joe the Fish earlier.'

Geoffrey felt as if someone had thrown a bucket of cold water over him. 'What do you mean, tried to murder him?'

'Exactly what I say. And knowing how close Mickey is to him, I thought we had better let him know.' The older officer was trying to goad him.

Unlike Anthony, Geoffrey could keep a lid on his temper. Deliberately misconstruing the policeman's words, he shook his head sadly and said, 'Mickey's like a son to that man. This will come as a great shock to him. What exactly happened?' He had to know what was going on. Half of his mind was saying silent prayers. He'd been sure Joe was dead when they left him.

'Someone tried to run him over a few hours ago. He's fighting for his life in St Charles's Hospital. The hospital said to try and get his next-of-kin. We assumed that was Michael Ryan. Two men couldn't get any closer than those two have been over the last couple of years, could they?' The policeman raised his eyebrows and his colleague laughed.

Geoffrey was saved from answering by his mother's voice. She had been carrying Maura down the stairs and had heard the policeman's remark.

'What are you trying to say? I know you lot with your dirty insinuendos.' She hitched her daughter up on to her shoulder, holding her steady with her free hand. The other was gripping the banister rail, her knuckles white and bony. 'My Michael is a decent clean-living individual. Now I'll thank you two to get out of my house.'

Hiding a grin, Geoffrey took the heavy child from her as she came to the bottom of the stairs. Maura sat in his arms, an alert expression on her face. At seven she was already wise to the likes of the police. Sarah pushed angrily at the two policemen. She looked so tiny beside the two men, yet so ferocious, that Geoffrey laughed out loud.

'That's it, Muvver. Tell the bastards to sling their hooks.'

Opening the front door, Sarah let the men out. She was fuming. How dare they say that of her Michael! Her temper was caused by the fact that she had a terrible suspicion that what they said was true. Slamming the door on them, she turned her anger on her son.

'Well, don't stand there like a gormless eejit! Go and get dressed and find Mickey!'

Placing Maura carefully on the floor, Geoffrey ran up the stairs. Maura followed her mother into the kitchen, curling up on one of the easy chairs by the fire.

'Can I have a standing up egg, Mum?'

Sarah nodded. 'Of course you can have a boiled egg if that's what you want.'

She filled the kettle, her mind racing. If Joe the Fish died then it would be a murder charge for somebody. But who? Michael? She pushed the thought from her head. Whatever she thought about her boys, there was one thing she knew: they were not murderers. They were just tearaways. High-spirited tearaways. Or, at least, she hoped that's all they were. Putting the kettle on the gas, she went to her daughter and hugged her tightly.

Joe was lying in the hospital bed. Nurse Walton looked down at his battered face. She shook her head and turned to see the policeman by the bed grimacing at her. She blinked and sighed.

'Who would do such a thing?' Her voice sounded very young.

PC Blenkinsop pushed out his narrow chest and tried to look like an all-knowing, sophisticated officer.

'You'd be surprised. It's a wicked life out on the street these days. He might look like an old man who's been run over a few times to you, but to me . . .' he puffed his chest out even further '. . . he's a vicious criminal.'

Nurse Walton looked suitably impressed. 'Just wait until I tell my mum!'

PC Blenkinsop looked as if he was readjusting his shoulders inside his tunic top. He thrust out his chin and smiled.

Joe groaned and immediately had the attention of both of them. 'Mickey . . . Mickey.'

PC Blenkinsop was writing down Joe's words with a flourish of his pencil. Licking it, he waited expectantly.

Michael stood in the entrance to the ward. He had known that a policeman would be in attendance. Squaring his shoulders, he walked down the ward towards Joe's bed. He could see the young PC and the nurse through the inadequate screens. Putting a sober expression on his face, he went to the bed.

PC Blenkinsop noted Nurse Walton's reaction to Michael Ryan and it annoyed him. He thrust out his lip like a petulant schoolboy.

'And who might you be?' He stood up and seemed to roll on the balls of his feet. Michael gave him a scathing glance. He picked up Joe's hand which was heavily bandaged. He turned to the nurse and smiled sadly at her.

'How bad is he?' His voice sounded wretched. Nurse Walton stared into his dark blue eyes and was immediately filled with pity for him.

'He's very bad. The doctor says he'll be surprised if he lasts out the day.' If she had known Michael, she would have noticed the glimmer of relief that came into his eyes.

'Has he said anything at all?'

The PC interrupted. 'He has been calling for a . . .' he glanced importantly at his notebook '. . . Mickey.'

Michael nodded. 'That's me.'

The young nurse brought Michael a chair and he sat beside Joe, holding the old man's hand and stroking it every now and again. The PC watched him. So this was Michael Ryan. He couldn't wait to get back to the station and brag about how he'd seen him.

The nurse brought Michael a cup of tea and he thanked

her, giving her one of his radiant smiles. PC Blenkinsop could have cried. She didn't even know he was there now.

Shortly before seven in the evening Joe opened his eyes and immediately recognised Michael. He passed his tongue over his cracked lips and tried to speak. Michael could see by the look in his eyes that he knew who had ordered his accident. Agitated, Joe tried to lift his head off the pillow.

'Mickey . . . Mickey . . . you . . .' Then his head fell back and he died.

Michael closed his eyes, a feeling of euphoria surging through him. He had got away with it! Then, as could happen with him, he felt a deep despondency replace his feeling of elation. Tears welled up in his eyes, spilling over on to his cheeks. In his own funny way he would miss Joe who had been his passport into the real world. For that he would always be grateful to him. He would give Joe the Fish the best send-off anyone had ever seen.

PC Blenkinsop looked embarrassed. Later on in the station canteen he had everyone hanging on his words.

'Yeah, I'm telling you. It was quite touching. Michael Ryan cried like a baby. Well, it was to be expected really. After all, the old boy died calling out his name.'

At Joe's funeral a week later, the police noted that all the gang bosses stopped to pay their respects to Michael Ryan. He was well and truly established now. That, together with the fact that Joe had willed him everything he possessed, made Michael Ryan a very happy man.

Chapter Five

1960

Sister Rosario looked at the pinched face of Maura Ryan and her heart went out to the child. She had noticed her being teased mercilessly all through the dinner hour, no doubt due to the fact that her brother Benjamin had been expelled the day before. The nun realised that now the child had no one to protect her, some of the other children were making up for lost time. She watched Margaret Lacey lean forward across her desk and pull hard on one of Maura Ryan's long blond plaits. Sister Rosario didn't like Margaret Lacey. She didn't like any of the Laceys, with their carroty red hair and green malicious eyes. And this Margaret Lacey was the most brazen strap of a child she had ever come across. The nun leapt from her seat, causing her chair to fly backwards. The noise brought thirty pairs of eyes to rest on her.

'Margaret Lacey, come out here at once!' Her voice reverberated around the classroom. Margaret, her face pale with fright, slowly edged her way from behind her desk and began to walk to the front of the class. Sister Rosario was without doubt the hardest nun in the school. No amount of tears could shake her. Margaret stood before her, trembling. Tapping a ruler across the palm of her hand, Sister Rosario stared at the child for a few seconds. She knew from thirty years' experience that bullies were a breed apart. Most were inherent cowards who picked only on people who they knew were frightened of them.

The nun's countenance and dark brown close-set eyes challenged the child before her.

'Did I see you pull Maura Ryan's plait?'

Margaret's big green eyes seemed to have taken possession of the whole of her face. Her tiny pink mouth was trembling. Already, tears were beginning to glisten in her eyes.

'N . . . N . . . No, Miss . . . I mean, Sister.'

In her fright she had begun to stutter. This caused some of the other children to titter, quickly putting their hands over their mouths to stifle the sound.

Margaret Lacey was the class bully and the children enjoyed seeing her get, for once, what she doled out so often.

'Are you calling me a liar?' The nun's eyes had narrowed.

'No, Sister!' Margaret's voice was stronger now. Whoever heard of calling a nun a liar? It was unthinkable. Her own mother would kill her if she knew. Her eyes were now riveted on the ruler in the nun's hand. She knew that it was liable to come swishing down on her hands and legs at any moment.

Sister Rosario was enjoying Margaret's discomfiture. Running her tongue across her teeth she glared down at the object of her annoyance. Her white wimple covered nearly all her head, revealing only wrinkled yellowing skin that, combined with her dark eyes, had earned her the epithet 'Lizard Features'.

'So . . . you admit to pulling Maura Ryan's plait then?'

Maura watched Sister Rosario completely demoralise Margaret Lacey. She sat in her chair, her face scarlet. She did not thank this nun for making her the centre of attention. She knew that whatever Margaret got she would make sure Maura got it back one hundredfold.

'Yes, Sister . . . I pulled Maura's plait.' This was said so low as to be virtually inaudible.

'Speak up, child.'

'Yes, Sister. I pulled Maura Ryan's plait.' The high piping little voice was trembling with fear.

Smiling smugly at the class, Sister Rosario lifted the ruler. 'Hold out your hand then.'

The thin little hand came out. Margaret closed her eyes tightly as the ruler came down hard six times across her palm. Against her will, hot scalding tears burst from her eyes and down her cheeks. She held her injured hand to her breast as if frightened it might drop off, and at a nod from Sister Rosario made her way back to her desk, rubbing at her injured palm with the thumb of her good hand.

Sister Rosario's beady eyes scanned the classroom for about twenty seconds before she said, 'Let that be a warning to any would-be bullies in this class. Next time it will be twelve strokes of the ruler and your name read out at mass.'

Thirty faces looked scandalised at the thought of having their name read out by Father McCormack. Picking up her chair, the nun turned to her blackboard and began writing on it.

Seizing her opportunity, Margaret leant forward across her desk and whispered to Maura.

'You're dead, Ryan. Come hometime I'm gonna kill you.'

Maura closed her eyes, a knot of fear already forming in her stomach. Everyone was frightened of Margaret Lacey, even some of the boys. Which was surprising really because she was so small. But small or not, she could fight and that was all that counted.

Maura sat back in her chair and looked out of the window to the side of her. A group of younger children were playing rounders. The voice of Miss Norman, the games teacher, drifted in at the window now and again. Always encouraging, never reprimanding. As Maura watched the dust motes flying through the air in the rays of the June sun she wished that she was outside with the younger children. That she was anywhere away from Margaret Lacey and her cronies who would without doubt be waiting for her as she left the school. Why was it that time always flew when you didn't want it to? The minutes sped by until the bell that heralded hometime.

Slowly Maura went to get her coat, hoping against hope that if she took long enough Margaret would get fed up and go home. She walked slowly from the school, across the playground and out of the gates into Latimer Road. Sure enough, Margaret was waiting for her, about twenty yards past the school gates. She had three of her cronies with her: Jennifer Howard, Betty Leeds and Vanessa Rouse. Maura began walking towards them like a condemned man on his way to the gallows. Prickles of sweat had broken out along her backbone. She bit down hard on her lip as she watched the four girls.

She saw that Jennifer and Vanessa were laughing at her

and something inside her stirred. In all her ten years she had always had one or other of her brothers watching out for her. Now here for the first time she was fighting her own battle. And fight it she would! She swallowed deeply. She could hear her heart crashing in her ears. She decided then and there that she was not going to stand for it. She had eight brothers and had had to fight or argue with every one of them at some time or another. Holding her head high, she walked faster, swinging her schoolbag menacingly.

The four girls looked at each other, puzzled. This wasn't supposed to happen! First they were going to make her squirm, then Margaret was going to hit her . . . Betty Leeds began to hop from one foot to another, a sure sign of agitation. Vanessa and Jennifer stepped back behind Margaret. Maura stopped in front of them, still swinging her schoolbag. She gave a loud sniff.

'Well?' The insolent way she said it made the other girls gasp with astonishment. Margaret Lacey soon found her tongue.

'I'll "well" you, you ugly bitch you! I'm gonna smash your face in!'

The other girls smiled. This was more like it.

'Well then, don't just stand there talking about it . . . do it!'

All eyes were glued to the swinging schoolbag. Margaret was silent for a few seconds. She could feel the others losing their nerve. If she didn't do something, and soon, they would desert her. She spat on to the pavement casually.

'I will when I'm good and ready!'

Margaret Lacey was getting more worried by the second. She had thought she'd give Maura's long blond hair a few good tugs, a scratch or two on her face, and then home to tea, basking in the other girls' admiration. Now she wasn't sure what to do. She might even get hit herself! She decided on a delaying tactic. Kneeling down on the dusty pavement, she made as if to tie her shoelaces.

The next thing she knew, she was lying sprawled across the pavement. Maura's schoolbag had hit her straight in the side of the head. Next, her long red hair was pulled so hard she felt as if it was going to come out by the roots. Finally, she felt a kick on the knee that brought a shocked cry to her throat. She lay on the pavement staring up at Maura Ryan, amazed. Her three friends had already run off. As soon as Maura's schoolbag had hit Margaret in the head, they had made their escape, frightened in case Maura decided on a repeat performance on one of them!

Maura just stood there stunned, staring at Margaret lying at her feet. She had done that! She had knocked Margaret Lacey down! She could feel her chest swelling with the joy of it. She had actually defended herself against Margaret Lacey, the school bully, and she had won. She had done it alone without one of her brothers to defend her!

Seeing Margaret begin to pull herself up, Maura's natural kindness came to the fore. This would be all over the school tomorrow. She tentatively held out her hand to help Margaret up. The smaller girl looked at her long and hard before accepting it. Maura pulled her to her feet and began to brush down Margaret's uniform, which was covered in grey dust. This was all done in silence, except for the occasional sniff. Maura saw the small swelling on Margaret's grubby knee and felt ashamed of herself. She had kicked her very hard and Margaret *was* smaller than her. In silent agreement they walked together down

Latimer Road, into Bramley Road and then through to Lancaster Road, where both girls lived. They stopped outside Margaret's house first and stood looking at one another.

Margaret sniffed loudly and said, 'Come in if you want. Me mum's at work.'

It was the hand of friendship. Maura shrugged nonchalantly. 'All right then.'

They walked up the steps that led to the front door. Margaret's house was the same as Maura's except it had been made into flats. Margaret's family lived on the top floor. Being large town houses they were three storeys high with large basements. As many as five families lived in them. As they made their way up the stairs the smell of cooking and urine seemed to overpower them. Margaret's flat had no lock on the door. There was no need for one, there was nothing to steal.

'You take off your things and I'll make us some bread and Marmite.'

'Ooh, lovely. I love Marmite.'

As Margaret made the sandwiches and a pot of weak tea, Maura glanced around her. The room was filthy, clothes and newspapers strewn everywhere. Unlike her own home that was stoved regularly, cockroaches were on everything. A particularly adventurous one with large quivering antennae was being slowly buried in the rancid margarine. Maura shuddered inwardly. The last few years her mother had been waging a war on all vermin, including bed bugs. Money was now plentiful in her home, thanks to Michael's employing her brothers in his business, while the majority of the people in Lancaster Road were still no better off than they had been before the war. Margaret's mother worked at the new Black Cat cigarette factory out in Harlow and her father still worked in Lyons bakery. Maura watched with distaste as Margaret flicked the cockroach out of the margarine with the breadknife. It landed on the floor where it lay on its back, its numerous legs doing cycling motions as it tried to right itself. Wrinkling her nose Margaret stepped on it, the crunching noise sounding like a gunshot in the hot evening air.

'I hate them bloody things.'

'So do I.' Maura's voice sounded small.

Soon the girls were eating their sandwiches and drinking weak tea. Neither of them mentioned what had taken place outside the school and neither of them would. From outside, the sounds of a game of cricket floated into the hot airless room. Finishing her tea, Maura got up to go. Margaret offered Maura her little finger with a shy smile. Maura linked it with her own, vowing that the two girls would be best friends for always – through thick and thin. This was the female way of becoming blood brothers – unlike the boys they did not cut each other's thumbs.

Margaret walked Maura down the stairs to the street. 'I'll be here in the morning to walk to school. OK?'

Margaret nodded her head vigorously. 'See you then, Maura.'

' 'Bye.' Maura walked towards her own house. She felt lighthearted and gay. What had started out as a bad day had suddenly become brighter.

In the road a gang of boys with a makeshift cricket bat stopped their game to look at her. Already the news was travelling fast. Dinny O'Brien, one of Garry's friends, smiled at her.

'That right you podgered Margaret Lacey, Maws?'

She nodded, feeling herself blush.

'We're friends now, Dinny.'

He looked away, disgusted. Trust girls! In Dinny's code, if you beat someone in a fight you made their life misery for as long as possible. You did not become friends with them.

Maura hurried home. As she let herself in at the front door her mother's voice came booming out of the kitchen.

'Is that you, Maura!'

'Yes, Mum.'

She went into the kitchen where Sarah was standing, hands on hips, her face like thunder.

'Where have you been, you bloody little sod? I've been out of my mind with worry about you.'

Maura chewed on her lip, staring at her mother. She very rarely got told off and when she did it upset her.

'Well? Answer me, you little cow.' Sarah's face was haggard.

'I went to me friend's house and had a bit of tea.' Her enormous blue eyes had tears glistening on their lashes. Sarah saw her daughter's face crumple and her heart melted. Pulling the child into her arms, she hugged her close.

'I'm sorry, love, but you gave me such a fright. It's not like you to stay out like that. You're normally the first one home. I was worried.'

'I'm sorry, Mum, I won't do it again, I promise,' She tried to smile at her mother, genuinely sorry to have vexed her.

'I sent Benny, Garry and Lee out looking for you.' As if her words had conjured them up, all three burst into the kitchen.

'Mum . . . Mum!' They were all talking at once. 'Have a guess what!'

'One at a time . . . One at a time.' She held up her hands for silence then pointed at Garry, the most honest of the three.

'Right then, Garry, you tell me what happened.'

He pointed at Maura who was beginning to panic.

'It's her.'

'What about her?' Sarah looked at Maura, a frown on her face.

'She's been and gone and smashed Margaret Lacey's face in!'

Sarah's eyes widened. 'She's what!'

The tone of her voice frightened Maura. She pulled on her mother's flowery apron.

'I had to, Mum. She was gonna kill me 'cos Sister Rosario gave her the ruler for pulling me plaits.' She looked into her mother's face, pleading for understanding.

'Am I hearing right? You . . .' she pointed at Maura '. . . had a fight with Margaret Lacey.' She screwed up her eyes as if she was having difficulty seeing her child.

Maura was gabbling with fright. 'I hit her with me bag but we're friends now, Mum. That's where I was earlier when you were looking for me.'

Sarah shook her head slowly as if to clear it. So this one had gone too, another fighter in the family.

'Go on, all of you . . . out in the street to play. Your dad will be in soon and I haven't got a bit of food on.' She pushed the children towards the kitchen door. She wanted them all away from her.

The three boys ran out. Maura stood for a second looking at her mother. 'I'm sorry, Mum . . . honestly.'

Sarah's voice was tired. 'Get yourself outside, Maws. Go on now.'

When she had gone, Sarah poured herself out a large

mug of thick black tea. She spooned four heaped spoonsful of sugar into it and some condensed milk and sat at the kitchen table. She sipped her tea and her body seemed to sag in the chair. Her mind was racing, though.

Leslie, aged twenty, was doing three years for robbery. Anthony, aged twenty-two, was with him, doing five years for robbery and malicious wounding. Michael was like the local Mafia, everyone was frightened of him. He now had all the older boys working for him. Over the years she had forced these thoughts from her mind, telling herself that her sons were the product of their father. And now this! Her only daughter, the apple of her eye, had been brawling in the street. It just wasn't fair. Her mother used to say that what was bred in the bone came out in the blood, and she had been right.

Oh, Sarah had plenty of money these days and the house was lovely. After the lean years, she had been only too happy to take the money her sons thrust on her. She had never questioned where it came from, though she knew deep inside. But if their lifestyles affected her daughter, she would murder the lot of them. Maura was going to have the chances that she herself had never had. One of her children would achieve something in this world. She was determined on that.

Outside in the summer evening, Maura was the centre of attention.

'Well done, Maws.' This from Garry, who was very fond of his sister.

'I hit her with me bag, that's what done it.'

They all looked across the road as they heard their father call. Maura's eyes lit up and she skipped across the road to meet him. Benjamin Ryan had had a skinful, that much was evident. He was flushed around his ample face and neck. Under one arm he had a large box of crisps and a bottle of Tizer. He passed the box to Lee who had followed Maura over the street and picked his daughter up in his arms. The old man, as they called him, worshipped his daughter and they all knew this and accepted it. In their own way they all felt the same. Maura rubbed her face against his cheek and felt his stubble scratching against her smooth skin. She breathed in his familiar odour of best bitter and Woodbines and snuggled against him, safe and secure.

'How's me best girl then?'

'All right, Dad. Had a win?'

He laughed at her cheek.

'How do you know I've had a win?' He asked the question in a mock stern voice.

'The box of crisps and Tizer for a start, and your beery breath.'

Benjamin looked at his sons, a theoretical scowl on his face. 'Hear that, boys? Typical woman! She'll drink the Tizer and eat the crisps, and still complain where they come from!'

Benny laughed with Maura, but Garry and Lee just smiled wanly. The memory of empty bellies because their father had gambled away all the National Assistance was still fresh in their minds. They all walked up the steps and into the house.

Sarah had started the evening meal. She completely ignored her husband until he fell asleep in his chair, whereupon she woke him up and berated him all the way up the stairs, their shouting and swearing affecting the children not one iota. Half an hour later they sat down to their tea. Maura was once more in high spirits. As they sat chatting around the table there was a loud knock on the front door. Garry answered it and came back into the kitchen with two policemen.

'Go and wake your dad up.' Sarah's voice was heavy.

The elder of the two policemen smiled at Sarah but she dropped her eyes and tried to busy herself at the sink. Every nerve in her body was jangling. Every time the police visited her house she felt a heavy sickness inside her. Maura and Benny carried on eating.

Benjamin Ryan shuffled into the kitchen in his trousers and string vest, his braces hanging down the sides of his legs.

'What the fuck do you want?' His voice was menacing.

The older policeman looked at the children, a question in his eyes.

'Never you mind them, they'll hear what you got to say sooner or later. Now spit it out, man. I ain't got all day.'

'Very well. We've got some bad news for you, concerning your son Anthony.'

'What about my Antney? Escaped, has he?' Benjamin's voice sounded hopeful.

'No, not exactly. I'm sorry to tell you, Mr Ryan, that your son is dead.'

'He's *what*!' Sarah's hand went to her chest and she struggled to find breath. Lee went to her and folded her in his arms. The younger children were pale and silent.

'He was stabbed to death this morning in Pentonville prison. In the showers. We're doing everything possible to find the people responsible.'

Sarah's sobbing was building to a crescendo. The younger policeman was watching her, fascinated.

'Jesus H. Christ!' Benjamin was trying to clear his drink-fuddled brain. 'Who would want to kill my Antney? Everyone liked him . . .'

The younger policeman dragged his eyes from Sarah and looked at Benjamin.

'Well, someone didn't. You don't stab your mates.'

Benjamin went for him. 'Why, you dirty little bastard!'

The other officer intervened, all formality forgotten now.

'Calm down, Benny. And you, Brown, shut your bloody big gob!' He pushed Benjamin back against the kitchen wall. 'Look, Ben, we've been questioning Leslie all morning and he won't say a dicky bird, but we think he knows who done it.'

Benjamin pushed the man away. 'Of course he won't tell you. He ain't a grass.'

'Grass or no, Ben, this person has killed his brother.'

'And that person will pay. Thanks for coming, Bill, but you can go now. I need to speak to me wife.'

His tone held dismissal and the two officers left the house. Benjamin pointed at Lee.

'Go up West to Mickey's and tell him what's happened. Tell him, Geoffrey and Roy to get their arses home – now.' Lee nodded. Still holding his mother, he walked her to his father. As Benjamin tried to comfort her, Sarah pushed him violently away.

'Don't you dare touch me! You've brought us to this, you conniving old bastard.'

Getting up from her seat, Maura ran to her mother. The two held on to each other tightly. Benjamin looked frightened by his wife's attitude. The hatred in her voice had shocked him.

'Garry, nip round and get the quack for your mother.'

The boy ran from the room, frightened. His mother's wailing, following him down the front steps, seemed to spur him on. Maura, tears running down her face, was frightened out of her wits. Anthony was dead . . . her brother Anthony who had alternately teased and comforted her was lying somewhere dead, never to come home again. Fighting Margaret Lacey seemed so futile now. Why was it that bad things always happened when you were feeling happy?

The voices had been going on all evening. Maura could not sleep. She slipped out of bed, where her mother was snoring softly. The doctor had been in and given her some sleeping pills. He had tried to give her an injection but it had only made her more hysterical. Pulling the cover up over her mother's shoulders, Maura crept from the room and down the stairs.

The front room door was slightly open and she pressed her face to the crack. Her eldest brother Mickey was walking up and down the room talking, his face set in a dark scowl. Maura loved Mickey. He was her favourite brother. She thought he was the handsomest of them all. All the boys were dark, with deep-set blue eyes, but Mickey was magnificent. He had something that attracted people to him – men as well as women. Maura adored him. He was like a god to her. Now, though, she was seeing a Mickey that she didn't know. His teeth were gritted together and he had dark circles under his eyes. He looked ferocious.

'I swear I'll kill the bastards! So help me God, I'll kill them.'

'Calm down, Mickey. Calm down.' This from Geoffrey.

'Calm down, you say? When them bastards have stabbed our brother to death?'

Geoffrey took a long drink of his whisky.

'Calm down and think clearly, that's what I'm saying. Think with your head and not your heart.'

Michael stopped abruptly in his pacing and punched the wall.

'I'd rather have given the bastards the cab ranks than see Antney dead.'

Geoffrey sighed.

'Well, it's done now, Bruv. What we've got to decide is how we retaliate.'

'We'll blow the fuckers off the face of the earth, that's what we'll do!'

'I was thinking along those lines.' Everyone in the room stared at Gerry Jackson, one of Mickey's closest friends, and he coloured slightly.

'What I thought was, right, they've got a rank in Ilford, ain't they? In the High Street.'

All heads nodded in agreement.

'Well, on Saturday night, Lee here and a few of his mates can go up the Ilford Palais, right? Later on in the evening they go into the Greek bastard's can rank, as for a cab to say . . . Wanstead. Anywhere, just so they can get a good look in. If he's there, one of them can trot off and let us know, then we can poodle round and petrol bomb the place. We can sit round Green Lanes waiting for word. It must be someone they won't recognise. That would teach the saucy gits a lesson.'

Mickey nodded his head.

'Yeah, that sounds dawdy, Gerry, I'll have some of that. Meantime, me and Geoff and Roy, who'll be the main suspects, can be causing a disturbance somewhere else.'

'Brilliant! That's it then.'

Maura, listening to all this, was frightened. Her brothers were planning to blow someone up! She had heard people talk about her brothers. Tearaways and out of control, had become the prevalent opinion in Lancaster

Road. Yet she realised that people were always nice to their faces, especially Mickey's. A couple of Saturdays previously, she had walked with him along the Portobello Road. They had stopped to get some fruit for her, and the stall-holder had insisted that it was a gift, refusing Michael's money as if it was the norm to give his produce away for free. Now she knew why people acted like they did. It was because her brothers blew people up.

She started to hop from one foot to the other. She was scared. Anthony was dead and her brothers were going to blow someone up. Suddenly, the door opened and Roy was standing in front of her.

She saw his face go pale.

'What's this then? Can't you sleep, Princess?' His voice was very loud. He picked her up and carried her into the front room. It was heavy with cigarette smoke and she coughed. Michael held out his arms to her and she shrank away from him, clinging to Roy. This Mickey frightened her. This was not her brother who cuddled her and bought her things . . . this was a man who blew people up. She looked fearfully into his face. He was so hurt by her attitude he was nearly in tears. With all that had happened with Anthony, he was near the end of his tether. Suddenly sensing this, Maura slipped out of Roy's arms and ran to him, big dry sobs bursting from her throat and bouncing off the walls.

He scooped her up into his arms and holding her tightly, rubbed his face into her soft, sweet-smelling hair.

She cried hard, wracking sobs distorting her voice. 'I want Antney to come home . . . I want Antney to come home! Blow the bad man up, Mickey. Blow the bad man up!'

He looked at the other men in the room, his eyes

resting on his father. Through her tears Maura heard someone mutter, 'Jesus Christ!'

Michael held her until her sobs subsided. Holding her away from him so he could look into her face, he spoke to her. His voice sounded worried.

'Listen, Princess. You must never . . . ever . . . tell anyone what you heard here tonight. Do you understand what I'm saying? If you tell anyone, even a friend, then the police will come and take us all away. Even Dad. Do you understand me?'

She nodded at him solemnly. 'I won't tell anyone, Mickey . . . not even Mum.'

Instinctively she knew that this was what he wanted to hear. He blinked and the relief in his eyes was evident. 'Good girl. You're a good girl. Now, let Dad put you back to bed.' He kissed her on the forehead and lips tenderly, then placed her on the floor. 'Good night, Princess.'

She took her father's outstretched hand and began to walk from the room. At the door she looked back over her shoulder at Mickey, her face serene. In her white nightdress she looked like a golden angel. She opened her mouth and spoke.

'I meant what I said, Mickey . . . get them that done in Antney.' With that she carried on walking with her father. Benjamin looked at her sadly. His little girl was learning the realities of life. He just wished she could have been spared them a little longer.

On 20 July 1960 they buried Anthony Ryan. The funeral cortège went slowly past Wormwood Scrubs prison, up past the wagon works and on to Saint Mary's Roman Catholic Cemetery at the top of Scrubs Lane. There were five cars from the funeral parlour following the coffin.

Behind these were two dozen other cars containing friends and relatives. A police car containing Leslie, handcuffed but in his best suit, was last in the line.

In the first car Sarah sat dry-eyed, staring out at the passing roads. As they had passed by Du Cane Road, where the entrance to Wormwood Scrubs prison was, she had been reminded of how many times she had been there, visiting either her husband or one of the older boys. Her husband had been proud of how he had lived his life. 'I'm a ducker and diver.' How many times had she heard him tell someone that? Well, the result of his way of living was upon them today. Her lovely boy dead. She felt the hot tears bunch in her throat.

Looking into her troubled face, Benjamin placed his hand gently on her arm. She smacked it away. She blamed him for all this. He had encouraged the boys to be villains. Even when they had been little more than babies he had started to corrupt them. If they had been beaten in a fight, he would give them a good hiding and send them back out to do the job properly.

'None of my boys are Nancys,' had been one of his favourite expressions, coupled with, 'All my boys are hard.' He had dragged them to dog tracks, pubs, bare knuckle fights. He had taught them how to pick a lock, steal a car, to shoplift . . . The list was endless.

What had he done? she asked herself. She felt an urge to fell him to the floor of the car, strike his face and hurt him as she was hurting inside. Her big manly husband – at this moment she hated him. She crossed her arms across her breasts and hugged herself. Her gaze lighted on her only daughter and her face softened. This one he could not touch. A beauty was her Maura. Sarah's pride in her daughter knew no bounds. With her white-blond hair and dark blue eyes, she was exquisite. Now Maura's hair was hanging in long waves, unaccustomed to being out of plaits, her eyes sad and shining with unshed tears. Sarah knew that the child was bewildered by all that had happened. She leant across the car and grasped Maura's hand, forcing herself to give her daughter a little wink. The cars stopped and everyone got out, standing around in little groups, talking in hushed voices.

Sarah's seven remaining sons carried Anthony's coffin to the graveside. The main mass and requiem mass had already been said in the RC Church in Notting Hill. Now all that was left was to bury her boy. The youngest, Benny, although only thirteen, walked with his brothers, carrying the coffin. Michael had placed Maura, dressed in white, at the front of the coffin. She led them slowly through the graveyard to the burial site.

Father McCormack was standing silently by the yawning hole. The sun was high in the sky and beating down on the mourners' heads. In the yew trees nearby, birds sang and the hum of traffic and smell of exhaust fumes carried on the air. Outside the cemetery walls were carts carrying totters from Shepherd's Bush. The rag and bone men were grim-faced and silent. Benjamin Ryan's eldest brother was leading them. Their horses had the old-fashioned black plumes rising up from their harnesses. The carts had been washed down and polished for the day's event. Paddy Ryan wiped a tear from his eyes as he watched his brother's son being lowered into the ground.

Bees were quietly going about their business, bumbling from flower to flower, the hot summer day bringing them out in force. The priest's voice droned on. The police had once again handcuffed Leslie. Funeral or no funeral they were not taking any chances. Maura was holding Michael's hand tightly, her face pale and troubled.

The policeman to whom Leslie was handcuffed was impressed by the turn-out. The Krays, Richardsons, and many more villains had come to pay their last respects. It showed the respect accorded to Michael Ryan.

Mickey stared stonily into the grave. Anthony's oak coffin had a large brass crucifix on the lid. The INRI above Jesus's head was glinting in the sunlight. In his mind's eye Michael could see Anthony's face inside it, staring upwards at darkness for the rest of eternity. He clenched his teeth together before he lost control and cried out. He prayed for the first time in years to the Holy Spirit to come and take his brother's soul. To care for him and protect him. He prayed to the Immaculate Conception and Holy Saint Anthony, the patron saint of miracles. He prayed to every saint and martyr he could remember from his years of Catholic schooling. Somehow, today, there being a God was important.

Out of the corner of his eye, he saw a movement. He turned his head. Being so tall he was head and shoulders above most of the mourners. To the left of him, standing about ten yards from the small crowd around the graveside, was a man. Michael stiffened. Feeling the change in him, Maura looked up into his face. She noticed that he was staring across the graveyard. She followed his gaze, through a small gap in the mourners opposite her, and saw the object of Michael's scrutiny.

The man was dark – not dark like her brothers but swarthy. His thick black curly hair seemed to grow around his head like a crown, leaving his forehead exposed where it had receded. He reminded her of the mad professor in her comics. The sun was behind him and she could see the glare that shone on his bald pate. Instinctively she knew that this was Stavros, the Greek man that her brothers had been constantly talking about since Anthony's death. The man was smiling slightly.

She looked from him to Michael and realised that her brother was going to go over to the man. He was pulling back his shoulders in his arrogant way. Holding Michael's hand tightly, she pulled on it. He looked down at her. When they both looked back a split second later the man was gone, but his face was stamped on Maura's memory. Then she felt the hot, scalding tears come into her eyes, spilling down her face and entering her mouth, their saltiness exploding on her tongue. From far off she heard shrieking. It was a few seconds before she realised that it was coming from her.

Michael picked her up in his arms and held her tightly to him, murmuring endearments into her hair and stroking her back until she was spent. After what seemed an age all that could be heard were little hiccups. Even the hardest of the men there was sobered by her outburst. Reggie Kray, always a lover of children, had tears in his eyes as he watched Michael comfort the girl. Like most Londoners from working-class backgrounds, family was important to them all. You looked after your own, no matter what.

A little while later, still holding Maura in his arms, Michael threw his handful of dirt on to the coffin. When the service was finished, he put her down gently by their mother and, picking up a shovel, filled in Anthony's grave, helped by Geoffrey and Roy.

One of the rag and bone men's wives, Lilly McNamara, had been asked to sing while this was being done. She was noted throughout Kensington and the surrounding areas as a fine singer. In the hush, broken only by the scraping of the shovels in the dirt and the soft thuds as it landed on the coffin, she sang 'Amazing Grace'. To outsiders it would have looked incongruous: men in black zoot suits, all with fashionable elephant's trunk hair styles, filling in a grave, surrounded by more men and women dressed in black. The women's hats and bright make-up made them look like exotic birds. To the Ryans and their like, Anthony had been given a magnificent send-off.

Sarah stood dignified and erect as her sons buried their brother. She would not cry here; she would wait until after the wake, when she was alone. In the scorching heat she had felt as if she would pass out; now she wished she had. It would have saved her having to watch this grisly ritual, the burying of her son's remains. She closed her eyes, her hand on her daughter's soft and springy hair.

When the singing was over and Anthony buried, the mourners went to the family and paid their respects. Diana Dors, the secret object of the young policeman's desire, hugged Michael long and hard. She was a firm favourite of everybody there, a kind, loving, generous woman who never in all her life judged anyone. Freddie Mills and his boyfriend Michael Holiday each clasped Michael to them. Freddie Mills had been Michael's boyhood hero. It had been worship of him that had aroused Michael's interest in boxing. Nowadays he met him socially, as an equal. A few days before Anthony's death they had been together at the Lancaster Road Baths watching local semi-professional boxers.

It did not escape Sarah's notice that Michael was treated as the head of the family and her husband relegated to second position. That was how it should be. After all, Michael was the main provider. He made sure that she had ample money. More than enough in fact. She did not feel overawed by the company at her son's funeral. She had known Violet Kray for many years. The Richardson boys had been visitors to her house for a long time. Many of the mourners were young men who had grown up with her sons. Petty criminals most of them, but good boys all the same.

Roy's wife looked depressed as usual. Sarah knew that it was not the funeral that had put the sad look on her daughter-in-law's face, but something quite different. Janine and Roy had problems, she was sure of that. Neither of them looked happy these days. Their daughter, Carla, nearly five now, looked as if she hadn't been washed for days. Sarah made a mental note to go and see Janine. Even in her grief she could still look out for her remaining children.

Finally, they began to make their way back to the cars. Sarah noticed Roy trying to take Janine's hand and being shrugged off. She frowned. As if there wasn't enough unhappiness in the family, they had to bring their petty squabbles into the cemetery with them.

Benny was staring at the mound of dirt that covered his brother. Benjamin walked back to get him, his old face looking more haggard and careworn than usual. He had been drinking steadily since the early morning.

'Come on, son.' His voice was slurred but gentle.

Benny was staring intently at a large worm wriggling on the pile of damp earth. In his mind's eye he saw it boring its way into the earth, down, down, until it reached his brother's face. Covering his own face with his hands, he was overtaken by silent sobs that made his shoulders shake. He was as tall as his father, and as Benjamin took his namesake into his arms, he felt the strength of him.

Sarah was watching them. She realised for the first time how Benjamin must be feeling. After all, Anthony had been his son too. A feeling she had not known in over a decade slipped through her body. All animosity towards her husband dissolved and a spark of affection for him seemed to light up inside her, as it had in the old days. She couldn't blame him entirely for what had happened. Children would go their own way in the end. In the environment they lived in it was inevitable that kids would turn to crime. All she could really blame him for was not working hard enough to get them out of it. She sighed heavily. How could he? He had never had the chance.

All this flashed through her head in an instant. She looked around the cemetery. The brilliant sunshine seemed to be mocking her. It was too nice a day to be burying a young life. It should have been cold and raining as befitted a funeral. She saw the flowers gently swaying in the light breeze, the lichen-covered gravestones that hid their contents from the world, and was overcome with sadness. The birds were still singing as she made her way slowly to the cars. Her body seemed to have shrunk since Anthony's death, giving her the appearance of an old woman. She was only forty-four.

Back at the house everyone was drinking. Maura pushed her way through the adults and stationed herself in the front room next to the table piled high with food. Presently she was joined by Margaret Lacey. This had been arranged the day before. That morning Margaret had complained of a bad bout of sickness. Her mother, anxious to get to work, had given her the day off school. Now she was up and dressed and holding her new best friend's hand. She could not even imagine what it must be like to have a brother who had been murdered. Her mum and dad had talked of nothing else for days. According to them it was a wonder something like this had not happened before. Margaret, though, wisely kept this bit of information to herself.

Mickey came up, and, taking the two girls by the hand, led them out of the house and into the back garden. He could not bear to be away from Maura today. She was so innocent and trusting. With his guilt over Anthony, he felt that at least she loved him and didn't blame him for the death. No one would dare say that it was his fault outright, but he knew what was going on in everyone else's mind.

He sat in an old deck chair and the two girls sat on the ground, each leaning against one of his legs. He was already half drunk. The sun was so hot it was impossible to open his eyes without being blinded. Eventually he dozed. Maura and Margaret sat by him for hours. The friendship of a lifetime was bonded that day. Maura and Margaret became a pair, the friendship only to end with the death of one of them.

That night in bed Maura had her first nightmare. It was of the man in the cemetery coming after her with her mother's bread knife. She was to have the same dream intermittently for the rest of her life.

Chapter Six

Carla Ryan opened her eyes. The sun was streaming in at the windows of her room. She lay for a few moments watching the patterns it made on the ceiling. A cool breeze drifted over her thin little body. She rubbed her arm, where she had a large bruise above the elbow. Her mother had picked her up bodily the night before and dragged her into her room where she had then thrown her on to her bed. She had bumped her arm on the little bedside cabinet. The pain had made her lose her breath for a few seconds. Lifting up her pink nightdress her mother had then smacked her behind as hard as she could, afterwards putting her face next to Carla's and telling her that she had had enough. Her mother's breath had been sour as it always was when she had been drinking.

What exactly her mother had had enough of Carla was not sure. All she had done the night before was make herself a sugar sandwich. She had asked her mother for something to eat over and over again, until finally she had decided to get it herself. She supposed it was the sugar all over the table and floor that had made her mother cross.

She sat herself up in bed and swung her little legs over the side. She yawned and her long brown hair fell over her face as she stretched her arms out. She winced as her bad arm was stretched. This was going to be a sore one, she reflected. Like the one she'd had on her leg a few weeks previously. Slipping off the bed she crept across her room, opening the door as silently as possible.

She looked through the crack into the hallway. Opposite her bedroom was the kitchen. She waited a few seconds for any sounds that might tell her that her mother was in there but out of her range of sight. Nothing. She walked across the hall and into the kitchen. The sugar she had spilt everywhere the night before was sticking to her bare feet. She was hungry again. She was always hungry. Sneaking across the kitchen she made herself some bread and margarine.

She was kneeling on a kitchen chair, her long hair trailing in the margarine, when she heard the steps. The heavy thudding steps that meant her mother was getting up. She froze. Her heart was fluttering in her chest. Her breathing came rapidly. Remembering the night before she threw her knife from her hand as if it was red hot, then tried to push the sticky mass of bread and margarine underneath the bread wrapper. In her haste she was clumsy and only succeeded in pushing the loaf of Dinkum bread and the sandwich off the table and on to the floor, already sticky from the sugar.

Tears of frustration stung her eyes. She felt her mother's presence before she turned and faced her, her little grubby hands clenching and unclenching with nerves. Janine looked at her coldly. Her daughter's face was exquisite even when she was terrified. Her eyes were a startling violet colour that made her look incredibly strong-minded.

Coupled with her dark brown hair and high cheekbones, she looked like a miniature woman. Janine watched her daughter sweep her hair away from her face with a gesture that was more fitting to a sexy movie star than a four-year-old girl. Her long neck and strong pointed chin were shown to advantage by the gesture.

Janine chewed her lip, staring spitefully at her child. She knew that if she didn't speak Carla would get more and more nervous, eventually breaking the heavy silence herself. She noticed the black bruise on her arm and a wicked light glowed in the back of her eyes. She would have to keep the child's arms covered, because Roy would go crazy if he thought his little angel had been whipped. She gritted her teeth and, aping the child's earlier movement, theatrically swept her own thick red hair off her face. She looked like a sleek, tawny cat about to pounce on its prey. Carla stared back at her, every nerve in her body tensed and waiting. As her mother swept back her hair in a parody of her own action she dropped her eyes. Everything she did annoyed her mother. How she sat, how she stood, how she ate, how she spoke. Every movement was ridiculed and parodied.

She wished her father was home but he was very rarely around much these days, and when he was her mother fought with him. Carla would curl up on his lap and hold her hands over her ears desperately trying to block out their arguing. She loved her father and missed him when he was away. She thought of him as a big tree, with strong branches that enabled her to climb him, which she did when he was home. With Roy holding her by the arms she walked up his body until, reaching his shoulders, she flipped over and landed on her feet, screeching with laughter. She wished he was here now. Her mother daren't touch her when her father was at home. The tension in the kitchen had reached its peak and, stuttering in fright, the child spoke.

'Where's me dad?' As soon as she spoke the words she flinched inside. Why had she mentioned him? She closed her eyes tightly. Somewhere inside her was a weak hope that she had not spoken. She heard her mother's slippers crunching across the sugar-strewn floor. She squeezed her eyes shut as tightly as possible. As she felt her hair being yanked, she screamed. The pain was searing through her scalp. Shaking her like a rag doll, Janine began to shout.

'You want your dad, do you? You little slut! He's out whoring as usual. Shacked up with some woman somewhere. He don't care about you.'

Carla was trying to drag her mother's fingers from her hair. Crying now, and frightened, she screamed back at her mother, 'Please, Mum . . . Please . . . Let go of me hair . . . You're hurting me!'

Sarah heard the screams from the entrance hall of the flats. Grabbing Maura's hand she ran up the stairs and banged on the front door with her fists, demanding to be let in. Janine heard the banging and shouting and went cold with fright. She threw Carla from her and looked around her wild-eyed, like an animal seeking an escape route. The state of the kitchen registered inside her mind somewhere. Carla lay sobbing where she had landed, holding her poor injured head in both hands. Her granny's banging on the door was like music to her ears.

She watched her mother walk out of the kitchen as if in a trance and a few seconds later Carla was nestled in her granny's arms. Little kisses were planted on her wet face, and murmured endearments and gentle strokes administered. Gradually the child calmed down. A handful of her hair was lying on the floor.

Maura watched the whole thing wide-eyed. Janine was now sitting at the kitchen table smoking a cigarette. Maura took in the dirty sugar floor and the loaf of bread now scattered everywhere, the filthy table and the stacks of dirty dishes. She dragged her eyes from it all, disgusted. She didn't like Janine. Taking the weeping Carla out of the kitchen Sarah motioned with her head for Maura to follow her, which she did gratefully. Going into Carla's room, Sarah laid the child on the bed. Maura watched as her mother checked the little girl from head to toe, shaking her head and tutting as she did it. Finally, Sarah turned to her own daughter.

'You stay here with Carla. Find some half-decent clothes and get her dressed. I'll call you if I need you . . . all right?' Her voice was thick with emotion. Maura nodded worldlessly. In the kitchen Janine sat at the table smoking yet another cigarette. Pulling herself up to her full height, Sarah glared at her.

'Now then, Janine. I think you'd better tell me exactly what's been going on here.' Her voice was determined.

Janine glanced at her and, all the hatred and animosity falling from her, began to cry. Groaning as if in physical pain, she rocked herself back and forth in her chair – her teeth bared as if she was grinning at some diabolical joke. Sarah stared at her. Where on earth was the beautiful, vital girl her son had married? How did this scruffy, dirty-looking individual come into being? The girl was only twenty-two years old. She looked at the filthy kitchen. The windows were so grimy it was difficult for the sun to penetrate them. The whole place stank. She had always understood that Janine's mother was never off the doorstep, that's why she never came herself. Say what you like about Eliza Grierson, she was a very particular housewife, so how come the flat was in this state? She shook her head in puzzlement. And just how long had Janine been beating the child? By the looks of Carla she had not had a decent meal for weeks.

Sarah blamed herself. She should have come over sooner, she should have spoken to Roy, but how did you ask a grown man about his home life? Once they left home it was up to them surely? That had been her own mother's philosophy. She was distressed, unsure how to go about sorting this situation out. Suddenly Janine spoke.

'No one ever said it would be like this!' Her voice was high. 'I hate it all . . . I hate the cooking and the cleaning and the dirt and the washing and the mending. I hate this flat – it's like a prison to me. Sometimes I don't see anyone for weeks on end. I'm so lonely.'

Sarah was nonplussed. Janine took a deep breath and all the fears and worries inside her came tumbling out like a great canker that had finally burst. 'Roy's never here. He leaves me for days on end. And Carla . . . that bloody Carla is like a permanent reminder of my bloody mistake! If it hadn't been for her I wouldn't be here . . . I wouldn't be here!'

She began crying again in earnest. Sarah went to her. She hesitated a few seconds before putting her arm around the girl's thin shoulders.

'What about your mother, Janine? I thought she came to see you.'

She gave a harsh bitter laugh.

'Well, you thought wrong, Mrs Ryan. My mother . . . my darling mother . . . has nothing to do with me anymore.'

'But why, Janine? Why?'

'Oh, it's a long story. She told me that if I left Roy and went home she would forgive me having Carla and everything . . . forgive me bringing shame on them by marrying a hoodlum. That's her choice of word not mine. And as much as I hate Roy at times . . .' she began to cry again '. . . I know that if I left him, I would never be happy again. I can't live without him, Mrs Ryan! I love him so desperately yet I can't seem to make him happy. When he's here I start fights and drive him out of the house. I want him to want me and he doesn't. I know he doesn't . . .'

'Dear God, Janine. What on earth's the matter with you, girl? Look around you, for Christ's sake. Who'd want to come home to this? It's like a bloody pig sty.' Janine's declaration of love for her son had softened Sarah up. She reasoned that if she could help the girl, she could save their marriage as well as the child. 'Look at yourself. You look like the wreck of the Hesperus! No woman likes house-work, but it's got to be done. At your age I already had five children living and not the hope of a decent wage coming. You've got it made if only you'd realise it.' She began rolling up the sleeves of her best dress. 'I'll tell you what we'll do. First we'll have a cup of tea. Get ourselves nice and calm. Then we'll go through this place like a dose of salts. Scrub it out from top to bottom. With the two of us working like blacks we'll have it done in no time. What do you say?' Janine nodded but Sarah could see her heart wasn't in it. She tried a different tack.

'Then you can go and get your lovely hair done while I get some food cooked. Can you imagine Roy's face when he comes home to everything nice and clean and homely? I'll take the little one home with me for a few days to give you a break. Now what do you say to that?'

Janine brightened up and Sarah smiled but deep inside she was worried. The only reason Janine had cheered up was because she was taking her child from her. She sighed. Even when your children grew up they still made demands. You were never free of them. Wearily she put on the kettle for the tea. Already she was tired, and by the looks of the flat by the time she was finished she would be exhausted. Well, soonest done soonest mended, as her mother used to say. She made the tea.

In the bedroom Maura had dressed Carla in a fairly clean pinafore dress. All the child's socks were dirty so she had turned a pair inside out and put them on her. They looked pretty clean. She was sitting on the bed cuddling Carla when her mother came in and told her to go to the shops and get some bits and pieces. She was instructed to take Carla with her and get her a big ice cream, and one for herself also.

She was amazed at how quickly Carla seemed to get over what had happened to her. At the mention of ice cream the little girl became excited and animated, bouncing up and down on the bed. Maura felt so sorry for her. Her arms were like sticks and the purple-black bruise looked swollen and painful. Yet jumping on the bed she could almost be a normal, happy little girl. She had seen the pity in her mother's eyes and a great rage against Janine had rushed through Maura. If she was older she would go into that kitchen and tear her apart.

Instead she took the money from her mother and walked sedately down to the shops with Carla, playing with her and making her laugh. She knew that Carla was coming home with her and decided that she would take the little girl into her bed with her. After all, she was her aunt. She had a responsibility towards her.

*

Three hours later the little flat was sparkling clean. Janine seemed to get up some enthusiasm as her mother-in-law chatted to her, telling her about her own difficult marriage, and how it was hard when one was young and unsure of oneself. For the first time Janine felt that she had an ally, and it made all the difference to her. Sarah was consciously getting her confidence, telling her what she knew she wanted to hear.

When Janine finally opened up to her she felt the loneliness and unhappiness emanating from her. Sarah reproached herself. She should have visited her more often, should have taken more of an interest in her – and just wait until she went around to Eliza Grierson's! She'd floor that bitch with what she had to say to her! The supercilious old cow! Sarah was looking forward to it. She'd 'hoodlum' her before she was much older! Next on her agenda was that galloping big son of hers. Letting the girl get into this state, and neglect that little child. She'd annihilate him as well! When she got her hands on the bugger, that was. From what she'd gleaned from Janine he came and went like a bloody ghost, flitting in and out as it suited him. Sarah's mouth set in a grim line. He wasn't too big for a clout round the ear hole, whatever he thought.

Janine came into the kitchen dressed up for her trip to the hairdresser's. Sarah smiled at her.

'You look a picture, love. Like one of them girls on the adverts! Now get yourself off and I'll fix you something for your dinner.'

Janine smiled shyly at Sarah. She felt better than she had for months. 'Thank you, Mrs Ryan. You've been so good to me.' Her voice was trembling with emotion.

Sarah waved her hand impatiently. 'Don't you think it's

about time you called me Sarah? As for thanking me . . . for what? I should have been here for you a long time ago. I'm ashamed of meself.'

Janine went to her and kissed her on the cheek.

'Thanks . . . Sarah.' She said her name timidly, as if it felt strange to address her so. Sarah just grinned at her.

'Get yourself off and I'll have a lovely meal waiting for you, OK?'

Janine nodded and left the flat, feeling lighter hearted than she had for many days. Sarah watched her go and wiped her arm across her brow. She was sweating. It had been a hot and sultry summer. In a way she was grateful to Janine. Today had been the first time since he died she had not been tortured with thoughts of her Anthony. She looked out of the now sparkling window and heaved a deep sigh. She began to cook the meal, briefly wondering how her own household was coping without her. She pictured Benjamin waiting for the food to run out of the cupboard and into the frying pan, and smiled. It would never occur to him to cook himself anything. Well, he would just have to wait. She had more pressing things on her mind.

As she prepared the vegetables, she heard the front door open. Thinking it was Maura and Carla she called out: 'I'm in here, lovelies.'

'What you doing here, Mum?' Roy was standing in the doorway, staring at the kitchen as if he was in the wrong house.

Sarah smirked at him nastily. 'Well, well. The Wandering Jew's returned to his home at last!'

She looked at his crumpled clothing, and the dark shadow on his jaw. 'Obviously your new lady love isn't looking after you very well.'

She slammed the saucepan of potatoes on to the draining board. Roy stared at her warily. There was something funny going on here.

'So, now that you're home, are you thinking of staying at all? Or are you just going to get a change of gear and go off again on your merry way?' She gripped the handle of the saucepan.

Roy looked at her, bewildered. 'Are you being funny? Where's Janine and the kid?' Too late he realised his mother's intention. The saucepan and potatoes hit him full in the chest, the water drenching him.

Sarah ran to him, slipping on the wet floor. Righting herself she slapped him across his face, a white hand print appearing as if by magic. 'I'll give you where's the kid . . . she's your daughter, Roy Ryan, and you fought hammer and tongs to marry her mother. When I think of the trouble you caused because you couldn't keep your private parts to yourself! You've driven that poor girl to distraction.'

'I've what! Now you hold up a minute, Muvver.'

Sarah screamed at him: 'No, I bloody well won't, you gormless eejit! Before that girl took up with you the most she ever did in her life was get dressed up for church. She wasn't brought up to do all this.' She gestured around the flat. 'She's been slowly going out of her mind stuck here day in day out, and do you care? Not on your bloody nellie! I'm ashamed to admit that you're my son! That poor innocent little child has taken the brunt of everything. She's got a bruise on her arm like she's been ten rounds with Dempsey . . . and it's all your fault.'

Roy's mouth was hanging open with disbelief.

'Shut your bloody gob up! You look like a mental deficient standing there gawking.'

Roy's mouth snapped shut. 'Janine won't do anything around the place.'

'Shut your trap, I said, or you'll be getting another smack off me otherwise. You're not too big for a good hiding, you know.'

Roy wanted to laugh. He towered over his mother. He had to admire her though. She stuck by her guns. Inside him there was a little nagging doubt. What his mother had said was true. He didn't try to understand Janine. Slowly bending down Sarah picked up the saucepan. It was dented on one side. She stifled an urge to brain her son with it, and instead placed it in the sink. In unspoken agreement mother and son began clearing up the debris. Potatoes had flown to all four corners of the kitchen. Water was everywhere. When it was all put right, Sarah pushed Roy into a chair. Outwardly, she looked her old formidable self. Inside, she was gloating. She was actually enjoying herself! She had not had so much fun for a long time, since before she buried Anthony.

She made a pot of tea. Putting a cup in front of Roy, she said, 'I came here this morning because I knew that something wasn't right. I sensed it at the funeral. The child looked like the orphan of the storm, and Janine looked terrible. I admit that I'm as much to blame, I should have come to visit her, but I understood her mother was never off the doorstep, so I left her to it. When I came here this morning she was pulling the child's hair out of her head.'

She watched Roy's mouth harden. 'And don't you come the old biddy with me! If *you* had done your job properly, been a decent husband, then all this could have been avoided.' She poked him in the chest. 'You are going to get yourself sorted out, my man, and you're going to start coming home at nights. I sat in many a night myself when you were all younger, waiting for that piss artist of a father of yours to come home, knowing in my heart that he was down the Bayswater Road, spending desperately needed money on old brasses. How I never got a dose of clap I'll never know! Well, I won't have any of my sons going the same way.'

Roy sat staring at her. He knew, as all the boys had always known, that she had not had the best of lives with his father, but she had never before spoken to him like this. He knew that she was trying to help him save his marriage, and in a tiny part of himself he knew that she was right. He had left Janine to fend for herself. He had chosen to ignore the fact that she took out her frustrations on Carla. But he just didn't know what to do. He was ashamed that his mother had so accurately put her finger on where he spent his nights. Since Michael had opened a hostess club in the West End, he had literally had his pick of women to spend the night with. It had been easier than coming home to fighting and arguing. To a dirty home and an unhappy wife.

But he still loved Janine. He had thought that taking her away from her mother's influence would have encouraged her to stand on her own two feet. Instead she had leant even more on him and he just couldn't take it, so had chosen the easy way out. Now he had to face not only Janine and little Carla, but his mother. He heard the front door open and braced himself, looking at his mother for support. As Janine walked into the room, Sarah stood up and smiled at her.

'You look an absolute angel, doesn't she, Roy?' She poked him in the shoulder, her bright smile belying the force she had used. Janine smiled uncertainly at him. The tension in the kitchen was like an electric current. Janine did look like an angel. Her hair was swept up off her finely boned face, emphasising her long neck. Her deep green eyes were made up expertly and there was a wistfulness in them that pierced Roy's heart. She was a cracker, he thought. She really looked the business. His mum was right, Janine was like a high-spirited thoroughbred. She needed gentle guidance. He got up from his chair and held out his arms to her. Janine hesitated for a few seconds before she slipped into them.

Sarah watched, a satisfied expression on her face. Now all she had to do was go and see Father McCormack and get him to sort out her Michael and she would be happy. Half an hour later she left the two love birds, Maura and Carla in tow. Her next stop was the Church and Father McCormack. She looked at her watch. If she hurried she would catch him as he finished six o'clock mass.

Sitting in the refectory with a glass of wine in front of her, Sarah poured out her heart to the priest.

'I feel ashamed to tell you this, Father, but Michael has bought himself another club, this time a bordello.' She sipped her wine to steady her voice. 'Men go there to . . . Well, I don't have to paint a picture, now do I?'

Father McCormack looked at her through shrewd eyes. He was sixty years old and had been the parish priest for over thirty years. His hair was grey and cut in an American crew-cut. He had heavy grey-flecked eyebrows that gave him a wise demeanour and looked on religion the way some men looked on marriage: as a necessary part of life. You made the best of it. He put his large, soft hands together.

'I see, I see.' His Irish accent was still thick even though he had left Ireland over forty years previously. 'Sure that

Michael was always a difficult one. I can see why you're worrying.'

'I think that if *you* had a word with him, Father . . .'. Her voice trailed off.

'Well, Sarah, I'll do my best. But your Michael was always a strong-minded fellow. He might not like the interference.'

Sarah was determined that before she left this room she would have an appointment to save her son's eternal soul! She tried a different approach.

'Oh, Father, I know what people say about my Mickey, but as you know yourself, stories get stretched in the telling. All he needs is a little gentle guidance. If you were to talk to him, I'm sure he would listen to a fine man like yourself. Even when he was an altar boy, he always had a high regard for you.'

The priest raised his eyebrows. When Michael had been an altar boy he had also stolen the lead from the church roof! But he had the glimmer of a plan forming in his mind, and it would please this poor soul sitting before him. He decided to do as she asked.

'Hostess club, you say? Well, I think that a few words from me are called for, as you say.' Sarah jumped in before he could change his mind.

'If you come to my house at eleven o'clock tomorrow morning, I'll make sure that he's there.'

He smiled at her, showing tobacco-stained teeth. 'Eleven o'clock it is then. Now tell me, how are the other children? I hear that all the older boys are driving big expensive cars and living the life of Riley. They all work for Michael, I take it?'

'Yes, Father, that's true. But if you can help to sort out Mickey, the others will follow suit, I'm sure.'

'Well, Sarah, we can only put our trust in the Lord.' He looked up at the ceiling as if expecting to see him floating there. 'As it says in the Bible, "God is no respecter of persons", Romans 2:11. Michael Ryan may be a big man on earth but in heaven he's just another of God's children.'

Sarah smiled at him. There was nothing, she thought, like a chunk of the Bible when spouted by a true believer. She left a little while later, happier than she had been for a long time. Over the years her religion had been a great comfort to her. As she had suffered one setback after another – no money, another still birth, one or other of the boys in trouble with the police – she had turned more and more to the church. Benjamin was no good at all. If she relied on him for anything, it never happened. Whether it was her housekeeping or anything, he always let her down. Michael, God love him, had been a good son in many ways. He had looked after his younger brothers and sister, he had made sure that she always had enough money, but she had been hearing things of late that had frightened her. Anthony's death had been the last straw. She knew that her eldest son was involved in all manner of criminal activities, that he was thought of as a kind of mobster. She shuddered. She was all for a bit of ducking and diving, that's how everyone lived in her estimation, but from what she had gleaned recently about her sons, it was a completely different lifestyle they were after. She had seen the effect that Michael had on the people around and about. She herself was now treated like visiting royalty when she went anywhere.

She could, to an extent, understand Michael's craving for recognition. She was shrewd enough to understand that the way he had been treated as a child would give him the added drive and determination to better himself. But she herself drew the line at prostitution. In her mind it was the ultimate degradation, and any man who could live off the proceeds of it was the lowest of the low. She fervently hoped that Father McCormack would be able to talk some sense into her son. The robbing was bad enough though the insurance companies could afford the losses and money had no soul. But the wilful destruction of young lives was a different kettle of fish altogether. She had been shocked to read in the *News of the World* about the drugs that were available now to youngsters. What on earth was the world coming to? Young girls selling their bodies for drugs.

In the war years and after, women had sold their bodies to feed their children. That fitted in with Sarah's creed. You could do anything to feed the children, to keep the family fed or clothed. Even sell your body. But that had been for women with no man to protect them, so they had to do whatever they could and were respected for it. Sarah herself knew many women who had moonlighted down the Bayswater Road to supplement meagre war pensions or National Assistance. What Michael was doing was disgusting. He was putting them on the game, women and young girls who would otherwise never have dreamt of doing it. He was offering easy money, a far cry from the days when it was a means to an end.

She watched Maura and Carla skipping in front of her. Maura looked huge beside the tiny Carla. Dear Maura, she had taken the poor little thing under her wing. Sarah only hoped now that Janine and Roy sorted themselves out. That it wasn't too late for her to take to her daughter. Oh, the worry of having children! A Jewish woman Sarah had been friends with, before the war, used to say to her, 'When your children are young they tread on your feet.

When they get older they tread on your heart!' How right she had been! The poor woman had died when she had been bombed in the blitz. A direct hit. Sarah often thought of her. Too many good people had died in the war, had suffered in one way or another. She sighed. She was dead tired. Now she had to go home and start her own cooking and cleaning. Still, she consoled herself, Father McCormack was coming in the morning and hopefully everything would right itself.

Father McCormack sat opposite Michael and appraised him. There was no doubt about it, he was a fearsome-looking individual.

From his dark expertly cut hair to his hand-made shoes he was the epitome of the new young man. His single-breasted suit was made of mohair and he flicked a trace of ash off his trousers with a perfectly manicured hand. His closely shaven face was tense and his usually sensuous mouth set in a grim line. The priest had guessed that he was well aware of the object of this visit.

Sarah had made a pot of tea and left them together in the overcrowded room. It was as if, after years of having no furniture at all, Sarah had gone mad for it. The room was filled with tables, knick-knacks, chairs, and a large horse-hair three-piece suite. Religious paintings were all over the walls. The Sacred Heart, the Last Supper and the Crucifixion stared down at them. Our Lady of Lourdes looked at the doorway opposite her in a gesture of supplication. On the large sideboard that covered nearly the whole of one wall statues of the Virgin and Child, as well as the holy family, stood silently. One particularly macabre statue of Saint Sebastian, arrows poking out of every limb, was given centre stage. The priest found his eyes drawn towards it and made a conscious effort to stop staring at it. He picked up his cup of tea and turned his gaze back to Michael.

'I expect you know why I'm here?'

Michael sniffed and uncrossed his legs. 'Yeah.' His voice was wary.

The priest nodded as if in understanding. 'Well, Michael, if you know then it's pointless me droning on now, isn't it?'

'Yeah.' This was said insolently. Michael's fear of priests and nuns was long gone.

Father McCormack sat forward in his chair and replaced his cup on the table. His face hardened. He spoke in a low voice. 'What I am here for today is something completely different. When your mother, good woman that she is, came to see me yesterday I was not shocked to hear what she had to say. I guessed that you were breaking the law in some way. I'm not a fool, you know. Anyway, that's all neither here nor there . . . I want to speak to you as a man of the world.'

Michael looked at him. His blue eyes were sceptical.

'What I'm after is a little donation.'

Michael sat up in the chair, stunned. 'A what!'

The priest became agitated. 'Whisht now, whisht. You'll have your mother galloping in here else. As you know, I am rather sympathetic to my countrymen. There's poor Paddies in London even now, God love them, who have been driven out of their homes by the Proddies. It's every Irishman's duty to help these poor unfortunates.'

'Look, Father, just because my name's Ryan don't mean I'm Irish.'

The priest banged his fist on the little table, causing the cups to jump in their saucers.

'Listen here, you, since nineteen-twenty the Catholics have been discriminated against in Ulster, Belfast, all the North. They can't even get a council house out there! The bloody Protestants run the whole fecking sheebang! I collect money for the IRA so we can build up an army and fight the bastards at their own game. One day, my laddo, we'll be ready for the eejits. We forced them out of the South and we'll fight the buggers in the North. We want an Irish Free State that spans the whole of Ireland.'

The priest's eyes were alight. Michael stared at him as if he was mad. He had heard stories of Ireland from the cradle, as most Catholic children had. He could still hear his granny singing 'Kevin Barry' on Saint Patrick's Day, still remember the stories of the Easter Uprising and the Famine. How his ancestors had left the meat that Queen Victoria had sent over to them to rot in the streets rather than accept help from the English. But this was nineteen-sixty, for Christ's sake. Who gave a toss what was happening out there?

Father McCormack drank his tea. Wiping his mouth with the back of his hand he spoke again.

'I know an awful lot about you, Michael Ryan. There's nothing I can't find out if I want to. All I am asking is a little donation now and again. You'd be surprised at how many people give money to the cause. The Americans have regular collections in their bars and churches. Ireland is a poor country and needs all the help it can get.'

Michael laughed.

'Supposing I give you some money . . . now and again . . . what would you do in return?'

The priest took a handkerchief from the pocket of his black cassock and mopped his forehead.

'I would tell your mother exactly what she wanted to

hear. If it came from me she would believe it. I can be a very persuasive man.'

Michael ran his tongue over his lips, and shook his head.

'What about the poor orphans and the starving blacks?' His voice was sarcastic.

'Sure, they would get a bit as well, God love them. Though I think most of the blacks are in Notting Hill.'

Michael burst out laughing.

'All right then, Father. You've sold me. But I'm warning you now, you've got to keep my muvver sweet.'

Father McCormack smiled.

'I will, Michael son.' He sighed heavily. 'Sure, it's a terrible world we're living in today. Money makes it so much easier. I remember this room when there was hardly a thing in it . . . except children, of course. Your mother always seemed to have plenty of those. Well, I must be off. It's been grand chatting to you, Michael. I'll expect you at the Presbytery in a few days with your donation.' He held out his hand. 'I won't give you a blessing . . . I don't think you need one!'

Michael shook his hand. 'I have a feeling I've just been conned, Father. An Irish Catholic Northern Ireland? Donations to the IRA . . . ?' He smiled. 'If it was anyone else I'd kick their arse out of the door.'

The priest's face straightened and he looked meaningfully at Michael.

'Don't mock what you don't fully understand. Your religion is the mightiest in the world. Remember this? *Dominus illuminatio mea, et salus mea, quem timebo?*'

Michael translated it for him, smiling as he did so. 'The Lord is the source of my light and my safety, so whom shall I fear?'

'Would you listen to that! You remembered your Latin.'

'Yeah, I remember it all right. And I don't fear anyone, not even God. *You* remember that.'

Father McCormack digested the veiled threat gracefully. 'How could I forget? But I'll tell you one thing before I go. One day the troubles in Northern Ireland will be known all over the world, and the British will have to listen to us. When that day comes you remember my words, Michael, because we won't forget our friends, whoever they are.'

With that the priest picked up his hat and left the room.

Michael watched him leave. He felt like laughing out loud. The old boy had lost his marbles somewhere along the line. Still, if it kept his mother off his back, he didn't care. He picked up the tray of tea things and took them to the kitchen where he glanced at the clock. If he got his head down for a couple of hours he would be nice and fresh for the evening. His new club was raking the money in. After the lean war years, people wanted a bit of fun. And he would make sure they got it!

Chapter Seven

1966

'You look nice, Maws. Where you off to?' Sarah's voice was tight.

'I'm going up Tiffany's with me mates.'

'Tiffany's? Where's that?'

Sarah's voice had taken on the tone of an interrogation. Garry answered for Maura.

'It's in Ilford. The old Allie Pallie.'

'What's she going up there for? What's wrong with the Hammersmith Palais?'

Maura sighed and tossed back her hair. 'There's nothing wrong with round here, Mum. I'm just meeting some of the girls from work, that's all.' Her voice was beginning to rise and she tried in vain to control it.

Sarah wiped her hands on her apron and stared at Maura, her face wrinkled in concern. 'Well, it's a bloody long way to go if you ask me.'

'Well, I'm *not* asking you, Mum. I'm nearly seventeen and I can do what I like.'

Sarah walked towards her daughter. Garry tried to pull her back, holding her arm gently.

'Let me tell you something, Madam. You *can't* do what you sodding well like . . .'

Her diatribe was cut off by Michael who stormed into the kitchen. The constant bickering between Maura and his mother was beginning to get on everyone's nerves.

'For Christ's sake, Muvver, give it a rest. Let the girl go out if she wants to. Anyway . . .' he put his arm around his mother's shoulders '. . . Garry's going up there tonight. He can give her a lift on the back of his scooter.'

'I'm not getting on the back of his scooter with all my new gear on!' Maura's voice was horrified.

'Just as well, 'cos I ain't going up the Palais.'

'Tiffany's.'

'Tiffany's then. I'm going to the pictures with me mates.'

Maura smiled triumphantly. 'Well, that's settled then.' She picked up her shoulder bag. 'Gawd Blimey, it's worse than living in Scotland Yard here. Where you bin? What you been doing? What did you talk about? Did he kiss you? I wouldn't mind, but I can't get a bloody boyfriend! As soon as they find out who I am they shy off.

'"You Mickey Ryan's sister?" they say. "Yes," says I, and watch them poodle off down the road. So stop worrying about me getting in the club, Muvver, I don't get the bloody chance!'

She snatched her coat off the kitchen table and stormed out of the kitchen, shouting, 'And if by any chance I do need an escort, it won't be my bloody brother. Ta rah!'

She walked out of the front door and gave it a satisfying slam behind her. In the kitchen Michael and Sarah stared at one another, shocked. Garry went to the sink and washed his hands. In the back of his mind he was cheering Maura on.

'Well, I never, Michael. Did you hear the way she carried on?'

He sighed heavily. 'I think the whole of Notting Hill heard it.'

Garry wiped his hands on a tea towel and faced his brother. 'She's got a point though, ain't she?'

Michael looked at him. It was like looking at a miniature version of himself.

'What do you mean by that?' His voice was cold.

Garry plucked up every bit of courage he had.

'Well, the way that everyone's at her. If I was her, it would drive me up the wall.'

'If you was her you'd be getting the same treatment. She's our sister, our responsibility. If we don't look after her, who will? You want to put your brain in gear before you open your trap, Garry. Our Geoff was right about you. He said an original thought in your head would die of loneliness. After hearing the crap you just come out with, I'm inclined to agree with him.'

Garry's face was scarlet with embarrassment.

'Come on, you two, get a move on or you'll be late.' Sarah was worried. She knew that Michael was capable of attacking Garry for what he had said. In Michael's mind it was tantamount to mutiny and he would not stand for anyone disagreeing with him.

He took a comb from the pocket of his suit and stood at the sink. Looking in the mirror that was perched precariously on the windowsill, he combed back the hair that hung over his eyes. Then, turning to Garry, he pointed the long steel comb at him.

'In future, Bruv, keep your nose out of what don't concern you.'

He kissed his mother lightly on the forehead and walked out of the room. Garry was fuming inside. Sensing this, Sarah went to him.

'He don't mean it, Gal. But he's right about Maura, you know. You should all look out for your sister.'

Garry shrugged her arm off and picked up his crash helmet. 'We're not looking out for her, Mother. We're trying to own her, and that's a completely different thing.'

When he had gone Sarah carried on with her chores, but Garry's words stayed with her all evening.

Maura breathed a sigh of relief as she slammed the front door. It was getting more claustrophobic in that house by the day. If it wasn't for Margaret she would go mad. They were as close as two friends could be. They worked in the same office, they ate their lunch together, they went down the Lane on Sundays and the Roman Road on Fridays. The only cloud on the horizon was a boy called Dennis Dawson. Margaret had been seeing him for nearly a year and Maura had the feeling that they were going to get married. Still, she consoled herself, she would always have Margaret as a friend.

Tonight the two girls were meeting Dennis and one of his mates up Tiffany's. She had nearly had heart failure at the thought of Garry going up there. That was all she needed. The only reason they were going there was because they could be pretty sure that one or other of her brothers would *not* be up there and Maura would have a bit of privacy. How she hated the way her brothers protected her, and her mother was all for it. She was beginning to dislike her mother. The last few years Sarah had practically suffocated her only daughter. Maura wished that she could meet a nice bloke and get right out of it. If she married, at least she would have a life of her own, away from prying eyes. She daydreamed sometimes about finding a little flat but knew they were just that – daydreams. There was no way she would ever be allowed to go and live alone.

She saw Margaret waiting for her outside her house and she gave her a little wave. They made a funny pair. Maura was tall, nearly five ten, and big-boned. She was what her father jokingly called 'a good eyeful', with her large breasts and wide hips. Her long blond hair was backcombed up into a beehive, kept firmly in place with sugar and water, making her look even taller – like an amazon. Her eyes, still a startling blue, were now heavily made up, with black liner and white eye shadow, the false eyelashes giving her a startled doe look. In her short shirtwaist dress and white winklepicker shoes she was the height of fashion.

Margaret on the other hand was still under five feet tall. Her orange-red hair was worn bouffant, and her orange lipstick made her look like a small circus clown. She was very flat-chested but had big legs and a large behind. When they were younger the boys in the streets whistled the Laurel and Hardy music as they passed. Nowadays they took no notice if people stared at them, they were used to it.

'You managed to escape then?'

'Oh, don't talk to me about it, Marge.'

Margaret laughed her billy goat laugh.

'You'd better check in your bag. It might be bugged.'

'Don't even joke about it, Marge, I wouldn't put it past them.'

They began to walk to the bus stop.

'What's Dennis's mate like?'

'Well, he's tall and very good-looking. He's twenty-four years old.'

'What job's he got?'

Margaret shook her head. 'Dunno. Dennis did tell me but we was too busy . . . well, you know.'

'No, I don't know. And you know that. Come on, Marge, tell me. What's it like?'

Margaret pursed her bright orange lips. 'What?' Her voice was innocent.

'You know very well, Marge. A bit of the other?'

'Maura Ryan! I am not discussing my sex life at a bus stop!'

Maura burst out laughing. 'Why not? It's never stopped you before!'

Both girls laughed and pushed each other in the chest.

'Come on, tell me.' Maura's face straightened and she looked earnestly at her little friend.

'Well, I've only done it a couple of times as you know. But . . . I like it. It's nice, but a bit embarrassing. Dennis said that I'll get over that. In fact, he says I'm a natural!' The last piece of information was given with a toss of her head.

'Oh, hark at the Duchess of Duke Street.' They both laughed again. The bus pulled up and they jumped on it, going upstairs so they could smoke.

'Two to Holborn, please.' As they lit their cigarettes Maura felt the familiar annoyance wash over her. This was another bugbear. Her brothers all smoked yet when Mickey had seen his sister smoking he had snatched the cigarette from her hand, grinding it out with his heel, shouting at her that only slags smoked. He had done it in the street in front of everyone. She had thought that she was going to die of shame. Now she could only smoke when well away from them.

They got off the bus at Holborn and got a train to Mile End, from there taking another train to Ilford. They were in Tiffany's at nine forty-five. If they got in before ten it cost only a pound. They went straight to the toilets and repaired their make-up and hair. As they came out of the toilet and into the bar Maura's heart stood still in her chest. Standing beside Dennis was the best-looking man she had ever seen in her life. She looked at Margaret with a question in her eyes and when she nodded felt a burst of happiness like she had never felt before.

'Hello, darling.' Dennis kissed Margaret on her cheek. 'Maura, this is me mate Terry. Terry, this is Maura.'

She shook the stranger's hand timidly. Terry Petherick was well over six foot. It seemed strange to Maura to look up at someone. He had dark blond hair yet his eyes were a light brown. Maura was besotted after one smile.

'Would you like a drink?' His voice was deep and it sent her pulses racing.

'Please.' Her throat was dry with nerves. 'I'll have a scotch and dry.'

She was surprised at her answer. What on earth had made her say that? She drank half of bitter normally, but somehow she couldn't say that to him. He would think her terribly unsophisticated.

'Ice?'

She nodded at him. As he took Margaret and Dennis's orders she watched him. When he went to the bar she whispered into Margaret's ear, 'He's gorgeous!'

At the bar Terry Petherick was thinking about Maura. He had been surprised at how big she was, but she was absolutely fantastic. She was incredibly sexy and didn't even realise it! As she had walked towards him he had felt a physical pain in his guts. She was like one great big present, just waiting to be unwrapped. He paid for the drinks and took them back to the others.

Maura gulped at her drink. The music seemed very loud all of a sudden. They were playing a Beatles number. 'Love Me Do' seemed to be reverberating off the walls. Maura could see Terry's lips moving but could not make out a word. She smiled and gestured that she couldn't hear him. He laughed, showing perfect white teeth, and putting his mouth to her ear, he shouted: 'Another drink?'

She looked at her glass and was amazed to find it was empty! She smiled and nodded.

When he brought her back another drink he moved close to her trying to have a conversation. 'Do you come here often?'

'No. Only in the mating season.'

The record ended just as she spoke and her voice caused people to stare at them. Terry's eyebrows went up and she felt herself blushing furiously. Why had she said that? It was a silly saying of Margaret's. Now he would think she was a tart. She could have kicked herself. She concentrated on her drink to hide her embarrassment, deciding that whisky was all right. Just like drinking ginger beer really. She noticed that it was getting very hot all of a sudden.

Terry grinned at her ruefully. 'Another?'

She was aware of the disbelief in his voice even above the din. He bought her another drink and she sipped it. A slow dance came on. Putting her glass on the bar, she went on to the dance floor with him. As it was quieter now, he began to talk to her.

'I thought I'd better dance with you in case you wanted another drink.' His voice was jocular.

'I don't drink shorts very often.'

'I thought so. Are you nervous or something?'

'Yes . . . Yes, I am.'

He smiled a funny little lopsided grin and pulled her closer. She could feel his heartbeat against her breast and it gave her a feeling of longing she had never experienced before. She closed her eyes.

'What do you do for a living?' he asked.

'I work with Marge. We're typists for a firm of accountants in Charing Cross.'

'That's right. I remember Dennis telling me now. I'm a policeman.'

He felt the change in her.

'You're a what!' Her voice sounded shocked.

'I said, I'm a policeman. What's wrong with that?' He was puzzled. Maura could hear it in his tone.

'Nothing! It's just that I've never met a policeman before.' God forgive me for lying, she thought.

He relaxed. 'Well, don't worry. I'm not on duty so I won't arrest you. Not tonight anyway.'

She tried to smile at him. Bobby Darin was crooning 'Dream Lover' and Maura stepped back into Terry's arms. They finished the dance in silence. When they went back to Dennis and Margaret, Maura picked up her drink and slugged it straight back. She signalled to Margaret and both girls went into the toilets.

As soon as they were in there Maura said: 'He's only an old Bill.'

'He ain't!' Margaret was stunned.

'Oh yes he is, Marge. What am I gonna do?'

Margaret put her finger to her bottom lip. Her tiny heart-shaped face was screwed up as she thought the problem over. She looked up at Maura.

'Do you like him, Maws?'

'Oh, yes, Marge. But a Filth . . . Jesus!' Maura was nearly in tears.

'Then it's simple. Just don't tell him about your brothers.'

'Do you honestly think I could get away with it?'

Margaret grinned. 'It's a doddle!' Her green eyes widened as she thought of a plan. 'Look, Dennis obviously ain't said nothing to him about your family and I'll put him wise. He don't see that much of Terry anyway. You just carry on as if nothing's happened. Let's face it, your brothers are more well known on their own turf than around this way. Anyway, you're not responsible for them, are you?'

'No, Marge . . . I know that. But I would feel a bit snidey pretending that I don't know them.'

Margaret rolled her eyes at the ceiling. 'Look, pea brain, you're not denying them . . . you're just not mentioning them. There's a difference. Like in confession when I tell Father McCormack that I have sinned in a personal manner – I don't tell him I'm having it off, do I? It's just a matter of not letting on, that's all.'

Maura still wasn't convinced.

Margaret sighed. 'Well, it's up to you, Maws. But I think he's lovely, and you can tell a mile off that he likes you. Now let's get back to them before they send a search party out looking for us.'

Later in the evening Maura was sitting in a small Chinese restaurant with Terry. What Margaret had said earlier had been going through her mind over and over again. She tried to reason with herself. Just because he was a policeman didn't mean she couldn't go out with him, surely? She shook her head to clear it. It was all the whisky she'd had. She was drunk.

'Do you come from a large family, Maura?'

'Oh, the usual, Terry. A few brothers, that's all. How about you?'

'There's only me now. I had a brother but he died.'

Maura's heart went out to him.

'Oh . . . I'm sorry. One of my brothers died. I know how you must feel.'

'We lost Joey to cancer when he was twelve. I was sixteen at the time. Funny, though, I still miss him. How did you . . . ?'

Maura looked at the tablecloth.

'He got run over. I was only a kid. I don't really remember it.' Another lie, she thought. Not a day went by but she saw Anthony's face, and superimposed on it the face of Stavros, smirking slightly as he had been in the cemetery.

No one in her family had been the same since Anthony's funeral. Her mother and father had aged dramatically overnight. Michael and the boys had become harder, more violent somehow. As for herself, she just missed him. Sometimes in the middle of a celebration, Christmas or Easter, she would think of him and the knowledge of how he had been murdered would cast a shadow over everything.

The food arrived. As they served themselves from the many little dishes, Maura surveyed her companion. She could really get to like Terry and the thought frightened her. She was going to murder Margaret tomorrow, going off with Dennis and leaving them like that. Now he had to take her home whether he wanted to or not.

'Eat up, Maura.' She smiled at him and brightened up. He wouldn't have asked her out for a meal if he didn't like her, she reasoned.

'Sorry. I was miles away.'

'Maura?'

'Yes.'

'Can I see you again? I don't think I've enjoyed myself so much with a girl for ages.'

He smiled at her with that lopsided grin and she was undone. Her whole body seemed to tingle with expectation. He liked her!

'Of course you can. Whenever you want!' She popped a prawn ball into her mouth and bit on it, showering him with sweet and sour sauce.

'Oh, I'm sorry!' She leant across the table to wipe his face with her napkin and knocked his glass of wine into his lap. Mortified at what she had done she leapt out of her seat and collided with a waiter, sending the plate of egg fried rice he was carrying flying through the air. She stood in the restaurant with her hand over her mouth and tears in her eyes. Terry burst out laughing, causing all the people in the restaurant to take their eyes off Maura and begin staring at him. He laughed so hard that he had a fit of coughing which, in turn, caused big tears to roll down his face. He stood up and, throwing a handful of money on the table for the bill, led a scarlet-faced and humiliated Maura out of the restaurant and into the night air.

'Now can I trust you with my car? You won't knock my wheels off or pull my radio to pieces?' Although it was said in a jocular fashion it was too much for Maura. The whisky, the heat, the Chinese food, the humiliation, and finally the cold night air all took their toll. She threw up in the gutter.

Terry rubbed her back as she heaved. When she had finished she leant against his car, gulping in the cold air. Her forehead had small beads of sweat on it that glistened in the lamp light. Her mascara was smudged under her eyes. One of her eyelashes had come unstuck. Gently he pulled it from her eyelid. Giving her his hanky, he went back to the restaurant and came back with a glass of iced water.

She stood there dejectedly looking at him, convinced that he would never want to lay eyes on her again. She looked at the red wine stain on his trousers and felt tears prickling her eyes. She frantically blinked them away.

'Feeling better now?' His voice was gentle. He handed her the glass of water. 'Drink this down and you'll feel much better, I promise you.'

She shook her head.

'Come on, drink it.' The authority in his voice surprised her and she took the glass and drank the water. The coolness eased her throat which was burning. She handed the glass back to him and he returned it to the restaurant. She breathed deeply, trying to settle her nerves.

He came back and unlocked the car, helping her into the passenger seat. As he pulled away from the kerb, he said, 'I think you drank too much.'

'It was the whisky. I've never drunk it before. Normally I drink a half of bitter.'

She looked at his profile. He looked solid, not just physically but mentally, with an air about him that denoted an inner strength. He smiled.

'Well, if it's any consolation, it happens to us all! I can remember the first time I got drunk on Scotch. I threw up all over my mum's slippers! Never touched the bloody stuff since, so you're in good company.' He poked himself in the chest. 'I can't take my drink either.'

He felt in his jacket pocket and brought out a pack of Juicy Fruits. 'Have one of these. It will freshen your mouth up.'

She took one gratefully.

'Where do you want dropping off? I know you live in Notting Hill.'

'Do you know the Bramley Arms?' He nodded. 'Well, there will do. I live nearby.'

'I'll take you right to your door.'

'No . . . That's all right. It's my dad. You know.'

He glanced at her and grinned. 'I get it. You're supposed to be coming home with Margaret.'

'That's it. He's a bit old fashioned.'

They chatted on until they came to the Bramley Arms. The water and the Juicy Fruit seemed to have done the trick because she felt great. And better still, the big hunk of man beside her made her feel terrific. He stopped the car and turned to face her.

'When will I see you then?'

'Whenever you like.'

He smiled at her eagerness. 'Let's see.' He put his head to one side as if he was thinking, closing one eye and giving his little grin. 'Tomorrow's Sunday. How about Monday night? I'll pick you up here at about seven-thirty. Is that all right?'

She nodded and he pulled her into his arms and kissed her, then waved his finger in her face and said: 'And no drinking whisky!'

She grinned and got out of the car.

'See you, Maura.'

' 'Bye.' She watched the car pull away. He wanted to see her again! She felt as if she could float up into the starry night. It was two in the morning and she walked the short distance to her home as if on a cushion of air. He wanted to see her again! She couldn't believe her luck!

She had a little nagging worry in the back of her mind

about Mickey, but pushed it impatiently away. As Margaret had said, what people didn't know couldn't hurt them. Anyway, Mickey and the boys weren't really bad. They were just tearaways.

As she pushed the key into the lock of the front door she heard a row going on. She walked into the kitchen just in time to see Benny punch Garry in the face. She ran and stood between them.

'What on earth's going on?'

'Get out me way, Maws. I'm gonna kill that little runt.'

'Calm down, Benny. What's he done?'

'Calm down? You dozy cow! He's poached my fucking bird, that's what he's done. The no good dirty ponce!'

Garry pushed Maura out of the way and faced his brother. 'She ain't your bird. She can't stand you, she told me that herself.'

With that Benny launched himself at Garry. As they fought, their mother and father came into the room, followed by Leslie and Lee who separated their brothers.

'What the hell's all this row abaht?' Benjamin's voice was slurred as usual. He was still half drunk.

'That wanker's poached me bird, that's what.'

'For the last time, Benny, she ain't your bird.'

Leslie threw Garry across the kitchen where he fell against the fireplace. He pulled himself up slowly. Leslie pointed at him.

'What's her name?'

'Mandy Watkins.'

Leslie and Lee looked at one another and burst out laughing. 'Not Mandy Watkins from Bletchedon Street?'

Benny and Garry nodded warily. There was something going on here.

'What's she doing, Les, making a career out of the Ryans?' Lee and Leslie began hooting with glee.

'What do you mean?' This from a sullen Benny.

'Me and Lee's had her, and Geoffrey. Me and Lee had her at the same time. She's a dog.'

'You're lying, you . . .' Garry went for Leslie who grabbed his arms and held him tightly, pushing his arms up behind his back expertly.

'Ain't we had her, Lee?'

He nodded, still smiling, then picked up a pack of cigarettes from the table and lit one.

'I take oath that we've all had her. Christ almighty, she's had more pricks than a second-hand dart board!'

'That's enough!' Sarah's voice echoed off the kitchen walls. 'I won't have this kind of talk. If you have no respect for me, your mother, at least have some for your sister.'

All the boys looked shamefaced.

Leslie spoke. 'Sorry, Mum. We're out of order.'

'Who wants a cuppa?' Maura tried to defuse the situation. The boys all nodded but Benjamin and Sarah went back to bed. Maura put the kettle on.

'Have a good time, Sis?'

'All right, Garry, I suppose.'

As she made the tea she thought about the way her brothers had talked about Mandy Watkins. She had known Mandy all her life. The papers might talk about the swinging sixties but the nearest most girls of Maura's age got to it was in the clothes they wore. If her brothers even suspected that she had been with a boy, all hell would break loose. She put their tea on the table. Benny and Garry were bosom pals once again. Kissing all the boys, she made her way up to bed, taking her tea with her. Her last thought before she fell asleep was the reaction she would get if they knew that she had been out with a policeman. She didn't care, though. She couldn't wait until Monday!

Chapter Eight

Margaret and Maura were in Maura's bedroom, painting their nails. They had worked out a system. On the nights that Maura saw Terry, Margaret would come to the house and they would get ready there as if they were going out together. In reality, Maura was meeting Terry and Margaret, Dennis. Maura had been seeing Terry for nearly five months, and miraculously had managed to keep him a secret. Sometimes though a terrible feeling of dread came over her. She knew that she was playing with fire but couldn't help herself. She was absolutely besotted with him.

'How's you and Den these days, Marge?'

'Great! We're getting engaged.'

Maura's eyes rounded. 'You're joking?'

'Oh no I ain't! We get on so well. He's got a good job and mine ain't that bad. We're thinking of saving up a deposit for a little house.'

Maura was impressed.

'Good luck to you, Marge. Dennis is lovely, and you can see how much he thinks of you.'

'He's all right, I suppose.' Margaret was embarrassed. 'How about you and Terry? You doo-dahed yet?'

'No, we most certainly have not!' Maura's voice sounded shocked even to her own ears. 'No disrespect to you, Marge, but I want to save myself for when I get married.' Even as she spoke she knew she was being a hypocrite. She wanted to do it more than anything in life.

Margaret laughed. 'You can't fool me, Maws. You're more worried about your brothers. It's 1966, for Christ's sake. Saving yourself for marriage, my Aunt Nellie!'

Maura ignored the jibe and started to apply mascara. 'I have all me life to do that.'

'That's just it though, ain't it? You don't! Imagine still doing it at forty!' Both girls laughed. To them forty seemed positively ancient.

'I'll think about what you said, Marge. Now can we drop the subject?'

'Be a damn sight better if you dropped your drawers and got it over with!'

'Marge!' Maura's voice had lost its joviality now and she sounded annoyed.

'All right, all right, keep your hair on! I'm sorry!'

'I should bloody well think so and all! You're obsessed with it.'

Margaret glanced at her watch and jumped off the bed. 'Come on, Maws. Get a move on. It's nearly a quarter past seven.'

Both girls scrambled into their coats. It was October and the nights had turned very cold. They hurried down the stairs. Michael and Geoffrey were in the hallway. Geoffrey whistled at them.

'You two look nice. Who's the lucky lads then?' Maura thought she was going to faint with fright.

Mickey glanced at Margaret and chucked her under the chin. 'You might be little, Margie, but you poke out in all the right places.'

Sarah's voice stopped Margaret from having to answer. 'Will you leave the poor girl alone! I don't know what comes over you sometimes, Michael. You can see she's embarrassed.'

He picked Margaret up and hugged her. 'She knows I'm only joking, don't you, Margie?' Margaret smiled shyly and nodded her head. He placed her gently on the floor and turned to Maura.

'Now you, Princess, you look absolutely gorgeous!' He frowned. 'I wish you'd lay off the make-up, though.'

Maura rolled her eyes up to the ceiling. 'Everyone wears their make-up like this, Mickey. It's the fashion.' Her voice, as usual when talking to Michael, was strained.

'Well, I think it suits her.' This from Garry who had just come in the front door. 'You look a cracker, girl.'

'Thanks, Gal.' Maura smiled gratefully at him. He was the only brother who allowed her to live her own life. He worked for Michael but wasn't as subservient towards him as the other boys. And though Michael acted as if he was annoyed with Garry when he spoke out of turn, Maura also got the impression that he admired Garry for it. Geoffrey snatched the books Garry was carrying from under his arm.

Garry and Geoffrey were the only readers in the family. They shared a common bond, a love of literature. The other boys revelled in baiting them about it, but in a good-natured way.

Michael put on his best voice and said, 'And what is one reading this week?'

Garry grimaced at him.

'I've read this, Gal. It's quite good. Heavy going at first, but then you can get into it.'

'I've read it before, Geoff. I like Voltaire.'

'I like revoltaire.' Michael parodied Garry's voice.

Everyone laughed. Geoffrey looked at Michael.

'In *Candide* it says, "If we do not find anything pleasant, at least we shall find something new." A very astute man. It's for that reason people like us read, ain't it, Gal?'

'Oh, for Gawd's sake, don't start on all that crap!' Mickey's voice was full of fun. 'I've read a few books in my time, and there's one thing I've learned . . . there's a difference between education and being well read.'

'Come on, Marge, before Robin Day turns up to join in the debate!'

'You saucy cow! Where you off to and we'll give you a lift?'

'Oh . . . we're just off to get the train to Holborn.'

'We'll drop you off. Come on then, Geoff, let's make tracks.'

Maura and Margaret exchanged dismayed looks.

'That's all right, Mickey. We don't want to put you out.'

'You're not. See you all.' He kissed his mother on the cheek. As he passed Garry he pretended to punch him in the arm. 'See you later, book features.'

'Tah rah, Mickey.' Garry took his books back from Geoffrey.

Inside the Mercedes, Margaret and Maura sat quietly in the back. Maura felt panic building inside her. She was meeting Terry at Holborn, and prayed her brothers would not see him there. If he came over to them she would have to introduce him, and that thought was enough to bring on near hysteria.

Michael's 280 sports car pulled out of Lancaster Road and into Bramley Street. It was already dark. As he turned the corner a police car pulled out in front of them. Slamming on the brakes, the car skidded to a halt. It was obvious to Michael and Geoffrey that the car had been waiting for them. A policeman waved Michael over to the side of the road. His face dark with temper, he parked the car.

A plainclothes policeman got leisurely out of the Panda car and walked across the road to them. He looked at the tax disc on the windscreen and motioned Michael to wind down his window. 'Insurance certificate, please.' Michael already had it in his hand.

The policeman took it and studied it.

'Well, well, well. I never thought I would see a Ryan driving a new Merc with all the rent paid.'

'Well, officer, we live and learn, don't we. Now fuck off!'

'That's not very nice, Mickey. You should have a bit more respect for the boys in blue.' The voice dripped sarcasm. 'It looks like pimping in the West End is a lucrative business. Who's that in the back? A couple of new girls?'

The policeman was knocked off his feet as Michael jumped from the car.

Geoffrey was trying to drag him back by holding on to his overcoat. He could see what the police were trying to do. They wanted Mickey to lose that famous temper of his so they could legitimately nick him.

'That's my sister you're talking about, you ponce!'

Two uniformed policemen got out of the Panda car and joined their boss. Geoffrey got out of the car and stood in front of Michael, willing him to calm down. If

Mickey went berserk here there were too many witnesses.

Michael pushed him out of the way. 'No one talks about my family like that and gets away with it. Do you hear me?'

The two uniforms stood in front of their boss to protect him. They were both terrified. It was true what they had heard: he was crazy all right. 'Mad Mickey' they called him. Since the Krays had been sent down, Mickey Ryan was the Number One. The only one left of all the big-time crooks. And unlike the Krays and the Richardsons, Michael Ryan was as cunning as a fox.

'So that's your sister in there, is it? I'm sorry, Michael. It was an easy mistake to make. I should have guessed because you don't have a lot of time for girls, do you?' He was goading again. He noticed that the veins were standing out on Michael's forehead and against his will felt a surge of apprehension. Geoffrey tried to save the situation. He grabbed Mickey's arm.

'They're trying to wind you up. Ignore them. If you blow your top, they'll nick you double quick.'

Michael's breathing was returning to normal. Geoffrey faced the plainclothes officer. 'Look, what do you want?'

The man ignored him and carried on talking to Michael. 'Can't your club run without you? I heard you had a very good doorman. Gerry Jackson, ain't it? Another brainless Mick . . .'

Michael shook his head in disbelief.

'If I'm not mistaken, you're Detective Inspector Murphy, ain't you? So you would know all about brainless Micks, wouldn't you?'

The two uniforms laughed and the Inspector was annoyed. 'I wasn't born in Ireland, Ryan.'

'Neither was I, nor any of my brothers. Neither was

Gerry Jackson, by the way. Now why don't you take these two little boys home? It's way past their bedtime.' The two uniforms sobered up instantly. Michael was calm now. Maura got out of the car and went to him.

'Can my brothers and I go now, please?'

The uniforms were giving her the once-over. One of them smiled at her.

'Who are you smiling at?' Michael's voice was loud. The young uniform was in a quandary. He didn't want to answer Michael, but at the same time didn't want to look like a coward. He was saved from answering by the DI.

'Very attractive girl, Michael.' He smiled at Maura, feeling a little bit sorry for her. He looked at her feet. In her winklepicker shoes they looked enormous. 'Do your feet go right to the end of those?'

He tried to sound jocular. She was only a kid. He had a daughter about that age himself. Maura looked at him with the arrogance of youth.

'Do their heads go right to the top of their helmets?' She jerked her head in the uniforms' direction.

Everyone looked at her in amazement. Michael and Geoffrey burst out laughing, surprised at Maura's front, but proud of her all the same.

'Now, Mr Murphy, can we go? Or would you like to ask us some more questions? Only I don't know about you, but we're very busy people.' She was as surprised as everyone else at her outburst. But she was annoyed. What gave this man the right to speak to people like he did! She would bet her last pound that her Terry didn't carry on like that. She got back into the car with Margaret. Now the excitement had worn off she was shaking.

She heard the DI saying, 'I'm gonna have you, Ryan.'

Michael laughed softly. 'Yeah, Murphy. Of course you are.'

Without bothering to speak again Michael and Geoffrey got back in the Mercedes. The three police stood watching them. Murphy knew when he was beaten and decided to retreat on this occasion. He made a mental note to have Maura Ryan checked out. Young girl she might be, but she was as streetwise as her brothers. She had made a fool of him and he wouldn't let that go. Once the uniforms had told their version in the canteen, he would be a laughing stock.

In the car everyone was congratulating her.

'Oh, Maura, how could you?' Margaret's voice was filled with awe.

'She's a Ryan, Margie. And she showed that tonight! I thought I was going to piss myself. Murphy's face!' Michael was roaring with laughter. 'I'll tell you something though, Geoff. I'll do for that bastard one day. I take oath on that. He winds me up!'

'You get wound up too easily. They can't touch us, Bruv. They can't prove nothing!' Geoffrey stressed the last two words.

'I thought we was all gonna get nicked!' Margaret's voice was still quavery. Michael looked in the mirror and caught her eye.

'I can just see you in Holloway, Marge. Them big butch warders would all be after a little thing like you!'

'Aaow, don't!' She put her hand over her mouth.

'Don't be rotten, Mickey. Marge, he's winding you up. What on earth would they nick us for?'

'That Murphy's all talk. He couldn't nick himself shaving.'

They all laughed and joked until they got to Holborn.

Maura was praying that Terry was not about. Her prayers were answered. When she and Margaret got out of the car, Michael and Geoff drove off immediately.

'Sod that, Maura, I thought we was goners there!'

'I know Mickey's my brother, but he scares even me when he gets annoyed.'

'Don't you think he's a bit weird, Maws? I mean, one minute he's foaming at the mouth and the next . . . laughing and joking.' Michael's quicksilver temperament made Margaret nervous. Maura was annoyed.

'No, Marge, I don't actually!'

'I wasn't criticising him, Maws . . .'

'He likes you, Marge. He always makes you feel welcome when you're round our house. There's nothing wrong with Mickey. He's just . . . highly strung.'

In her heart Maura agreed with Margaret's opinion of Michael, but she would never admit it openly. Maura was more like her brothers than she cared to think about. There was a loyalty in her family that would not, and could not, be understood by outsiders.

Margaret was contrite. 'I'm sorry, Maws. Here, imagine the old Bill thinking we was old brasses!' She tried to lighten the atmosphere between them.

Maura giggled. 'Bloody cheek!'

They stood outside the station until Dennis came up.

When Margaret and he had gone, Maura thought about what had happened. Tonight she had discovered a new side to herself. She had not intended to say what she had. It just came out. She shrugged and pulled her coat tighter around her. It was getting cold. She saw Terry walking towards her and smiled at him. The familiar lurch in her breast that always heralded his approach left her breathless. She ran into his arms for a kiss.

'Hello, Princess!' Maura froze in his arms then pulled away from him.

'Do me a favour, Terry. Don't ever call me that again.' Her voice was frosty. Terry couldn't believe her attitude.

'I'm sorry, Maura. I . . .' He held out his arms in supplication. Maura could see that he was bewildered.

'Look, it's no big deal. It's just that I hate that expression, that's all.' Her voice was rising.

'All right. Keep your hair on!' He was annoyed and she knew it.

'Terry.' She drew his name out softly and slipped her arm through his.

'What?' His voice was flat and expressionless. He had really been looking forward to seeing her tonight. Then, within two minutes, she had started an argument with him. He couldn't believe it.

'I'm sorry, Terry.' Her voice was small.

He relaxed. 'Let's forget it. I've booked a table for us up West in a snazzy restaurant.' He saw her face fall again. Now what was the matter with her?

Maura was in a state of acute agitation. She couldn't go up West with him! Supposing Mickey saw her? Or one of her other brothers? Not to mention all the people who worked for them. They all knew her. Michael might come into the restaurant to say hello! She felt faint just thinking about it.

'Are you all right? You've gone very white.' His voice was all concern. Maura's mind was reeling.

'I feel a bit under the weather. I haven't eaten all day. Can't we eat around here?' She knew she was clutching at straws but nothing would get her up the West End.

'But I booked the table especially. We're celebrating.'

'Celebrating what?'

'Never you mind. I'll tell you when we get to the restaurant.'

Oh, God, please help her.

'Oh, let's stay around here . . . please. I don't fancy travelling back up West.' Her voice was wheedling. He couldn't help smiling. She was some girl! Not two minutes in his company and she was biting his head off. Now she didn't want to go to an expensive restaurant in the West End. He shook his head at her.

'All right. You win as usual. What's it to be? Indian? Greek? What?'

Maura felt the tension drain out of her. She kissed him hard on the mouth.

'Greek, please. I just love taramasalata!'

She tucked her arm into his. Twenty minutes later they were sitting in a little restaurant drinking retsina.

'So what are we celebrating then?'

'I've been given a transfer. I applied for it about six months ago. Anyway, today I was told that it had been passed. From next month I will be at Vine Street! That's why I wanted to go up West tonight. Get the feel of the place.' He grinned at her.

Maura felt herself smile in response. She felt the muscles in her face moving. 'What exactly will you be doing up there?'

'It's hard to explain really. There's a lot of illegal gambling up there, always has been, as well as prostitution and drugs.'

The waiter placed two moussakas in front of them.

'Anyway, some firms – that's gangs to you – are using the hostess clubs as a front for many other things. Guns, blackmail . . . the list is endless. Well, I'll be a very small cog in the wheel that's trying to stamp it all out.'

'I see.' Maura was finding it increasingly difficult to swallow.

'You don't see, but never mind, love. You'll never have to worry about it. Or are you a closet villain?' She laughed with him, amazed that she was still able to function normally while her insides were doing the Twist!

'How about a toast to your new job?'

'I'll drink to that, Maura.'

They clinked glasses and Terry chattered on.

'It's so exciting. Do you know that there's men running clubs up there who would murder somebody like you or me would have a cup of tea? It's unbelievable. I tell you.'

She stared into her glass of wine. What was she worried about anyway? Michael wasn't involved with anything like that. And drugs? Never!

But a little nagging voice at the back of her mind kept reminding her of the way he had blown up the taxi rank after Anthony died. A little voice was whispering: 'They all work for Michael now.'

She pushed the thoughts firmly from her mind, forcing herself to concentrate on what Terry was saying. All the while icy fingers were touching the back of her neck – ghostly reminders of the past. Later on, when they left the restaurant arm in arm, she shivered. Terry pulled her closer to him.

'I want you, Maura.'

'I want you too, Terry.' And she was surprised because she meant it. At this moment she wanted him more than she had ever wanted anything in her life.

'Really?' His voice was husky with longing.

'Yes . . . really.'

'Oh, Maura, you don't know how much I wanted to

hear you say that.' He clasped her hand and pulled her to his car. 'Come on, before you change your mind.'

'Where are we going?'

'You'll find out.'

She felt the thrill of sexual anticipation sweep over her body, wiping everything from her mind except Terry, herself, and their need.

Inside the car he kissed her, long and hard. He fumbled in his pocket and took out a key.

'Do you see this?' Maura nodded. 'Well, it's a key to a flat in Islington. I rented it today. Not for this, Maura, I swear. But to be nearer my job. All that's in it is a bed and a camping stove, but it's home for us . . . if that's what you really want.'

Maura loved him just for those words. He wasn't trying to force her into anything.

'I want to go to your flat in Islington, Terry.'

He kissed her again and then started up the car. Tonight was his lucky night.

On the way to the flat, Terry had stopped and bought a bottle of wine. Maura sat nervously on the edge of the big double bed while he opened the bottle and brought her a glass. She took it from him. The bedroom had large bay windows covered with grubby nets. Grantbridge Street was the centre of bedsitterland. Even now, record players and radios could be heard. Occasionally a shout or a loud laugh broke the gloom. There was no light in the bedroom, only the moonlight and the subdued glare of the streetlights outside the window. Maura was glad. She drank the wine and placed the empty glass on the floor by the bed. Terry walked out to the kitchen, talking as he moved.

'It doesn't look much now, I know, but you wait until I've finished it – decorated it, I mean. Hey, why don't you help me? We could go to Camden Market together and pick out some furniture.' He walked back into the bedroom with the bottle of wine. 'What do you say?' His voice was eager.

Maura caught some of his enthusiasm. 'I'd love it.'

He refilled her glass and gave it to her.

'Look, Maura, you don't have to sleep with me, you know.' His voice was caressing. 'I'll understand if you're not ready.'

She looked up. In the half-light he looked boyish. She traced the contours of his face with her finger.

'I am sure, Terry. In fact, I'm positive!'

He sat on the bed beside her and kissed her gently. 'Well, as long as you're sure.'

He stood up and removed his shirt. Maura watched him, fascinated. The muscles of his arms and chest were rippling as he moved and she felt a hot flush creeping over her body. She took a deep breath and slipped off her coat. The room was not very warm and she felt goosebumps on her arms. Her dress fastened up the front and she began to undo the buttons. She could sense his eyes on her and felt a sudden bashfulness. She had never in her life undressed in front of a man – not even a doctor. She came to the last button and, plucking up all her courage, slipped the dress off her shoulders and let it drop to the floor.

Terry watched her. His throat was dry and his breathing heavy. Standing there in the moonlight in her underwear she looked magnificent. Her breasts were huge – like giant orbs in the confines of her bra, spilling over the top like overripe melons. He couldn't believe his luck. She was like a larger than life fantasy that had just come true.

He dragged his eyes from her breasts to her long legs. He was surprised at how small her waist was. She was like some voluptuous painting by Titian. He could feel himself hardening.

He slipped off his trousers and went to her. Putting his arms around her back he unhooked her bra, letting her opulent breasts free. He pulled the brassiere from her body and dropped it on to the floor. Instinctively her arms crossed over her chest. He gently pulled them away, staring down at her body. He groaned.

'Oh, Maura. You're beautiful . . . You're so beautiful!' He pressed his lips against her nipples and she jumped. She could feel them hardening under his tongue and was caught between pure ecstasy and an urge to run from the room. Her heart was hammering in her breast and her breathing was irregular. She could feel herself panting. He squeezed both her breasts together and licked and chewed on her nipples, sending delicious waves of euphoria through her. He pulled her gently on to the bed. They fell together, their arms and legs entwined. He loomed over her.

'I love you, Maura. God, I love you.'

If he never said it again, the way he had just expressed himself to her would last for the rest of her life. She felt his fingers hook into either side of her panties, and as she felt him pull them down her body she closed her eyes. It was finally happening. The mystery of man and woman was about to be unfurled before her. She bit on her lip, an exquisite agony tearing her apart. Her natural shyness was trying to overcome a new, bigger, and more intense feeling.

Unaware that she had even done it, Maura opened her legs wide. As his tongue flicked over her thighs she groaned out loud. Slowly, he pushed his forefinger inside her. She was like a juicy peach.

Terry was in a fever of excitement. Who would have dreamed she would be so fiery the first time? She was like an experienced woman, the way she moved her body and opened herself up to him. He loved everything about her – the way she looked, the way she acted – everything. He especially loved the smell of her.

Maura felt him push himself up on his arms. She opened her eyes, and as he straddled her watched his swollen member trying to push into her. Her eyes opened wide. It was too big, surely? She pushed her elbows into the bed to pull herself up, but she was too late. She felt a tearing pain as if Terry pushed against some kind of obstacle. Then she felt a wave of dizziness as he slipped right up inside her. As he moved backwards and forwards she thrust her hips up to meet him at every stroke, a jumble of feelings and emotions raging through them both. Suddenly, she felt a shuddering somewhere in her bowels. It seemed to be slowly creeping into her groin and up . . . up into her stomach. She arched her back, and as she lost control in the final throes of orgasm felt Terry biting on her breasts. She called out . . . All self-consciousness seemed to dissolve in this all-encompassing feeling. She was aware that she was wailing and moaning, but she didn't care. This feeling was too good, too exciting to let go of. She felt her legs grab Terry's thighs and was trying desperately to push him further inside her.

Above her Terry was watching her, fascinated. As he felt his own orgasm beginning to pulsate he felt her legs gripping him and drove his penis into her as hard as he could, bursting inside her like a dam.

They lay together, their bodies bathed in sweat, their

hearts beating a tattoo on each other's chests. Terry kissed her gently, little tiny kisses, all over her face and neck. He licked her throat and tasted the saltiness of her.

'That was fantastic, Maura.'

She lay beneath him, shy again, amazed at her own feelings.

'Thank you, Maura. For letting me be the first. And if it lies with me, I will be your last. You're my girl now. You'll always be my girl.'

He kissed her again and was surprised to find that she was crying gently. He was immediately concerned. 'I didn't hurt you too much, did I?'

'No, you didn't hurt me. I'm crying because I'm happy. That's all.'

He gathered her into his arms and held her tightly. He had promised himself that he would not get too involved with her, but at this moment he could no more have parted from her than he could have cut his own throat.

Maura felt the heightened awareness that comes with love-making. That feeling of infinite perception that envelops lovers in its embrace. She was acutely aware that she had burnt her boats. That she now belonged to the man lying with her. That her family had taken a back seat in her life. But she was also aware that no matter how she felt, her family would never allow her to relegate them to second place. The fact that Terry was a policeman would be enough for Michael. He would never countenance her having an association with one. He would take it as a personal affront.

She felt Terry's hand running over her body, kneading her breasts and shoulders, and was caught up in a feeling of presentiment. They were doomed and she knew it. She closed her eyes tightly, praying to her God to take pity on them. To help them find a way out of the morass they had jumped into. She wished fervently that they might be allowed to be together, that nothing would happen to make them part. And even as she prayed and wished, she knew, deep inside, that it was all useless. But with the foolishness of youth, she convinced herself that somehow, somewhere, there was an answer to their problem.

Finally, she abandoned herself to him once again, the moonlight playing on their bodies as they loved each other with a strength that surprised them both. Their whispering and low moans echoed around the empty flat, like ghosts that danced on the ceiling with their shadows.

Maura had never dreamt that she could feel like she felt at this moment. She had indeed burnt her boats. But she smiled while she did it.

Chapter Nine

Benjamin Ryan pushed his wife out of his way. He was drunk as usual, but today, instead of his normal boisterous drunkenness, he was in a violent, vindictive frame of mind.

Sarah watched him warily. Ever since Anthony's death her husband had suffered these fits of depression. His face was bloated and red-veined. His large nose was reddened and bulbous. His dark blue eyes, inherited by all the children, were now listless, the whites a sepia colour, like an old photograph. He looked terrible. His once black hair was grey, hanging across his face in greasy tendrils. Sarah shook her head sadly. He was grey-skinned and the weight that had once given him an air of affability had dropped off him, leaving only a large beergut that hung offensively over his trousers. He stalked across the bedroom to her. Sarah put her hands up to her face through years of habit. The chances were that she was going to get a good hiding. She braced herself for the blows.

'I want some money, Sar . . . I'm warning you.'

His breath was sour and she tried to turn her face away from him. He grasped her chin with his hand and pulled her face towards him. He grinned at her, showing yellowing teeth. 'What's the matter then? Turning your face away from me these days?' He squeezed her chin in his large hand, causing her to flinch. 'That's right, my lovely . . . You be scared of me, because if you don't give me some of the money you've got stashed, I'm gonna beat you all around this room. Now where is it?'

Sarah was trying desperately to pull herself away from him. He pulled his right arm back and punched her in the stomach. He used such force she fell to her knees, winded.

He grabbed her hair, forcing her head up to look at him. 'That's just a taster, Sarah.'

She nursed her injured stomach with her arm, feeling sick. She stared at her husband, and gathering all her strength she spat at him. She saw his lips draw back over his teeth.

'You old trout! I'll bloody murder you for that.'

As his fist was raised to begin his beating she screamed, holding her arms over her head. His first punch hit her on her wrist, causing her to cry out in pain. Somewhere above the din she heard the bedroom door opening, then she felt Benjamin being pulled away from her bodily. It was Garry and Lee.

Lee felt a rush of emotion he had never known before. Seeing his mother kneeling there while his father beat her caused him to lose control. He was aware that he was punching and kicking his father. He could feel the surge of adrenaline as his arms and legs came into contact with Benjamin's body. He could easily kill this man who had fathered him. Eventually Garry pulled him away, forcing him to sit on the big double bed. His breathing was loud and noisy. The effort he had used on his father had exhausted him. He felt his mother's arm go around his shoulder. He grasped her rough workworn hand. His knuckles were bleeding.

Benjamin was too drunk to feel anything. He lay on the bedroom floor staring up at a picture of Our Lady's Ascension into Heaven. Her pale blue and gold gown was swimming before his eyes. He could taste blood in his mouth. Running his tongue around his gums, he found that one of his few remaining teeth was loose. Garry looked at his father with a feeling of disgust coupled with distress. The older man's woeful face was like an open book. All the setbacks, troubles, humiliations and causes for discontent were there for anyone who wanted to look. Only nobody ever wanted to. Even his own sons regarded him as an object of derision, tempered with a love that came more from duty than any feeling of filial affection. Garry sighed.

'Help him up, son. We'll put him to bed to sleep the worst of it off.' Sarah's voice was flat, resigned. Before the boys had grown up, she would have endured the beating; years of experience had taught her that it was preferable to giving him the money.

Garry and Lee, calmer now, put their father to bed. Benjamin was pliable. He allowed his sons to strip him and bundle him under the covers. Within minutes he was asleep. The three went down the stairs together. In the kitchen Lee examined his mother's arms and face. She shrugged him off.

'I'm all right, Lee. Give it a rest now, for Gawd's sake.' She made one of her endless cups of tea.

Garry took his and went back upstairs to his room. He placed the tea on his dressing table and went back to what he had been doing before his mother's scream. He was making a car bomb. The main work had already been done in one of Michael's lock-ups. Now he was perfecting the detonator. He took his glasses off the bed where he had left them earlier and slipped them on.

Garry's years of being the inventor of the family had paid off. Michael had taken his expertise and channelled it to his own advantage. Garry made everything, from Molotov cocktails to delayed-action devices for robberies or personal revenge attacks. His natural misanthropy and lack of interest in possessions gave him the perfect temperament for an explosives manufacturer. In Garry's mind there was no black or white, just fuzzy grey areas that he could interpret to his own advantage. Like Michael, he was a psychopath. He could champion causes with a fervour that amazed those around him. He could also see two sides to an argument, could balance the debate in his mind or that of whoever happened to be interested. But there was another side to him that even his own brothers did not realise. He would not stand for anyone or anything getting in *his* way. He had no real feelings about anyone, except his sister Maura. He was incapable of deep feelings or emotion. If Garry had a girlfriend, she was his property. He would be jealous and moody. The girl always seemed to think this was because he felt deeply for her, but Garry felt the same way about his car or his record player. It was *his*. Until the time came when he tired of it.

The bedroom door opened and Lee came in. 'Mickey just phoned and said that we're all to meet him at the club tonight. Nine-thirty, OK?'

'All right, Lee. Thanks.' Garry carried on with what he was doing. Lee walked out of the room. The earlier trouble with their father was now forgotten. In the Ryan code, if you didn't mention it then it had never happened.

When Benjamin had slept off his drink and emerged once again into their world he would be treated with the usual haphazard affection.

Garry had finished his detonator and smiled to himself happily. He began clearing away. His room was so tidy, Garry would know if anyone had been in while he was out. He had everything strategically placed.

Like all the rooms in the house, this also had a religious print on the wall and a small crucifix over the bedroom door. Garry's religious painting was of Jesus's entrance into Jerusalem on Palm Sunday. Jesus sat on a donkey, the marks of the stigmata on his outstretched hands, his face as always serene with a hint of sadness. Around him were crowds of people holding their palm leaves, expressions of ecstasy on their faces. The print was in beautiful pastel shades of blue and pink. Picking up the detonator, Garry went to the picture. Holding the device under the Donkey of Christ, he laughed softly.

'Bang fucking bang!'

Jesus still sat there, the yellows and golds of his halo shadowed by Garry's body, still serene and still sad.

Mickey, Geoffrey and Roy sat in the offices above their club, Le Buxom, in Dean Street. All three were wearing the usual dark suit, brilliant white shirt and thin black tie. It was their uniform. Michael's tie had a grey stripe going through it horizontally. It was his way of being just that little bit different. He lit a cigarette and blew the smoke out noisily.

'So what else have you found out then?' He stared at Geoffrey.

'Plenty. He's a bit of a rogue, is old Hanley. He likes the gee gees for a start, and he's not averse to a bit of skirt now and again either. Both expensive pastimes for old Bill. He usually goes round to the wives of convicted criminals offering them a bit of consolation.'

Mickey laughed. 'In return for a bit of the other, I suppose.'

'Exactly. He now owes us about three hundred quid. He was betting quite heavily in our South London shops. I tipped the lads the wink to give him as much tick as he wanted, which they did. Now we have him right where we want him. By the short and curlies.'

'Good work, Geoff. Arrange for him to come and see me next week. Another face would be to our advantage. Especially a prat like Hanley.'

'How about we give him a free night here, before you see him? Let him have his leg over with one of the girls for nix. That should soften him up before you give him the bad news.'

'Yeah, I think that's what we'll do, Roy. Bent Filth are ten a penny these days. What we want are the ones who can do us the most good. Hanley's at Vine Street, from what I understand. He's the one who liaises with all the other nicks. We'll cultivate him, I think.'

Geoffrey and Roy nodded in agreement.

'Now about the loan sharking. I had a visitor today . . . do you remember old Moses Mabele?'

Roy nodded. 'The old West Indian bloke who lived in our street?'

'That's him. His wife Verbeena was mates with Muvver. Used to help her out now and again with money. Old Moses used to work in the Docks.'

'Yeah. What about them?' Geoffrey's voice was puzzled.

'Well, they moved Plaistow way. They got one of the

old Dockers' Mansions – he was working in the East India Docks. Anyway, to cut a long story short, Moses popped off a bit sudden like . . .'

'What's this got to do with us?'

'Well, if you'd listen, you might learn something, Roy. Now where was I?'

'Moses had popped off.'

'Thanks, Geoffrey. Moses popped off a bit sharpish and Verbeena couldn't afford to bury him like. So she went to one of our "borrowers" – no prizes for guessing who that was.'

Geoffrey groaned. 'Not George Denellan!'

Mickey smirked. 'The one and only. Anyway, the rub is she couldn't pay it back quick enough and Georgie boy sent round some heavies . . .'

'You're joking!'

'I wish I was, Roy. I bunged her a couple of ton for her trouble and told her the debt was scrubbed. What I want you two to do is go and see Denellan. Put him straight about a few things. She's an old lady, for Christ's sake. I want at least an arm broken. He's got to learn that he works for me, not the government. You don't belt old dears. In fact, you don't lend money to old dears, period, not without querying it with one of us first. He takes too much on himself and he's beginning to aggravate me.'

'I'll go, Mickey. I don't like Denellan anyway, he's a ponce.'

'All right then, Roy, you can sort him out. What an advert for us, eh? Beating up old ladies!'

They all laughed.

Geoffrey got up and poured them all a drink. 'What's happening with that Smithson, Mickey?'

Michael took the glass off him and sipped the brandy.

'Our Garry's made him a little surprise present. He should be getting it some time over the weekend.'

'You're definitely trouncing him then?'

'Yep. I don't like doing it, Geoff, but that saucy bugger's asked for it.' He poked his finger in the air. 'Nobody tucks me up and gets away with it. It'll be a lesson to all the blokes who work for us.'

'How much exactly did he poach?'

'Nigh on two grand.'

Roy whistled softly. 'That much?'

'It's not so much the money as the principle of the thing. One bloke owed us a monkey. He paid three oners over, and then the last two hundred plus the fifty quid interest. Next thing he knows he's got three blokes waiting for him as he leaves for work. They'd trashed his motor.' Mickey laughed softly. 'The poor bastard is informed that he still owes three hundred smackers. Anyway, he paid it . . . but he came to see our Lee and he told me about it and that's how we uncovered the little bastard's game. Fuck me! It ain't as if we don't pay him enough. For a bloke who came out of the South London slums he's done bloody well. Do you know, his kids go to private school? Straight up.'

'That don't surprise me, Mickey, he always fancied himself. He still brags in pubs about how he worked for the Richardsons.'

Michael snorted. 'Don't talk to me about him. He's history now.'

The three men were quiet for a few moments. Geoffrey got up from his chair. 'Shall I bring the other lot up then? See what's happening with their teams?'

'Yeah. Hang on, what's the time?'

'Eleven-thirty-five.'

'I bet you a tenner Benny's sitting in the club watching the stripper. She comes on at half-past.'

They all laughed.

'He's sex mad. Most of the girls don't have to "go case" with the punters, they can go home with Benny!'

Still laughing, Geoffrey made his way down the stairs to the club's foyer.

Gerry Jackson, the doorman, nodded at him. 'We're pretty full tonight, mostly Americans. Must be a convention on somewhere.'

'Plenty of money then?'

Gerry nodded. 'The touts reckon that the streets are full of them. I bet a few get rolled, don't you?'

'Bound to, ain't they? Stupid bastards. They flash their money about like it's going out of fashion. Someone's got to stomp them, it stands to reason.'

Geoffrey walked into the club itself. The air was thick with cigarette smoke and cheap perfume. At the bar area seats lined each wall to either side. They were plush red velvet, were upholstered and fixed to the wall. On them sprawled women and girls of every shape and colour. On entering the club, punters were able to see the merchandise and if a particular girl took their fancy, she accompanied them to their table. The hostesses were only allowed to drink champagne – which they tipped on to the carpet when the punter wasn't looking. With a different stripper on every twenty minutes this was not difficult. At the moment a tall blonde of about thirty was dancing semi-naked to 'Pretty Flamingo'. She bent over almost double and her long bleached blond hair touched the floor. She swayed her buttocks suggestively before hooking her fingers into her sequinned panties and slowly pulling them down her legs.

Geoffrey smiled. Sure enough there was Benny, sitting on the edge of his seat, his tongue poking out of his mouth as he watched the girl in a state of hypnotic fascination. Stepping out of her panties, the stripper stood up and turned to face the audience. Her pubic hair was black, in stark contrast to the whiteness of her hair. She raised her arms above her head and once more set the tassels on her small breasts spinning.

The music ended and she nonchalantly picked up her discarded clothes and walked from the stage. She would strip in six or seven different clubs during the course of the evening. She passed by Benny and Geoffrey saw him squeeze her buttocks. The girl smacked his hand away and glared at him, shouting at the top of her voice, 'When you're old enough, Little Boy!'

Benny laughed good-naturedly. Geoffrey called him and he walked over, his moon face wreathed in smiles.

'You never give up, Ben, do you?'

Benny grinned. 'Old slag! She's got a face like a carpenter's nailbag. Let's face it, I don't want to *marry* her, just fuck her.'

'Well, she obviously don't want to fuck you.'

Benny tapped his nose with his finger and winked lewdly. 'She will. It's just a matter of wearing her down! She'll come round in the end.'

Geoffrey laughed. 'You'll wear your dick out if you're not careful. Where's the others?'

'In the back bar as usual. You know they don't like sitting with the peasants!'

'Get upstairs, you ponce. Mickey's waiting for you. I'll go and get the others.'

He walked across the dance floor. All round the walls were large photographs of women in various stages of undress. Geoffrey stopped at a table where a small bald-headed man was sitting with two girls. He smiled at the girls warmly and shook the man's hand.

'How is everything, sir?' His voice was solicitous.

The small man grinned, showing expensive-looking teeth. 'Just fine, son. These here two ladies is just about as fine as you could get.' His voice had a southern drawl. The two girls giggled. Geoffrey noticed that one of them was high.

'I'm glad to hear it, sir. We like all our guests to enjoy themselves.' He nodded at the man and moved away from the table, his eyes taking in everything that was going on around him. One of the hostesses, a young lady who called herself Shirelle, had her head buried in a man's lap. Geoffrey sighed with annoyance and, pulling back a curtain at the end of the dance floor, walked into the back bar.

'What on earth's going on here?' His voice was loud. Two hostesses were sitting at a table. Geoffrey recognised them as Liverpool twins who Denise, the head girl, had taken on a few days previously. They were tiny little things with wide brown eyes and mousy blond hair. They were not particularly pretty but their attraction was that they only worked together. They had little half-formed breasts and were no more than fifteen. From what he had gleaned they had been toms for quite a while. Looking at them, it was obvious they had been roughed up.

Garry spoke. 'We caught these two "doing a dolly".'

Geoffrey was stunned. 'You're joking!'

'Oh no I ain't! Me and Lee were walking across the dance floor to come in here and I saw them, as plain as day. One of them slipped her arms around the bloke and kissed him on the mouth. While she was doing it she lifted his wallet and passed it to the other one. They've obviously done it before because it was all over in a split second. In fact, if I'd have blinked I'd have missed it. The slags!'

Both girls looked at Geoffrey with frightened eyes. In Soho you could be striped up for less. No clubs liked their punters rolled. It brought them to the attention of the police – the last thing a hostess club needed.

'Where's the wallet now?'

'I've got it, Geoff. It's got over three hundred quid in it.'

He gave a low whistle.

'Look, Lee, go back in there and tell the punter that the girls had to go somewhere. I noticed as I passed through that Monique and Cynthia are still up in the meat seats. Bring them to him. They're good girls. Pretend to find the wallet under the table. Make a big thing out of it. Oh, you know what to do.'

'What about these two?' Garry nodded at the girls.

'Sling them out. Give them a slap, Garry, but don't go too far. All right.'

Garry nodded at him.

'When you've finished, get your arses upstairs. Mickey's waiting for you.'

He stormed out of the back bar and went to where Denise was standing. She was nearly fifty years old and weighed in at seventeen stone. Her face was heavily made up and she wore too much rhinestone jewellery. She had been a prostitute for over thirty years. Her bright orange hair was piled up high on her head, and somehow she had squeezed her enormous bulk into a lurex two-piece. Her huge pendulous breasts spilled over the top. She smelt of gin and Parma violets.

'I want a word with you, Denise. Garry and Lee just caught those scouse birds "doing a dolly".'

'Look, sonny, I ain't got eyes up me arse, you know. There's over thirty brasses in here. I can't watch them all.'

'Well, my advice to you, Denise, is to get some eyes put up there then! And in the back of your head. That slag Shirelle was giving a punter a blow job earlier. Now either get your act together or you get another job! This is my last warning.'

He stormed off before she could answer him. Shrugging her ample shoulders, she cursed him in her head.

One of the girls on the meat seats had heard the exchange. She shouted to Denise: 'What's the matter then? You been a naughty girl?' All the other girls laughed.

Denise curled her lips back from her broken teeth. 'Oh, go fry your shite!'

The girl made a face at her and called out, 'She's a silver-tongued bastard, ain't she, girls?'

Denise picked up her Sobranie cigarette from an ashtray and pulled on it, stifling an urge to put it out on the girl's face.

She'd murder that bloody Shirelle!

Detective Inspector Murphy was driving home to his house in Putney. Since his run-in with Maura Ryan he had been doing some snooping and what he had found out had given him food for thought. She was as clean as a whistle, never even been cautioned, but she had an Achilles heel and he had found out what it was. Tomorrow morning a certain young DC was going to get a shock. He smiled to himself. He quite liked young Petherick as well! He began to whistle a little tune. He would teach Maura Ryan a lesson she shouldn't forget. If there was one thing he hated, it was mouthy young women.

*

Maura got out of bed and began to get dressed. Terry lay for a while watching her. She was the sexiest girl he had ever known. The secret of her allure was the fact that she was completely unaware of it. She sat on the edge of the bed and smoothed her stockings up her legs. He pulled her backwards and kissed her, fondling her breasts.

'Is it my imagination or are your boobs getting bigger?'

Maura pulled away from him. 'Don't be so rude!' She pursed her lips. 'Come on, Tel, get dressed. You've got to run me home.'

He got off the bed and stretched himself lazily. 'I wish you didn't have to go.' His voice was childlike.

'Well, I have. And soon. So hurry up.' She picked up a pillow and threw it at him. He caught it and threw it back, knowing it would cause a pillow fight. Five minutes later they lay semi-naked on the bed, both trying to catch their breath.

'I love you, Terry.' Maura's voice was low.

'And I love you, Maura. More than you think.'

She smiled at him. She hoped that what he said was true, because tomorrow she was going to find out whether she was indeed pregnant. She bit her lip. There was going to be murder, she could feel it in her bones.

Michael arranged to see Lee on his own. His brother stood in front of him, his face pale. As far as he knew he had done nothing wrong.

'That right you give the old man a hammering today?'

Lee swallowed noisily. 'He was belting the old woman.'

Michael smiled one of his radiant smiles that seemed to light him up from inside. 'You did good, Lee. Remember this . . . you always look after the womenfolk. You never,

ever let anyone hurt them, no matter who they are. I'm proud of you, Lee.'

Lee smiled with relief.

'I'll bung the old man a few bob tomorrow. He'll be as sweet as a nut. Now get yourself off home.'

Lee left the little office with his heart singing. He could hear the first few bars of 'Jailhouse Rock' and hurried down into the club. The girl who stripped to this particular record was a six foot amazon with olive skin, jet black hair, large brown eyes, and the biggest tits he had ever seen in his life! He settled down next to Benny, who being a thoughtful kind of boy had saved him a seat!

Chapter Ten

'Detective Constable Petherick, the big boss wants to see you.'

The WPC who gave Terry the message was grinning all over her face. He looked across his desk at Detective Sergeant Jones and made a little face. Far from being amused DS Jones just stared at him sadly and shook his head.

'You must have been barmy, lad, if you thought you could get away with it.'

Terry looked at him nonplussed. 'What are you on about?' His voice was genuinely bewildered.

Jones picked up some papers from in front of him and pretended to sort through them. 'Get yourself into the office, son. The Chief Inspector doesn't like to be kept waiting.'

Terry stood up. The WPC who had spoken to him was standing with one of her cronies and laughing. He had a sneaking feeling that the object of their amusement was himself. He racked his brains trying to think what he had done wrong. As far as he knew all the reports he had typed up were fine. He'd had two 'collars' in the last few weeks, and neither of them had been in any way abnormal. There was nothing that he could think of that would merit being seen by the Chief Inspector. He made his way across the crowded office to the glass partition that served as the Chief's office when he was down 'below' with his men and tapped on the door.

The Chief Inspector was deep in conversation with DI Dobin when he motioned with his hand for Terry to enter. He walked into the office tentatively, shutting the door quietly behind him. The two men stopped talking as he entered and the Chief told him to sit down. Both the Chief and the DI regarded him stonily. Terry sat down opposite the Chief. He could feel sweat coming out of every pore in his body. He wiped the palms of his hands on the front of his trousers. As far as he knew he had not done anything wrong. He was trying frantically to think of any slip-up he could have made when the Chief Inspector spoke.

'Well, Petherick. This is a nice kettle of fish, I must say.' His voice was hard. Never had Terry been reprimanded before, not even when he had inadvertently written down a suspect's numberplate wrongly and it had led the inquiry team to go to the house of a respected judge.

He cleared his throat. 'I'm sorry, sir. I'm not with you.'

'I've been wondering the same thing myself, young man.'

Terry watched his superior. He was not loved by his men but he was respected, which in Terry's mind was a much better thing. Chief Inspector Harris was an ample man who ran his squad along the lines of an army platoon. Indeed, he had been a colonel in the Lancers. He still sported large handlebar moustaches that had earned him the nickname 'Flying Officer Kite'. He was a large, extremely corpulent individual, much given to brightly coloured clothes that made him look like a confidence trickster. But for all that he was shrewd. Very shrewd indeed.

'I am sorry, sir. I really don't have any idea what you're talking about.'

The Chief looked up at DI Dobin, a smirk on his chubby red face.

'Hear that, Dobin? The cheeky young bugger's begging me pardon.'

Dobin nodded. Personally he thought that the Chief was an arsehole. He would not have given Murphy house-room, but the Chief *was* the Chief, and if he saw fit to listen to Murphy . . . Dobin mentally shrugged. What could he do? He felt sorry for the boy. He was getting caught up in one of Murphy's little vendettas. Dobin had heard the chat in the canteen about how Maura Ryan had wiped the floor with him verbally. He had laughed, along with most of the others. Now it seemed Murphy had done a bit of digging and had uncovered poor Petherick's association with the girl. He was to be Murphy's sacrificial lamb.

Most of the plainclothes police had had associations with villains' female relations. There was nothing like a twelve stretch to bring the Casanovas out of the wood-work, especially if the villain's wife was a nice-looking sort, and the majority of them were. He felt sorry for the boy in front of him.

'Seen much of your girlfriend, Petherick?' The Chief's voice dripped with sarcasm and innuendo.

'I saw her last night, sir.' Dobin closed his eyes. He

couldn't look! The Chief linked his fingers together and leant on his desk.

'How long have you been seeing this Miss "Ryan"?' He stressed the 'Ryan' and suddenly Terry had a terrible sick feeling in the pit of his stomach. His mind was screaming 'No' but it was all becoming frighteningly clear.

Ryan . . . Ryan . . . Ryan . . . seemed to be swimming around in his head, like a rogue shark waiting to pounce on him.

He licked his lips.

'I have been seeing her for about nine months, sir.'

'Nine months. How thrilling for you. Taken you home to meet Mummy and Daddy and the boys, has she? Especially her brother Michael . . . I bet he just loved you, didn't he?'

'No, sir, she has not.' He stared at the men defiantly. He was in a kind of limbo now. The officers in front of him had already tried and convicted him in their minds and he was quietly furious.

The Chief's voice rose a few octaves at the tone of Terry's voice.

'Well, young fellow me lad, you have a decision to make. I suppose you realise that her family between them have done more time than bloody Big Ben?'

'NO! No, sir . . . I didn't.'

The Chief's voice seemed to thunder from him. Terry and Dobin were aware that everyone outside had gone quiet and were listening to all that was taking place.

'Don't you take the piss out of me, sonny. I was doing this job when you were just a drunken twinkle in your father's eye!'

Suddenly it was all too much for Terry. The enormity of what he had found out, coupled with the humiliation of being bawled out in full earshot of his colleagues, took its toll. He lost his temper. He stood up and, putting his hands on the desk in front of him, palms flat, shouted in the Chief Inspector's face.

'I'm not taking the piss out of you . . . you can't take the piss out of shit! Surely *you* know that? You seem to know everything else. As for Maura Ryan, it never occurred to me to run her through Interpol. Let's face it, if every bit of skirt that got pulled around this place was checked out for credibility, there wouldn't be any time to catch criminals. And another thing: Maura Ryan is a decent law-abiding girl who never mentioned her family. Now, I might add, I bloody well know why!'

He stood staring at his boss, flecks of spittle at the corners of his mouth. Somewhere in the distance he heard the sound of clapping. He guessed, rightly, that it was his partner, Jones. Obviously the whole of their slanging match had been witnessed. He felt his heart sink. He had just thrown away his career, all that he had worked for. He felt an insane urge to bang his head repeatedly on the desk in front of him.

DI Dobin was having trouble keeping his face straight. He wished he had the nerve to clap the boy. It was about time someone gave the sanctimonious old bastard a taste of his own medicine. Then, to the amazement of everyone, the Chief Inspector actually smiled. His large moustaches seemed to crawl upwards towards his eyelids and he was showing small, even white teeth.

'Good lad! The fact that you lost your rag shows me that you're not guilty of anything. You must understand that the last thing we need here is a bent copper. I know they exist, but please God not in my division.'

He sat back in his chair, placing his fingers together and

resting his elbows on the arms of his chair. He stared at Terry for a while before he continued speaking. Then his voice was low and adamant.

'It's either her or the force. You realise that, don't you? I can't have one of my men running around with the sister of the biggest villain London's ever known. It would cast doubt, not only on your integrity but on the integrity of your colleagues. You can understand that, surely?'

All the fight had left Terry and he dropped into his chair, defeated. He nodded. Dobin handed him a cigarette and he took it gratefully. Taking his matches from his pocket he lit up, aware that his hands were shaking.

Dobin spoke for the first time. His gravelly voice was quiet. 'Has she ever asked you about your work, Terry?'

'Never, sir. In fact, she hated me even mentioning it. Now I know why. It's all falling into place. Why I could never pick her up from her house . . . never phone her there . . . Oh, lots of things.'

The Chief was sorry for the boy.

'Well, lad, I'll give you twenty-four hours to make your choice. I hope you decide to stay with us.' He held out his hand to show that the meeting was over. Terry shook hands with both men and left the office. In the main office, the hubbub of conversation had begun again. A few of his friends smiled at him and patted his back. WPC Lomax, who had brought him his summons, winked at him saucily. Terry ignored everyone and went to his desk. He picked up his jacket.

'I'm going home, Jonesy. I don't feel very well.'

'Go home, lad, and come in tomorrow. He's given you an ultimatum then, has he?'

'Yeah.' Terry's voice was tired. He needed time to think. Away from this place.

'Well, if it's any consolation, son, I think you have the makings of a good copper. Don't throw away a perfectly good career for a piece of skirt. They're not worth it.' Jones's wife had been one of an army of long-suffering women who, faced with the loneliness of being a policeman's wife, had got herself an alternative wage packet. Jonesy still carried a torch for her though he would never admit it.

'Thanks for the vote of confidence. God knows I need it at the moment.'

'That slag Murphy had told everyone before he saw the old man. Never could stomach the bastard. There was talk once . . . a few years ago now . . . that he was in on the Train Robbery. Nothing was ever proven against him, mind, but he's had a hard job living it down, I can tell you. What's this Maura Ryan like?'

'She is one of the sweetest girls you are ever likely to meet. I just can't believe that she is in any way related to that shower.'

'Well, you know what they say, son. You can pick your friends, but not your relatives. I reckon the bloke who said that had never been in the police force.'

Terry tried to smile. 'See you tomorrow.' He slipped on his jacket and left the building. He sat outside in his car for ten minutes before pulling away, his mind screaming one question: Why?

Margaret and Maura walked into the little chemist's. They had both had the day off work and had spent the morning walking aimlessly around the shops. It was twenty minutes before they plucked up the courage to enter the chemist's shop, standing outside waiting for it to empty of people. Now they were finally inside, Maura felt as if she wanted to scream. An Asian man stood behind the counter.

'I . . . I would like the result of my test, please.'

The little man smiled, showing decaying teeth. 'Surely you would, madam. And the name?' He spoke with the inbred politeness particular to the Pakistani race.

'Miss . . . I mean, Mrs Ryan.'

He grinned at her. Oh, they were all Mrs in this country, he thought. Even those who were not. He went into the back of the shop and looked through the test results that had arrived that morning. He walked back into the shop and looked at Maura pityingly before he said, 'I am pleased to tell you that the test was positive.'

It was the standard reply that was hardly ever what the woman wanted to hear. 'You are three months pregnant.'

Maura's face dropped. Under normal circumstances she and Margaret would have had a laugh at this man's expense. Mimicked his voice to each other and remarked on his rotten teeth, saying he had a mouth full of dogends, the standard expression for tooth decay. Now she very much doubted if she would ever laugh again. She had a terrible feeling, as if her head was filling up with hot air. She felt much too hot, and prickles of warmth crept up her back to her neck. She was having trouble breathing. She put her hand up to pull her blouse away from her throat . . . As she fainted away on to the floor the last thing she heard was Marge's voice, coming from somewhere in the distance, high and croaky.

'Oh my Gawd! The bleeding shock's killed her! She's dropped down dead!'

Maura woke up on a little couch in the back of the chemist's shop. As she opened her eyes and took a deep breath she vaguely wondered how on earth the two tiny people looking at her anxiously had managed to carry her in there. Margaret's face had tears and mascara running down it.

'Oh, Maws, you gave me such a fright . . . I thought you'd copped it.'

The little chemist pointed at a cup of hot sweet tea beside her. 'Come along, madam. Be drinking it up, it will make you feel much better. It's the best thing for shock. And it's a terrible shock you had, I am thinking.' He looked at the two girls closely.

Maura pushed herself upright on the little couch and picked up the cup of tea. Her dress had somehow risen up over her thighs and she noticed the chemist staring at her legs. Hastily she tried to pull her dress back down, spilling her tea as she did so.

'I am having a friend who can help ladies like yourself . . . young ladies who cannot tell their mummies and daddies what has befallen them. I will write his name and address down and give it to you. Tell the man that Mr Patel sent you. It will cost you only eighty-five pounds. That is very cheap price.'

He hurried back into the shop. The two girls stared at his retreating back. Maura felt as if she was trapped in some kind of nightmare that would never end. She glanced around the room. It was chock-a-block with boxes and packs of shampoo, disinfectant, bleach, and all manner of weird-looking instruments. The only nice thing about it was that it smelt lovely . . . of pine-scented bath cubes and perfume.

The little man rushed back in with a piece of paper. 'This man is very, very good, madam. A very nice man indeed.'

Maura took the piece of paper, because she didn't know what else to do, and placed it in her shoulderbag.

The man kept chattering on until finally Maura put down the tea and stood up. She felt absolutely terrible and as if he read her mind he pointed to a small door in the corner of the room. Entering the tiny toilet, Maura retched for what seemed like ages, the dank and musty smell of the carpet tiles mingled with the overpowering smell of urine seeming to spur her on. Cold droplets of perspiration were standing out on her forehead and she wiped them away with the back of her hand. She staggered out to the smell of the pine bath cubes.

'Come on, Maws, we better make a move.' Margaret took her arm and, thanking the little man, they left the shop. They walked for a while in silence before Margaret said: 'You should have seen that skinny little sod trying to lift you on to that couch . . . If I hadn't have been so worried. I'd have pissed myself laughing!'

Maura, seeing in her mind's eye the incongruousness of the situation, started to laugh. Margaret laughed with her, and soon the two girls began to scream with laughter. Passersby paused to stare at them, smiling to themselves and thinking it must be a great joke. Maura's laughter was tinged with hysteria. They held on to one another, screeching, until Maura's laughter turned to deep racking sobs.

'What am I gonna do, Marge?'

Margaret led her into a small coffee shop and sat her down. She ordered a pot of coffee from a fat bored waitress and went back to her friend. When she was seated Maura repeated her question.

'What the hell am I gonna do? There's gonna be murders committed over this.'

'There's not a lot you *can* do, Maws, except tell everyone. People are funny like that. Remember Gina

Blenkinsop? She got in the club by some bloke who had it on his toes. Well, she had her baby and now her mum and dad absolutely dote on the poor little thing.'

Maura snapped at her friend, 'Oh, yeah? I can just see Mickey, can't you? Holding the baby at the christening . . . every villain in London on one side of the church and the best part of Vine Street nick on the other. Use your bloody head, Marge. This baby will be as welcome as a pork chop in a synagogue.'

The waitress brought over their pot of coffee. She laid out the cups and saucers and the two girls sat quietly until she had finished. When she went Margaret tried again. 'I still can't understand why you never went on the pill.'

Maura sipped her coffee and banged the cup back in the saucer.

'Oh, don't be so bloody ridiculous! How could I go to O'Reilly? He would have been straight round my mother's!'

Margaret swallowed her temper. Maura was in one of her moods and in fairness, Marge admitted, she would be the same if the boot was on the other foot. She took a deep breath.

'I told you to go to that doctor in Hampstead where I go. He'll give you slimming pills . . . anything you want, as long as you can pay.'

Maura screwed up her eyes and stared at Margaret. Her weight was a touchy subject. 'Are you being bleeding funny?'

'Of course not! Anyway, slimming pills would be a bit of a waste of time now, don't you think?'

She looked meaningfully at Maura's waist. The look brought Maura back to reality and she wailed: 'Oh, Marge, what am I gonna do!' Her voice held a plaintive note. She put her hands on her belly. She had a little life in there, and somewhere inside her she was pleased. She loved children. Her brother's daughter Carla had always been like a little sister to her. She had never resented the amount of time she spent at the house. Maura was aware that Janine did not really like her only child, but it had never mattered because Carla was doted on by herself and her brothers. Now she had a child growing in her own body and knew that it would be hated, despised, because its father was a policeman. The biggest cloud on her horizon was not Terry's reaction but Mickey's. He would want to kill Terry stone dead just for sleeping with his sister, and when he found out that Terry was a policeman . . . she felt sick with fright. He would kill Terry, then herself – in that order. He would take it as a personal affront. She closed her eyes tightly to block out her brother's image.

'I tell you what I'm going to do, Marge. I'm going to go and see Terry and tell him everything. About the baby . . . the boys . . . everything. He loves me, I know he does. We could go away together somewhere. I know that he'll stand by me. He's got to!' Her voice was full of panic. Margaret wondered who she was trying to convince with her talk about going away.

'I hope he stands by you, Maws.' Her voice sounded sceptical.

Maura wailed, 'Oh, don't put the mockers on me, Marge! As if I haven't got enough troubles.'

Margaret stretched her hand across the table and held on to Maura's. Squeezing it tightly, she smiled at her best friend. They had come a long way together since the fight outside their school. She just wished that she had as much faith in Terry Petherick. She liked him well enough, but couldn't see him standing by Maura, somehow. She might not have any qualifications but she was cute enough to realise that Terry Petherick would not want relations like the Ryans in his job. She said a quick Hail Mary, as she used to when she was a child, and prayed that Maura would not come unstuck. Though another part of her mind said: She already has.

Terry was sitting in his flat in Islington. The chair he was sitting on had been a present from Maura. They had been strolling through Camden Market when they had seen it. It was large, high-backed, and upholstered in green leather. They had homed in on it together, both of the same mind. Instead of a settee they would have the chair, then they could cuddle up in it together. Something they had since done many times. They had bartered with the stall owner for it, laughing and joking until a compromise had been reached. For the grand total of six pounds they had got their 'lovescat'. Maura had then bought some material, a riot of green and blue brocade, and had made the curtains for the windows. He remembered thinking as he watched her sewing them: She's a natural homemaker.

Over the months they had been together he had fallen deeply in love with her. Her smile, her cheeky quips, her long legs and incredible breasts . . . Now he had to decide whether that love was strong enough. All day a little voice had been nagging at him, telling him that if he really loved her he would have thrown in his job there and then . . . Oh, he had defended her, but not vehemently enough to tell his boss where to stick his job, and logic told him that's what he would have done if he really, really loved her.

He stood up and went to the window. It was cold outside and a solitary little boy was kicking a football around the road. He turned abruptly from the window and walked into the bedroom. He stared at the bed. Maura had really abandoned herself there. She had shocked him at times with the intensity of her loving. She wasn't a girl who would give herself lightly, he knew that. Was that why he was feeling such a bastard? Because deep inside he knew that there was no competition really. Maura Ryan was an also-ran.

He went back into the small living room and opened the bottle of Teacher's he had bought on the way home from work. What he needed was a stiff drink. He poured himself a large Scotch. He needed something to numb his mind for what he was thinking of doing. He checked himself. What he was *going* to do. He had decided then, and not even realised it.

He took a large gulp of his Scotch, grateful for the burning sensation it created in his throat. All his life he had had one ambition: to be a policeman. He had studied long and hard with that one thought in mind. Now he had to choose between the job he loved and the woman he loved, and the woman had lost. He had to admit that to himself . . . Oh God!

If she had been anyone's sister but Michael Ryan's! The thought of Michael brought his heart leaping into his mouth. He took another long pull of his whisky and sat back in the armchair. Everyone knew about Michael Ryan and his brothers – they were notorious. There was talk of their being involved not just with drugs and whores, but arms too. Not just the odd sawn-off either, but high velocity rifles, rocket launchers, and anything else that the British Army wouldn't miss. Jesus Christ, how did he ever get personally involved with all this! He was starting to sweat. He had before him the awesome task of giving

Michael Ryan's baby sister the Big E. He put the glass he was holding to his forehead. The enormity of it all was breaking into his consciousness.

All day he had been worried about Maura . . . Her reaction. How to let her down gently. In his worried state he had concentrated wholly on Maura. Now the thought of her brother invaded his mind. He rolled the glass along his skin, savouring the coldness as he became unbearably hot.

He sat back in the chair. Everything in the room seemed to be mocking him. Even the TV set in the corner. Once again the dreadful feeling of foreboding pervaded his being. Michael Ryan would not like his sister being with a policeman, he would lay money on that.

He closed his eyes again. In his mind he could see Michael standing over him, threatening him with bodily harm. Suddenly he tensed. He could hear the scraping noise of a key going into a lock. His whole body was taut. In his mind's eye he could see Michael Ryan letting himself into his flat. He sat in the chair paralysed with fright, the knuckles of his hand white as he clutched the glass. He heard the door swing open with its familiar creaking groan. Every nerve in his body was jangling. For the first time he knew the smell of fear. It seemed to rise up into his nostrils, an overpowering aroma of hot sticky stale sweat. Supposing Ryan had taken the key off Maura? They could have been seen out together. A hundred different thoughts whirled around in his head, leaving him breathless and dizzy . . .

Instead of Michael's heavy footfall, he heard the familiar clatter of Maura's heels as she stepped into the hall on to the worn linoleum. He collapsed into the chair like a rag doll. A thin trickle of sweat slipped down his forehead, over his eyebrow and down on to his cheek. A feeling of euphoria swept over him. It was Maura . . . Maura . . . Her name bounced around inside his head like a crazy pattern in a child's kaleidoscope. She walked into the lounge and smiled at him.

'You all right? You look as if you've seen a ghost.'

He stood up awkwardly. Placing his glass on the small coffee table he went to her. Maura was in the process of putting her key back into her bag. Reaching out, he took it from her gently and slipped it into his trouser pocket. Maura looked at him.

'What did you do that for?' Her big luminous eyes held a hint of fear. He tried to smile and succeeded only in grimacing.

As he looked at her he didn't see her lovely trusting face. Terry saw only Michael Ryan. A very angry Michael Ryan.

'I think that we're getting a bit too serious, love.' It sounded lame even to his own ears. 'I think we should cool it for a while. We're both young . . .' His voice trailed off. He felt so bad he could not meet her eyes. Maura just stood there thunderstruck.

'I beg your pardon?' Her voice sounded small and hurt.

Terry still could not bring himself to look at her so he walked back over to the window.

'It's quite simple really, Maura . . . I don't want to get involved right now. I want to be free. Go out with other women. I don't want to get tied down just yet.'

'I see.' Her voice was flat. Pride had taken over. 'And just when did you come to this earth-shattering conclusion, may I ask? Only I was under the impression that you was my bloke . . . My chap, if you like that expression better. Now I find that I was just a screw.' She stormed across the room to him, pulling him around to face her with considerable strength. 'Let me tell you something, Terry bloody "I want to see other women" Petherick! I'm . . .'

She stopped herself there and then. How could she tell him about the baby? Her eyes darted around the room, looking for a chance of escape. It was all going wrong. All the words she had practised on her way over here dried up inside her head. The picture she had built up in her mind of Terry taking her in his arms and whispering that they would always be together, no matter what, faded in front of her eyes like chalk paintings in the rain. He was dumping her. He had had his bit of fun and now she was ancient history.

The fight left her as quickly as it had come. The urge to rip his face open with her nails dissolved along with all her dreams and hopes. She felt the hot salty tears come and forced them away. If she had to go, she would go with dignity. She glanced around the room. She had experienced so much pleasure in this little flat, the result of which was inside her at this very moment. Should she tell him? Should she scream it out into his face? Make him take the responsibility? Even as the words formed in her mind she knew that she would never say them to him. She would never tell him about the child. Having him on sufferance would be far worse than not having him at all. She bent down wearily and picked her bag up off the floor. She had not even realised that she had dropped it. She turned to leave and his voice stayed her.

'Believe me, Maws, I am really sorry about this.'

His voice sounded so sincere. She laughed bitterly. He had the knack of sounding sincere. Last night in bed he had told her that he loved her, and had sounded sincere. The lying, two-faced bastard!

Without facing him, she said: 'Terry.'

'Yes?' His heart was breaking.

Gathering up every ounce of strength and hatred she could muster she turned to face him, launching herself at him with arms flying. She felt his skin tear beneath her nails. Felt the pure rush of pleasure as she made him hurt, as she was hurting. As quickly as the attack began, it stopped. The sudden urge of energy left her drained.

'You can fuck off, Petherick!' She saw his hand go up to his face. Four deep grooves on his cheek were bleeding simultaneously. She smiled at him, a nasty evil smile, and pointed her finger at him. Her long scarlet-painted nails made him flinch.

'I never thought I would ever say this to you. You're a dirty rotten swine. You took me and you used me. I trusted you, Terry.' Her voice broke. 'But I tell you something now, boy. The day will come when you will want me . . . when you will need me. You'll live to regret this day, because if you live to one hundred years old you'll never find anyone to love you like I do.'

With that she turned away from him and left the flat, slamming the door behind her.

Terry watched her leave. In his heart he knew that what she said was true. She deserved much better than the treatment he had given her. She was his first love, the first woman to meet him on an equal plane, and he had destroyed her with a few simple words. He was not surprised to feel that he was crying. The tears were running into the scratches on his face, making them sting. He had a terrible feeling that although he had destroyed Maura, somewhere along the line he had also destroyed himself. He saw droplets of blood falling on to his shirt, their deep crimson colour spreading over the material.

Suddenly he couldn't let her go. He ran to the window. Pulling back the net curtain, he looked out on to the street. She was on the other side of the road, her head tucked into her coat. He knew that she too was crying. Fumbling with the ancient catch on the window he finally opened it and leant out, calling her at the top of his voice.

'Maura . . . Maura . . . come back!'

His voice carried to her on the wind.

He knew that she could hear him, saw her hesitate before walking away faster, her white-blond head tucked even further into the collar of her coat. He watched her until she turned the corner, the hum of the traffic grating on his ears.

Pulling his head back inside, he closed the window. The once friendly little room looked alien now, and hostile. Everywhere he looked was Maura Ryan . . . He could see her flitting about, putting up the curtains, making sandwiches or curled up with him on their special armchair. He could breathe in her perfume and taste her musky body. She was everywhere around him. He sat in the chair.

He was still sitting there thinking about her when he passed out much later in the evening. He had drunk the whole bottle of Scotch.

Maura was devastated. If someone had told her that Terry would dump her like that she would have laughed at them. 'I want to see other women.' Those words kept echoing in her head. They would stay with her for the rest of her life. Anything he could have said, even that he hated her, would not have had the profound effect that those few words had. Well, let him see other women! She hoped to God that he caught a terrible disease from them.

She passed the Angel and made her way along the

Pentonville Road. The fact remained that she was still pregnant. She had an urge to go and drown herself but dismissed it. It was getting dark and she wandered aimlessly, trying to figure out what on earth to do. All around her were couples, holding hands, laughing, kissing. She pushed her hands further into her pockets and carried on walking, letting her legs carry her wherever they wanted to go. Terry's face was fresh in her mind, his softness and his tenderness welcome memories to her in the cold evening wind.

She found herself at Kings Cross Station and was surprised at how far she had walked. A black cab came along the road and she hailed it, telling the driver to take her to Notting Hill. She sat in the back, huddled into a corner of the seat, staring listlessly out of the window at the rapidly moving landscape. A lone tear rolled down her face and she wiped it away impatiently. She was done with crying, she had more important things to think about.

The cab driver looked over his shoulder at her and asked cheerfully, 'Whereabouts in Notting Hill, love?'

'Lancaster Road, please.' She wouldn't go home just yet. She would go to Margaret's. Margaret would know what to do. She rested her head on the window, her breath coming in little gasps that barely managed to create steam on the glass surface. She felt so lonely, so frightened. Her bottom lip quivered as she tried to stop the tears of frustration and rage. She loved him so much!

'You all right, love?' The driver's voice was concerned.

She sat up in her seat and saw him watching her in the mirror above his windscreen.

She gave him a small childish smile. 'No, actually, I'm not.'

He had a broad good-natured face. 'You listen to

me, girl. If it's boyfriend trouble that's put that frown on your boat, remember this. Us blokes ain't worth it!' He laughed at his own wit.

Maura looked back out of the window, then forced a large smile on to her face. 'Don't I bloody know it!'

Chapter Eleven

Michael Ryan was in the Valbonne nightclub in Kingly Street having a quick drink with his boyfriend, Jonny Fenwick. It was a well-known fact that Michael Ryan was a 'brown hatter'. Not that anyone would call him that to his face. Far from taking anything away from his street credibility it enhanced it, because queers were known to be nasty bastards. They had a cruel twist to their nature and the best thing to do was to keep on the good side of them. There was no queer bashing when Michael Ryan hit the streets. He also took a woman now and again which further puzzled his friends and adversaries alike. It was proof of his ever changing habits. He treated his friends like he treated his lovers. He could go one way or the other.

At the moment Michael was besotted by Jonny Fenwick's youth. He was a beautiful boy with thick blond curly hair and large, wide-spaced grey eyes. Mickey had put him up in a flat and paid him an allowance. He was Jonny Ryan now. Michael owned him, lock, stock and barrel. Jonny loved it, and loved being seen with Michael.

Tonight, though, he was in a dilemma. He had heard a bit of gossip today concerning Michael's sister and was not sure whether to tell him or not. He certainly didn't want any comebacks off Michael if what he said turned out to be false. But Michael was in fine fettle tonight, full of laughter and jokes, and Jonny decided to risk it. Not only that, but that bitch Tommy was looking at him all gooey-eyed and Michael was loving it, so Jonny would use it as an excuse to get him away from the bar *and* Tommy! He tapped Michael's arm.

'What, mate?' Michael's voice was warm.

'It's a bit private, Mickey. I heard a bit of news today . . . I don't want to talk about it here.' He looked meaningfully at Tommy and pursed his lips. Michael nodded.

'Come and sit down then.'

He picked up their drinks and led Jonny over to an empty table away from listening ears. Jonny sat down and crossed his legs, placing his hands one on top of the other on his knee. He leant towards Michael theatrically.

'It's about a member of your family. But first I want your solemn promise that you won't go ape shit in here.'

Michael's eyes narrowed. 'I won't lose my temper. Now tell me what you heard.'

Jonny flicked his hair out of his eyes with a girlish gesture and said, 'I asked you to promise me, Michael.'

He gritted his teeth. 'For fuck's sake, Jonny, spit it out. I ain't got all night.'

Jonny licked his lips nervously. He wasn't at all sure that he was doing the right thing now. Michael spoke of his little sister as a mixture of the Virgin Mary and the Queen. Either way, she was completely beyond reproach.

'It's about your sister . . . She's got herself a boyfriend.'

Michael relaxed. 'Is that all? Who?'

Jonny took a sip of his gin and tonic before answering. 'It's a policeman from Vine Street.'

Michael looked as if he had been hit by a bus.

'A what!'

'Keep your voice down! Do you want the whole world to know? He's a young Detective Constable. Remember my friend little Mo, the fat queen from Kensington?' Michael nodded. 'Well, apparently he has a few friends at Vine Street, though myself I'd call them customers. Anyway, one of them told him. It seems a bigwig there . . . some bloke called Murphy . . . pulled the rug out from under him today. Told his Chief Inspector that he was seeing her . . . your sister. Apparently there was a big to-do about it. Anyway, little Mo rang me. And being a good boy, I thought you ought to know.'

Michael was staring at Jonny without seeing him. His face was dark with fury. The conniving little bitch! She'd been knocking about with a Filth right under his nose. He felt a blinding compulsion to wring her neck.

'Phone this little Mo and find out who his customers are. Names, ranks, the works. Tell him from me that if he decides to become coy I'll break his fucking neck.'

Jonny nodded. 'All right, Mickey. First thing in the morning.'

Michael was in the throes of a violent rage. Maura had never even brought a fellow home. A small rational thought broke into his reverie. It said to him, Well, she wouldn't, would she? Of course not. She had a bit more sense than to bring an old Bill straight into her family of criminals. He could easily walk out of this club and smash her to a pulp. At least one good thing had come of it. He had the means to blackmail a few of the shirtlifters on the force. He consoled himself with that thought.

'Look, Jon, I have to get around to me own club now. I'll see you later on tonight.'

Jonny smiled his best smile. He had been the teller of very bad news and now he was scared. Michael was capable of taking the whole thing out on him.

'All right, Mickey love.' He fluttered his eyelashes as a woman might. Watching him, Michael experienced one of his lightning changes of mood. He laughed softly, guessing what was going through the boy's mind. Wagging his finger in Jonny's face, he said: 'Behave yourself, you!'

To which Jonny answered seriously, 'I don't have much choice do I?'

Michael squeezed his shoulder affectionately and left the club.

As he made his way to Dean Street he thought about what Jonny had told him. The doorman of the Pink Pussycat hailed him and he waved back halfheartedly. His arrogant, strutting walk and dark countenance were familiar features around Soho. Unlike most of his contemporaries Michael didn't feel the need to be surrounded by minders. His immense size, coupled with the fact that he was known to carry a piece, was warning enough for any would-be assassins. Since Michael had taken over as the Baron of the West End he had not had one serious threat. He was, to all intents and purposes, the business – the highest accolade that a villain could be awarded. As he walked to his club he was hailed by touts, prostitutes, bouncers and pimps. He crossed Shaftesbury Avenue into Dean Street itself and slowed his pace. If Maura was knocking about with a Filth he would kill her. He hadn't fought tooth and nail since he was seventeen to have his little baby sister blow it all wide open for him. He gritted his teeth in temper. He had worshipped her, would have given her the earth if she had asked for it. But he wouldn't allow her to have this bloke. Never! He would find out everything he could about this copper and then he would nip it in the bud. He stormed into Le Buxom at ten-fifteen.

The club was just picking up. A few stray punters were having a drink. They were 'weekend warriors' – the nick-name given to men who saved up their meagre earnings as civil servants or bank clerks and came up West once a month for a drink, sex and excitement. An experienced tom could tell them a mile off from their off-the-peg suits to their Freeman, Hardy and Willis shoes. The older women gravitated to them, secure in the knowledge that it would be an easy lay. These men were too scared of their wives and the police ever to cause any trouble. They were seldom rough, and because they had to make their money stretch were hardly choosy. The only bugbear for the club was the fact that they only ever bought one bottle of champagne, making it last all night, until the final stripper had departed. A weekend warrior was the only sort of punter who provided the women with an opportunity actually to drink the stuff.

Michael looked around the club. It was half empty. He noticed Benny sitting at a table with one of the younger girls, a pretty little piece known affectionately as Pussy. Despite his anger Michael smiled. Benny had a permanent hard on. As soon as a new hostess arrived, Benny was there, cock standing to attention. There was a longstanding joke in all the rival clubs that without Benny, Le Buxom would have gone bankrupt years ago. Michael stood by the meat seats. For once the girls there were subdued. He had that effect on people. The girls rarely spoke to him unless he addressed them personally. The stench of cheap perfume was overpowering. Michael nodded to them and made his way out into the foyer and upstairs to the offices.

Geoffrey, Leslie and Garry were already in there having a drink. He greeted them and poured himself a large brandy. Sitting behind his desk, he looked directly at Garry. If anyone knew Maura's whereabouts it would be him.

'Do you know if our Maura's got a boyfriend?'

Garry looked at his brother in bewilderment. 'What if she has? It's none of our business.'

Michael was out of his seat and round the desk, knocking Leslie flying out of his chair as he pushed past him to get to Garry. He grabbed him by his shirt front, pulling him up out of the chair with considerable strength.

' "None of our business" you say . . . I heard a whisper on the street tonight that our sister is knocking about with a Filth!' He threw Garry back into his seat. His temper was seething. If he didn't get some kind of answer soon he would explode.

Leslie stared at Garry, who was gasping for breath. There was no doubt about it . . . Mickey was an awesome bastard. There was no one to touch him. Mickey was the business. Well the business.

'Who told you all this then, Mick?' Geoffrey tried unsuccessfully to defuse the situation.

'Never you mind who bloody well told me! It's enough that I've heard. I want you two –' he pointed at Leslie and Garry – 'to find out how true it is.'

Geoffrey tried again. 'It's not definite then? What I mean is . . .'

Michael screwed up his face and bellowed at his brother, 'Oh, for fuck's sake, Geoffrey . . . I don't want a government White Paper on it all. I just want the facts! Now do what I fucking well told you to do!'

Leslie and Garry scrambled from the room. When Michael was in one of his tempers, you did not argue with him.

Geoffrey poured himself a brandy. When Michael was like this, it was best not to rock the boat in any way.

Michael swallowed his own brandy in a gulp and grimaced. 'So what do you think, Geoffrey?' His voice was once again steady.

'Who told you?'

'Jonny actually.' He sounded wary.

'In that case . . . no way. Not our Maws.' His voice was dismissive. He did not like Jonny. He did not like the fact that Michael was homosexual, though he would never say it outright.

Michael guessed, rightly, exactly what had gone through Geoffrey's mind.

'I know you don't like Jonny. That's tough. But I'll tell you this much – for all his faults he ain't a liar. And there's one thing that seems to have escaped your notice . . . most people don't even know we have a sister.'

Geoffrey digested this bit of logic, watching Michael sitting at his desk chewing his thumbnail. Geoffrey knew from experience that Michael could sit like that for hours. Sighing, he poured himself another drink. He hoped for Maura's sake that what they had heard wasn't true.

Downstairs, Leslie and Garry had told Benny what had happened. He was still sitting with Pussy, except now the night had lost some of its enchantment. Sensing that she had lost his attention, the girl stroked his thigh, pouting at him prettily. He smiled at her with a crafty little grin guaranteed to melt the hardest of hearts.

'Pussy.' His voice was caressing.

'Yes?' She looked into his eyes. Their blue depths mirrored her features.

'Let's go, shall we?'

'All right then.' They stood up together. Benny wanted out of here before Michael decided to rope him in on everything. There were many things he would do for his eldest brother, but even he drew the line at a witch hunt on his only sister. Gathering up their things, they left the club. Hailing a cab outside, Benny jumped in, pulling Pussy in after him. There was a little hotel just off Leicester Square where he could hole up with her for the night. And that's what he intended to do. The thought of ringing home and warning his sister crossed his mind, but he soon dismissed it. He didn't want any part of this whatsoever.

The girl snuggled up to him in the back of the taxi, and for the first time in his life Benny wondered if he would be able to get it up.

The way he was feeling, he would need Charles Atlas to lift it for him.

Garry and Leslie got out of their car. They were going to see another policeman. This was their second visit in two hours. The first had been to a young PC who had been as bewildered as they were. They had left no wiser to their sister's antics than they had been before. It had cost them twenty quid to keep him quiet, but it was worth it. He was going to keep his ear to the ground. The man they were going to see now was a sergeant in Notting Dale police station. He had been on the Ryans' payroll for about five years. Well, now he could earn his money.

They knocked on his front door. It was nearly twelve-thirty. The small terraced house was in darkness. A light came on upstairs and Sergeant Potter's grizzled head appeared from a window.

'Who the bloody hell is it?'

He peered myopically down at them.

'It's Leslie Ryan. I wanna see you, Sarge.' Leslie's voice was a theatrical whisper.

Grunting and moaning, the old man retreated back inside the room. Leslie and Garry heard him clumping down his stairs. The hall light went on and the door was opened.

'What the hell are you playing at? Coming round here at this time of night?'

Garry and Leslie walked into the hallway.

'We've got a few questions, and we want you to give us the answers.'

The old man looked at them maliciously. He had a sneaking suspicion that he knew what they were going to ask. 'Would the questions be about your sister by any chance?'

'That's right, Sarge. What do you know about her then?' Garry sounded menacing and the man realised that he had forgotten for a moment just who he was dealing with. He licked his lips.

He started talking in a self-righteous tone of voice. 'Now you listen to me . . . I didn't know anything until today, I take oath on that. A friend of mine who's now at Vine Street gave me a ring at Notting Dale. He told me that there had been a bit of malarkey with one of the plainclothes there. He got hauled over the coals because he was knock— I mean, seeing your sister.'

He was fiddling with the cord of his plaid dressing gown, his short stubby fingers tobacco-stained. Leslie and Garry stood quietly staring at him.

The man began to babble. 'Honestly, boys, I didn't think you would be interested in it. I mean . . . I assumed you knew about it all.' He was getting desperate.

'What's the bloke's name?'

'The bloke who rang me or your sister's fancy man? Sorry, I mean boyfriend.'

Garry closed his eyes wearily. He spoke slowly and deliberately. 'Who was the man who rang you up?'

'Oh, it was an old friend.'

'Listen, you!' Garry pushed him across the hallway. 'I just want his name, not his fucking life story. Now who is he?'

The old man had fallen back on the stairs and sat there watching the two boys. Upstairs he could hear his wife getting out of bed. Her high-pitched, nasal voice floated down the stairs. 'Who's that down there, Albert? Sounds like an 'erd of bloody elephants from up here.'

He groaned. That was all he needed, his wife awake and sticking her oar in where it wasn't wanted.

'No one, dear. It's police business. You go back to sleep.'

'Well, just you tell them to keep their great big galloping feet off of my clean floor.'

'I will.'

Leslie had an urge to laugh and stifled it. 'The name of your informant?'

'It was a bloke called Jones . . . He's a DS at Vine Street.'

'Is he reliable? I mean, if he said something was true, would that be the case?'

'Oh, yeah. He's a rare one, old Jonesy. If he told me he had seen old Nick himself I'd believe him. He's not a spinner.'

Garry snorted. 'That makes a change in the police force. I thought you needed a degree in being a lying bastard before they would have you?'

Albert pursed his lips. Even though he was on the take, he still took a pride in being a policeman.

'What was the bloke's name who's been seeing my sister?'

'Petherick. Detective Constable Terence Petherick.'

'That's all we wanted to know. You can go back to bed with old vinegar tits now.'

As they left the house, Leslie slipped the old man a ten-pound note.

'Listen, Sarge, we want his address. If you can get it there'll be a pony in it for you, all right?'

'OK, son.' All his animosity was forgotten now. He could do a lot with twenty-five quid. Anyway, he reasoned, they'd get their information one way or the other so he might as well feather his nest while he had the chance. 'I'll keep me ear to the ground. Don't you worry.' He closed the door behind them.

His wife's voice came once more from above him. 'Al . . . bert!' She had the knack of singing his name out in such a way that her voice carried for about three miles.

'Oh, shut your row, you stupid old bitch!'

His wife sat in her bed, her face a mask of Pond's cold cream and abject disbelief. Her curlers were placed strategically around her head like a crash helmet. She hitched up her ample chest, her mouth settling to a grim line. A malevolent gleam in her eye, she pulled the covers off her. Swinging her legs out of bed, she placed her feet in her carpet slippers, stood up and picked up the heavy chamber pot from underneath the bed. She walked out of the bedroom on to the landing. As her husband reached the top of the stairs she flung the contents into his face . . . that would teach him to answer her back!

She clumped back into her bedroom leaving her husband clutching a soggy ten-pound note in his hand. He spat. Only his Gladys would have the nerve to empty an 'Edgar Allen' all over him. Sod them bloody Ryans! If they hadn't got him out of bed none of this would have happened.

Garry and Leslie drove back to Dean Street. It was just on one o'clock. They arrived at the club at one-thirty-five. The balloon went up at one-forty.

Maura was lying in bed wide awake. It was nearly two-thirty in the morning and she was no nearer sleep than she had been at nine o'clock when she had got into bed. Her mind was turning in circles, her thoughts drifting away on different tangents as she tried to see a way out of her predicament. There was none. She had talked everything over with Margaret, but neither girl could find a solution to her problem. A problem that was getting bigger in Maura's mind with every passing second.

She was in a quandary. If she told her family who the father was there would be murder. Especially if she told them he had dumped her. As much as Terry had hurt her, she wasn't going to be the cause of his getting beaten to death. And if she knew Mickey that would be the outcome. She placed her hands on her belly. There was a tiny little person in there, a completely new life waiting for her to bring it into the world. She turned over the bed again. The blankets and sheets were tangled around her.

How could he have dismissed her like that? She was still reeling from the shock. She had thought he would have been over the moon once the news had sunk in. She had seen him picking her up in his arms and kissing all her fears away. Telling her that he loved her. That they would go away and get married, away from her brothers, to Scotland or somewhere. Now, in bed, in the dark, she could see her plans for what they were: childish fantasies. Terry had no more need of her than he had of his car. When it was old hat, you traded it in for a newer model.

She felt the familiar sting of tears. Well, he wouldn't hear about this child from her. She wouldn't lower herself. If he didn't want her then he didn't want his child either. But what was she going to do about the baby? She couldn't see herself as one of these unmarried mothers, brazenly having their babies and sod the neighbours. If it had been anyone else, her brothers would have been round the boy's house, given him a good hiding, and then the wedding would have been arranged, quick smart. But this was a situation that could not be resolved so easily. Even if Terry wanted to marry her, Michael would move heaven and earth to stop the marriage taking place.

She was hot again so she pushed off the blankets. In her short nylon nightie she looked far more seductive than she felt. Her long smooth legs were spreadeagled on the blankets, her arms were hugging her breasts. She had combed out her long hair before getting into bed and it fanned around her head giving her an ethereal appearance, like a saucy angel.

She rolled her head from side to side on her pillow. Oh, why was she being plagued like this! It was bad enough being pregnant without all this added worry. She turned herself over again in the bed. This time she was facing the window. She stared out into the darkness, only the light of the streetlights to illuminate her room. Earlier she had prayed – to the Immaculate Conception and Saint Jude, the patron saint of no hope! Above her bed was the Sacred Heart, a large golden vessel pulsing outside Christ's body. He had looked benevolently down on her for years. She began to pray to him again. In the half-light she could see his golden heart glinting. She began to murmur the Eucharistic prayer.

' "Father, you are holy indeed, and all creation rightly gives you praise." '

As she prayed she heard a car drive into Lancaster Road. She saw the car's headlights cast long shadows over her bedroom ceiling as the engine died down and guessed, rightly, that her brothers were home. She heard them coming into the house and carried on praying.

' "All life, all holiness comes from you . . ." '

They were coming up the stairs. She could hear the thud of their shoes.

' "Through our son, Jesus Christ our Lord." '

Her bedroom door was thrown open and the light turned on. She pulled herself up in the bed and put her hand over her eyes to shield them from the sudden glare. Michael and Geoffrey stood at the end of her bed like avenging angels.

She squinted at them. 'What's going on?'

'I was just gonna ask you the same thing.'

'I don't know what you're on about, Mickey. I ain't done nothing!' Her voice was full of fear.

With one bound he was across the room. He grabbed her hair, yanking her head back. 'You bloody tart! You've been knocking about with a Filth, ain't ya?'

'No . . . Mickey, I swear!' She was screaming with fear.

'Don't lie to me, you slag.'

He pushed his face closer to hers. She could smell his breath as he shouted at her, 'Lover boy got an ultimatum today, Maura. Either his bit of skirt or his job. I understand the job won.'

Maura's head was reeling. That was why he had dumped her! That was why he had taken the key from her. He knew who she was!

'He was called into the Chief's office. Told what a naughty family you'd got. I'm the fucking laughing stock of the Metropolitan Police Force over you. Every villain from here to Liverpool will be laughing up their sleeves at me. I could bleeding well murder you!'

Maura was not listening to him. All she could think of was the fact that Terry had known about her when she had gone to him. It was the name Ryan that had created the rift between them. Somewhere deep down inside her a grain of contempt was forming. It was her family that he objected to, not her. Even though it proved that it was not anything she had done that had caused their rift, instead of pleasing her she felt a disdain for him that was so strong she could actually taste it. The gutless bastard! The dirty gutless bastard . . .

He didn't even have the nerve to tell her why he was dumping her. He'd said he wanted to see other women when in reality he meant: I am frightened of your brothers. He had destroyed her and didn't have the decency to tell her truthfully why. She was carrying his child inside her. The fruit of their so-called love. If he walked into her room now, Michael wouldn't be in it. She would rip him to shreds, Terry Gutless Petherick would be a dead man, and it wouldn't be her brothers who killed him.

Michael and Geoffrey were watching her, fascinated by the changing expressions on her face.

'Leave me alone, you!' she screamed at Michael at the

top of her voice, all fear of him leaving her at the thought of what Terry had done to her. Michael brought back his fist. As he went to slam it into her body, Sarah's voice stayed him.

'Oi! What the bloody hell's going on in here? It's a wonder you ain't woken up the whole bleeding street.' She took in the picture before her and ran to her son. Raising herself up on her toes she grabbed hold of Michael's hair, shaking him like a dog with its prey.

'Don't you dare raise your hand to your sister, you great gormless bastard! Leave go of her hair before you pull it all out.' She pummelled Michael's chest with her fists. It said a lot for his feelings for her mother that he didn't strike her, but instead threw Maura back against the pillows.

'Go back to bed, Mum, and let me sort this out.'

'No, I bleeding well won't!' She looked at her husband who had followed her into the room. 'Tell him to leave her alone.'

She pulled her daughter into her arms.

Benjamin, as usual, was half drunk. He looked at everyone in the room with his drunken leer and, finding it difficult to concentrate, waved his hands at his wife. 'Leave Mickey alone. He knows what he's about.'

Sarah lost her temper.

'That's right, Ben, do what you always do. Pass the bloody buck. This time to your son. You drunken bastard! Get out of me sight.'

She turned her gaze on Mickey.

'Now you tell me what's going on here. Your father might be scared of you but I ain't. I'll never be frightened of something that came out of me own body, so just you remember that. Come on, I'm waiting. What's going on?'

Geoffrey answered for him. 'She's been seeing an old Bill.'

Maura's little sob was the only other sound. Sarah stroked her daughter's hair gently and sat herself on the bed.

'So what? Why should that worry you lot? Who the hell do you think you are . . . the Krays? You're nothing, do you hear me. Nothing!

'Out on the street you might be hard men, but in here . . .' she gestured around the room with her free hand. '. . . you're just my boys. That's all. And I never thought I would see the day when you raised your hand to your own sister.'

Sarah was aware that she was speaking for effect. She knew enough about her boys to know that they were greatly feared. She had found guns hidden in the coal house and had sat beside her sons in courtrooms. She had even read about them in the papers. The *News of the World* had had a big spread a few weeks earlier about the hostess clubs in Soho, and one of the clubs mentioned was owned by this great handsome son of hers. A son she was finding it increasingly difficult to love these days. And now on top of everything she had this – her only daughter, her pride and joy, being attacked in her own home. Just because she was seeing a policeman. A decent man more than likely. Yet she knew that her daughter's lovelife was doomed.

She looked down into Maura's tearstained face. 'Is it true, Maws?'

Maura couldn't lie to her mother so she nodded.

Benjamin, more alert now, said, 'Oh my God!'

Sarah turned on him like a mad dog.

'I'll give you "Oh my God", because your daughter's decent. By Christ, it's a wonder we haven't got a whore on our hands, being brought up with you lot. You're all whoremasters, the lot of you!' Her voice was thick with tears. 'I can't hold me head up in the street because everyone knows about you all . . . everyone knows my sons are glorified pimps.' She turned on Michael. 'Well, my lad, I hope you get your just deserts in this life. That you pay for all that you've done. For the innocent lives you've ruined and for the death of my Anthony. I've always blamed you for that.' She wagged her head at him. 'If he hadn't been working for you he would be at home with me now.

'I also happen to know that you're a queer, Michael Ryan. And I hear that they're very good to their mothers. So perhaps you could make me a happy woman now by getting out of this house and not coming back. It's high time you left anyway, at thirty-one. Go and live with your boyfriend, and take that little snipe with you!' She pointed at Geoffrey. 'Yes, you. You always walked in his footsteps, tried to emulate everything he did. Well, you can follow him out of this house tonight. Go on. Get out, the pair of you.'

Michael was staring at his mother as if she had grown another head right in front of his eyes. He worshipped her, lived for her. If she turned her back on him he had nothing. He stepped towards her, his voice wheedling.

'Mum? Don't be silly, Mum . . . I don't want to leave you.'

Sarah cut him off. 'It's a fine thing we bred between us, Benjamin. A cruel, sadistic mummy's boy.' She put up her arm to push him away. 'Get out of my sight, Mickey. You're making me stomach turn. While you kept your violence outside this house I could ignore it, but to see you attacking your own sister . . . and her no more than a child. That's finished you as far as I'm concerned. Now just get out.'

She turned her back to him and pulled Maura tightly to her breast. Michael stood there, dazed. Geoffrey went to him, taking him gently by the arm and leading him from the room. Neither looked at their father who stood staring at his wife as if she was a stranger. He had never heard her say so much in one go, in all their years of marriage. He heard the front door slam. Turning slowly from his wife, he went back to their room.

Maura and Sarah cried together.

'Oh, Mum . . . poor Mickey!' Even after what had happened Maura could still find it in her heart to feel sorry for him. She knew that her mother was the most important thing in his life. For her to say all that to him, and for him to stand and take it, spoke volumes. Anyone else would have been dead.

'Don't waste any pity on him, Maws. He's no better than a wild animal. The thought of him with another man makes me sick to me guts.'

Sarah made herself comfortable on the bed and smoothed back her daughter's hair from her face. She loved Maura. She admitted to herself that she had been overprotective towards her, had allowed Michael and the other boys to run her life. But when she had walked in this room and seen Michael attacking her, something inside her had snapped. Garry had been right all along. What she had done was try and take over Maura's life, and this had been the outcome. Her daughter had found herself a man, a decent man more than likely, and the boys wanted to tear it apart.

She said softly, 'Who's the lucky man then?'

Maura sniffed and wiped her eyes with the back of her

hand. 'That's the ironic part about it, Mum. As from today I'm not seeing him any more. He packed me in.'

Sarah smiled to herself. 'Listen, child, you will meet a lot of fellows and think that you love them. It's human nature, part of growing up. Don't make the same mistake as I did and marry the first man that comes along. I've regretted marrying your father all my life. You get yourself a decent man with a decent profession. Let me sort out Mickey and the rest of them.'

Maura cried harder. 'You don't understand, Mum. Terry . . . he was the one for me. I really loved him. When he finished with me today, I wanted to die.'

Sarah did smile now. Maura sounded so young and naïve. 'That'll pass. And in a few months someone else will be "the one". It's all part and parcel of growing up.'

Sarah's patronising tone made Maura angry. Rising up on her elbow she shouted, 'In a few months' time I'll be out here!' She gestured with her free hand.

Maura had a sneaking feeling of triumph when she saw the shock on her mother's face.

'Oh no, Maws! Never that. Is that why Michael . . . ?'

Maura collapsed back on to the pillows. 'No, Mum. He doesn't know. I only found out myself today.' Her voice broke. 'I was gonna tell him . . . tell Terry everything. About the baby, Mickey . . . But before I got the chance he dumped me. Said he didn't want to get tied down. Wanted to see other women.' Her face screwed up into a mask of tragedy. 'Oh, Mum! What am I gonna do!'

Sarah was stunned. She sat on the bed staring at her daughter, the word 'pregnant' echoing inside her head. It made her squirm inside. She had become pregnant at eighteen. Her father had gone round to Benjamin's house and given him the 'hiding of his life', as he had boasted afterwards. Then the marriage had been arranged. Her life had been ruined because of a furtive, fumbling, sexual exploration up a dark alleyway. Well, that was not going to happen to her daughter. No, by Christ! Her only daughter would get a decent crack at life. She personally would see to that. She made a decision. 'You're going to get rid of it.'

'What!' Maura thought she was hearing things.

'I said, you're getting rid of it!'

'But, Mum!' Maura's voice was shocked. 'I can't do that. It's a sin!'

Sarah's thin-lipped mouth set in a grim line.

'It's a pity you didn't think of that when your knees were pointing at the ceiling. That was a sin as well! No, I've made up my mind. The child must go.' Seeing her daughter's sad face, her voice softened.

'Believe me, Maws, you will thank me for this some day. Could you imagine the trouble this would cause with Michael? His sister pregnant by a policeman – of all things – who'd dumped her? There'd be murder done.'

Maura felt numb inside. 'That's why he dumped me, Mum . . . because of who I am. A Ryan. He never told me that – Mickey did. That's how he found out about it all.'

Sarah kissed Maura's forehead lightly. Suddenly she felt weary, old. 'Get yourself off to sleep now. We'll make our plans in the morning.'

When her mother had settled her down and left the room Maura lay for a while in the darkness. Everything had gone wrong for her. Now she was not only pregnant, she was the cause of Michael and Geoffrey being thrown out of the house. She felt the useless tears run from her eyes and thought, I'll never sleep again. But she did. Only to be plagued by the old nightmare . . .

Downstairs Sarah had made herself a pot of tea and was on the second cup. There would be no sleep for her tonight, that much she was sure of. She finished her tea and settled herself into her chair. Closing her eyes, she began to pray to our Lady of Perpetual Succour.

'"Most holy Virgin Mary, who, to inspire me with boundless confidence, has been pleased to take that sweetest of name, Mother of Perpetual Succour . . ."' Sarah's lips were barely moving in the dimness of the kitchen. '". . . I beseech thee to aid me at all times . . ."'

Chapter Twelve

It had finally been agreed between Maura and her mother to use the address given to her by the little chemist. Old Mother Jenkins would normally have been the one chosen to perform the operation but her encroaching senility, coupled with the fact she couldn't keep her mouth shut, had made Sarah chary of even approaching her. Though abortions were sometimes performed in the local hospital, the fact that the Ryans were a well-known family had put the damper on that idea as well. So it was that at three and a half months pregnant Maura finally went to the little flat in Peckham, accompanied by her mother. It was a high rise block, and Mr Patel lived on the tenth floor. Sarah had already visited the flat to arrange things. After the long journey up in the lift, she knocked on the front door.

Both women had been silent throughout their journey from Notting Hill. Maura felt sick with nerves. There was a part of her that was rebelling against all that was happening to her. Whenever these thoughts entered her head she reminded herself what Mickey would do if he knew, and the knowledge that he would commit a murder generally brought her back to her senses.

The door was opened by an Asian woman. She wore a canary yellow sari and smiled at them constantly, as if trying to make up for her lack of English with courteousness. Maura and Sarah found themselves nodding their heads at her like marionettes.

She showed them into the lounge. Maura had never seen so many colours in one room in all her life. There were greens and blues and reds of every shade imaginable; the walls had brightly coloured carpets hanging on them like paintings. Maura caught her mother's eye and felt an irresistible urge to laugh. She wasn't sure who was the more nervous.

A small untidy Asian man came into the room. 'How are you doing, madams?' He shook their hands and smiled at them so that the whole marionette game began again. 'If you plis follow me?' He led them through a small door into the kitchen.

The place stank of stale curry and there was a nasty undersmell that Maura couldn't pinpoint. It could have been blood. She wasn't sure. Whatever it was, it caught in her throat, burning it. The kitchen was small and in the middle was a large Formica-covered table. It was yellow with a small black pattern going through it. Maura stared at the table fearfully. To the right of her was a work surface and an array of stainless steel tools upon it. She was beginning to sweat. She felt her mother pull her coat and slipped it off her shoulders, letting it fall into her mother's arms.

'Please would you make sure your bladder is empty?'

'Er . . . I . . . it is.' Maura was stammering with fright.

'Good. Please be removing your undergarments and get on to the table.'

'What? You're going to do it in here?'

The man looked at her, puzzled. 'But of course.'

'Come on, Maws. Slip off your drawers.'

Burning with embarrassment, Maura slipped off her panties. With her mother's help she climbed on to the table. It wobbled under her weight and Maura had an awful vision of the whole lot collapsing underneath her. She closed her eyes for a second. On the ceiling above her she could see the naked light bulb. Years of cooking had left the flex with a coating of grease and fly droppings. She closed her eyes again. She must have been mad to come here.

'Mum . . . Mum! I've changed me mind.' Her voice was urgent.

'There now . . . there now. Quieten yourself. It will all be over soon.'

Maura pulled herself up with difficulty and Sarah forced her to lie down again.

'For goodness' sakes, Maura! Will you behave yourself?'

She was a child again, in the dentist's or the doctor's. Only this time it wasn't a filling she was having done, or a few stitches in a cut, it was to be the slaughter of her unborn child.

'Money, please.' The little Asian man had his hand outstretched.

Sarah took an envelope out of her bag and handed it to him. He ripped it open and took the money out. He counted it. Then putting the money back into the envelope, he pushed the lot into the pocket of his cardigan. He used such force he pushed the garment out of shape.

Sarah, watching him, was aware that his fingernails were filthy. She forced herself to look at her daughter.

Maura was now gripping the sides of the table. Her long hair was hanging over the edge, nearly touching the floor.

Mr Patel smiled at his wife. He was happy now. He had the money, even if this silly girl changed her mind.

'Put your ankles together and let your legs drop open.'

Maura did as she was told, fear taking over. Mr Patel stood at the end of the table staring at the opened body for a long while. He was sweating. The palms of his hands were damp and he wiped them on his grubby cardigan. He parted her pubic hair with his finger. Sarah saw him lick his lips and turned her head away in disgust, the bile rising up inside her. The man picked up one of his instruments and slipped it inside Maura. She felt the cold intrusion into her body and stiffened.

'Relax, madam, it will soon be over.'

Maura felt the stinging pain as the steel tip probed for the neck of the womb. When she felt the hard aching agony as he opened the cervix, she gasped. Picking up the curette, a long piece of metal with a strange-looking loop on the end, he began the scraping.

Sarah could hear the animal-like grunts coming from her daughter, could see large beads of sweat appearing on her forehead.

The man worked fast, scraping into the depths of her body. Sarah heard him mutter something in his native language as Maura tried desperately to sit up.

'Oh, Mum . . . please . . . the pain! I can't stand the pain!' Maura's voice was drenched with agony. Then she shrieked like a dog caught in a trap. The woman tried to clamp her hand over Maura's gaping mouth. Tears were rolling down her cheeks and into her ears. She could feel the wetness as she rolled her head from side to side on the hardness of the table. Pushing harder now, the man carried on his scraping. Sarah and the woman held Maura's shoulders to stop her rolling off the table. Sarah felt as if she was caught in some kind of nightmare.

'Just relax, Maws . . . relax.' Someone in the next flat turned their radio louder to drown out the screams. The strains of 'I wanna hold your hand' filled the little kitchen.

Maura tried to close her legs and Mr Patel forced them apart with his shoulders. 'Goodness gracious, woman. Will you keep still?'

'Mum . . . Stop him, Mum . . . I can't stand it. Please!'

Maura felt herself urinating. A bubble seemed to have burst inside her. Then she felt the hotness of the urine and blood. The man yanked out the instruments and shouted to his wife in their native tongue. Mrs Patel went to the sink and, tipping the dirty cups out of the washing up bowl, brought it over to the table. Somehow, between them, the couple managed to get Maura to squat over the bowl.

She felt a lump slowly leave her body, looked down through her sweatdamp hair and saw a baby, about four inches long, lying in mucus and blood at the bottom of the Dayglo orange washing up bowl. It was perfect. Her shoulders began to shake uncontrollably. She felt the hysteria rising up inside her like a tidal wave. That was her baby. She began to cry, harder now, a high piercing crying that was tinged with mania.

Snot was hanging from her nose in long fat lines that dripped into the bowl and mixed with the blood and urine. She could see her white thighs smeared with blood on either side of her baby's orange coffin. She fainted, dropping forward on to the table, sending the washing up bowl and its grisly contents all over the kitchen floor. Sarah stared at the tiny foetus, her grandchild, and felt shame crawl over her body. It began in her legs and crept up her body to her heart. What had she done? Dear Lord, what on earth had she done?

Mrs Patel shook her arm and somehow Sarah was snapped back to life. She dragged her eyes from the tiny corpse and began to help the couple to clear up.

When Maura woke later her panties were back on and she could feel a sanitary towel between her legs. She felt dreadful. She noticed that she was lying on a strange bed in a strange room. She gazed around her, dazed. Then she remembered where she was, the scraping of the cold steel inside her, and felt the familiar panic return. The image of her baby rose up before her and she began to cry again.

Sarah, hearing that her daughter was awake, went into the room. She gathered her into her arms, her own heart breaking. Now she knew why her church outlawed abortion. Why it was considered a sin. She had been the instigator of a horrific deed. She had brought all this pain and suffering on to her daughter. She kissed Maura's head softly.

'It's all over, my love.' She helped her daughter to sit up.

'Oh, Mum, I do feel rough.'

Her stomach felt as if it had been ripped open. She had just had an abortion without any anaesthesia whatsoever. Although neither of them knew it, Maura would never be the same girl after what had happened that afternoon.

Half an hour later she and Sarah were in a taxi, on their way back to Notting Hill. Both sat in silence until, once again tucked up in her own bed, Maura said: 'I wish I'd had the guts to have kept it, Mum. Every time I think of it lying there . . .' Her voice broke. Sobbing, she turned her face into her pillows.

Sarah left the room. She could not face her daughter. She went down the stairs and into her front room where she poured herself a large whisky. She would not forget this day's work in a hurry.

Later in the evening, when she went to her daughter, Maura was asleep with the tears she had cried still glistening on her long lashes. Sarah pulled the blankets up around her daughter's shoulders, praying that her child would find some comfort in her rest, would wake up restored a little. She knew that it would be a long time before either of them felt their old selves again. If indeed they would ever feel anything again.

It was not until the next morning that Sarah found out why her daughter had slept so peacefully and for so long. Finding that she could not wake Maura, Sarah pulled the blankets from her, disturbed by her daughter's whiteness. A mass of deep red blood had seeped from her, till it covered nearly all her lower body and soaked the sheets and bedding. Maura Ryan was haemorrhaging her life's blood away.

Sarah's screams finally brought her friend Pat Johnstone running into the house. She took one look at the scene before her and phoned for an ambulance. The two women sat together as Maura was operated on, united in grief and worry.

Pat Johnstone had known immediately what had happened and she swore to her friend that the knowledge would go to her grave with her. After phoning the ambulance she had phoned Michael, not knowing what else to do. Now she held her friend's hand.

Sarah sat in limbo, waiting for the operation to be over. She would wish to her dying day that she had not taken her daughter to that little flat in Peckham, that she had let her have the baby in St Charles's hospital where they were fighting so valiantly to save her life. She closed her eyes tightly to blot out the troubling visions that kept disturbing her . . .

She heard the swish of the swing doors that led to the operating theatre and turned in the direction of the noise. It was the surgeon. His gown was covered in blood and his face strained. For one awful moment Sarah thought that her daughter had died. Then he spoke.

'Mrs Ryan, your daughter is over the worst now.'

Sarah heard her own voice. 'Thank God! Oh, thank God.'

'I wouldn't be so quick to thank him if I were you, Mrs Ryan. Your daughter was very badly smashed up inside. We've had to remove her ovaries. An infection had set in and I'm afraid she was in no fit state to fight it. Whoever the person was who operated on your daughter, they should be facing a life sentence.' He shook his head slowly. 'By rights she should be dead. As it is she will never have a child . . . another child. She still hasn't regained consciousness yet. But as I said before, the worst of it is over. Though how she will react mentally, I really couldn't say.'

'Thank you, Doctor. Thank you.' Sarah's voice was low and full of shame.

'Whoever it was who did this to your daughter should be put away. I have never, in all my years, seen anything like it. It was as if they had used a battering ram inside her. I'm afraid I must insist that you give me the address. I won't tell the police anything about your daughter. I feel she has been punished enough. But I cannot allow this ever to happen again.'

Sarah nodded. Opening her bag she gave the surgeon the piece of paper the chemist had given Maura. He took it. Patting Sarah's shoulder, he said, 'I know that sometimes the easy way out looks inviting. But it never works out, you know. In the end it pays to do things properly. Your daughter's being taken to Intensive Care if you would like to see her.' He walked off with the paper clutched in his hand.

When Sarah and Pat got to the Intensive Care Unit Michael was already there. He had just arrived in the hospital. Seeing him, Sarah forgot all the harsh words and ran into his outstretched arms. Michael held his mother to him, tears in his eyes. While all the staff looked at the big handsome man comforting his mother, Terry Petherick was being beaten mercilessly by two hired thugs. It would be three months before he came out of hospital and nearly a year before he went back to work.

Sitting his mother down, Michael asked one of the nurses to get her a cup of tea. He wiped her eyes with his handkerchief and then went into the little ward to see his sister. He stared down at her, shocked by what he saw. The years seemed to have been piled on her overnight. Her high cheekbones stood out starkly against her white skin; her cheeks had sunk into her face, leaving deep hollows. As he looked down at her he made a solemn vow to himself. No matter what she did, or what happened, he would always be there for her. He knew that if it had not been for him, she would not be lying there. That Petherick would not have dumped her. Now she was hurting and it was his fault. If it was left to him she would never know hurt again. Petherick was being paid out for his part in it, even as he stood there. Paid muscle was beating him to a pulp. And that was as it should be. As he had told Benny, you looked after your womenfolk.

He took her hand gently in his and Maura regained

consciousness. She opened her eyes and looked up into Michael's face. She ran her tongue across cracked lips, trying to speak. He put his head nearer to her face and what she said caused him to sob into her shoulder.

'My poor baby, Mickey. My poor innocent baby.'

He gently enfolded her in his arms, their tears mingling together. If it cost him his life, she would never know sadness again.

A week later the surgeon, Mr Bernard Frobisher, was told by the police that the address he had given them had been firebombed three days previously. The tenants of the flat, Mr Ahman Patel, his wife Homina and eldest daughter Naimah, had been killed.

The police thought it was probably a racial attack; they had no idea who could have done it. Mr Frobisher wisely kept his opinion to himself. He had no intention of putting his own family in jeopardy. Especially not for a back-street abortionist.

Chapter Thirteen

Maura had been out of hospital six weeks and the whole family agreed that she was a changed girl. She had a brittleness that sat uneasily on her now slim shoulders. She had lost so much weight that Benny playfully nicknamed her 'Beanpole'. With her height and new svelteness she looked like a fashion model. Except for her breasts. Somehow, although they had shrunk with the rest of her body, they were still large enough to make her feel 'top heavy'. She had smiled at Benny's jokes about her body, but deep inside felt she had paid a high price for her newfound slimness.

She was sitting by her bedroom window looking out at the children playing in the street. She remembered when she had played the same games with Margaret. Tin Pan Alley, Hopscotch, Five Jacks. She longed for that safe world now, when the only worry she'd had was what time she had to be in by. Maura's profile, as she looked down on the children, showed the extent of the change in her. Her nose was more sharply defined, a Roman nose, her cheekbones looked as if they had been carved from ivory.

Her dark blue eyes were deeper set. Earlier, she had creamed her face and hands, still unaware of how lovely she really was. Although she saw herself in the glass, she never really took any notice. It was as if the day she had left the hospital, Maura Ryan as was had ceased to exist. Now a beautiful outer shell, inside she felt nothing. Nothing at all. Until today. Today she had the beginnings of a plan forming in her mind, and she needed Michael's help to fulfil it.

She smiled as one of the children below her screamed and pointed to something on the pavement. She guessed, rightly, that it was some kind of insect. It brought back a memory from her subconscious. She could smell the dampness of the scullery, that cold dampness that seemed to seep into the bones. Anthony had locked her in there when she was a small child. Turning out the light, leaving her in the darkness. She had been far too small to reach the light switch. She had stood in the dank world he had created, knowing that the army of cockroaches was scrambling beneath her feet. She shuddered as she thought of it. The fear and panic it had created rose up inside her again, as it had on that day. She had imagined they were running up her legs, into her knickers. Until she had felt the hot wetness as the urine had run down her chubby legs, soaking her socks and shoes. That's when the screams had been forced from her throat, high piercing screams that had brought her mother and father and Michael . . . a very angry Michael who had taken off his belt and laid into Anthony until his screams had matched her own.

Again the image of her baby in the washing up bowl filled her head. She forced the picture away, shaking her head as if it would help to make it disappear. She did not blame anyone but herself for what had happened in that tiny flat. She told herself that at least twenty times a day. Not her mother or Michael. Not anyone but herself. And Terry.

She blamed him with all her heart and soul. From the moment she had seen the body of her child, their child, lying in that dirty bowl, hatred for him had entered her body. A seed had been planted that day, and Maura had nurtured it and cultivated it, until now it had grown tall, like a bedraggled beanstalk in a fairy tale. She had read about his beating in the *Daily Mirror* and felt nothing for him. No pity. No sorrow. Nothing. She was as empty where he was concerned as she was about herself. As the seed of contempt had grown inside her, it had strangled the memory of every nice thing he had ever said or done, until she had forgotten his goodness. Forgotten the fun they had had and the closeness they had shared. She knew that if he had not dumped her that day, she would have had the baby. Somehow she would have found a solution to her problems. She chose to forget her fear of Michael. Her fear of having a baby alone. In Terry Petherick she had found the perfect scapegoat. She knew that the police knew exactly who had ordered his beating but like so many things that happened thanks to the Ryan family, they could not prove it. She smiled to herself. Well, if everything went as she planned, she would soon be a real member of the Ryans. An active working member . . .

She hoped that Terry was in agony. That he was so badly hurt no one would ever look at his handsome face again. That was her prayer. The only good thing to come out of the whole sorry business was that Michael was back in her mother's good books. Although he had not come back home to live, he still visited frequently. It seemed that the day he had moved out had started the ball rolling for them all. Geoffrey, Leslie, Lee and Garry had all moved out. Only Benny and herself remained at home. Lee and Garry shared a flat off the Edgware Road; Geoffrey had bought himself a flat near Michael's, in Knightsbridge. The house was quiet now, unlike the old days when they were all young and it was noisy from early morning to late at night. In a funny way she missed the hustle and bustle of her younger days.

She was roused from her reverie by a tap on the bedroom door.

Michael walked in carrying a large box of chocolates. She gazed at him affectionately. There was no doubt about it, he was one hell of a good-looking man.

'You keep buying me chocolates, Mickey, and I don't eat them.'

'No . . . but I do!' He grinned at her mischievously, and then, throwing himself across the bed, rolled off on to the floor, rolled again sideways and was kneeling in front of her, offering the box of chocolates in a gesture of supplication. Arms outstretched, eyes raised to the ceiling, like a Japanese Geisha girl.

'And all because the lady loves Milk Tray!'

Maura burst out laughing. 'I wouldn't mind but they're Black Magic.'

'That's right, laugh at me after I risk life and limb for you.'

He sat back on his heels and looked at her. 'How are you feeling?' His voice was gentle.

Maura sighed. 'I feel OK. Though I would feel a damn sight better if everyone stopped asking me that, I just want to forget it.' She slumped into her chair, her face closed again. She stared at him warily. 'Actually, Mickey, there is something I want to ask you.'

He shrugged. 'Ask away, Princess. Anything you want, you can have.'

'Honestly, Mickey? Anything?'

He put his hand on his heart. 'I give you my word, as they say on the telly.'

Maura leant forward in her chair and grinned at him. 'I want you to give me a job!'

Michael stared, his face a study in dismay. 'I don't know about that, Maws.'

'You promised me, Mickey.' Her voice was hard and shrewish. 'You promised me anything. Anything!'

'Yeah. But I never expected this.'

'Look, Mickey.' Her voice was wheedling now, cajoling. 'I have been thinking about this for a while now . . . I want to take over the ice cream and hot dogs.'

'You!' He sounded as if he had been poleaxed.

'Why not? I worked them often enough as a kid.'

He pushed her back into her seat. 'You don't understand, Princess.'

She pushed herself forward again, her voice desperate. 'Oh, but I do understand, Mickey. That's just where you're wrong. I know exactly how to run them. A bloody kid could do that. If you're worried that I ain't got the bottle then you can stop. I have got it, Mickey. More than you would think. I've spent the best part of my life listening to you lot plan and scheme. I could piss it, Mickey, if you gave me the chance.'

'Look, Maws, it's a dangerous business for a bloke. Let alone a bird.'

'I know that, Michael, but I'm your sister. Not some nonsense bird out to make a few bob. I could do that on me back like your hostesses. I know that if you give me the chance, I could make a go of it. At first I would be respected because I'm your little sister, but I guarantee you that within a few months I'd be respected for myself.'

'But you don't understand, Maws . . .'

'I do! That's just what I'm trying to tell you if you'd listen to me. I know that if someone puts a van on one of our pitches, licence or no licence, they get warned off. Or you try to buy them out, depending. If they won't play your game, you petrol bomb them. They soon get the message. If you happen to know the person and like them, and the pitch isn't major, you arrange for a little percentage. Christ Almighty, Mickey, we're all from the same stable. If you can't trust me, who can you trust?'

Michael digested this bit of logic.

'I don't know, Maws.' She sensed that he was thawing towards her, and pressed home her advantage.

'I swear to you, Mickey, that I will make you proud of me. I'll run those pitches better than they have ever been run before!'

Seeing her face, so full of hope and anticipation, Michael couldn't deny her. After all she had been through, the pain and heartache, it seemed small compensation. He grinned. 'All right. You win.'

Maura threw herself into his arms, pulling them both to the floor. She kissed him full on the mouth.

'Oh, Mickey, thanks. Thanks! I'll work like a nigger for you, I promise. You won't regret it.'

I've got the ice cream and hot dogs, she thought, thrilled at the implications. If Terry Goody Two Shoes Petherick wanted to catch criminals . . . let him try to catch her!

'I promise you, Mickey, you will never regret this.'

And he didn't.

*

Maura walked across the Yard towards the small crowd of men. They were all staring at her. Some watched her with hostility, others with curiosity. She was their boss, and like most workforces they were waiting to see the outcome of a new regime. They were all aware that she was Michael Ryan's sister. Just seventeen years old. Most were amazed at the sheer size of her. She was taller than most of the men there. She smiled at them all, hiding her nervousness behind a façade of friendliness.

'Right, I expect you all know me, and over the next few weeks I hope to get to know you. I'm new at this business, I admit, and I will be open to any friendly advice you may wish to give me. But I must stress this one fact . . . at the end of the day it's my decision that counts. Now if any of you gentlemen find that hard to accept, I suggest you see me after I've finished the rotas. OK?'

She scanned the sea of faces before her, looking for any hint of trouble. Everyone looked neutral. Not bad for starters, she thought.

'Now if the runners would all stand aside, I would like to see the actual drivers and workers.'

Most of the younger men in the crowd broke away and made a smaller gang by themselves. The runners were the young men who kept a look out for the police. They stood at strategic points near the vans watching not only for beat policemen but also Panda cars. They also eyed up any competition that came on to their patch, reporting all back to the drivers – the mainstay of the business. It was not unusual to see an ice cream van wheelspin away, dragging a runner into the service hatch as it went, especially on the police patches: Westminster, the Houses of Parliament, Knightsbridge, outside Harrods, and Baker Street where Madame Tussaud's brought so many tourists.

The drivers and servers stood quietly. They employed and paid their own runners, the Ryans only paid these men. Eventually, if the runners proved any good, they were given new pitches as and when they came up. It was a close-knit community that these men lived in. If they were caught, and hauled into Bow Street court, they gave 'moody' names and Michael paid their fines. It was an arrangement that suited everyone. In the summer, especially, there was an awful lot of money to be made. And as with any lucrative business, many people who wanted a piece of the action.

Maura coughed to clear her throat. 'I think that for the time being, we stick to the usual rota. So you can all go to your usual pitch today. I will be looking over the takings and popping along to see you now and then.' She smiled again. 'I hope you will all bear with me on this.'

The men nodded at her, happier now they knew where they were to be stationed. Most knew their pitches like the back of their hands. They knew every road, alleyway, and escape route on their own particular manor.

'Off you go then. If you have any trouble, ring me. If I'm not here, someone will find me.'

She turned away and walked to the caravan that served as her office. Michael was watching her from the window. He had been listening to her address the men and was impressed. Against his better judgement, he began to think that she might just be able to do the job after all.

The men all gravitated to their vans. Most were subdued. None had ever worked for a woman before. All had lived on the fringes of crime, were petty burglars, car thieves or 'kiters' – people who bought stolen cheque books and then used them to buy goods that could be sold off to fences. Maura's advert into their masculine world was a shock. But she was Michael Ryan's sister and so they would afford her a trial period. If she didn't work out, and they were all sure she would not, Michael, being a businessman first and foremost, would 'out' her and they could all get back to normal!

Maura walked into the caravan feeling sick with apprehension. It had gone much better than expected. Michael laughed and shook his head slowly. 'Sure you want all this hag, Princess?'

'Yes, Michael, I'm sure. Now, if you don't mind. I have some books to look over.'

'Oh, well. Pardon me for breathing.'

Maura laughed. 'Have a quick coffee before you go. There's still a few things I'm not sure of.'

'Okey doke. But I'll say this much to you now, Maws, you did well out there. They're the scum of the earth but they're good workers. But for Gawd's sake, watch them! If they kiss your hand, count your fingers. And if any get a bit too saucy, you let me know. Most of them would put their granny on the streets if they thought she could pull a few bob. Start as you mean to go on, love. Be fair but hard. That's the only law they know. Show that you're stronger than them and you've got friends for life. Show a chink of weakness and . . . well, to put it bluntly, you're fucked.'

'I'll remember that, Mickey. Now about these books?'

'You sort out the books, Maws. I know sod all about it. I told Benny to get his arse down here this morning and show you what he'd been doing. All I ever did was pick up the overall total. How Benny got to it, I don't know. So you'll have to sort that lot out yourself.'

'Well, Benny should be here soon. I'll ask him.'

'You do that. Now one last thing, Maws. In the drawer of your desk, on the right hand side, is a gun.'

'A gun?'

'Yes, a gun. I told you this was a dangerous business. But don't worry. I've left one of my best boys outside. No one will bother you while he's there. But just in case, that's where the gun is. If the Filth come snooping about, tell them that they're paid up to next month. If they see you here they might try it on. On no account get rid of that firearm. Right?'

Maura nodded. She looked troubled and Michael laughed. 'Still think you can hack it?'

She straightened in her seat. 'Yes, I bloody well can. Now do you want a coffee or not?'

As she went to put the kettle on she had a fleeting feeling of being involved in something way over her head. She pushed the thought and the feeling firmly from her mind. This was her inauguration into the world of the Ryans. This was to be her career and she would make her name synonymous with villainy. Her brother Michael wouldn't be in it once she got started!

Danny Forster had been a runner for nearly two years. He worked for 'Big Bill' McEwan, a large extrovert Scotsman. He was standing at Baker Street tube station, watching for roving policemen and Panda cars. It was a bright spring day and the tourists were just arriving in force. He saw a strange van parking just down the road from him. It was a Milano Bros ice cream van. He frowned. Within minutes they were open for business. He walked quickly past the van. Inside were four men. He could not see any runners so he assumed that two of the men were breakers. He walked slowly back to Madame Tussaud's and told the Scotsman what he had seen.

Big Bill McEwan was not known for his quiet

temperament. He was once described by a judge as 'a most obnoxious individual who should not be walking the streets with innocent people'. Big Bill had taken this as a compliment. He saw himself as different from the average person and was gratified that someone educated, as the judge so obviously was, should agree with him. Getting his considerable bulk out of the ice cream van he meandered down to the rival camp. When he arrived he realised that he had been expected.

'This is my patch. I want you lot to piss off – and sharpish!' His large stomach, hanging over his trousers, quivered as he spoke.

A very good-looking Italian smiled at him, displaying perfect teeth.

'We have a licence. Legally we are allowed to be here. I think it is yourself who is maybe . . . how you say? . . . in the wrong.'

Big Bill stared at the man through small piggy eyes. He decided that the Italian was probably a simpleton. Everyone in the 'creaming' business knew who he was. That's why he got to work 'The Sword', one of the best pitches in London.

'Are you going to fuck off or not?' His voice brooked no argument. By now a crowd had gathered to watch the exchange. Tourists and Londoners alike sensed that a battle was taking place and stood waiting to see who would be the victor.

'No . . .'

Before the Italian could finish his sentence, Big Bill was already walking away and hauling himself back into his van, a bright pink and yellow affair with 'Dingle Dells Ice Cream' written in green letters along the sides. Without speaking to his server he started up the van and reversed out of his parking place. The server was still trying frantically to get a lid on the hotplate, which was covered in chopped onions and half-cooked hamburgers. He turned off the gas and the ice cream valves. He was not taking any chances.

Big Bill drove his ice cream van straight at the Milano Bros vehicle. The four men inside stood rooted to the spot as they realised his intention. He hit the back of their van so hard a box of flakes that had been standing on one of his own back shelves shot forward into the front seat, crumbling its contents all over Big Bill's trousers.

He reversed back again and once more rammed the Italians' van. They were hanging on to anything they could grab. Then, pulling his van up beside the driver's window. Big Bill shouted at the four men: 'I'll be back tomorrow with shooters and anything else it takes to shift you. This is your one and only warning.'

Then he drove away at a leisurely pace. The Hot Dog War of 1967 had started.

Maura listened to all that Big Bill had to say. In the few weeks she had been doing the job she had begged for, she had gained an insight into the world of the 'creamers'.

'So what are you going to do, Mrs?'

Maura sighed. If he called her 'Mrs' once more she would strangle him.

'Well, Bill, I'm not sure exactly what action I'll take yet, but I promise you that I'll have it sorted in the next twenty-four hours, OK?'

'You'd bloody well better have, Mrs. I've lost an awful lot of money today.'

Maura cut him off. 'I'm quite well aware of that, Bill. Now you shoot off home and leave this to me.' He turned to go and she called him back.

'One more thing. My name is either Maura or Miss Ryan. I don't care which you use. But, please, don't call me Mrs.' She smiled at him icily.

'Fair enough, Mrs. I'll let you know what I decide to call you.'

Maura mentally chalked one up to Big Bill.

Left alone she pondered what he had told her. This was the chance she had been waiting for. If she could successfully pull this off alone, without any help from her brothers, she would be set. She called in her minder, a large black man called Tony Dooley after his grandfather, an Irishman who had taken a West Indian woman as his wife. Tony stood in front of Maura as she outlined her plan. When she had finished, he smiled. Maura took the gun from the drawer and placed it in her shoulderbag. It was time to go and see the Milano Brothers.

George Milano surveyed the young girl before him. He let his gaze roam over her body. He decided she had good tits. He was disappointed that Michael Ryan could make such a bad decision. He had always understood that Michael was an astute businessman. He had respected him. Then this! It had hit the street that he had given his little sister the ice cream and hot dog business. Now she sat here, in his office, making veiled threats. It was laughable! He smiled at her.

'Listen, Miss Ryan, I appreciate you coming here today to speak to me, but I'm afraid that you are wasting your time. I have legitimate licences for all those vans of mine. My advice to you is to go and see your big brother . . . or has he given control of the rest of his businesses to your mother?' He spoke in a sarcastic manner, causing Maura to grit her teeth.

'So you won't listen to what I have to say?' Her voice was soft. He shook his head, still smiling that maddening smile. Maura stood up. She noticed him looking at her legs.

'Very well, Mr Milano. We shall have to come to some other arrangement.'

She left the office with Tony Dooley following her, her head held high. Milano might have won the first battle but she was determined to win the actual war. She went from the Milano Brothers' offices in Aldgate East to Brixton where she had a meet with one of Tony Dooley's brothers. Two hours later she left the meeting smiling.

Back in the caravan she had a telephone call from Michael. She assured him that it was all under control. All he had to do was wait. Tony made her a cup of coffee and they sat together companionably. News came in all day of different pitches that had been encroached on. Maura told each driver the same thing. To go home and come back the next day.

Geoffrey was annoyed and Michael knew it. 'She can't cope with all this on her own!'

'Let's just see how she gets on, Geoff. I think she might surprise us.'

'What if she gets hurt? Have you thought of that?'

Michael laughed. 'She won't. Why do you think I gave her Tony Dooley? Just leave her be, Geoff. If she cocks it up we can easily take over. If she gets a result, she's proved herself a worthy asset. Now let's forget it.'

Geoffrey was livid with Michael. How could a young girl like Maura be expected to cope with the likes of the Milano Brothers? 'Have you any idea how she's going to sort it all out?'

Michael lost his temper. Sometimes Geoffrey was like an old woman!

'No, I ain't! Now for fuck's sake give it a rest. She asked for twenty-four hours and she's gonna get it, all right?'

'All right . . . all right. Keep your hair on!'

They sat together in silence. Michael hoped that Maura did not let him down. He was well aware of the stir her appointment as head of the creamers had created on the street. He had been a laughing stock, not only among rival villains but among his own workforce. Not that anyone would ever say it to his face. In their world women were either wives or mistresses. They were not thought capable of running a 'moody' business, unless they were brasses; then they sold the only asset they had, their bodies, and nine times out of ten a man was behind that – either a pimp or a boyfriend. He crossed his fingers as he thought about what he had done. A lot lay on Maura's performance in the next twenty-four hours. He just hoped that he had not overestimated her.

George Milano was forty-five years old. His wife was twenty-two. She had flown over from Palermo two years earlier, a week before he married her. She had already given him two sons, and was lying beneath him passively as he puffed and panted on top of her when the telephone by the bed rang. George glanced at the clock. It was two o'clock in the morning. Not letting his stroke falter, he answered the phone, still pumping away at her. She watched his face, a detached expression in her eyes. She had been quick to learn that if she lay quietly he was soon finished. Even though she felt nothing for this fat old man on top of her, it annoyed her female pride that he answered the phone while he made love to her.

'Yeah?' His voice was breathy and stilted.

'Is that George Milano?' It was Maura Ryan's voice! He was so shocked he nearly missed his stroke.

'What do you want?'

'I just thought I'd let you know that your yard was blown up five minutes ago. I happened to be there when it went up.' The line went dead.

As did George's erection. He lay on top of his young wife with his mouth hanging open, the telephone receiver still in his hand.

Magdalena Milano brought up her long slender arms and, putting a finger under her husband's chin, pushed his mouth closed. She had to endure his nightly assaults, she accepted that, but she did not have to look at his false teeth and his yellow tongue.

The action spurred him back to life. He leapt from the bed, his flaccid penis lost in the roll of fat that was his stomach. Screaming abuse in Italian, he began to dress himself. Magdalena rolled over and closed her eyes, grateful to whoever was on the phone for cutting her husband's sexual appetite short. When he left the house five minutes later she was asleep.

By the time George got to his yard in Aldgate East the worst of the fires had been put out. He saw a police car and went straight to the officers standing by it.

'I know who did this thing! It was the Ryans! They rang me up to tell me . . .' His voice trailed off. Sitting in the police car was Maura Ryan.

She looked at him innocently. 'I beg your pardon?'

Suddenly George Milano realised exactly what he was up against. His vision of usurping the Ryans' position in London was replaced by one of his body floating in the Thames. He heard the two officers laughing. Turning from their grinning faces he went to what had once been his yard. Nearly all his vans were destroyed. As Maura watched the man's shoulders slump inside his suit she felt a moment of pity for him. She had just ruined his business. Then her heart hardened as she reminded herself that if he had had his way the boot would be on the other foot. She got out of the police car. Her brother owned most of the officers in this area. She went to George Milano and put her hand on his shoulder.

'I did try to warn you, Mr Milano.'

He nodded imperceptibly. 'I know that.'

'I'm not sorry for what happened here tonight, but I am sorry it had to come to this.'

He nodded again. She left him. Getting into her car with Tony Dooley, she went to her own yard. She would stay there for the rest of the night with Tony and a couple of his friends. If there were going to be any comebacks she would sort that out herself as well.

Tony bought the *Daily Mirror* at five-thirty. The explosion in the Milanos' yard had made the middle pages. It said that following the ramming of rival ice cream vans in Baker Street, a well-known Italian ice cream merchant's yard had been firebombed. The police believed it was the work of another Italian family. The Italians were known to be the main distributors of ice cream in London and the surrounding areas. The story went on to describe George Milano's father's rise to riches. From an ice cream barrow-boy in the late eighteen hundreds, he had built up the Milano Brothers business empire . . .

Maura, Tony and the other men laughed. They had done it!

*

Michael took the call from George Milano at nine-fifteen.

'Hello, Michael. It is George . . . George Milano. How are you?'

'I'm fine, Georgie. Which is more than I can say for you, ain't it?'

'I did not realise your sister had your protection . . .' His voice sounded desperate. Michael cut him off.

'My sister has my protection, Georgie, but only when she asks for it. Whoever done that bit of business last night works for *her*, Georgie, not me. It's her you've got to pacify.'

The line went quiet.

'I know what you was thinking, Georgie. Chatter always gets back to the person being chattered about. I know what the word was on the street. That I was a nutter for allowing my sister to take over the creamers. But it paid off, didn't it? She pissed all over your fireworks, didn't she? Well, I'll tell you again. If you wanna bargain, you do it with her.'

He replaced the telephone in its cradle, then laughed out loud. He looked at Geoffrey, and, pointing to the newspaper on his desk, said, 'She's a fucking girl ain't she?'

At six-thirty that morning Maura's workforce turned up for work. They greeted her warmly. She had not only their respect but their friendship. To Maura this was an added bonus. As she watched them sorting out their vans and stocking up, she felt a sudden pride in what she had done. They drove from the site with her watching. Then, as if all of one mind, they began to play their jingles. The noise was deafening. The Dingly Dell music was a clanging rendition of the old music hall favourite: 'How much is that doggy in the window?'

Maura laughed out loud as she placed her hands over her ears to blot out the noise. All that day she found herself humming the tune. It was a turning point in her life. Within eighteen months she ran every site in London. Thanks to her own natural friendliness, coupled with a ruthless use of pickaxe handles and muscle men, Maura Ryan was well and truly on her way.

Book Two

Pecunia non olet
(Money has no smell)

– Emperor Vespasian, AD 9–79

I fear the Greeks,
even when they bring gifts

– Virgil 70–19 BC

Chapter Fourteen

1975

Roy walked into the Lotus House Restaurant in Dagenham. It was three-thirty in the morning, 1 December 1975. He walked up to the tiny bar in the corner of the restaurant and banged on the counter. He frowned. Mr Wong was usually there to greet him, offer him a complimentary drink and pay him his money. Instinctively, Roy's hand went into his jacket, to the gun that he kept there. With his free hand he banged once more on the counter.

'Oi, anyone at home!'

He sensed rather than heard two men step from the shadows of the dimly lit room. He turned to face them.

'Mr Ryan? Mr Roy Ryan?' A short swarthy man stood there smiling at him – an oily smile that dripped from his face. Looking at him, Roy knew that if he got close enough the man would stink of garlic. His hand tightened on his gun. 'You have no need of your firearm tonight, Mr Ryan. I am intending to be very nice to you. Very friendly. I am a very generous man.'

He snapped his fingers at the large muscular young man beside him.

'Dimitri, get Mr Ryan and myself a drink.' As the younger man walked to the bar, the smaller one offered Roy a seat.

'Who are you?' His voice was careful and controlled.

'I am Mr Dopolis. You may laugh if you want.' He paused to allow Roy to chuckle. Roy ignored him. 'Normally you English hoot with laughter when you hear it.' He shrugged. 'Unfortunately, that was my father's name and his father's before him.' He smiled again. 'I could not have changed it.' His voice was conversational, as if they were old friends.

'Look, Mr Dopolpolis, or whatever your name is, what do you want and how do you know who I am?'

Mr Dopolis shook his head sadly.

'You young men! Always in a hurry!'

He snapped his fingers again and the boy brought over their drinks.

'Please, Mr Ryan. Sit down and have a drink with me.'

Roy sat down opposite the man. Up close he realised that his first thought had been correct. Dopolis *did* stink of garlic.

'Drink your whisky, Mr Ryan. We are going to have a little chat.'

Dimitri stood between the two of them and Roy noticed that he was carrying a gun. In his padded leather jacket it would have been virtually undetectable by anyone else. However, Roy was unnerved to observe that it was no ordinary handgun the youth was carrying. He would bet his last pound that the thigh-length leather the boy was wearing had a special 'long pocket' fitted inside it. That meant only one thing. Young Dimitri was carrying a sawn-off shotgun.

He glanced at the door, weighing up his chances of escape. Mr Dopolis laughed out loud, bringing Roy's head round to face him again.

'I know what you are thinking, young man.' Dopolis held his hand up as if to stop Roy leaving. 'You are free to go when you have heard what I have to say. You won't need *your* gun. Not tonight anyway.'

The man's voice was cold and calculating, as if he took great pains to pronounce his words properly.

Roy leant back in his chair nonchalantly and took a long sip of the Chivas Regal Dimitri had placed in front of him. He was well aware that he was not Brain of Britain. Roy had never overestimated himself. He could work the bookies, the hostess clubs, the minding. He was also first in line for any armed robberies that were in the offing. Roy was the eternal heavy. That's why he was in the Lotus House now. He was collecting the 'rents', the protection money. What he did not know was that Dopolis had picked him out for these very qualities. He wanted a message taken to Michael Ryan and Roy seemed to be the perfect messenger boy.

'I want you to tell your brother something for me, Roy. May I call you Roy?' He did not wait for an answer, but carried on as if taking everything he said for granted. 'I want you to tell Michael that although he has run the West End satisfactorily for many years, people are getting . . . how shall we say? . . . upset at the way he has gradually taken over East London and even parts of Essex!'

He laughed as if it was all a big misunderstanding. 'He collects the "rents" on the restaurants and bookies, not to mention the pubs and the clubs. He owns all the cab ranks. He even has the monopoly on the ice cream and hot dogs. Not forgetting that he gets a percentage of any blags that take place on the manor. Now I ask you, is that fair? My friends and I would like to know what is left for us? We want to earn a living as well. We have all joined forces, so to speak. We have only one avenue left for making money – drugs – and the blacks have always had the edge where they're concerned.'

His voice became low and conspiratorial, as if Roy was his dearest and oldest friend. 'You must tell your brother what we have been discussing. Tell him that myself and many others have joined forces. We will fight him if needs be. Tell him that we want the East End. The pubs, the clubs, the restaurants. Everything. He must make do with the West End, North London and South of the water. Surely that is enough for him? Tell him that he has my word we will not interfere with him.'

Roy burst out laughing. He sat and literally roared with laughter. Great bursting gales of merriment that rendered him incapable of talking. This man was some kind of nutter. He had to be. Everyone in the East End who was employed in a 'fringe' business, whether it was a jellied eel or a market stall, worked indirectly for Mickey. Even the blaggers, and they were getting more and more as the years went on, came and saw Mickey or one of his intermediaries before nipping into their local Tescos waving their sawn-offs at everyone. Now this little Greek twat wanted him to take a threatening message to Michael. He bubbled over with laughter again, forgetting the youth with his shotgun, forgetting everything except the crazy man before him.

Dopolis stared at him icily.

'You can laugh, Mr Ryan, but I am afraid that I and my

friends are very serious. Very serious indeed. As you will soon find out.'

Roy wiped his eyes with his handkerchief. 'Listen, Cocker, Mickey has not, as you put it, muscled in on the East End. We fought for this shitheap and we won it fair and square.'

The little man sat straighter in his chair. 'Your brother –' he pointed at Roy – 'firebombed a taxi rank belonging to my cousin Stavros. Only two days after your brother's funeral my cousin was crippled for life. He was so badly hurt he could not control his armies.' Dopolis's face was red with temper and he had flecks of spittle at the corners of his lips.

Roy interrupted him rudely.

'Armies! What fucking armies? He couldn't control a bumper car. He had my brother murdered!' Roy was losing his own temper now. The last shred of fear dissolved in the face of Dopolis's argument. Anthony's death was still an open wound with all the Ryans.

Dopolis forced himself to remain calm. He smiled. 'That famous Irish temper of yours . . . it will be your downfall one of these days. Remember this – when you are in a temper you do not think straight. Michael should have worked out an agreement with my cousin. Something that would have been satisfactory to both parties. If he had done that your brother would be alive today.'

'Bollocks!' Roy stood up. 'Let me tell you something, Mr Oppodopolis or whatever your fucking name is . . . Mickey will rip your ears off and shove them up your arse. And he'll smile while he's doing it. So do yourself a favour and piss off. I'm a very busy man.'

He pushed Dimitri out of the way. 'As for your Action Man, if you're gonna use your weapon, do it now. You've been standing there like the orphan of the storm . . . you big prat!'

The boy looked at Dopolis who shook his head slowly. Roy walked through the service door into the kitchen of the restaurant.

Mr Wong was sitting in there with his wife and daughter clutching him, frightened. His son was standing behind his father. He had recent bruises around his face. They all stared at him pathetically. Roy's blood was up now and taking his gun from its holster he stormed back into the restaurant. These people paid protection money. The least he could do was protect them. The restaurant was empty. He walked back to the kitchen.

'What happened?'

All four started talking at once, the mother and daughter in Cantonese. Roy put his hands over his ears and shouted: 'SHUT UP!' at the top of his voice. They all stopped speaking abruptly. Roy pointed to the son, Hap Ki, who spoke reasonable English, and said: 'You tell me what happened.'

'I tell you, Mr Ryan. The man took monry we had for you. In future, he say, you pay monry to us. Get bugger! I say we pay Mr Ryan. We always pay Mr Ryan. Nor anymore they say. If we no give monry, then place burned to ground by weekend. Still we not pay. My father tell them that Mr Ryan good friend and will protect us . . . So they start to bash me in face.' He pointed to his swollen eye. 'So my father gave them monry. We can't pay you now.'

Roy nodded. 'Never mind about that now. Look, I'll be back at the weekend as usual. If they come to see you before I get back here, phone me at this number.' He took a small card out of his jacket pocket. 'Now don't worry.

This will all be sorted out in a few days.' He nodded to the women and walked out of the kitchen. He put his gun back in its holster. Then taking a serviette from the counter, carefully picked up the glass that Dopolis had used. Now, he thought, we'll see how good our friends at the Met are.

He left the restaurant and went to his car. Tessa, his Doberman, was lying on the back seat asleep. She shot into action as he unlocked his car, barking and growling. Roy spoke to her gently until she calmed down. She had been lying asleep on more than sixteen thousand pounds. As the dog settled back down Roy smiled to himself. He collected over sixty-four thousand a month. There was no way Michael was going to let that go, especially not to a relative of Stavros, the man who'd murdered Anthony. Roy started up the car. That Dopolis had to be some kind of head banger.

Michael Ryan was pacing up and down his office, a sure sign he was agitated. He pulled on his cigarette and blew the smoke out noisily from between his lips.

'Did he look familiar like? Have you ever seen him about?'

Roy shook his head.

'Nah, never seen him in my life before. He was a saucy fucker, though. The big bastard, Dimitri, was carrying a sawn-off, I'm certain of it. They'd collected old Wong's rent before I got there so they were definitely waiting for me.'

'What exactly did he say about Stavros?'

'Just that he was his cousin, that we had bombed him out and while he was hurt . . .' Roy laughed again '. . . he couldn't control his "armies". Armies, I ask you! Then he went on about you having the whole of London. Oh, Mickey, I tell you. He was a right prat.'

Geoffrey got up from his seat and glanced at his watch. 'How about we let Roy get home and get some shut-eye? It's nearly half-past four.' He looked at Roy. 'I expect you're dying to get home. The baby's due any day, isn't it?'

Roy nodded, a big grin on his face.

Michael rubbed his eyes with his fingers and leant against the wall of the office.

'I'm sorry, Roy. You get off home, mate. Tell Janine that she's got to phone the old woman as soon as she comes into labour. The old Dutch is like a cat on a hot tin roof over this baby.'

Roy laughed.

'If you could see the bloody stuff that they've got for it. Cots and cribs and bleeding layettes. It's enough to drive a man to drink, I tell ya!'

Michael smiled. 'You love it, mate. Is Carla going home when the baby's born?'

Roy's face dropped.

'I don't think so, Mickey. Maura's house is nearer her college and that.'

There was an embarrassed silence. It was a well-known fact that Janine could not stand her daughter around her. Carla gravitated between her grandmother's house and Maura's. Geoffrey coughed loudly.

'Anyway, mate, we'll see you later on. Give Janine our best.'

'I will, Geoff.' He got up to go. Michael took a package off his desk and passed it to Roy.

'One last thing, would you drop this off at Black Tony's house? Tell him it's a pound bag and I want the money for it by Saturday latest. Give it the big'un while you're there. He's been getting a bit lairy lately.'

Roy took the package.

'Okey doke. See you later then.'

When he had left, Geoffrey poured out two brandies. Giving one to Michael, he sat himself in the easy chair opposite the desk. Michael sat at the desk rolling the brandy in his glass.

'So, Mickey. What do you think? Trouble?'

Mickey sipped his drink. 'With a capital T, Bruv.'

He tossed back the rest of the brandy and stood up. 'Let's get off home, Geoffrey, I'm knackered. I can't think when I feel like this.'

Geoffrey gulped his own drink down. By the time he had pulled on his overcoat, Michael had already turned off the lights and made his way down the stairs. Outside the club they stood on the pavement, both gulping in the cool night air. Michael touched Geoffrey's shoulder before getting into his car and driving off.

As Geoffrey watched Michael's Mercedes pulling away he was aware of a feeling of annoyance. He walked slowly to where his own car was parked. He knew in his heart that Michael wanted Maura's opinion on the night's aggravation and he resented it. Over the last few years she had gradually moved up in the firm, until now, at only twenty-five, she practically ran the lot with Mickey. She was his right hand, as he never tired of telling anyone who would listen. She was the only person who could openly disagree with him and get away with it. This fact alone had earned her the respect not only of all her brothers but of the entire workforce, every man Jack of them. She had also masterminded a bank robbery that still had the police baffled eighteen months after the event. Geoffrey was beginning to hate her. Marvellous Fucking Maura . . . the Woman of the Century. He unlocked his car and sat in it for a few minutes, staring out into the night. His whole life had been built around Michael, and he was realising more and more each day that his brother did not really need him. It was a frightening thought. Without Michael, Geoffrey was nothing and he knew it. He started the car up. As he pulled away he turned on his radio. The soothing sound of the Carpenters filled the car. Geoffrey smiled to himself. Maura was like most women . . . give them enough rope and they generally hanged themselves. Eventually she would foul her nest and Michael would give her the bad news. All he had to do was wait.

He relaxed his grip on the steering wheel and allowed the strains of 'We've Only Just Begun' to wash over him.

Michael had driven from the club to Maura's house in Rainham, Essex. He had to see her about the events of the night. Maura had something that he would never have in a million years: she had a calculating nature. She never let her emotions interfere with her work. Michael respected this trait in her. Where he would lose his temper, Maura would calmly sort out a crisis. Her favourite expression was, 'Think with your head, not your heart.'

He looked at the house. It was in darkness. He got out of his car. When Maura had bought this house he had laughed at her. It was a large Georgian monstrosity that had seemed to be falling down. Now, a year later, it was beautiful. She had put in new windows, new doors, and the large overgrown frontage was now an in-and-out driveway. She had bought the place for pennies and if she sold it she would more than double her investment. In Michael's eyes this was another of Maura's clever schemes.

Something that, until she had looked into and studied, he would never have dreamt of investing in.

He crunched across the pea-shingled drive up to the large double front door. He rang the bell. About five minutes later a bedraggled Carla opened the front door to him, her face lighting up as she smiled.

'Hello, Uncle Mickey. Auntie Maura's just getting dressed!' Michael playfully slapped her behind. 'Don't you let Maws catch you calling her "Auntie"! She'll skin you alive!' They walked into the lounge.

'Don't worry, I won't.' Her voice was full of fun.

In fact, Carla was one big bundle of fun and laughter. She was a natural mimic, and had the gift of making people laugh. It always amazed Michael that her own mother had so little time for her. Still, he reflected, she had Maura and his mother. They more than made up for Janine's indifference.

'Shall I make a pot of tea?'

'Yeah. There's a good girl.'

He watched her as she left the room. At twenty she was a lovely girl. She still had reddish-brown hair and freckles, but now had the grace that her mother had always had. She walked like a cat, with a long-legged stride. As she was now, in a shortie nightdress, her legs looked impossibly long. Michael sat himself on the Chesterfield and waited for Maura. When she walked into the lounge she looked as if she had never even been asleep. Her blond hair was now cut in a bob and it was immaculate. She wore a pink silk robe that barely covered her full breasts, and high-heeled mules. She grinned at her brother.

'So what brings you here at daybreak?'

'There's been some trouble, Maws.'

'I guessed as much. Ah, here's Carla with some tea!'

She took the tray and placed it on the Edwardian table to the left of the sofa. As she poured the tea Carla kept up a stream of chatter.

Michael smiled and answered Carla's seemingly endless supply of questions, relaxing back into his seat. Maura had good taste. The room was decorated in a mixture of peach tones and pinks. The carpets and heavy drapes were a deep burgundy. It was a cosy room. Even though it was full of expensive furniture it was a room that looked lived in, from the magazines on the coffee table to the Jacobean bookcase full of every title imaginable. Dickens and Trollope rubbed shoulders with Harold Robbins and Len Deighton. Maura's tastes in reading were as extreme as everything else in her life.

Carla did not think it at all strange that her uncle should get them out of bed at six in the morning. It was like everything else in her life with them. The unexpected was the norm around here and you had better get used to it or you were liable to go up the wall!

Michael and Maura allowed Carla to chatter to them. She was like the family mascot. Loved by them all, as if the rejection she had experienced when her mother had literally handed her over to Sarah, had made her their communal property. In their own ways, they tried to make up to her for what her mother had done. Though with Maura, Michael guessed, it went deeper. Carla was the child she had had aborted from her body. She was funding Carla through college. Maura made sure that Carla had everything, from decent clothes to a small car.

Carla finished telling them about her latest boyfriend and glanced at the ormolu clock on the mantelpiece of the Louis XVI fireplace.

She squealed: 'Oh, no it's nearly seven o'clock! I'd

better get a move on. I've got to leave at eight!' She flitted from the room, all legs and hair. Michael laughed.

'She's a nice kid, Maws.' Even though Maura was only five years older than Carla, no one ever alluded to that fact. It was as if Maura had always been a woman. In Michael's eyes anyway she had never been any different. She had been a little sister for a long time, then she had become the mainstay of his life. There had never been an inbetween. Maura had never seemed to have that coltish look that Carla had. That magical illusion that was the turning point from adolescent to woman. Maura had become a woman overnight and had been one ever since. Maura Ryan had been a women from the age of seventeen.

'She's a good kid, Mickey, as well as a nice one. I miss her when she's at Mother's.'

'I bet you do. She's company in this great big rattling drum of yours.'

Maura laughed. 'You leave my house out of it. You're just gutted that you didn't buy it. Now what's all this about? What's happened?'

Michael explained to her. She sat curled up on the seat beside him, chain smoking as she listened. She did not interrupt him once. When he had finished, she smiled.

'So it's Stavros's cousin is it?'

He smiled too.

'Well, we'll give the fat little bastard a run for his money!'

Michael grinned at her. Maura had said the words that he wanted to hear.

'That's exactly what I thought! Listen, Maws, I want you to think over what I've said. Get a few ideas together and then meet me later at the club. I'll get off home now or Jonny will think that I've been topped by someone. I'll see you later then.'

'All right, Mickey. What about the glass that Roy nicked? Shall I have it sent over to the Met? They might come up with a name . . . a legitimate name and address.'

Michael slapped his hand on his forehead. 'Bugger me, Maws. That went right out of me mind. I've left it in the club.'

'Never mind, Mick. Just you get home and get a bit of sleep. I'll sort that out.'

When Michael left, Maura went to her kitchen and made herself some tea and toast. The more she thought about what Michael had said, the more impossible it seemed. Who would wait over fifteen years to regain a territory? This bloke might be Stavros's cousin, but his story did not ring true.

Carla breezed into the kitchen and pinched a slice of toast from Maura's plate. 'I'll be late tonight, Maws. All right?'

'All right, love. Drive carefully.'

'I will.'

Then she was gone. As always when Carla left the house, it felt empty. She seemed to breathe life into it. Still pondering what Michael had said, Maura went up for a shower. She had a busy day ahead.

Chapter Fifteen

Maura walked into Le Buxom at ten-thirty-five. The hostesses were, as always, pleased to see her, unlike some of the men who worked for the Ryans who were wary of Maura. She was regarded as a hard-hearted bitch by the majority of them. Though if any one of them got hurt during the course of their work, it was Maura who saw to it that their wives were amply provided for. She half guessed what was said about her and made a conscious effort to keep the myth alive. Maura was happy enough with their respect, she did not want their love. She wanted to be known as a hard bitch. It suited her. The only people she could not con into disliking her were the hostesses.

They loved her. She always made sure that the girls with children got a good bonus around Christmas time, which was much appreciated. Also, most hostess clubs left the girl to sort out her hostess fee with the punter. Maura had a rule that the hostess fee, which was twenty-five pounds, went on the overall bill. Then, if there was a row over it, which was what frequently happened in the clubs, the bouncer would ensure that the hostess fee also was paid. A girl who had sat all night with a punter and talked him into buying champagne at two hundred pounds a bottle and cigarettes in packs of fifty that cost three times their retail price, could help run up a bill of over seven hundred pounds. If there was a fight over the payment she was hardly likely to be going on to a hotel with the punter. Therefore all she had for her efforts was the hostess fee. At least in Maura's club they could guarantee that. It was not unusual for a customer to be taken to the back bar where he was punched and threatened until the bill was paid.

Consequently, Le Buxom was known as the place to work. Maura offered them a degree of protection that had gradually wiped out pimping on their girls. For that they respected and loved her. They also kept their ears to the ground and let her in on anything that they heard. If they got any kind of venereal disease they were out, that was Maura's main stipulation, along with drugs and drinking. She had seen the effect that these things had on the prostitutes. It made them violent and aggressive. All prostitutes looked on one another as rivals. Hostess clubs were alive with gossip and back biting and trouble. Whores would rip one another apart, yet defend a sworn enemy to the police; would show a young 'greenie' the ropes, then try and muscle in on her punter. They lied, cheated and stole from one another.

All clubs had 'head girls', older, over the hill prostitutes who were as hard as nails. They were employed to keep order among the girls and liaise between them and the punters. In some clubs, if the head girl was offered a 'drink' – a percentage of the girls' 'case' fees – they would book these girls before their allotted time. (Hostesses generally lived by the rule that first into work was the first to be booked at a table.) So if a girl was offering a 'drink' she would be more likely to get a generous punter, either Arab or Chinese, both races known to be well heeled and unafraid of large fixed bills.

This form of hostessing had been gradually stamped out in Maura's club and the girls were grateful for it. Maura's club had waiting lists of girls who wanted to work for her. She ran her club like she ran her cab ranks and her hot dog stalls – fair and square. She was always on the right side of the police and had never had so much as a parking ticket herself. She was a very different person to the naïve young girl that Terry Petherick had known. She was frightened of no one. Even the large, hard-faced prostitutes, known lesbians and violent streetwalkers, held no terror for her. She walked the streets of Soho without a trace of fear. She had established her reputation long ago.

Tonight, an ex-hostess had brought in her baby and every woman in the club was clustered around the tiny bundle. Punters were left sitting alone while the child was duly praised and cuddled. The girl, Jenny Randle, had left the club a year earlier to marry one of her regular customers, a banker from Chiswick. She was radiantly happy. Maura took the baby into her arms and breathed in the smell of Johnson's baby powder and urine. The baby was wrapped in a white shawl and all that was visible was a tiny heart-shaped face, still red and wrinkled. The child opened its eyes and yawned, its tiny little rosebud mouth making a perfect 'O'. Maura felt the familiar longing rising inside her, and was embarrassed to find tears in her eyes. That was all she needed in front of the hostesses! Proof that she was soft.

'Oh, Jenny, she's beautiful . . . Gorgeous.'

'Thanks, Miss Ryan. I'm so happy.'

Michael walked down the stairs and into the club. All he saw was twenty-odd women huddled together at the entrance to the meat seats.

'What's going on here? A bloody union meeting?' His voice was annoyed. At his words the girls broke away from Maura. Michael was astonished to see her standing there, in a hundred-pound suit, holding a baby! As he looked into her face he saw the naked longing there, as did most of the hostesses, and suddenly he could not be cross with her. Maura treated the girls as if they were valued employees. Sometimes it drove him mad. She listened to their stupid quarrels, helped them when they were in trouble, financial or otherwise, arranged abortions for them, even paid for their baby-sitters if the woman was having a hard time getting 'case'. He admitted, grudgingly, that the club ran smoothly, but this was the ultimate piss take. It was like a secretary going into her office with new offspring. The bird was a brass, for Christ's sake. Next thing they'd be having Tupperware parties. Maura smiled at him.

'Jenny's new baby, Michael. Isn't she lovely?'

All the hostesses were on their guard, waiting for his reaction. Maura gave him a penetrating look that begged for his co-operation in front of the girls. He smiled to himself. She had so much front! Only Maura would expect him, Michael Ryan, the most feared man in London, to make a fuss of an old tom's baby. With all the aggravation they had at the moment with that nutty Greek, Maura expected him to act like the benevolent uncle! He took out his wallet, and pulling out a couple of ten-pound notes thrust them at Jenny. He smiled his most winning smile that secretly melted all the women's hearts.

'Get the baby something from us, Jenny.'

She took the proffered money and grinned at him.

'Thank you, Mr Ryan. I will.'

Feeling embarrassed, he left the women to carry on their inspection of the tiny scrap of humanity and went upstairs to his office.

Maura grinned at the hostesses who were all smiling at each other. It was at times like this that they were made aware of how lucky they were to have Maura Ryan's championship. She treated them as real people, not just whores. Even though they sold their bodies for a living, a fact that automatically made them second class citizens to the legitimate section of the female community, Maura made them feel like honest working girls. Like real people, doing a respectable job.

She handed the tiny baby back to Jenny and pulled down the jacket of her pale gold silk suit.

'She's a diamond, Jenny. You're very lucky. Now then, you lot!' She made her voice jocular. 'There's some lonely-looking punters sitting at the tables! Back to work!'

The girls who had left men sitting alone went meekly back to their tables, glad of the change in their nightly routine. Jenny's baby had been a little light relief.

Maura, leaving the other girls still cooing over the baby, followed Michael upstairs. In the office she put her finger to her lips and laughed.

'Not one word, Michael Ryan!'

He sat behind his desk, scowling at her.

'Well, Maws! What next? National Insurance stamps and baby showers?'

'Oh, shut up, you old bastard! What you seem to forget is that those women down there . . .' she pointed a perfectly manicured finger to the floor '. . . bring us in an awful lot of money. Jenny was one of the best hostesses in the West End. She brought thousands into this club.' Maura started to giggle. 'Not to mention a few highly respectable customers. If you remember rightly she worked the New Rockingham club before we poached her . . . *and* she brought her customers with her. So there!' She poked her tongue out at him saucily.

Michael ran his hands through his thick dark hair. There was a little glint of malevolence in his dark blue eyes. 'Have you by any chance thought over the problems of last night? Or was you out visiting the waifs and strays at Routen House?'

Maura walked behind her brother and slipped her arms around his neck. She kissed his cheek lightly, breathing in the smell of Old Spice aftershave.

'I love you when you're angry, Mickey. And Routen House was closed down years ago. They don't have workhouses no more. They have to go to the Salvation Army.'

Michael grabbed her hands and squeezed them. He laughed. 'You've got an answer for everything. And that Carla's getting just like you. Another trappy bird in the family is all I need!'

Maura pulled away from him and got herself a drink. She needed one. Holding Jenny's baby had unnerved her more than she liked to admit to herself. As she had clasped it to her breast she had felt a squeezing sensation in the pit of her stomach, similar to the feeling that preceded driving fast over a large hill. Her tummy had turned over. What she would not give to have a child of her own! She sipped her whisky.

'Well, down to business. What do you think about all that last night, Princess?'

Maura settled herself in the chair opposite her brother.

She crossed her silk-clad legs and leant her right arm on the desk, staring at Michael.

'Well, it sounds to me like the bloke wants us to split territories. Let's face it, we've got our fingers in a lot of pies, haven't we? I sent the glass over to the fingerprint boys this morning.' She shook her head. 'I don't know, Mickey. They make me laugh. They want their money for their little flutters and bits of skirt, then when you want them to return the favour, their arsehole goes. Well, I made a few go this morning, I can tell you! We should have a result late tonight. Realistically, Mickey, until this Dopolis makes his next move, or we find out something about him, we can't do much anyway.

'As for the protection money, he obviously knew that Wong's was Roy's last call, so taking the old boy's rent was just a token thing. A little bit of defiance. Roy had over sixteen grand in his motor. Even though he had Tessa in the car, if this Dopolis had wanted the money he could have got it. If what Roy said was right, and the young bloke had a sawn-off.' She shrugged. 'Well, they could have taken the lot, couldn't they? No, I think we had better wait until this Dopolis gets in touch. Then I bet if we offer him a little bit of action, he'll be as happy as Larry. The fact that he's Stavros's cousin does put the mockers on it a bit . . . it means we all hold grudges. But for Christ's sake, Bruv, who would be mug enough to take us lot on?' She waved her hand dismissively. 'We'll just wait and see, I ain't too trashed about it all.

'Now then, what about those houses out in Essex? Have you thought about them at all?'

Michael nodded. 'If you think they're worth it, it's up to you.'

He was digesting all that Maura had said. It made sense.

'Well, the thing is, Mickey, they're all knockdown rebuilds. And I've got a smashing little firm of NHBC housebuilders who would love the work. We'll make a fortune, Mickey. There's no doubt about it. Property is the business to be in these days.'

'Like all the old "tut" you've bought around the old docks?'

Maura smiled tolerantly.

'You crack me up, Maura. Imagine buying a load of old warehouses and Dockers' Mansions!'

'Those old Dockers' Mansions will be worth a fortune one day, boy. You mark my words.'

'Oh, yeah, Maws! I can just see everyone dying to live in a two up two down, with a carzey in the garden and a tin bath in the front room. I bet you'll have queues of people just dying to buy them!'

Maura laughed. She sat back in her chair. She had never regained the weight she had lost after the abortion and was fashionably thin. In her gold silk suit and matching shoes and shirt she looked as if she had just stepped from the pages of a fashion magazine. Her white-blond hair was freshly washed and framed her face like a platinum halo. Her bright blue eyes were expertly made up. She was, Michael reflected, a very beautiful and sophisticated woman. Yet she had never, to his knowledge, had a boyfriend. Not since the policeman. Michael guessed, rightly, that she still held a torch for him. Though they had never, ever discussed it. It was the only taboo subject between them. They discussed everything under the sun, except Terry Petherick.

'Do you remember Auntie Nellie's house, Mickey? I used to love staying there when I was a kid. I remember one New Year . . . the old man was in the 'ville, I think, and Mum dropped me off there for a couple of nights.' Maura closed her eyes as she remembered it all. 'I was only about six or seven, and as the clock chimed in the New Year Uncle Bertie opened the front door. It was foggy that night. I can see it so clearly. All of a sudden all the ships' hooters began to blast. It was as if all the boats were going to sail straight into their little front room. The noise was deafening. Uncle Bertie gave me a hot toddy to help me sleep . . . I loved that little house.'

Michael grimaced at her comically. 'Turn it up, Maws! You'll have me crying in a minute!'

'You rotten sod! You've got no soul, that's your trouble! For your information, Michael Ryan, those old places will be worth the National Debt in a few years. There's talk of them building a marina there, everything.'

'On the old docklands?' His voice was sceptical.

'On the old docklands.'

'Well, I still can't see it, Maws.'

She sobered as she looked at him. 'Property is the money making scheme of the future. I'm telling you, Mickey. Houses don't eat nothing and they make you a fortune. You buy them cheap and you sit on them until the prices rise.

'There's so much building going on in London at the moment, soon there'll not be any building land left except what can be reclaimed from the old dock areas: Wapping, Woolwich, all up the Thames.' She smiled. 'You just wait and see.'

'Do you know something, Maws?'

She looked at him, puzzled. 'No. What?'

'You are one clever bird. If you had been a bloke you could have taken over the world.' His voice held genuine admiration.

'Well, I've got you and the whole of London. That's all I want, Mickey.'

'You'll always have me, darling.' Michael's voice was soft. Maura smiled at him. As long as she had Mickey she didn't need a husband, a lover – anything. As she looked into his dark blue eyes she was aware of how much he had changed over the years. At forty years old he was still a handsome man but his body was more bulky now than it had been. He was beginning to run to fat. Yet he was still good-looking enough to gather glances wherever he went, from men as well as women. His dark hair was touched with grey. His face still had the high cheekbones and deepset eyes of his youth, except now he had the crow's feet and lines that denoted middle age. Like most handsome men, his age suited him. Unlike women who tried to keep young for as long as was physically possible, men like Michael wore their age with a panache that made it look like a desirable attribute. Maura poured them both out a whisky.

'Before I forget, Mickey. I had Mahoney on the blower today. He wants some more hardware, mainly MI6 rifles. He said that Father McCormack would get them to Eire as usual. Don't ask me how. Probably by boat. He wants them by the end of the month and I said that was fine . . . provided he paid the money up front. I don't really like dealing with them, Mickey. But as you say – if we don't, someone else will.'

He nodded. Father McCormack's predictions in Sarah's front room all those years ago had proved startingly accurate. Now they dealt with many aspects of the Irish Republican Army's operations. Not only arms, but also providing safe houses and, when possible, safe conduct for its soldiers.

'How much are they willing to spend?'

'A lot. The arms from Libya have dried up since the Arabs started fighting amongst themselves, but the money from America is astronomical now. They can't spend it quick enough. Shall I get in touch with Dixon then?'

Michael sighed. 'Yeah. Use Billy Bootnose as a go-between. I don't want you or me seen with them.'

'I will do. While you were sleeping the day away, Michael, I –' she poked herself in the chest – 'have been sorting out the monthly accounts . . . as well as sorting out the fingerprint men!' She laughed. 'We've had a few big bets placed at the bookies, but no harm's been done. The club's doing all right. Considering it's nearly Christmas, the hot dogs are bringing in a small fortune. Especially on the new sites we took over.'

'You bought them out then?'

'Oh, yeah!' Her voice was indignant. 'It was all done legally and above board.'

'Except Roy had an axe in his hand when you went to negotiate!'

Maura made a little moue with her lips.

'Well, I think that did help. But I gave them a good price, Mickey. Well above the pitches' value. The cab ranks are booming, thanks to the cold weather and armfuls of Christmas presents. All in all, life is good. Once we sort the Greek prat out, we'll be laughing!'

'Thanks for sorting all that for me, Maws. What's the SP on the family front?'

She frowned. 'Not too good actually, Mickey. I had word today that Benny and Garry have been getting lairy in pubs and clubs all over town. Shouting their mouths off about you, me, and anything they can think of.'

'That don't sound like our Garry, Maws!'

'I know, but it's the truth. They haven't been working, Mickey. Sammy Goldbaum said he hadn't seen either of them for days. He's been running the ranks himself. I think we should give him a drink for that. I thought we could slip him a monkey as a Christmas box.'

Michael slammed his fist on to the desk.

'All right, do that. Fucking marvellous, ain't it! A pissing front wheel skid running me businesses, and me own brothers, who get paid a hefty portion, are doing fuck all! Well, I've just about had it this time. If they don't pull their socks up, they're out on their arses. I can't afford to have lazy bastards on my team.'

'I know what you're saying, Mickey, and I'll get Geoffrey to have a word with them. By the way, have you heard from any of the boys, today?'

He shook his head. 'No. Why?'

'Oh, nothing. It's just that I haven't seen hide nor hair of any of them, that's all.'

She yawned.

'You get yourself off home, Maws.'

'I might just do that, Mickey. I'm shattered. Not surprising considering I was woken out of my sleep this morning. Six o'clock this morning, to be precise.'

Michael laughed.

'I'll wait here for the bloke from the Met. As you say, we can't do anything until Dopolis makes a move or we find out more about him. We've got to find out exactly what we're dealing with.'

Maura walked around the desk and kissed his forehead. 'See you tomorrow, Mickey. Goodnight.'

'Goodnight, Princess.'

Maura left him and made her way to her car. As she drove home she hoped that Carla would be in when she arrived. She worried about her, especially with Janine having another baby. Though Carla seemed happy enough about the impending birth, Maura was worried that the baby would further push her out of her parents' life. It was this overshadowing worry that made Maura shelve thoughts of the trouble with Dopolis. She wasn't to find out for a few days that he was a very dangerous man indeed.

Chapter Sixteen

Benny sat at the kitchen table eating an enormous breakfast. He insisted that his mother made him two eggs, five pieces of bacon, black pudding, mushrooms, and three giant sausages every morning. He ate this with five pieces of toast and washed it down with a whole pot of tea. He wiped the last of the toast around his plate and popped it into his mouth. He sat back in his chair replete, holding his stomach with both hands.

'That was handsome, Muvver.'

Sarah laughed. He was the last child to live at home and she was dreading the day when he, too, flew the nest.

'I don't know where you put it all, Benny.' She picked up his empty plate and placed it in the sink.

'I think I'll have a quick fag and then be on me way. It's about time I showed my boatrace at the betting office.' His voice sounded worried. Sarah turned to face him. Benny was her baby. She was aware of all his faults and still she loved him.

'Michael won't put up with you skiving off, you know. Or Maura.' Sarah's voice was tight when she spoke about her daughter. She could never get used to the fact that Maura ran the business with Michael. It bothered her more than she cared to admit. In Sarah's mind women married and had children. She admitted to herself, grudgingly, that Maura could not do that. But she still felt that no woman should live or work in what was to her a man's world. The shady life of Soho and hostess clubs was, to her, the lowest in the world, filled with the dregs of humanity.

Benny lit his Benson and Hedges cigarette and finished his cup of tea. He glanced at the old kitchen clock. It was nearly eight-thirty.

'I'm off then, Muvver. I'll see you tonight, about sixish.' He got up from the table and kissed his mother lightly on the cheek. Sarah smiled at him and said what she said to him every day.

'You be careful now, Benny. And do what our Michael tells you.'

'I will. See you.' He went from the house. Sarah carried on with her washing up. She'd had a bad feeling on her since she had got out of bed – like a dragging pain in her side. She wiped her hands and turned on her radio. Jimmy Young would be on soon and she liked him. She began her day's work. Janine would be around at about ten and they were going to plan the Christmas celebrations.

She now looked on Janine as her daughter and Maura as a distant relative. Sarah would never admit to herself or anyone that she actively disliked Maura these days, it seemed blasphemous somehow. She did not like Carla living with her either. She wished she could get Janine and Carla to become close, but she had resigned herself long ago to the fact that Janine would never like her child. That she could not stand being in the same room as her.

She sighed. Children were a bind really. You loved them but they never seemed to be out of your life. Wherever they were they demanded your time and energy. She consoled herself with the fact that at least there would be a new baby soon. If she waited on the other boys to make her a grandmother she would be disappointed. None of them seemed to want to settle down, Michael for obvious reasons. She knew he had a man living with him. She closed her eyes and shuddered. As for Geoffrey and the rest of the boys – they gravitated from woman to woman. Now here was Janine, in her thirties, having another baby – though she had a sneaking suspicion that if Janine had been able to get rid of this child she would have.

Sarah began to wipe the kitchen table with a damp cloth. She'd better get a move on. She wanted to get the house sorted before Benjamin decided to get out of bed. He was another one. At fifty-nine he was like a man of ninety, shuffling about the house waiting for the Bramley Arms to open. She carried on cleaning, unaware that before the day was out there would be trouble the like of which she had never even dreamed of.

It was eleven o'clock and Michael and Maura were in the small offices above Le Buxom. The glass had been sent back late the night before from West End Central police station. The prints on the glass were not known to them. Whoever it was had no criminal record. Michael and Maura were no nearer to finding out exactly who Dopolis was and what he dealt in than they'd been at the beginning.

'Well, we've had our people out on the street but this Dopolis is an unknown face. I don't know, Maura. The more I think about what went down in old Wong's, the more shirty I get.'

The phone rang and Maura answered it. While she took the call Michael lit himself a cigarette. There was something funny about all this and he could not put his finger on it. No one was an unknown quantity. There had to be someone who knew them, or of them. Yet this Dopolis seemed to have appeared out of thin air.

Maura put down the phone and stared at Michael. 'That bloody Benny has gone on the missing list again. He ain't turned up for work.'

Michael groaned.

'What about Garry the boy wonder? 'As he turned up?'

'Funnily enough, he has. And according to Sammy Goldbaum, he was surprised that Benny hadn't turned in.'

'If I know Benny, Maws, he's got himself a new bird and he can't keep away. Well, I'm gonna dock the sod's pay this week. See how far he gets with the women then!' He laughed. 'As much as he annoys me, I have to laugh at him. He'd travel miles for a new conquest. He's like one of them wolves. He sniffs the air and can smell a bitch on heat from ten miles away.'

'Sex and food . . . that's our Benny. His two main occupations. Well, all joking aside, Mickey, he's got to be taught a lesson this time. He's twenty-nine, for Christ's sake, and he follows his dick like a teenager.' She pointed across the desk at Michael. 'You've got to put the hard word on him. He'll listen to you.'

'All right. When he finally turns up. Now, any more business before I shoot off home?'

Maura shook her head. 'I did the main work yesterday. There's just the usual today. Where's Geoffrey, by the way? I ain't seen him.'

Michael chewed his bottom lip and Maura, seeing this, sat back in her chair. She looked annoyed.

'Not again!'

'I'm afraid so, Maws. He thinks that I give you too much of my time. I had another row with him this morning.'

Maura lit herself a cigarette. She was fuming. 'What's it this time then?'

'He thinks you should be doing the cabs, not him.'

Maura pulled on her cigarette and stared at her brother. Geoffrey was beginning to get on her nerves. Although he was brought into everything that they did, was informed of every transaction that was made and was generally thought of as the main brother after Michael, he still kept up a petty coldness towards Maura. He acted as if she was just there to be humoured. At first Maura had accepted this. Now, nearly eight years later, he was getting on her nerves. Geoffrey could not be made to see that she was an asset to the businesses. That she was trying her hardest to make them more or less legal. Whatever she did he poured cold water on it. If she told him to do something, he nodded and smiled and then did exactly the opposite. What Geoffrey did not realise was that Michael was getting fed up with it all as well.

'Look, Mickey, can't you have a word with him?' Her voice was desperate. 'I understand that he feels put out, but if he would only try and work with me, instead of against me . . . I'll tell you something now that I was going to keep to myself. He goes through all the files.'

Michael's eyebrows rose and Maura laughed. 'Honestly, Mickey. He comes in here in the middle of the night and checks over all that I've done.'

Michael grinned. 'Sometimes. I think he's a few

sandwiches short of a picnic. Still, do me a favour and swallow. I've got enough on me plate at the moment, without you two going ten rounds.'

'You will have a word with him though?'

'Oh yeah, yeah, yeah.' He stood up, exasperated. 'Fucking real, ain't it? What with him and Benny, it's a wonder we ever get anything done!

'Well, I'm off, Princess. Unless there's anything else?'

'No, nothing, Mickey.'

'I'll be off then. See you.' He kissed her cheek. Maura watched him pull on his overcoat.

'See you later then, Mickey.'

She sat at the desk chewing on her pen. Outside the window she could hear the steady hum of traffic. It had been a bitter cold morning, but inside the office it was baking. She slipped off the suede shoes and wriggled her toes. In her plain green suit and white silk blouse, she looked very young and carefree. Like an office clerk. It always amazed people when they met her that she was Maura Ryan. Her name always preceded her, and though they were prepared for her height and magnificent bosom, they were always unprepared for her looks. They soon found, though, that behind her pretty face was an analytical brain that could pick up and dissect whatever was being said to her. She sat for a while thinking about Geoffrey. She had tried so hard to work with him and he would not play along. The jangling of the telephone broke into her thoughts.

'Hello.'

'Hello, Maws!' Margaret's nasal tones were instantly recognisable.

'Hello, Marge! I was going to ring you tonight. How's the kids?'

'Oh, they're all right, Maws. Looking forward to Christmas. The twins have got their Nativity play next week, that's why I was ringing you. They want you to come down and see them both in it. Can you make it?'

'Tell them it's a date. I wouldn't miss it for the world. I'll bring Carla. She should be on her holidays from college by then. How's baby Dennis?'

Marge groaned. 'He's in his playpen now, but about ten minutes ago he flushed the toilet roll down the loo. Honestly, Maws, he's worse than the girls ever were. You need eyes in the back of your head!'

Both women laughed.

'I must see them soon. I really miss them.'

'Well, don't come and spoil them. The girls are already too big for their boots.'

Maura's voice was cynical. 'Marge, girls can never be too big for their boots – or anyone else's come to that! Now, have you spotted any more houses?'

'Funnily enough, I have. Three. Two in Southend and one in Shoebury. They all have knockdown rebuilds on them.'

'Great. I'll have a look when I come over to see you.'

'How's your house coming along?'

'It's finished, Marge. You and Den must come to dinner one night. You'll love it.'

'Oh, I bet it's gorgeous. You're lucky, Maws.'

Maura went on the defensive. 'Luck don't enter into it, Marge. I work bloody hard for what I've got.'

Marge's placating voice came over the line. 'I know, I know. I didn't mean it like that and you know it. I meant lucky to have a good job, a nice home, and a lovely bank account! Especially the lovely bank account. Me and Den seem to spend the money before the poor bugger's even earned it!' Margaret was laughing.

'Listen, Marge, I'd swap everything I've got for a nice bloke and a couple of kids.'

'I know that, Maws. I wish you would meet someone.'

'Oh, Margie, get real, will you? Blokes my age want to settle down, have some babies. I can't give that to anyone so it's not worth the aggro. I mean, I can't see me being allowed to adopt, can you? No, Marge, I accepted that a long time ago. I'll have to make do with me wheeling and dealing!'

'Well, you certainly seem to have a flair for it.'

'Long may it last, Margie! Look, I've got to go. I'll give you a bell and let you know when I'll be over, all right?'

'Okey doke. See you.'

She hung up.

Maura lit herself another cigarette. What she wouldn't give to be Marge! She smiled to herself at the thought of little Dennis and his tricks. He was a case . . .

Geoffrey burst into the office.

'Where's Mickey?'

'He left a while ago. What's wrong?'

'We had a call at the cab rank in Manor Park. Some nutty bastard reckons there's bombs in all the ranks we've got. I've phoned around and had the places cleared, sent all the drivers home.'

'You what!' Maura stubbed her cigarette out. 'On the strength of one bloody crank call!'

Geoffrey lost his temper.

'It was a crank all right . . . a crank called Dopolis. Can't you see this is the start? The prat wants war!'

Maura sat back in her chair, her face a study in disbelief. She stared at Geoffrey blankly for a moment then she shot into action. 'Get all the boys together at my warehouse in Wapping. Tell them me and Mickey will meet them there.'

Geoffrey stood looking at her. He curled his lip in contempt.

'I ain't your fucking messenger boy!'

Maura closed her eyes and said, through gritted teeth, 'It's bad enough we have this crisis with a nutty Greek. The last thing we want is to be arguing amongst ourselves. Now will you do as I ask . . . please?'

Geoffrey turned on his heel and stamped from the room. Maura turned her attention to the telephone and dialled Michael's number.

'Is that you, Jonny?'

'Oh, hello, Maura. Mickey's not . . .'

'Shut up and listen to me. Mickey will be home at any moment. You tell him that I am on my way over. Do not open the door to anyone except Michael or myself. Do you understand?'

The urgency in her voice communicated itself to him.

'What's going on!' His voice was high and frightened.

Maura slammed the phone down on him. She was in no mood to console that little faggot. She took a deep breath to control her heartbeat which was hammering in her ears, feeling a wave of apprehension wash over her. Slipping her shoes back on, she quickly left the office.

Michael and Maura walked into the club at eleven o'clock. It was a freezing night and a fine covering of snow was glistening in the light from the doorway. A surge of hot air hit them as they entered the club. Gerry Jackson took their damp coats from them.

'Brass monkey weather, ain't it?'

Michael nodded. 'Any news from Benny?' Everyone

else had turned up at the warehouse meeting. Benny was the only exception. No one seemed to know where he was.

Gerry Jackson smiled.

'If I know your Benny, he's shacked up with some old bird somewhere!'

'Maybe, Gerry. Tell Geoff to come straight up when he gets here, OK? And get one of the hostesses out on reception.' Michael gave Gerry a small green address book. 'Tell them to try all these numbers. They'll get a ton if he's located. All right?'

Gerry took the battered address book. 'Will do. Shall I have some coffee sent up?'

Maura rubbed her hands together. 'That'll be just the thing, Gerry. How's Anne and the boys?'

He smiled sheepishly. 'She's pregnant again.'

'So I heard. I reckon she'll be like my mum. She won't get a girl for years!'

Gerry rolled his eyes at the ceiling.

'Oh, don't dare say that, Maura! We've got five boys already.'

Maura smiled at him. 'You shouldn't have married a good Catholic girl then.'

She followed Michael upstairs to the offices. As she entered behind him the telephone rang. Maura picked it up, hoping that it was Benny.

'May I speak to Michael Ryan, please?'

'Who's calling?'

'Tell him it's concerning his younger brother.'

Maura handed the phone to Michael and gently picked up the extension. She listened to a man's voice.

'Mr Ryan, I imagine you are missing one brother by now. Correct?'

Maura looked at Michael's set face and implored him with her eyes not to lose his temper.

'I have not missed my brother at all actually . . . Mr Dopolis. This is Mr Dopolis, I take it?'

The man laughed gently. 'How very astute of you, Mr Ryan.'

'Well, it wouldn't take a fucking contender for Mastermind to sus that much out, would it?'

'I hear from your voice that you are worried. I notice that you English always resort to bad language when you are in a tight corner . . . But I promise you that if it rests with me, no harm will come to your brother whatsoever.'

The words were spoken sincerely, but with a small underlying threat.

'Well, Mr Dopolis, what have you got my brother for? The rents and rates are fuck all to do with him.'

'I understand that, Mr Ryan. We want to use him to bargain with you. I know that you are a . . . how shall we say? . . . temperamental fellow. I want you to realise that we mean business. I knew that you would guess that the bomb threat was a hoax. I was just showing you my power, if you like. I know, for example, that you had a meeting at the warehouse today. I know everything that you do.' His voice was smug. He was obviously enjoying himself. 'Perhaps we could meet at your warehouse tomorrow?'

Maura and Michael were astounded. How could he have got that kind of information?

'When do you want to meet?'

'Tomorrow at six-thirty. It will be nice and dark by then. Also, I want you to have plenty of time to think over my terms. I must stress to you here and now, Mr Ryan, that I am open to negotiation, providing it is in my favour . . .'

'And just what are your terms?' Michael was having trouble controlling his temper.

'Firstly, I want the East End of London for myself and my family. We have a few legitimate businesses there but it is not enough for us. We are not happy being such little fish. We are willing to make you a payment of half a million pounds for all your businesses there. A reasonable offer, I think.' He waited a few seconds before continuing.

'Secondly, I want your word that there will not be a gang war. Very sordid in this day and age, don't you think? We are both reasonable men. And, lastly, I will give you my word that we will never, ever, try and muscle in on the West End. That would remain wholly your domain.'

Michael chuckled, a grating phlegmy chuckle that should have warned Dopolis that he was not really amused.

'You don't want much, do you, cocker?'

The man's voice went cold.

'I want what I am entitled to, Mr Ryan. My cousin Stavros was willing to negotiate with you but you were young and hot-headed. You did not have the wisdom to talk things out. Sadly, you lost your brother and my cousin was crippled for life. I do not want a repeat of all that. But I am warning you now, I will fight if necessary. I have taken your young brother as a token, to show you that I know all that you do. I could have picked you all off one by one, your sister included, and have had the lot. The East and the West. But I am not a greedy man. No one can have everything. It just causes greed and envy, Mr Ryan.'

Michael listened to the man's voice as if fascinated by it. His eyes held the malevolent gleam that heralded one of his tempers.

'Yeah, well, the only thing you're causing right now,

Mr Dopolis, is my blood pressure to rise! If anything should happen to my brother, either accidentally or deliberately, you will pay. Believe me, mate, that is a solemn promise.'

'Nothing will happen to your brother, Mr Ryan. Provided you do what I ask of you. I will see you tomorrow at six-thirty.'

The line went dead.

As Michael and Maura replaced their receivers, Gerry Jackson came into the office with a tray of coffee.

'Any news, Mickey?'

'Tell the hostess who's ringing around not to bother. We've found him.'

'Where?'

Before Michael could answer, Maura spoke.

'We'll tell you later, Gerry, OK? Now if you don't mind I want to speak to Michael alone.'

Offended, Gerry placed the tray on the desk and walked out. Michael was annoyed.

'Here, hold up, Maws. Gerry is like family. You can't just dismiss him like that.'

Maura walked to the desk and began to pour the coffee. 'Mickey, that Dopolis just said that he knew where we all were today, right? He also said that he could have picked us off one by one, right? Now doesn't that tell you anything?' Her voice was peeved.

'Obviously someone in the firm is grassing.'

'Precisely.'

Michael banged his fist on the desk, causing the coffee to slop over the rim of the cups.

'Listen, you, Gerry would no more grass me than he would cut his own throat! You're out of order, Maura.'

She banged her own fist on the desk.

'Look, Mickey, I don't want to argue with you. All I'm thinking of is the fact that these people have got our Benny and I ain't taking any chances where his safety is concerned. We must play this one very close to our chests.'

Michael sighed and ran his hands through his hair. He looked old suddenly.

'Maybe you're right, Maws.'

She went to him and put her arms around his waist. 'We'll beat the buggers at their own game. With all the feelers we've got out in the street, something's bound to come up. It always does.'

'And what about his "terms", as he put it?'

'What about them?'

'Well, what are we going to do?'

'We play along with him, Mickey. To be honest, I wouldn't care if we let the East End go. It's pennies and halfpennies to what we can make once the building begins in London.'

Michael clenched his fists. 'Docklands . . . docklands, always the bloody docklands! Your brother is being held captive by a fucking nutter and that's all that you can think about. It's like a cancer with you!'

Maura was stunned. She looked up into Michael's face and what she saw there made her flinch. He was really worried about Dopolis.

She lost her temper again, this time deciding to tell him what she had been putting off for months.

'Can't you see further than that big hooter of yours? Sometimes you bloody well amaze me, Mickey. We are paper millionaires. We should take his money and get Benny back. Whoever controls the West End, controls the whole of London. It's always worked like that. Let the silly old bastard have it if he wants it so bad. He'll only be working for us anyway. Think about it, Mickey. We'll still get a pull off any blags that go down. We'll just be shifting the aggro, that's all. Then once the building starts, we'll be laughing all the way to the bank. Legally.'

'I ain't so sure about that . . .'

Maura clenched her fists. This was like a gift from the gods if he could only see it! She had wanted to lease out the East End anyway. Get rid of it. Now she had the perfect opportunity.

'Mickey, all that talk about luxury flats and the marina is true. I know for a fact that certain people have been buying up the place. They've been collecting money to fund the project for years. Oh, for God's sake, Michael. Do you want to be a hoodlum all your life? Well, do you? Answer me!' She pushed him in the chest.

Michael grabbed her hand and pushed her away from him. 'Why not? I ain't done too badly, and neither have you.'

Maura had tears in her eyes. If only he could be made to see. 'So you want to duck and dive all your life, is that it? This is a chance for us to be somebody in our own right. A legitimate way to spend our cash. I know that to the likes of you and me, living in the old dock areas would be anathema. We grew up in post-war slums, no better or worse than Tobacco Road or the Isle of Dogs. To us, you ain't made it unless your address has West One on it. But things are changing, Mickey . . . this country is going building mad at the moment. Everywhere you look, new housing estates are going up. People are even buying their council houses. We're cultivating a nation of home owners, and you can't see it! Soon all the sites will be played out, except for the old dock areas. And I want to be in on it. I want that *and* the West End.' Her voice trailed off. She could have cried her eyes out, but her pride stopped her.

Michael poured them both a large brandy. He passed Maura her glass and shook his head slowly. 'All right, Maws, you win. I'll take the half a mil. When Benny's back home I want to see all you've got on this docklands scam. I just hope that Dopolis hasn't roughed Benny up. For his sake . . . As you say, indirectly Dopolis would be working for us anyway.'

Maura put her glass on the filing cabinet beside her and ran into his arms.

'Oh, Mickey, Mickey . . . you little darling! I promise you won't regret it. I'll get on to our solicitor now and get him to draw up an agreement to take to the Greek bastard's meet. We'll show them! Just you wait and see. The name Ryan will be known the length and breadth of England. Just like Wimpey's!'

Michael laughed at her.

'What about Fitzpatrick's? Let's at least keep this thing Irish.'

Maura did a little dance of happiness. Michael smiled at her. She was right. They should let the East End go. Get Benny back safely. His dad had always said it was hard to own the two. That's what had happened to the Krays. He would let Dopolis have it, take his money, then pay him back one hundredfold for poaching his little brother. Dopolis would be made painfully aware of the fact that he worked for the Ryans.

He took a cigarette from his pocket and lit it. A thought had occurred to him. The only outsider to know about the meet today was Jonny. He made a mental note to have a word with his boyfriend. He was sick to death of him anyway. This had given him just the push he needed to out Jonny.

Michael drank his brandy and the two of them made their plans. When Geoffrey arrived the excitement was over. He realised that he had been too late. Again.

Downstairs, Roy, Leslie, Lee and Garry watched the strippers. When they were finally called upstairs into the office they were all glad to hear that their brother had been located, especially Garry. As Michael gave them their orders none of them realised that the real trouble was only just beginning. That events were being put into motion that would smash their world apart.

Chapter Seventeen

Benny watched as the man came into the room. It was the same man who had brought him some food earlier in the day. Benny smiled painfully, trying to get some response. In the fight that had occurred during Benny's kidnapping, he had lost two teeth and acquired a large black eye. The man was also sporting a black eye so Benny thought that evened things up. The man ignored Benny's smile and picked up the empty plate and cup. He checked that the handcuff which held Benny's right hand to the bedpost was secure. Then he left the room, banging the door behind him.

Benny tried to get comfortable on the bed. The muscles in his right shoulder were screaming. He reckoned that he had been in the room twenty-four hours. He could smell the urine that was in a bucket by his bed. He had just enough space to kneel up and urinate into the bucket. As yet he had not been allowed to open his bowels. Not that he fancied going in front of an audience, and he had a sneaking suspicion that was what would happen. He rubbed his shoulder with his free hand.

The room he was in was some kind of office, he was

sure of that. It had the hollow feel that was peculiar to Portakabins and the like. It was definitely not a house that he was being kept in. He felt the giant swelling above his eye and grinned – he had given them a run for their money. If they had not had the element of surprise he would have won the fight hands down. Now all he had to do was wait. He had been told briefly by his captors that he was being held until an agreement had been reached with Michael. He wasn't too worried about it. He knew that he was worth more to his captors alive than dead. He just hoped that someone had had the savvy to tell his mum that he was not coming home for a few days. She would be worried.

He tried to settle himself back against the bedpost. His round boyish face had a dark stubble around the jaw; he looked terrible. He ran his tongue over his teeth. He wished they would let him have a wash and brush up. He hated this dirty feeling. The bed was filthy and it stank. It was also damp. In the corner of the room was a paraffin heater which gave out a sickly smell as well as a sticky cloying heat.

He decided then and there that when he got home he would find out the names of the people who had held him here and would personally give each one a good hiding. This place was a dump. He wouldn't keep his dog, Driver, in conditions like this . . .

It never occurred to Benny that he was in any danger or that there was a good chance that he would never leave the room alive.

Maura and Michael walked into the warehouse at six-fifteen. Geoffrey, Roy and Leslie were already there. Garry and Lee arrived at six-twenty. Geoffrey had put up a set of spotlights. From outside the warehouse still looked empty.

Dopolis arrived, accompanied by two big men, at six-thirty-five.

The two men with him were, Michael guessed, just brawn merchants. He also noted, as did his brothers, that they were both armed. Dopolis looked like a dark-skinned dwarf standing between them. The Greek nodded to them all, giving a half bow towards Maura.

It was freezing inside the warehouse. It seemed colder in there than it did outside. The snow was coming down harder and had decided to settle. In the bright glare from the spotlights they looked like characters rehearsing for a play. Dopolis was the first to speak. He cleared his throat theatrically. Dopolis had a taste for drama that spilled over into everything he did.

'I am so glad that we could have this little chat. I hope that you have thought over my proposition.'

'Where's Benny?' Michael's voice was flat.

Dopolis laughed and Maura saw the tendons stand out in Michael's neck. She touched his arm lightly to remind him that he was not to lose his temper.

'Surely, Mr Ryan, you do not think that I would be so foolish as to bring him here? I must first find out how the land lies.'

Garry was staring at the three men in front of him. He stifled an urge to open his coat and blow them away with his shotgun. He could feel the sweat slippery on his palms.

Maura could sense the mounting tension. Her voice seemed to echo around the building. 'We have decided that we like your offer, Mr Dopolis.'

The three Greeks stared at her in amazement. Surely Michael Ryan was not going to allow a woman to negotiate for him?

'Young lady,' Dopolis's voice was gentle, 'I have come here to do serious business.'

Maura's voice was brisk. 'I am well aware of that fact, Mr Dopolis. My brother has every faith in me as I am sure you will soon realise.' She smiled. 'Now, shall we get down to business?'

Mr Dopolis was nonplussed. That much was clear to everyone watching. Never in his wildest imaginings had he envisaged discussing business with a woman. He had heard that Maura Ryan was a very astute businesswoman but nevertheless, he was a Greek and Greeks did not allow their women to interfere in men's business. It crossed his mind that this may be Michael Ryan's idea of an insult. Women were for pleasure or for childbearing as far as he was concerned. Maura could read the expressions on his face as if they were written on his forehead in indelible ink.

She began to talk in her best no-nonsense voice.

'You have offered to buy out our holdings in the East End for half a million pounds. We shall accept that offer with good grace. But only with the proviso that you work, indirectly of course, for us.

'We would only expect to be consulted on major issues. Everything else would be down to yourself. We shall keep our interests in the warehouses and the property . . .'

Dopolis seemed to have gathered his wits together.

'My dear girl, the half a million includes all this.' He gestured around the warehouse with his arms. 'I have a pressing need for these old warehouses myself. I want –' he paused for effect, 'everything you own from Dagenham to Tower Bridge. I want everything you have in Katherine Dock, East Dock. Around London Dock. I want all you possess on the Wapping Road, in Whitechapel and Shoreditch. I want Bethnal Green. In short, I want it all.'

Maura, Michael and Geoffrey were flabbergasted. Dopolis smiled coldly. 'Do not insult me by trying to negotiate with me. I have given you my terms. I would never work for you!' He spat out the words like bullets from a gun. 'I want it *all*, do you hear me? Every little bit, lock, stock and barrel. And if we can't settle this amicably then we will fight you. *I* will fight you to the death.'

He put a pudgy hand to his breast. 'I came here for an answer to my terms, that's all. Nothing else.'

'What about Benny?' This from Leslie, who was dying to start a fight.

'What about him?' Dopolis shrugged. 'He is my bargaining point. While I have him, I also have you.'

Michael stepped towards him, causing Dopolis to retreat; a fleeting expression of fear crossed his sallow face.

Michael pointed at him. 'You can't just demand, mate.'

'Oh, Mr Ryan, that's where you're wrong. While I have your brother I can demand all I want. And I will tell you something, Mr Ryan . . . I have a man behind me who is so big that he would scare even you. Yes, even you! I am a trusted friend of this man and I can tell you now that he has much money and arms to fight you with. I know you are a force to be reckoned with but I have at my disposal a larger, more dangerous force. Do you understand what I am saying?'

Dopolis had a demonic look on his ugly face. In his temper he had spoken so forcefully that long strands of spit hung from his lower lip.

'Listen, mate.' Michael went to him. As he walked he clicked his fingers and Geoffrey, Roy, Leslie, Garry and Lee brought out their shotguns from beneath their coats. Maura stepped back from them. Despite herself she was getting frightened. She had never thought it would get this far.

Michael picked Dopolis up by his camel hair overcoat, lifting him off the ground as if he weighed nothing at all. 'You are beginning to get on my wick. Comprendez? Or whatever it is you bubbles say.' He threw Dopolis on to the filthy floor and turned to the minders. He could see they were frightened. 'Don't even think about getting your little pop-pops out. You'd never walk out of here. So just button your mutton while I tell your short-arse little mate here the score.' He went to where Dopolis was sprawling on the cold floor, his face like thunder. Grabbing him by the lapels of his coat, Michael dragged him upright and pushed his face down to his.

'You tell your Mr Big that if my brother ain't home by ten o'clock tonight, I am coming after him. If as much as one hair is harmed on Benny's pretty little head, I will kill you all. Slowly and painfully.'

He punched the Greek to the ground again. Dopolis watched as Michael took a length of lead piping from his pocket. He tried to scramble away. Michael brought the piping down on his legs.

'You want everything, do you? All that I've got? Don't want much do you, you wanker?' He brought the lead down on Dopolis's elbow and a powerful crack echoed around the warehouse. The two minders were staring, fascinated, at Michael Ryan in action. Leslie and Lee giggled as they heard Dopolis try to stifle a scream.

'Well, you'll get nothing, mate. Not a brass razoo, as the Aussies say. You've got more chance of getting a dose of clap off the fucking Pope than you've got of getting a job off me cleaning out toilets. You made a fatal mistake, Mr Dopolis. You were stupid enough to annoy me. I want me little brother and then I'm coming after you and your Mr Fucking Big. So you had better start saying your prayers, OK?'

He smashed the lead piping into the man's face, felt Dopolis's nose collapse and smiled. The Greek was a bloody mess.

He looked to where the two minders were standing and said calmly, 'Pick him up and take him home. He's annoying me.'

The two men stood paralysed with fear. They had never seen a look the like of which was on Michael Ryan's face now. He had enjoyed every second.

Mickey shouted at them: 'PICK HIM UP AND PISS OFF!'

They did as they were told, their movements jerky and awkward in their fright. Carrying Dopolis between them, his legs hanging uselessly, they began to drag him from the warehouse. Michael called to them, and then standing in front of them pushed his finger into Dopolis's broken nose. The bone and gristle were open to the freezing air.

'This is just for starters. You wait until I really lose me rag. I want me brother. And I want him tonight.' He jerked his head at the two men and they dragged Dopolis from the warehouse as fast as they possibly could. Michael pulled a handkerchief from his pocket and wiped the blood from his finger.

'Coo, Mickey . . . you scared me.'

'Listen, Princess, I might rant and rave but I would never hurt me own.'

'What about if they grassed you up?' This from Leslie, who always asked the wrong thing at the wrong time.

Michael stared at him nastily. 'Why? Are you thinking of trying it?'

Leslie blanched. He dropped his gun in fright and Michael laughed.

'No . . . No, Mickey. Not me. N-never!'

'I was only joking, you nonce.'

Michael was on a high. He was always the same after a bout of violence. 'Well, Maws, it seems your ideas about the docks are spot on.'

Geoffrey nodded. 'This Mr Big, whoever he is, must want all this. It's got to be something to do with all this chat about redevelopment. Why else would anyone want this heap of shit?'

Michael shrugged.

'Once our Benny's home we'll rip this town apart. No one can hide from us. Not for long anyway. This has taught me one thing, though. If we're going to keep any sort of order we must rent out the East End in little pieces. Geoffrey, I want you to keep your ear to the ground. See if any old wags are out and about looking for a bit of action. I'm getting sick of the lot of it. What's it the Yanks call it?' He laughed out loud. 'A conglomerate. That's what we'll become – a conglomerate! Take a leaf out of the big knobs' books. Get loads of little firms to do the shitty work. Only there won't be any golden handshakes floating around!'

Maura was unnerved by how quickly Michael could forget what had just taken place. It was as if Dopolis had never existed. As if he had not been beaten to a pulp. She shuddered, and Lee put his arm around her.

'You cold, Maws?'

Michael carried on talking. 'I should have listened to you ages ago, Princess. We're going legal at last. Should please Mother anyway. Let's get back to the club. This place gives me the heebie jeebies.'

Ten minutes later they were all on their way to Dean Street. Maura and Michael travelled together and he talked to her all the time, not seeming to notice how quiet she was. They parked the Mercedes in Old Compton Street. For some reason Dean Street was cordoned off. There were people milling around everywhere. Maura and Michael saw that Geoffrey and the others had arrived before them. Maura walked up to Geoffrey. His skin looked grey in the twilight. She noticed police were everywhere. She heard the high screeching of an ambulance as it travelled along Shaftesbury Avenue. A large crowd had gathered, mainly bouncers and hostesses, a few punters and sightseers mixed in with them.

She felt Michael's breath on her neck as he spoke to Geoffrey. 'What's going on here?'

'It's the club, Michael. It was firebombed.' Geoffrey's voice was dead. As if he could not really comprehend what had happened.

'What!' Michael and Maura spoke in unison.

'I said it's been firebombed.'

'Is anyone hurt, Geoff?'

He shook his head. 'I don't know, Maura.'

She pushed her way through the crowd and stared at what had once been the entrance to Le Buxom. The wind was picking up and little flakes of snow were stinging her face. She could smell the burning.

Then her heart seemed to explode inside her chest. She felt her hands clench into fists and a breathlessness as if she had run for miles. Walking towards her, from the entrance of the club, was Terry Petherick. Even in the freezing cold she felt a wave of heat sweep through her body. He still had the same long-legged stride. The same dirty blond hair. The same lopsided grin. She was aware of her rapid heartbeat crashing through her body. For the first time in eight years she was seeing the man she hated. Only she did not hate him. She realised that she loved him . . . loved him with every ounce of her being.

The sights and sounds around her were blocked from her mind. All she was aware of was a feeling of being alive. Really alive. For the first time since she'd had the abortion she felt an overpowering urge to throw herself into his arms. Beg him to forgive her for what she had done to their child. He was getting closer to her. She could feel the heat creeping along her flesh . . .

'Hello, Maura. Long time no see.' His words were a vocal caress and she felt herself tremble. Her throat was dry and she knew that if she tried to speak to him she would begin to cry. The tears were already there, hot and aching behind her eyes. She bit down hard on her lip.

Terry Petherick was looking at her with his penetrating stare. He thought of the Maura he had known, the vulnerable young girl, and felt ashamed of what he had done to her. Through her sophisticated hair style and expensive clothes he could still see the girl she had been. The young woman he had made love to and whom he had nearly died for. She was still there, inside the new shell, looking at him through the blue stillness of her eyes. They would never change. When he had been beaten up he had lain in the hospital bed thinking about her. He had never held any grudge about what had happened to him. He had felt at the time that he deserved it. He deserved to feel the pain. He still felt that, especially now, looking at the face that had haunted him for eight long years.

Michael's voice broke into their private thoughts and snapped them both back to reality.

'Well, well, well. If it ain't the Casanova of Vine Street.'

Maura felt a flush come over her face and neck.

'Hello, Mr Ryan. I suppose you know that your club was firebombed?' Terry's voice was quiet and controlled. 'Your doorman, Gerry Jackson, was badly hurt, and a young lass, a young blonde girl called . . .' he looked at his notebook '. . . Sheree. No one seemed to know her surname.'

'Well, anything you want to ask you talk to my brother Geoffrey. He's over there.' Michael pointed to where Geoffrey was standing with Lee and Garry and Leslie. 'I want to get my sister home. This ain't no place for her. Especially now.'

'Quite.' Terry's voice was smooth. Maura noticed that he still had his baby soft skin. She wanted to reach up and touch his face. Feel his flesh beneath her fingers again. She closed her eyes and felt Michael's arm go around her.

'Come on, Maws. There's nothing we can do here.'

She wanted to throw Michael from her. She couldn't walk away from Terry now. Not when she had found him again. She felt Michael pulling her gently away and still she watched Terry, turning her head as Michael steered her through the crowd back to the car. And she knew in her heart that Terry felt the same as she did. It was written in his eyes and face. Suddenly all the noise and bustle around her became real once more. She came back to earth with a jolt that made her want to cry out in anguish.

'Come on, Princess. In the car, love.' Michael's voice was caressing, like a lover's. Only this time it was not enough for her.

In the space of a few minutes all the old longings had come back to haunt her. Long suppressed sights and sounds were rushing back. The little flat in Islington. Their favourite restaurant. The smell of his body as he slipped his maleness inside her. It was like a strong heady potion that had miraculously brought her back to life.

'Come on, Maws. Get in the car.'

She opened the door and sat in the car obediently. Leslie and Lee were already in the back, Garry squeezed in with them. For Maura the whole day's events had been wiped out by that one chance meeting.

Michael got into the driving seat and put the key in the ignition. He started up the car and pulled away. When they were driving along Shaftesbury Avenue, he spoke.

'I suppose you all realise what's happened, don't you?' Nobody answered him. 'The bombing of the club had already been arranged, well in advance. From five minutes after me belting Dopolis, the word had been sent out. It was a foregone conclusion. Whoever threw the petrol bomb was ready and waiting for word.'

Gradually, what Michael was saying penetrated Maura's brain.

'Benny ain't coming home, is he, Mickey?' Garry sounded as if he was going to cry.

'I doubt that very much, Gal. I doubt that very much indeed.'

'The dirty bastards! The filthy rotten dirty bastards . . .'

Leslie and Lee were both in shock.

'Well, I have an idea where some of Dopolis's information came from. And that's where we're all going now.'

They drove on in silence. Everyone was thinking about Benny. Michael gripped the steering wheel. Mr Big had better watch out. He was coming to get him.

The enormity of what had happened hit Maura like a bucket of icy water. Benny was probably dead already . . . She felt the shaking in her hands and legs that was caused by shock. As she looked out of the window of the car she saw that they were in Knightsbridge. Harrods had its Christmas decorations that brought people from miles around. Everywhere she looked were lights and Christmas messages, in the shops and the restaurants. And Benny was dead. Or about to die. She closed her eyes and saw his face. Then Terry's face.

Garry was sitting hunched up in the back, racking his brains like Michael, trying to come up with a name. Someone who would have the guts to take on Michael Ryan. Someone who held a grudge . . .

Michael parked the car outside his flat. They all followed him inside. Maura realised that Roy was missing and asked Mickey where he was. He put his key into the lock of his front door.

'I sent him home, Maws. He's the only family man among us. After what happened at the club, I sent him home.'

She nodded as he opened the door. They all followed him into his lounge.

Jonny was sitting on the couch. He was wearing his straight gear: grey polo-necked sweater and black Staprest trousers. He was very white. His blond curly hair had been freshly washed. It was still damp. He stared up at Michael and smiled. Maura noticed that he was a bundle of nerves.

'Get us all a stiff drink. Jonny . . . now!' Michael sounded ferocious. Jonny leapt out of his seat to do his bidding. He was shaking so much he nearly dropped the decanter of whisky. Everyone sat down on Michael's deep green Habitat settee. Jonny brought them all a drink. Michael stood at the fireplace and, as Jonny handed him his drink, said: 'How much did they pay you?'

Jonny tried to bluff his way out of it. He knew that his life depended on it.

'I don't know what you're talking about, Mickey!'

Michael threw the contents of his glass into Jonny's face. Then, grabbing his blond curls, cried: 'Tell me, Jonny. Answer my question.'

'I swear to you, I don't know what you're talking about. Please!'

Michael brought his knee up into Jonny's groin, using such force that the boy's whole body was lifted from the ground. Michael let him drop on to the carpet in front of him. Then, taking out the lead piping he had used on Dopolis, he waved it in Jonny's face.

'You can make this hard for yourself or easy, Jonny. Either way you will answer my questions. Now, I ask you again, how much did they pay you?'

Jonny lay on the floor, heaving. His hands were holding his testicles, which felt as if they had been forced from their protective sac. He was in agony. Michael had dropped his glass and Jonny had a fleeting image of him smashing it into his face. Michael kicked the glass at him as if he had read the boy's mind.

Jonny hunched his shoulders up and held his testicles tighter. 'Five . . . five gr-grand.'

Michael laughed a bitter laugh.

'Five lousy grand? You let my brother die for five lousy grand? I'd have given you that if you'd asked me. You fucking scum queen!'

He brought the lead piping down on Jonny, busting his head open with the first blow.

Maura jumped from her seat and grabbed Michael's arm.

'Not here, Mickey. Don't kill him here. Find out who approached him. Then let them have him.' She poked her head in her brothers' direction. They were all sitting on Michael's giant settee watching him.

Maura stared down into Jonny's face.

'Who bought you off, Jonny? You may as well tell me. You're a dead man anyway. If you don't start talking, I'll let Michael and Garry torture you. I mean it, Jonny.'

He was crying, his tears mingling with the blood that was dripping down his face from his head.

'Maura . . . I . . . I swear I didn't mean any . . . harm. He made me do it! He said . . . you . . . was all finished. That I'd better get away . . .'

'Who was it, Jonny? Tell me who it was.'

'It . . . was . . . Sam. Sammy Goldbaum.'

Michael spat in Jonny's face.

'Not Sammy. Never! You poxy little shit stabber . . .'

'I swear to you, Mickey. Please believe me.' Jonny was crying hard now. 'I loved you, Mickey. I did. I'm so sorry . . .'

Michael kicked him in the legs. 'Yeah, you loved me all right. You ponce! You loved me so much you done a deal for money. Five shitty grand you sold me and my brother for. Wanker!'

He nodded his head and Garry and Leslie picked Jonny up from the floor between them. They did not need to be told that Jonny was not to come home. They would enjoy putting him away, for Benny's sake.

Jonny screamed out in fear. 'Please, Mickey! Please . . .' Tears were rolling down his face and mingling with blood and the mucus from his nose. 'I only told him things because I thought you wouldn't be there any more to protect me. I'm begging you, Mickey . . . please!'

Michael raised the lead piping above his head and smashed it down with all his might across Jonny's head. Jonny was suddenly quiet. He would never utter another word.

Garry, Leslie and Lee carried him from the flat.

Michael sat on his giant sofa and put his head in his hands. 'Benny's dead, Maws. Because that slag sold him for a lousy five grand. I want Goldbaum next. Sammy, my friend. Well, from now on, it's family always.' He wiped his streaming eyes.

'Come on, Mickey. Me and you will sort out Sammy together.'

They left the flat. As they got into the car, Maura heard the high piping voices of a group of carol singers. They were singing for charity outside the restaurants in Beauchamp Place. Maura could have wept herself. This had been one of the worst days of her life. Instead she lit them both a cigarette and braced herself for the night ahead. She knew that tonight she was going to commit a murder, and instead of being frightened felt a deadness in all her limbs. Thoughts of Terry Petherick were a luxury she could not afford. She had come too far with Mickey ever to be able to live a normal life again. Together they would pay back everyone responsible for Benny's death. The familiar hardness crept back into her deep blue eyes and she put away her childish dreams for ever.

Terry was like the expensive present that all poor children wanted but could never hope to attain. She had felt for a few moments the agonising pleasure that he had always created in her, and she would have to make do with that for the rest of her life. She would think about it in her lonely bed when all this was over, but tonight they had a job to do.

As Michael's Mercedes sped through the streets of London Maura saw in her mind's eye the little baby in the washing up bowl and finally laid that ghost to rest.

She opened the window of the car and let the cold

night air whip at her face. Benny was dead, love his heart. Big lovable Benny was dead. Her mother and father would be devastated.

As they drove past the Giorgiou used car lot in Bethnal Green, they were completely unaware that Benny was lying not twenty yards from where their car stopped at the junction with Roman Road. He had died at seven-ten precisely.

Chapter Eighteen

Sammy Goldbaum was sitting at his kitchen table, looking around the familiar room, breathing in the same old smells: gefilte fish and kanadelach soup. His wife Noola made the best Matzo balls he had ever tasted. On the wall to the right of his chair was a photograph of his three daughters. The eldest, Rebekka, had his large bulbous nose – the only one to inherit his Jewish legacy. The other two, Beatrice and Ruth, both had the blonde prettiness of his wife. He wiped his forehead again with a large handkerchief. He had been sweating profusely since he had heard the news. He was aware that Michael would be coming for him and so he waited, patiently but feeling very frightened.

His wife Noola sat opposite him. She was more than worried by the look of her husband. He looked terrible. You did not live with a man for over thirty years without knowing his every thought and action.

'Tell me, Sammy, what is ailing you? You sit there like a statue, staring into space. Is it the police you are frightened of? Have you got into trouble again?'

'Noola!' Sammy's deep voice was exasperated. 'Keep your nose out of my affairs. Always you must know everything. I tell you, Noola, it's not always healthy to know too much. Go to bed. God knows, you could do with the beauty sleep.'

He tried to smile at her but it did not quite work. She reached across the table and gripped his arm.

'Sammy, in all the years we've been married I've always stood by you. I've lied to the police. Even to the Rabbi, may God forgive me. But I did it for love. Now I see you scared out of your wits. You've sent the girls over to my mother's house for the night, and all you can say to me is: "Go to bed, Noola." Do you think I am a fool?'

He shook his head. Trust her to begin one of her arguments, tonight of all nights. She had been a good wife to him, an exemplary wife. Over the years he had grown to love her more than he had thought possible.

'No, Noola, my darling. I would never think that you were a fool. But I tell you, you should have gone to your mother's with the girls. It could be very dangerous here tonight.'

'But why, Sammy? Tell me why?' Her voice was desperate. He looked into her faded eyes. Her grey hair was, as usual, rolled up in enormous curlers with a bright green chiffon scarf tied around them. Suddenly he saw her as she had been thirty-five years ago: a small thin young Jewish girl, with a trim figure and a bubbling, overpowering personality. She had made him laugh. Being a big man, he had wanted to protect the tiny scrap that was to become his wife; instead she had taken him over. But he had never once resented her for it. She would always be quicker than he to see the point of a debate or the way out of any trouble. He had begun to rely on her early in their marriage and it had never changed. Until tonight. No one could help him now. No one at all.

He took a deep breath. She deserved to know the truth.

'I sold out Michael Ryan, Noola.'

Noola's hand flew to her mouth. Her grey eyes screwed up into tiny slits until they finally closed, as if trying to blot out what her husband had said to her. She took her hand from her mouth and put it to her heart as if trying to stop its beat.

'Oh my God, Sammy! He will kill you.' Her voice cracked with emotion.

'I know that, Noola. I am waiting for him now. That's why I sent the girls away. I am sure he would not hurt them or you. But I think it would be better for all concerned if I was alone when he came.'

'But why, Sammy? Why?' Her voice was stronger now, truculent. 'He has always been a good friend to you, looked after you.'

Sammy wiped his forehead again.

'I know that. You think I don't know that?'

Noola sat back in her chair and stared at her husband. It all became as plain as day to her.

'God help you, Sammy Goldbaum. You've been gambling again. That's it, isn't it?'

He nodded his head.

'So, like Judas Iscariot, you betrayed your friend. Your very good friend.'

'I did not think that anyone would get hurt.' His voice was self-righteous. 'I swear, Noola. Then tonight I heard on the radio that his club, Le Buxom, had been fire-bombed. And I realised I had caused a lot of trouble. Now all I can do is sit and wait for my punishment. It is pointless trying to get away from him.'

Noola got up from her seat and went to her husband. She kissed his hot dry lips and sweaty forehead and she went to bed. She knew that she would never see her husband alive again. She took three Mogadon sleeping tablets, and when Maura and Michael arrived was out cold. As Sammy said, sometimes it was best not to know anything.

Janine looked at her husband Roy. He was eating his breakfast and it seemed to her that every mouthful was a trial to him. 'What's going on, Roy? I've already heard on the news about the bombing.'

He stopped chewing and glanced at his heavily pregnant wife. Then, putting down his knife and fork, he got up from the table and went to her, pulling her into his arms.

'Bombed!' He tried to make his voice light. 'It was a gas leak. You know what it's like if anything happens in Soho. The press always has a field day.'

'But a young girl died, and Gerry Jackson is seriously ill.'

'I know that, love. It was burns. Honestly, Jan, it was a gas leak from the building next door.' He caressed her swollen belly. 'You just worry about Junior here. I'll take care of everything else.'

'If it's trouble, Roy, I want to know.'

He turned her back towards the cooker and patted her behind. 'You just worry about making me a nice cup of Rosie Lee. Then I'd better be off.'

Janine filled the kettle and plugged it in. Then she turned the radio up. It was the eight-thirty news. The announcer's voice crackled around the kitchen as if unaccustomed to being listened to in this household.

'The bombing of the West End nightclub, Le Buxom,

was this morning said to be a terrorist attack. The owner of the nightclub, Mr Michael Ryan, has been seen over the years with various IRA sympathisers. Mr Ryan is a known gangland figure, though attempts to bring charges against him have always failed. He was not available for comment this morning. Mr Heath . . .'

The voice droned on and Roy carried on eating his breakfast. Janine placed his cup of tea in front of him. She did not know what to do. She felt the baby kick and her hands went to her swollen belly protectively. She thought of ringing Carla and dismissed it. She would wait for him to leave then she would phone her mother-in-law.

Sarah Ryan looked terrible. She had not slept all night. Her straggly grey hair had escaped from its usual bun and her round open face looked more wrinkled than usual. Her body had grown fatter over the years and now everything about her seemed to sag – her breasts, her stomach, even the folds of skin under her neck. She had always looked older than her years, but in the last twenty-four hours had become positively decrepit-looking. She was just fifty-nine. Her eyes, though, were alert and filled with a bright intelligence that seemed to glow out of her wrinkled face. She was worried out of her mind about her youngest son. She had not seen him for over forty-eight hours, not since he had devoured one of his Olympian breakfasts. She knew that something had happened to him. She had tried unsuccessfully to contact Michael and Maura. Both were nowhere to be found. Carla had told her that she had not seen Maura for a couple of days. She had not seemed too bothered about it, but Sarah knew that her nervousness had communicated itself to the girl and now she too was worried.

Since the news about the bombing of the nightclub she had had a sick feeling in her guts. She had spoken to Roy late the night before but he was closemouthed about everything she had asked him. Protecting himself and the others, she guessed. She poured out a large mug of tea and took it up to her husband, who as usual had drunk himself into a stupor and gone to bed. She placed the tea on the bedside table and shook him roughly, the sour smell of his breath adding to her feeling of nausea.

'What? What do you want?'

She stared down at his sunken face. He had not shaved for nearly a week. He looked what he was . . . like dirty Irish scum. She had to stifle an overpowering urge to throw the mug of steaming hot tea into his face.

'Benjamin . . . he still hasn't come home.' She tried to get some response. Benjamin opened his eyes and stared around him blearily.

'Oh, piss off, Sar. Benny's a grown man. He's probably out shagging. You know what he's like.'

He sat up in bed and looked at the clock. It was just after nine.

'Jumping Jesus Christ! What you woke me up for?'

Sarah sat on the bed and gripped his arm. 'I think something terrible's happened. Michael's club was bombed last night.'

'What!'

'It was on the news. Roy said it was a gas leak but the man on the news said it was a terrorist attack.'

She watched the different expressions flicker over Benjamin's face and sighed. In his state he would have difficulty even working out what day it was, let alone following all this. It had always been the same. She could never rely on him to be of help in any way, shape or form.

It was beyond him. For the first time in years she needed him and he was going to let her down. She heard the telephone ringing in the hallway and rushed off to answer it, hoping against hope that it was young Benny. It was Janine. Sarah felt the hope seep from her body as she heard her daughter-in-law's voice.

'Can you come over to me, Sarah? Please.'

'Yes, Janine, I'll come to you. Give me an hour.'

When she replaced the receiver she rang Carla. By ten-thirty the three women were closeted together in Janine's house. For once the atmosphere between mother and daughter was forged by a common bond. They were all frightened, but as yet did not really know what exactly they were frightened of.

Mr Desmond Buckingham Gooch walked his dog across Hampstead Heath every morning. He rose at five precisely and breakfasted on a soft boiled egg and one slice of toast. He then walked his dog Victory across the Heath. He was there by six o'clock every morning, come rain or shine. His neighbours called him 'Colonel Blimp', though never to his face. Victory was a cocker spaniel, a splendid animal, though scatty. She never came when he called her and completely disregarded his orders, and he loved her with all his heart. She was his sole companion.

This morning she had stopped by a litter bin attached to a lamp post. He called her in his most commanding voice. She ignored him as usual and stayed exactly where she was. She began to whine. She got up to her hind legs and tried to scratch the metal bin. The lamp post was giving out an eerie light. It was just becoming day in the cold twilight world of a winter's morning. A fine covering of snow had settled during the night and in the gloomy light of the breaking dawn the lamp post seemed to be radiating a burnt orange glow that barely illuminated itself. For a few seconds Desmond Buckingham Gooch felt a prickle of fear. Then, his natural common sense coming to the fore, he walked purposefully to the bin. Victory could probably smell one of those damned hamburgers that young people these days seemed to live on. If he had his way he would bring back the days of powdered egg and rationing. Youngsters today had it too easy, far too easy in his opinion. He looked into the bin.

A head stared up at him, covered with a layer of early morning frost. He staggered backwards, his hand going instinctively to his chest. He felt the vomit in his mouth, his boiled egg and toast mixed with bile burning his tongue and gums. He threw up on to the pavement. Taking deep breaths, he dragged Victory roughly away from the bin and put on her lead, then he half pulled and half kicked his beloved dog back to his flat. Inside his hallway he leant against the front door, trying to calm his heartbeat. He made his way into his bedroom and, sitting on his bed, opened his bedside cabinet and took out the pills the doctor had given him for his heart. He placed one under his tongue with a trembling hand. Victory sat staring at him, her bright red coat glistening with snow. When he felt the life coming back to his limbs, he picked up the phone by his bed and called the police.

The news of the finding of the head did not hit the streets until twelve-thirty.

It was Benny Ryan's.

Mrs Carmen De'Sousa, a West Indian woman, was coming home from a nightshift at Ford's in Dagenham. She walked slowly up Lower Mardyke Avenue towards her block of maisonettes. She had had a bad night. Their union representative had wanted to call them all out. She shook her head in its large woolly hat. This country amazed her.

She heard the rubbery screech of car tyres as somebody attempted a wheelspin in the frosty morning. She ignored it. Cars came and went at all hours of the day and night. You became immune to the sound, as you became immune to the noise of radios, record players and ghetto blasters. If you were sensible on the Mardyke Estate, you kept your nose out of other people's business.

She started to walk up the steps that led to her landing, gripping the rail that ran parallel with the steps. It was very icy, the snow had settled, and all around her the world was blanketed in a white layer that made even the Mardyke Estate look pleasant. As she reached the top step she stopped. She could hear a faint mewling. She walked past the entrance to her landing and began to walk down the flight of steps that led to the garages that ran the whole length of the block of maisonettes. No one in their right mind kept their cars there these days. They were full of junk, old furniture, old bikes, mattresses and general rubbish.

She heard the soft mewling again and called out in the darkness, 'Marley? Id that you, boy?'

She reached the bottom of the steps and felt rather than saw that there was something lying sprawled out in front of her. She squinted and peered at the ground. The lights had been broken down here for over five years. She felt in the pocket of her heavy blanket coat and took out a box of Swan Vestas. She lit one and held it in front of her. It was to be an action she would regret all her life.

Lying on the floor in front of her was the body of a

young man. A young blond man. She stared at the body for what seemed ages, a scream stuck in her throat. Then the match burnt her fingers and pain spurred her into action. She began to scream and wail at the top of her voice. Within five minutes nearly every resident from her block of maisonettes was with her.

Jonny's body had been found.

Denise and Carol McBridge walked to the bus stop together. Both girls worked at Van Den Bergh and Jurgen's in West Thurrock. Their bus came at five minutes to seven. Two stops later they alighted and made their way from the London Road to the dirt track that had always been used as a short cut to their factory. As usual they were joking around, barely able to see in the winter half-light. Carol tripped over something and swore softly. It was a large rolled-up canvas. Nothing unusual about that. This was a known dumping ground. What was unusual was what was poking out of the bottom end of it. On closer inspection, the girls found that it was a pair of feet. Rather large feet. As if of one mind they scrambled over the bundle and ran as fast as they could to work, fear giving their feet wings.

Sammy Goldbaum's body had been found.

Denise's and Carol's manager was very good. He gave them the rest of the week off on full pay.

Maura sat in the interview room at Vine Street police station. She lit another cigarette and pulled on it hard. She was frightened, very frightened. But outwardly she looked as if she did not have a care in the world.

The WPC who had been assigned to stay with her looked her over critically. She approved of the pale grey suit Maura wore. It was plain but, with the single strand of pearls and the pearl earrings, it looked what it was: exclusive and expensive. WPC Cotter approved of everything about Maura Ryan, from her shiny white-blond hair to her crocodile-skin shoes and bag. It was common knowledge that this was the woman who had nearly ruined DS Petherick's career. It was an old story that had been embellished over the years until now it was part of Vine Street folklore.

DI Dobin came into the room. He smiled at Maura and she smiled back. She had been here for hours and they still had not charged her. She had called her brief and he was on his way from Cambridge. All she had to do was keep a clear head. They had nothing on her.

She forced the events of the night before from her mind. Sammy Goldbaum had deserved everything he got. Sammy was to become another blank spot in Maura's mind, along with everything else she had ever done that was decidedly wrong. DI Dobin and the WPC and everyone who touched Maura's life in some way, however trivial, were never in any way aware that she was like a time bomb: a dangerous time bomb that would eventually explode. Her outer veneer of calm and friendliness hid a mass of emotions and feelings that would one day spew out like a festering cancer.

'Am I going to be charged with anything?' Her voice was calm and controlled.

DI Dobin cleared his throat. Against his will he had taken a liking to this girl. Which was more than could be said of his feelings for her elder brother. The sad part was they both had perfect alibis and not even an outstanding parking ticket between them.

'I am afraid, Miss Ryan, that I have some bad news for you.'

Maura's face remained neutral. She took a long drag on her cigarette.

'Oh? And what's that?' She braced herself for what she knew was coming.

'A head was found earlier today in a litter bin in East Heath Road, just off Hampstead Heath. It was your brother Benjamin's.'

He watched her face blanch. The corner of her mouth began to twitch upwards. It was the only outward sign that she felt anything.

'Now, Miss Ryan, I ask you again – have you anything to tell me about the death of Jonny Fenwick or Samuel Goldbaum?'

Maura stared at him blankly. She put out her cigarette and immediately lit another. She shook her head. DI Dobin watched the tears begin to gather in her lovely eyes. He could see what had attracted young Petherick to her. Even with her height and her woman's body, she still had a naivete about her that made men want to protect her.

He knew as sure as eggs was eggs that if this lovely creature sitting in front of him had not actually committed the murders herself, she, along with her brother Michael, had ordered them. And he also knew that they would walk out of this police station because there was no evidence to go on. Michael had been with a 'friend', a young barrister who had already been in and given a sworn statement, and this young woman had been with Timothy Repton, a well-known actor who starred in a twice-weekly soap opera called 'Crossways'. Mr Repton had also been in and given a sworn statement. Both the witnesses to their whereabouts were beyond reproach and both were, in DI Dobin's opinion, lying bastards.

It was always the same with the Ryans. They were more

slippery than a greased eel. Also, the Chief Super had been running around like a blue-arsed fly. He had received word from a big wig somewhere along the line, and now the Ryans were to be 'courteously' escorted off the premises. He sighed.

'Well, Miss Ryan, thank you very much for your time. You can go now.'

Maura stood up. She slipped her crocodile-skin clutch bag underneath her arm and held out her free hand. Dobin shook it gently.

'Is my brother being released?'

'Yes, Miss Ryan, he's waiting for you at the reception desk.'

'Thank you. Thank you very much. Have you any idea who could have hurt . . . murdered my brother Benny?' Her voice was low.

'No, Miss. But rest assured we will do all that we can. As we will to investigate the bombing of your brother's club.'

Maura bowed her head and followed him from the room. Unlike her, Michael was making himself heard. Maura could hear him before she saw him.

As she turned the corner and walked to him, he pointed at her. 'Don't you worry, girl. These bastards will pay for this day's work. My little brother's dead and *you* arrest *me*!' His voice was indignant. 'And my little sister! My club's been bombed and you lot don't give a toss about it. I'm a taxpayer and I want me rights!'

The Chief Superintendent was nearly in tears. 'Please, Mr Ryan. We must follow every lead.'

'Why ain't you out looking for the real criminals, eh? The rapists and the child molesters. Why ain't you out looking for whoever murdered my little brother?'

Maura slipped her arm into his. 'Come on, Michael. Calm down, love. Let's just get out of here.' She led him out into the afternoon air. 'Please, Mickey, let's get home. I think I'm going to be sick.'

Michael put his arms around her and cuddled her to him. 'Don't worry, Dopolis will pay for what he's done, darlin', and he'll pay bloody dearly.'

At this moment Maura did not want anyone to pay for anything. She just wanted to run away from it all. Instead she smiled wanly. The worst was yet to come. They had to face their mother.

Sarah had been sitting in the darkness of her front room for hours. When the police brought her the news about Benny she had walked into the room, pulled the heavy curtains and sat in the chair by the fire. She felt nothing. Nothing at all. But she would. Oh, she knew that much. She would. It was like Anthony all over again. She had made Benjamin go with the policeman to identify young Benny's remains. Let him do some of the dirty work for a change.

In the flickering firelight her religious statues looked lifelike. Getting out of the seat, she went to the large sideboard that held them all. She opened one of the drawers and took out her wooden rosary. She went back to her seat. Kissing the Cross of Christ, she began to pray.

She could hear Carla's sobs coming from the bedroom above her, but did not really care. It would do the child good to find out just what her Auntie Maura and Uncle Michael had caused. It might take some of the shine off them for her. She had already refused to see Geoffrey. He had arrived just after the police and she had told him to bugger off out of it. She did not want to see any of her children except Maura and Michael. Oh, she wanted to see them all right! She wanted to throw them out of her house and her life. They were filthy . . . putrid.

She heard the click of the front room door opening and glanced towards it. In the light from the hall she could make out Maura and Michael's silhouettes. She said nothing. They walked into the room quietly, shutting the door behind them. Sarah carried on praying.

'"Hail Mary, full of grace, the Lord is with thee. Blessed art thou amongst sinners and blessed is the fruit of thy womb, Jesus . . ."'

Michael watched his mother. She was so short that her feet did not touch the floor properly as she sat on the large horsehair chair. The room had its own distinctive cloying stuffiness, a sickly sweet smell of lavender polish and dusty velvet.

'Mum? Shall I turn the light on?'

'"Holy Mary Mother of God, pray for us sinners, now and at the hour of our death, Amen."

'"Hail Mary, full of grace . . ."'

'Come on, Michael. Let's leave her.'

Maura's voice sounded something in Sarah's head. It was as if her daughter's voice triggered an explosion. Sarah's voice came to them from the semi-darkness.

'So you want to leave, Maura Ryan, do you?' Her voice was low, conversational. As if they were having a friendly chat about the weather. 'Did you know that your brother's head was found this morning? In a litter bin, of all places.' She was amazed to hear herself laugh. 'Yes, a litter bin. Just the place to put rubbish, isn't it? In a dustbin. Where will they put you two, I wonder, when you're dead? Down in the sewers, I expect, with the rest of the shit and the effluent. Oh, yes. That will very likely be where you two will end up. In the filth and stink of the sewers!'

'Mum! For God's sake.' Michael's voice was shocked.

'Don't you "God" me, Michael Ryan. Because I'm finished with you . . . I should never have forgiven you over my Anthony.'

Maura listened to their mother's voice. She knew that what Sarah was saying would break Michael's heart.

'And what about me, Mum? What about me?'

Maura's voice was hard. Sarah felt its iciness and shivered in her seat.

'You filthy whore! I know all about you, Maura Ryan. You and him.' She poked her head towards Michael. 'Do you know what people say? That you two sleep together. Did you know that? Only I know that's not true because he's as queer as a fish and you're a neuter. You're not capable of sleeping with any man, Maura Ryan.'

Maura felt a hot flush creep over her body. She went to the lightswitch and flipped it. The room was filled with the glaring brightness of a one hundred watt bulb.

Maura walked to her mother, her lovely face twisted into a mask of hatred.

'So I'm a neuter, am I? And whose bloody fault was that? Yours! Call yourself a mother? *You* took me to the abortionist. And *you* held me down on the bloody table while that Paki bastard ripped my baby from inside me. You turned us all into what we are, Mother. Even poor Benny. Another Mummy's boy, still at home at twenty-nine years old! You made it impossible for any of your children to lead a normal life. You drove your husband to drink and your kids into being neuters.

'I may end up in the gutter or the sewers. Who knows? But at least if I go there I'll have finally told you what I think of you. You're a nasty vindictive old bitch! You're even jealous of me and Carla, ain't you? Go on . . . admit it!'

Sarah stared at her daughter, mesmerised. Of all the things she had envisaged at this meeting with Maura and Michael, this was not one of them. She had expected silence as she read them the riot act. Not this.

'Sitting in the bloody dark saying the Rosary! You old hypocrite. Well, let me tell you something. Your old darling Father McCormack is an active IRA member. That's how we all got involved. When you sent him to talk some sense into Michael, the priest dragged him into it all. He was laughing at you, you stupid old cow!'

'No! I won't have you say that about the priest. You're a dirty liar!'

'SHUT YOUR BLOODY MOUTH UP!' Maura's voice bounced off the walls. 'Do you hear me? Shut up for once in your life. We may not be pillars of the church but we ain't got anything on our conscience where you're concerned, Mother. Everything you ever had come from Mickey, later on from me and the other boys. You had nothing . . . NOTHING!'

Maura ran to where the religious statues stood bearing witness to their fight. Picking up the statue of Saint Sebastian, she threw it to the ground.

'Not even the money to buy this shower of shite!'

She stopped abruptly, gasping for breath. She saw her mother sitting in the chair. She looked like a very old woman. All the fight left Maura and she went to Michael.

'Come on, Mickey. Let's go.'

'Mum . . . You didn't mean what you said, did you, Maws? Mum, look at me.'

Sarah sighed heavily.

'Get him out of me sight, Maura, and take yourself with him. You both disgust me.'

Maura turned round to face the woman she had alternately loved and hated all her life.

'Not half as much as you disgust me, Mother.'

As Maura spoke, Michael seemed to snap out of his reverie. 'I worshipped you, Mother.' His voice was dangerously low. 'All my life it's been, "Michael, get me this, son." Or help with that. But you never really cared about me, did you? I was just a pair of hands as far as you were concerned.'

His eyes were moist and Maura felt her heart breaking as she watched him confront the most important person in his life. 'I helped you with the kids as they came along. I fetched and carried while you had your long . . . painfully long . . . pregnancies. Then as soon as you were delivered of yet another child, you allowed the old man back into your bed, didn't you? Even after the dead babies you were both back at it like a pair of dogs copulating.

'You wonder why I turned out like I did? Well, I'll tell you why. I never wanted a woman and all that it entailed. I never wanted an emotional leech sucking out my entrails like you did to all us. Anthony's dead, and our Benny – and I'd give anything to be with them! Away from this house and this family and *you* . . . especially you.

'Come on, Maws. Let's leave her to her prayers and her religious mania. It's all she's fit for.'

Sarah felt as if she had been stabbed to the heart. She'd never realised just how much she had come to rely on Michael's unquestioning support.

She sat still in her chair, trying to control her breathing. As Michael pulled Maura from the room they came face to face with Carla. She was standing in the hallway, her lovely face twisted in pain, arms hugging her slim body.

'Get your stuff together, Carla, we're leaving.'

She shook her head. Her long red-brown hair swirled about her face.

'I'm not going anywhere with you, Maura. I'm staying here with Nana.'

'I said, get your stuff together.' Maura's voice brooked no argument.

'No. I'm not going.'

Maura sighed. 'You do what you like, Carla. You know where I am when you want me.'

Carla curled her lips in contempt. 'I'll never want you. Never! You're nothing but murderers.'

Maura brought her hand back and slapped Carla a stinging blow across her face.

'You stay here with your precious Nana then . . . I don't give a toss any more. You can do what you like. Come on, Mickey. Let's go.'

As they left the house Benny's Alsatian, Driver, ran from the kitchen down the front steps. He leapt about in the snow, ecstatic to be out in the air.

Michael opened the door to his Mercedes and the dog jumped into the front seats then dived over into the back. He sat there with his tongue hanging out, his heavy tail thumping the seat as it wagged.

'I'll take him home with me, Mickey.'

They got into the car and Michael pulled away from the kerb with a heavy heart.

Inside the house Sarah and Carla held on to each other tightly.

Michael finally spoke as they drove along the Bayswater Road. 'When we get to your drum, Maws, we've got to round up the boys. The old Bill ain't got nothing on us but we have to plan our next moves cautiously.'

Maura did not answer him. He took one hand off the steering wheel and patted her leg.

'Listen, Maws, I ain't learnt much in this life but I have learnt this. When you hit a major setback you put it behind you as quick as possible. Benny's dead. Nothing will ever bring him back again. What we do now is decide when and how we retaliate.'

Maura nodded her head wearily. Her mum was right. Mickey was mad . . . and she had a sneaky feeling that she was as well.

Driver put his head on Maura's shoulder. She could feel his hot dog breath on her cheek and lifted her arm and caressed the dog's soft fur. Benny had loved his dog as he had loved his life – wholeheartedly. She realised with a curious insight that Benny had probably not even realised he was in danger. That fact would never have occurred to him.

She closed her eyes tightly and instead of the tears she had been expecting, began to laugh. A slight giggle at first that gradually built up into a deep rollicking belly laugh. A laugh that made her shoulders shake and her tummy hurt. Somewhere in the distance, far off, she heard the dog begin to whine, and for some reason this just made her laugh harder.

Michael stopped the car and pulled her towards him. She could smell the dank dampness of the material of his coat. Then the tears came at last. She saw Terry Petherick, Anthony and Benny, as clear as a photograph in her mind. Then she saw her mother's face, old and wrinkled . . . a feeling of panic welled up in her and for a few minutes she thought she really had gone mad.

How had this happened to her? And, more importantly, how had she allowed it to happen? Both questions were to remain unanswered for many years, but as she sat in the car with Michael and Driver that night, she realised for the first time just how lonely and unhappy she really was.

'All right, Maws. All right, my love. I'll look after you. Don't you worry.' Michael's voice was soft and husky.

She did not want Michael to look after her. She wanted Terry Petherick to put his arms around her and whisper his words of love, as he had done before. Long ago. Before she had become bad. But, like many other bad things in her life, she forced the thoughts away. Where they waited patiently for the day they would all creep out into the open and torture her, like the long forgotten nightmares of her childhood.

Chapter Nineteen

'Merry Christmas, Auntie Maura!'

Margaret's twin daughters jumped on to the little bed where Maura was sleeping. She opened her eyes, not sure for a few seconds where she was. Then seeing the two bright faces, she tried to smile.

She was at Margaret's. She sat up in bed and hugged Patricia and Penelope. The sleeping tablets she had taken the night before made her feel groggy. She yawned. 'Merry Christmas, my lovelies.'

'Thank you for our Christmas presents, Auntie Maura. They were lovely.'

The two identical little faces beamed at her and she felt the familiar tightening in her guts. What she wouldn't give to be the mother of these two! She hugged them both to her tightly.

Margaret came into the bedroom carrying a tray. Maura could smell eggs and bacon.

'Oh, Marge. Don't be silly. I can get up.'

Margaret pursed her lips and shook her head. 'Oh no

you won't, Maws. Oi, you two! Dad's got your breakfast waiting for you downstairs.'

The two girls got off the bed, their bright ginger hair telling anyone who looked at them who their mother was.

Patricia, the elder of the two by five minutes, grimaced. 'Oh, can't we stay up here, Mum?' Her voice had the whine that made Margaret feel like murdering her.

'N-O spells no. Now hop it, the pair of you.'

The two girls ran from the room.

'Honest, Marge, I couldn't eat a thing.'

The greasy smell of the bacon and eggs was beginning to make her feel sick.

'You *will* bloody eat it. After all you've been through this last few weeks!' Margaret's voice was scandalised. 'You'll end up ill if you're not careful. Smoke, smoke, smoke! Drink, drink. And then sleeping pills to blot out the world.'

'Oh, give it a rest, Marge, for Christ's sake.'

Margaret put the tray across Maura's legs as if to trap her in the bed.

'No I won't give it a rest! You're my best friend and I feel that it's down to me to tell you a few home truths.'

'Such as?' Maura's voice was sarcastic.

'For a start, you look old and haggard. You're drinking too much. It's impossible to get a civil word out of you. You're moody, sarcastic, and to be honest, Maws, you're beginning to get on my tits!'

Maura closed her eyes and yawned again.

'Margie, just in case it's escaped your notice, I recently had a brother murdered. He was spread all over London like a paper chase. His left foot and various other parts of his anatomy are still unaccounted for. I had a big fight with my mother and Carla who are under the impression that me and Mickey were to blame for Benny's murder. I was arrested by the police and kept for over three hours on suspicion of *two* other murders. And you have the nerve to sit there and tell me that I am not my old self!' Maura's voice rose. 'It's enough to make the Queen feel depressed.'

Margaret sighed. She loved Maura wholeheartedly. 'Look, Maws, all I'm trying to say is, pull yourself together. If not for my sake then for the kids. I can't stand them seeing you like this. Last night you was so pissed Dennis had to carry you up to bed.'

'I know. Marge, I'm sorry. It's just that with all that's happened, I feel responsible . . .'

'That's crap and you know it! I can swallow a lot. Maws, but not self-pity. That's a luxury none of us can afford.'

Maura looked at Margaret as if for the first time. Since having the kids she had become huge. In her pink candlewick dressing gown she looked like a little pink Buddha. Her red hair was pinned up untidily and her face had the harassed look that seems to be worn only by mothers of young children. It was only her eyes, the deep sea-green eyes, that still held the image of the girl she had been. They were as sparkling and mischievous as ever.

Cutting off a small piece of bacon, Margaret held it to Maura's mouth. Reluctantly she ate it. Slowly Margaret fed her the whole breakfast. When the last piece of food had been eaten she placed a mug of tea in Maura's hands. Then, picking up the tray, she made her way out of the room. As she opened the bedroom door, holding the tray against her side with one hand, she looked back over her shoulder at Maura.

'You can't plan and scheme on an empty stomach, you know!'

'And just what do you mean by that?'

Marge smiled at her cheekily.

'I'm not as silly as I look, you know, Maura Ryan. So I'll thank you not to act as if I am.' She lowered her voice. 'What I know and what I've guessed will go to my grave with me. Now, you need your wits about you at this time, and I intend to see that you have them.'

She walked from the room and let the door slam shut behind her.

Maura leant back against the pillows and sighed. Good old Marge. The only real friend she had. She sat up in bed, and, putting the tea on the night table, picked up her packet of cigarettes. She lit one, drawing the smoke into her lungs. Margaret was right. She did need her wits about her. If only Carla would talk to her she would feel better. Every time she tried to get through to her, the phone was slammed down. She had even tried ringing Carla's friends. But nothing. She had not answered any of Maura's messages. Maura could imagine her mother, in her element, poisoning Carla against her. Oh, she had guessed her mother's game all right . . .

She took another pull on the cigarette and felt a wave of nausea sweep over her. The combination of fried food, cigarette smoke and acute hangover was suddenly too much for her stomach. With her hand pressed tightly to her mouth, she ran from the bedroom into the bathroom. Dropping her cigarette into the toilet pan she retched. She heaved until she thought her insides were going to come up. A cold sweat broke out all over her body. She leaned against the wall, trying to gather her wits about her. Turning on the shower, she slipped her nightie over her head and stood underneath the shower head. She shivered as ice cold water ran over her body, making her teeth chatter. Still she stood there, trying to bring some kind of life back into her limbs.

After a few minutes she felt the delicious sensation of warmth that only cold water can bring. She felt the tightening of her skin as the blood vessels beneath the surface tried desperately to pump warm blood around her aching body. Her nipples were rock hard and as she turned the water on to hot she savoured the exquisite sensation of the heat gradually invading her bones. She put her face up to let the water cleanse her from head to toe. Gradually she felt the life begin to come back to her. For the first time in days she actually felt something that was real and tangible.

Then the tears came. A torrent of salty rivulets that mixed with the heavy water from the shower and ran away, down her breasts, over her empty stomach, on to her feet and into the shower tray.

In her mind she saw the loathing on her mother's face. The handsome carefree face of Benny, the young boy who had always been in some kind of prank. She saw the face of Terry Petherick, as it had been the night of the club bombing. She had known then that he still cared for her, that if she had not been Maura Ryan they would have married. She would have been like Margie, juggling the bills, looking after the kids and just being loved. As Dennis loved Marge, even with her large mauve and silver stretch-marks and empty breasts. And she, Maura, would have loved it. Every second of it.

Instead she had more money than she knew what to do with. She ran a business that was more crooked than the Government of Cuba, and had a brother who was at this time almost totally dependent on her. As for the younger boys, they blamed *her* for Benny's death. Not Michael but her. They believed that if she had not wanted her dock properties so badly, and had given them to Dopolis, Benny would still be alive. And she had to be honest and admit to herself that they were right. She cried harder. Whoever said that money made you happy was a liar. A dirty rotten stinking liar! She would give every penny she had at this moment to be just plain ordinary Mrs Terry Petherick. He was the only man she would ever want, even if she lived to be a hundred. If only she had kept that little baby! If she had nothing else now she would have had that. She would never have taken over the ice cream and hot dogs. She would never have become the person she was now. The person who had watched her brother murder an old man, Sammy Goldbaum, who had been waiting patiently for them to arrive. He had walked so meekly to the car. And now she had his blood on her hands and could never escape from any of it.

She had always thought that if she ever came face to face with Terry Petherick she would spit in his eye. Instead she had felt an urge to tell him all that happened to her. About the baby and her life with Michael . . . everything. She had wanted it to be like it had been once before. When she was young and free. She was still young, but too much had happened over the years ever to allow her to be the girl that she once had been.

She turned off the tap and stood in the confined space of the shower cubicle. The sudden silence was startling and broke her out of her reverie. Her tears were gone now and all they had left in their wake was a heavy tiredness. Stepping from the shower, she wrapped a large towel around her body. As she dried her hair she thought about what she was going to do next. Then she made a decision. All that she could do now was go forward into the future. No matter how exciting the past may have been you could never recapture it. What Margaret had said earlier was right. Self-pity was a destructive force. She would have to make herself stronger. Much stronger. What she really needed was to get laid!

She smiled to herself. That was what Marge had been telling her for years! She shrugged aggressively, as if throwing off all her previous worries and cares. She wiped the steam from the mirror on the wall opposite the shower and stared at her face. Her hair hung in limp, damp strands around her face which was puffy from crying. She smiled to herself. She was going to pick herself up and slowly mend all the broken pieces. She and Michael could take on the world. She had absolutely no one else now. She had lost them all, one by one. But she knew that she would always have Michael and Margie. Good old Margie.

She remembered that it was Christmas Day. Back at her own house she had the mother-of-pearl jewellery box that she had bought for Carla . . . She forced the thought from her mind. Let the ungrateful little bitch stay with her mother! Maura did not need her. She did not need anyone.

She ran her hands through her hair, feeling the silky softness of it. Letting the towel fall from her body, she ran her hands down her neck and over her breasts, travelling down her tight stomach to her pubic hair, enjoying the sensation. Picking up her nightie from the floor she put it back on, then went back into the bedroom where her overnight bag was. She felt a lot better. Much better, in fact. As she plugged in her hair dryer she was actually humming a little tune. Margie was right. Self-pity was a bummer. All that she could do now was go forward.

*

When she finally went downstairs she had her make-up on and her hair done to perfection. She was wearing a dress that would have cost Marge two months' housekeeping and was gratified to hear the long low whistle that came from Dennis.

'If I wasn't so happy with my old Margie I'd be after you myself, Maws!'

Marge laughed. 'Listen here, Dennis Dawson. You couldn't pull a ligament these days, let alone a beauty like Maura. Especially not since you lost your hair.' She smiled at Maura. 'All he's got these days is six hairs and a nit!'

Maura laughed with her. Dennis had lost his hair early, and Maura knew that it was a sore point with him.

'Come out here and have a cuppa. You look much better.'

Maura followed her out into her little kitchen. 'I feel a lot better, Marge. Thanks for letting me come.'

Margaret plugged in the electric kettle. 'What you on about, you silly cow? This is your home for as long as you want to be here.' She opened her arms wide and Maura walked into them. Margaret's tiny plump body held on to Maura's tall thin frame. Maura got upset again at the show of emotion.

'If you knew what I'd done, Marge!'

'Shh.' Margaret stepped back from Maura and raised her finger to her lips. 'Look, Maws, I know that you and Michael ain't strictly kosher. I've always known and I don't care. You're me mate and that's all I'm interested in.'

Maura looked at her and frowned. 'Sometimes, Marge, I don't think that I'm all the ticket. I get so moody and I think really weird things.'

'Maws love, you've been through an awful lot, you

know. Just let yourself heal naturally. Benny's death would make anyone feel rotten. It was horrific. You need time to get over it, that's all.'

'Maybe you're right, Marge.'

She wanted to tell Margaret what Mickey had done to Sammy Goldbaum and Jonny Fenwick. She wanted to tell her that she had helped him. She was experiencing that feeling again – as if she was on the outside of her body looking in. She had always known that Michael enjoyed inflicting pain on people. And until the night with Jonny Fenwick and Sammy Goldbaum it had not bothered her.

'Maura!' Margaret's voice broke into her thoughts. 'Mickey's on the phone for you.'

Maura stared around the kitchen blankly. Margaret looked at her curiously. 'You all right, girl?'

Maura nodded and walked out of the kitchen into the lounge. The twins were watching *Mary Poppins* on television and baby Dennis was now sitting on his dad's lap. Maura's mind registered the fact that the Christmas tree was falling to one side where the kids had been playing underneath it. She walked out into the hallway and picked up the receiver lying on the telephone table.

'Oh, darling. You'll never guess what?'

His voice was bubbling over with excitement.

'What?' Maura's voice was flat.

'I just had a visit from Sammy Goldbaum's daughter. You know her . . . the one with the big hooter?'

'Rebekka.'

'Yeah, that's it. Rebekka. Anyway, she said she had come to see me on Christmas Day to show that she bore me no ill will. Not that I give a toss anyway. Those front wheels are like the eye ties, full of crap. Anyway, the bottom line is she brought me some documents that belonged to Sammy. I've just been through them, and have a guess what I found along with a load of old betting slips?'

'What?'

'The name of the property developer we've been looking for. The mastermind behind Dopolis.'

'But Sammy said he had no idea who he was . . .'

'I don't think Sammy realised just what he had. You see, I found an old cutting from a newspaper. The *Daily Mirror* in fact. It was from the racing section and it had a picture of Dopolis. And get this bit, Maws. He's in the Royal Enclosure at Ascot! Now what, I asked myself, was he doing in there? Then I realised that he was standing with none other than William Templeton! That's when it hit me. He's the Mr Big that Dopolis was talking about.'

Maura was stunned. 'But he's a peer of the Realm!'

Mickey laughed. 'I know. Saucy bastard! I bet he's even in You Know Who . . . or whatever that book's called.'

Maura laughed despite herself. 'It's *Who's Who*, you wally. Christ Almighty, Mickey, if you're right . . .'

'I know I'm right. I've got a gut feeling about it. Look, can you get over to me now?'

'I can't, Mickey. I promised Marge and Den I'd have Christmas dinner with them.'

'All right then, Princess. But get your arse over here as soon as you can. All right?'

'All right then, Mickey. Merry Christmas.' Her voice was sad.

Michael's voice lost its excitement. 'I know it's been a bad time, the last few weeks, but I promise you, Maws – I'll make it up to you somehow. Merry Christmas, my darling.'

Maura put the phone down gently. The implications of

what Mickey had just said were phenomenal. She went back into the lounge and started to play with the children. She held them to the floor and tickled them till they screamed with laughter. Marge and Dennis watched her with amused expressions on their faces. This was more like it. This was the old Maura.

It wasn't until she was sitting at the dining table eating her enormous Christmas dinner that the excitement hit her. Lord William Templeton . . . Suddenly she could not wait to get started on him. Together Michael and she would eat him alive.

She picked up a bright blue cracker and pointed it at Patricia. 'Come on, Patty. Let's see who wins the paper hat!'

Lord Templeton was also sitting at his dinner table in his large rambling house in Kent. The house dated back to the fifteenth century and over the large inglenook fireplace was a painting of one of his ancestors. It had been executed by Holbein, one of Henry VIII's favourite painters. There was an old story in his family that it was this ancestor who had actually ordered the death of Sir Thomas More. William liked to think that the story was true.

At forty-five, he was a somewhat jaded man. Over the years he had used his vast wealth to engage in many pastimes, both sexual and otherwise. He had hunted big game in South Africa and had smoked hashish in Turkey. He had travelled to the Himalayas and had seen the Manta Rays leap from the sea in the Maldives. He had experimented with drugs, and did not think there was any country in the world that he had not visited. He had married once, when he was very young, a large voluptuous woman, years older than himself. She had left him after one year, taking with her a large amount of money and his good wishes. She had taught him much: that there was no pleasure without pain; that a man, especially a rich man, needs to use his wealth wisely. He had never, as far as he knew, fathered a child. Unlike most men, William Templeton did not have the urge to reproduce. He rather liked his solitary life. If he wanted a woman they were easy enough to find.

He picked at his expertly cooked Christmas dinner. At this moment he was a very worried man. He was regretting getting involved with the Greek, Dopolis. For a start it had not achieved his objective – the warehouses that the Ryans owned in the old docklands. Dopolis had turned out to be a penny ante type villain. Not at all the hard man he had said he was. The Ryans had completely obliterated him. If only he had had the sense to keep his eye on the proceedings, then the young boy, Benjamin, would never have died. He shuddered. He had been impressed with Dopolis at first. Had admired his plan of action. How was he to know it was all going to backfire?

He pushed his plate away from him. He had no appetite. Dopolis should never have ordered the boy's killing, and such a horrible death . . . Now he would have to be very careful. The only avenue left to him was to get someone harder than Michael Ryan and from what he could gauge that would be a very tall order indeed.

His manservant, a rather pinched-faced man called Rankin, cleared the table in front of him. Templeton sat back in his large comfortable chair. His dining table could easily seat twenty-four people. Normally he would have accepted an invitation from a friend for the Christmas festivities, but this year, after all the trouble with Dopolis, he had a hankering for his own company and his own hearth. He conceded that he had made a fatal mistake with the Greek. He toyed with the idea of going to see Michael Ryan and offering him a good price for the warehouses, but pushed the idea away as quickly as it occurred to him.

Some of his best friends had done a stint in Ford Open Prison; in the circles he moved in it was inevitable that you would eventually meet someone who had either embezzled money from the bank that they had worked for or been involved with some kind of fraud. But that was a fact of life. This Ryan, though, was a rough type and his sister wasn't much better apparently. He lit up a Cuban cigar and poured himself a large Remy Martin into the glass that Rankin had left conveniently by his elbow. No, he had made a tragic mistake. What he had to do now was try to recoup his losses. But he was sure of one thing. He *would* get those warehouses. He would get all the Ryans' properties along the Thames.

He smiled to himself. As usual he was absolutely amazed by his own intelligence. He thought of himself as the epitome of the upper class male. God in heaven, he was a cousin to the Queen! Only by marriage, he admitted, but it was a close enough connection to get Nigel Dempster practically wetting himself with excitement every time he appeared in public. He relaxed. There was nothing whatsoever to tie him in with Dopolis.

He sat in his chair, smoking his cigar and drinking his brandy, planning his next move. When the building finally started in the old docklands, every foot would be worth a small fortune. He sat all evening scheming how he would get the Ryans' properties.

Luckily for him he was not aware that Maura and Michael Ryan were also planning and scheming along the same lines – how they were going to get *his* properties, and his co-operation.

Maura and Michael were now certain that William Templeton was their man. An old friend of Michael's who worked on one of the gutter papers had run his name through the newspaper's computer and supplied them with every piece of gossip ever written about him, as well as some facts that had never been published. And their friends in the IRA had been very helpful. Their final recourse had been to some paid 'informers' in the Foreign Office who had supplied information that had shocked even Michael. It seemed that Templeton was a major shareholder in an arms factory that had been supplying anyone with the readies for years. Templeton was certainly no angel, that much was apparent. And that he was protected by the old boy network was more than obvious. Though as Maura had pointed out, there had to be more people involved with him, and with all his businesses. His main buyers were North African countries; Iran, Iraq, Libya – the list was endless. He also supplied Romania and the Czechs. All in all, Templeton seemed like their kind of guy!

Michael was jubilant! The only cloud on their horizon was Dopolis. Although they now had just about everything they wanted to know about him, plans for his demise were put on hold for the time being. He was the bait with which they were going to lure William Templeton. As Michael had playfully remarked to Maura, 'Let him get over his injuries first. He can pay for Benny when he's better!'

Sarah Ryan had still not acknowledged either of them. This had cut Michael deeply. His mother had been his life.

But the estrangement from her had brought brother and sister closer together. They spent every available minute in each other's company. Maura now needed Michael more than ever. When she was with him he could convince her that Sammy Goldbaum's and Jonny Fenwick's deaths were just the paying of a debt. While she was with him she could accept that. Away from him, she was frightened and lonely. Every day that passed was making her more bitter and confused. They had spent the days since Christmas following up their leads on Templeton, and decided they would pay him a visit on New Year's Day. Until then they would bide their time.

On the 29 December 1975 Roy's son was born. He rang the news through to Michael at seven in the evening. Maura and Michael arrived at St Mary's Hospital at eight-thirty. After looking at the new baby fleetingly, Michael and the rest of the boys took Roy out to celebrate, all feeling the loss of Benny more than ever.

Maura was left with Janine. She noticed that her mother was nowhere to be seen.

She held the baby, Benny Anthony, in her arms. 'He's beautiful, Janine. I hope you realise just how lucky you are?'

Janine smiled wearily. 'I'm a bit sore, Maws, but he was worth it.'

Maura nodded. She was staring at the baby so intently that Janine felt a prickle of fear.

'I nearly had a baby once, Janine. A long time ago.' Maura's voice was sad. For the first time ever Janine pitied her.

'I know, Maura. Roy told me.'

She held the baby tighter to her chest.

'It was a lovely gesture, naming the baby after Benny and Anthony. It brings them back somehow.' She kissed the baby's downy head. 'I think that if they'd at least let us bury Benny, half the battle would be over. I can't stand to think of him on ice.'

'Please, Maura. Don't talk about it.' Janine was nearly in tears.

Maura's sing-song voice as she spoke about her brother made Janine feel frightened. She had always been a little in awe of Maura. Now she was terrified.

Maura smiled radiantly at her.

'I'm sorry, Jan. I'm getting a bit morbid!' She kissed the baby's head again and squeezed him to her breast. It took all Janine's willpower not to snatch her baby away. Janine was sensitive and felt things very deeply. She did not want this woman anywhere near her child.

Roy had said recently that he did not think that Maura was right in the head. Looking at her now, Janine was sure that she was capable of anything. She had a terrible feeling that Maura would even kill a baby if it would get her what she wanted. Janine shivered.

'You cold?'

'No, Maura, just tired. It takes a lot out of you, having a baby.'

'Like shitting a football, is how Marge described it!'

Janine pursed her lips. She had never understood the Ryans' use of bad language. They swore in much the same way as her mother said 'God bless you'.

Janine took all her courage into her hands and decided to approach Maura with an idea that had been floating around inside her head for months.

'Maura?'

'What?' She was rocking the baby in her arms, completely engrossed in his little face. He was looking up at her with the dark blue Ryan eyes.

Janine picked at her bedsheet, watching her sister-in-law warily.

'It's about Roy.'

Maura laughed gently. 'He's like a dog with three lamp posts! I've never seen him like this. All the boys are ribbing him terrible. You'd think this was the first baby ever born!'

'I know . . . I know.' Janine was finding it difficult to find the appropriate words.

Maura sensed that there was something going on and looked Janine in the face.

'What's on your mind? Come on, spit it out. I'm not really an ogre, whatever my mum might say.' Her voice was bitter.

'I was wondering if you would help Roy set up a little business . . .'

Her voice trailed off as she saw the look of shock on Maura's face.

'You what! Roy work outside the family? You must be joking.'

Janine started to cry. 'Oh, Maura, I'm so frightened.' She put her face into her hands. 'I feel like a policeman's wife, wondering if he's going to come home. Then after what happened to Benny . . .'

Maura pulled her hands away from her face. 'You're just overwrought, that's all. Having a baby makes you go funny.'

'NO! It's not that!' Janine lost all caution. 'I don't want to be left a widow, bringing up the baby on my own. I want us to be a normal family. A real family. Roy's not meant to be a thug.'

Maura put the baby into the cot by the bed. Her face was set. She loomed over Janine and began to speak to her in a low and menacing voice.

'Shall I tell you something, Janine? In case it has escaped your notice. Roy, as much as I love him, is as thick as two short planks. He can barely count over fifty. He still reads *Marvel* comics, for Christ's sake! The best he could ever have expected out of life was a job on the council or with the Water Board. Either way, you'd not be spending the kind of hefty wedge you're used to now. Your father tried to turn him into a butcher and look where that got him. If Roy knew what you'd said here tonight he'd give you a well-deserved slap. Now about the other load of shit you was spouting . . .'

She pushed Janine back against the pillows hard and poked her in the chest. 'You want to be a real family, do you? You dumped your daughter on my mother if you remember rightly, love. If push ever comes to shove, you can dump your new arrival on her and all, can't you? Don't you ever try and bullshit me again. DO YOU HEAR ME?'

Maura's loud voice made the baby whimper in his cot. 'I'm going to forget what you've said in here tonight, Janine, because I know that having a baby can make you a bit distraught. I'm warning you, though, if I ever get wind that you've said this to anyone else, I'll come and sort you out myself. Get it?'

Janine nodded, her lips trembling. She realised that she had just made an enemy for life.

Maura watched her closely. Then she smiled a soft little smile that did not reach her eyes. Picking up her bag from the floor, she opened it, took out a blue velvet box and handed it to Janine.

'Well, open it then,' she snapped.

Janine was shaking so badly that Maura had to place her own hands on top of hers to help her open the box. Inside was a gold and platinum identity bracelet.

'I'll have his name put on it for you.'

Janine swallowed heavily. She did not want it. 'Tha . . . thanks. It's lovely. Beautiful.' A stray tear slid down her face. Maura wiped it away gently with her fingers.

'Cheer up, love. You just had a lovely little boy. You should be laughing, not crying.'

Janine forced a smile she did not think she had in her. 'As you say . . . it's my hormones or something.'

Maura laughed. 'That's the ticket. Now, I'm off to the Crown and Two Chairmen. If that lot are left on their own with Roy, he'll end up legless.' She put her bag under her arm and kissed Janine on the cheek.

'I heard a little saying the other day, Janine. It might give you something to think about. It was on a wall in some public toilets and Mickey read it. It said: "Life is like a shit sandwich. The more bread you've got, the less shit you have to eat." I'd think about that if I was you.'

With one last glance at the baby, Maura left the room. Janine was convinced that she was fuming inside and she was right. She sat in the bed staring at the identity bracelet. The tears came in a red hot rush. She felt like a trapped animal.

Her mother-in-law had been right. They would never let Roy go.

A while later a nurse came in and gave her a little talking to. And Janine sat in the bed silently as she was told all about 'the baby blues'. She was still crying when the nurse finally gave up and left her.

Maura drove to the Crown and Two Chairmen feeling better than she had for weeks. It had taken Janine's smugness and petty strivings for respectability to bring her out of her depression.

She was honest with herself, though. Holding the new baby had brought back all her maternal feelings and she had resented the fact that the baby was Janine's. Had she but known, Janine could not have picked a worse time to ask Maura for a favour.

Chapter Twenty

Maura walked into the Crown and Two Chairmen pub in Dean Street. As usual it was packed. She pushed her way through the throng of people and finally located the boys in the corner. Roy was already very drunk. The air was thick with cigarette smoke and camaraderie. Leslie saw Maura first and raised himself from his seat unsteadily. He was as drunk as a lord. Maura smiled at him.

'Hello, Mawsh.' His voice was slurred.

'Sit down, Les, before you fall down.' She looked around the table. Her six remaining brothers were all sitting, looking like clones of one another, all in different states of inebriation. Only Michael was even remotely sober. He stood up and offered her his seat.

'Sit down, Maws, and I'll get you a drink. What'll it be? Scotch?'

Maura sat down and nodded at him. He went to the bar.

'Well, you lot seem to be enjoying yourselves.' She made her voice sound jovial. Five pairs of eyes stared at her blankly. Maura felt for the first time the impact of their combined wariness and it hurt her. Only Geoffrey looked different and she realised that he looked smug. Smug and very, very sure of himself. Maura mentally chalked one up to him.

'Well, Roy, you got a son at last.'

He nodded at her, a silly grin on his drunken face. Maura began to search in her bag for her cigarettes. It was obvious that she was not welcome. In her present state of mind she was not sure if it was over Benny or because it was a boys' night out. Michael came back with a tray of drinks and she took the double Scotch he gave her and drank it straight down.

'That bad, Maws?' Michael's voice was soft.

'No. Actually it's worse. If you boys will excuse me, I have got some work to do in the club. OK?'

She picked up her bag and left as quickly as possible. Outside in the freezing night she breathed a deep sigh. It was still snowy, though most of it had turned to slush and black ice. She walked carefully up Dean Street to Le Buxom. The main damage to the club had been in the foyer. The little reception desk where Sheree Davidson had been sitting on the night of the bombing had taken most of the blast from the petrol bomb. The damage to the club had turned out to be minimal. Mainly cosmetic. But as Maura walked inside she was acutely aware of the fact that Sheree would never again walk in there with her tall stories and deep braying laugh. She had been popular with both punters and the other hostesses. She had left two children, who were now in the care of the courts. Their father, or fathers, no one was sure, were nowhere to be found. If indeed Sheree ever knew who they were.

As for Gerry Jackson, he had been taken to a Burns Unit in Billericay. His wife had already been made an interim payment of two thousand pounds to get her over Christmas and the New Year. She would receive a substantial weekly amount until it was decided by the doctors what would happen to Gerry. If he never worked again he would be more than amply provided for.

The club was once more up and running. It had been reopened less than a week after the 'trouble'. As Maura walked into the familiar blast of warm air she could hear 'My Eyes Adored You'. Her mind registered that Louise Barton was doing her act. Maura looked at her watch. It was nearly eleven and she was surprised that it was so late. She slipped off her fur coat and locked it in the little cloakroom just inside the entrance to the club.

Picking her bag up off the floor she went over to the meat seats and started her night's work. A new girl called Monique, for once a real Frenchwoman and not a phony, had started a few weeks previously. She was a very, very beautiful girl, very intelligent, and not at all the usual class of tom. There was just one thing that had puzzled Maura: she would take literally any punter. And another of the girls had told Maura that she would 'go case' for as little as fifty pounds. The minimum that her girls usually worked for was one hundred pounds plus their hostess fee. That told Maura one thing: Monique either had a violent pimp who insisted on a night 'quota', or she had a drugs problem.

Maura guessed it was the latter, and if it was, then it would not be long before they were busted. The busts were well staged. They were told at least a week in advance when one was going to occur so they could put off any well-known citizens, such as judges or more rarely politicians. The police had no qualms about arresting any of the girls that were taking, or happened to possess, drugs. It gave the so-called raid credibility. But Maura did not work like that. She would not, like some club owners, employ 'stooges' to give their busts a veneer of realism.

Monique was sitting with two black girls. They were chatting together amicably, which was unusual in itself. There was a fierce rivalry between the black and white toms, but Monique seemed to be liked by everyone. Maura went to where they were sitting, and smiled.

'Hello.' She nodded at the three girls. 'I wonder, Monique, could I see you upstairs for a few minutes?' Maura's voice was friendly. The other girls would assume that Maura had a 'homebird', a regular punter who had arranged to pay for the girl over the phone. That entailed stumping up for two bottles of champagne, fifty cigarettes, and a small administration fee. The girl would then be cabbed to the man's address.

Monique stood up and Maura noticed that she was very bright-eyed. Her pupils were dilated. She followed Maura upstairs to the office. Maura turned on the lights and, walking to the window, shut the venetian blinds. She turned back to face Monique and, smiling still, offered her a chair. The girl sat down. Instead of walking around the desk and sitting in her own chair, Maura stood in front of Monique, leaning on the edge of the desk.

'Monique, hold out your arms, please.'

'But why?'

Maura cleared her throat. She hated this. 'Would you please hold out your arms? You know why.'

Monique had long black hair and dark hazel eyes. In the bright light of the office Maura was surprised at how hard-faced she really was. In the muted light of the club she looked much younger. Maura had thought she was in her twenties. Looking at her now, though, she put her much nearer forty.

'Please, Monique. Don't make this any harder than it already is.'

Monique held out her arms. Maura checked them for track marks. There was nothing.

Monique looked at her triumphantly. 'You see, Miss Ryan. Nothing.'

Maura smiled apologetically. 'Take your stockings off, please.'

Monique's faced dropped. 'I beg your . . . how you say?'

Maura finished her sentence for her. 'Pardon. I beg your pardon. Now, if you don't mind, take your stockings off. I want a quick shufti at your calves and your shins, OK?'

Monique's eyes glittered with malevolence. She reminded Maura of a cornered rat.

'Take your stockings off, Monique. Either you do as I ask or I'll call one of the bouncers up here to have them forcibly removed. It's your choice.' She saw Monique's eyes go to the beaded bag on her lap. 'And don't even think about trying to shiv me, darling. It would only end in tears. And they wouldn't be mine.'

Maura's voice was as hard as concrete now. Monique surveyed her, weighing up the pros and cons. After a few seconds she dragged her tight black velour dress over her thighs. Slowly she began to undo the suspender belt. Monique rolled the stocking down to below her knee and held her leg out for inspection. Maura grinned. She was used to every ploy in the book. She took off the black patent leather shoe that Monique was wearing and pulled the stocking off completely. The bottom of her leg was a mass of needle marks. Even between her toes. Maura threw the stocking back at her and sighed.

'You're a bloody mug to yourself. You know that, don't you, Monique?'

The woman shrugged. She began to put her stocking back on.

Maura carried on talking. 'I know for a fact that you can speak German, Arabic, and even a smattering of Japanese. You're not a fool. Why do you take drugs?'

Monique slipped her shoe back on and took the cigarette that Maura offered her. Maura offered her a light. Monique puffed on the cigarette.

'You people make me laugh. Oh, don't look so . . . how you say? . . . shocked. I come here night after night and I sleep with strange men. Some of them are very nice men. Very kind. Some, they are rough and they want to hurt you.'

She saw Maura's face change and laughed. 'You are a very funny girl. You do not want me in your club because I take drugs. Well, let me tell you, I have been a prostitute since I was seventeen. Over twenty years. I have to have something to give me a bit of happiness and I find it in drugs. I have slept with thousands of different men and while I work for people like you, I make you very much money. How many of my men have refused to pay their bills, eh? None. I can sweet talk any man I want. So please don't lecture me!

'I will leave your club. It's shit anyway since the bomb was thrown in here. All the girls are nervous.' She stood up and put her cigarette out in the ashtray on the desk. 'I will say one thing before I go. Who is worse, eh? Me because I sell my body, or you for earning good money off that fact?'

'I give all the girls a good deal here. I offer them a degree of protection that they would not get anywhere else in London.' Maura's voice was defensive.

Monique laughed. 'True. True. But you are still a pimp in my eyes *and* theirs.' She gave her Gallic shrug. 'Goodbye.'

Monique walked from the room and Maura suddenly felt flat. It seemed that she was not 'Miss Popular' these days. Even her own brothers were wary of her. Except for Michael, of course.

She laid her arms on the top of the desk and rested her head on them. What she would really like to do now was walk out of this office, out of this club, and in to her car. Then she would like to drive and drive and drive until she arrived somewhere where no one knew her and she could be exactly what she really was – a twenty-five-year-old girl. Not woman . . . girl.

She was startled to hear the door opening. It was another of the hostesses, a very young girl by the name of Candy. Whether or not that was her real name was debatable. She was carrying a cup of coffee. Maura sat up in her chair and tried to smile at her.

'I thought you looked as if you could do with this, Miss Ryan.' She placed the coffee on Maura's desk. Maura could smell the aroma of whisky. As if reading her mind, Candy smiled.

'It's an Irish coffee. A very strong Irish coffee.'

Maura smiled, her first real smile for days. 'Thanks, Candy.'

Candy sat in the chair vacated by Monique. She was a natural blonde, her hair lighter than Maura's which was unusual as Maura's was nearly white. Candy's was a silver blond and she had the most amazing brown eyes. It was a startling combination. A few weeks earlier, all the hostesses had put in five pounds each and Candy had shown every one of them her pubic hair. It was exactly the same colour as the hair on her head. She had stopped all the arguments about herself, and made herself nearly a hundred pounds richer.

The girl hitched up her strapless dress. The movement seemed to accentuate her childishness.

'You look right done in, Miss Ryan.'

'I feel it actually, Candy.'

The girl sniffed loudly. 'I wanted to see you about something personal.'

Maura sipped the steaming and fragrant coffee and lifted her eyebrows in an invitation for the girl to continue.

'A bloke was hanging around outside the club earlier.'

'What was he – a pimp?' Maura sounded bored. This was the last thing she wanted even to think about. Let alone *do* something about.

Candy shook her head. 'Oh, no. He was nothing like that. He was a policeman.'

'A what!'

'An old Bill. You know, lily law.' Candy laughed.

'What was he asking about? The night of the bombing? What?' Her voice was anxious.

Candy relaxed into her seat. 'No, nothing like that, Miss Ryan. He was asking about you.'

Maura's mouth dropped open. 'Me?'

'Yes, you. He gave me this to give to you.' Candy took a slip of paper from between her boobs. 'He asked me if you would be in tonight. I said I didn't know and then he offered me twenty quid to deliver that to you. So I did. I hope I haven't done anything wrong?'

Maura's eyes were devouring the words on the piece of paper. 'No . . . No, Candy. You were right to take the message.'

She got up from her desk and, picking up her bag, slipped the note inside. Then she took out her purse and gave Candy three twenty-pound notes.

'Oh no, Miss Ryan, I couldn't. The bloke gave me a score.'

Maura pushed the notes into the girl's hands. 'You take it, Candy. You did very well tonight.'

Candy took the proffered money and smiled craftily. 'Well, if you're sure . . .'

Maura laughed out loud. She could feel the adrenaline pulsing through her body.

Candy stood up too and Maura did something that would make her a friend for life. She hugged the girl.

'Candy, can I trust you never to tell anyone about this?'

She put her hand gently on Maura's arm. 'Look, Miss Ryan, I don't know what was in that note. I didn't read it. And I'm not a grass. You've been good to me and if I can repay you somehow, I will.'

'Thanks, Candy. I appreciate it.'

Candy smiled and went back downstairs. She liked Maura Ryan. Whatever anyone said about her, she looked after the girls. And Candy, being honest in her own way, admitted that she would not get very far without her. It would be back to a pimp and either Park Lane or, when her looks went, King's Cross. At least at Le Buxom she had the chance to get herself a little stake. And for that she would be eternally grateful.

When Candy left the room Maura snatched the note from her bag. It was from Terry Petherick! She could not believe it! She read it again.

'IF EVER YOU NEED ME, CALL THIS NUMBER. LOVE, TERRY.'

Underneath was his phone number. Maura was ecstatic. He *did* still want her. Otherwise why would he bother to send her a note? She hugged the scrap of paper to her. Terry had put himself on the line to get this message to her. It crossed her mind that it was some kind of frame up but she had felt the attraction between them. And if nothing could ever come of it, at least she would always have the satisfaction of knowing that he had still wanted her, whatever she had done, because he must know everything that had transpired over the last few weeks. She sat back in her seat and drank the now stone cold coffee. The whisky bit into her taste buds and suddenly she realised that she was starving. She'd pack up here for the night and go home. Home to her own house. Not Michael's flat.

She felt as if she was on a high. Monique, the reaction of her brothers to her in the Crown and Two Chairmen pub, Benny, Sammy, Jonny, Janine – all was wiped from her mind for a few precious moments as she thought about Terry. She wrote a note to Michael saying she would see him in the morning and, humming to herself, got her stuff ready to go home.

She sat on the edge of her desk and stared at the telephone. She glanced at her watch. It was twelve-fifteen. Was it too late to ring? She opened up the slip of paper and stared at the words. 'Love, Terry' seemed to leap off the paper. Love . . . She picked up the phone and dialled the number. Her mouth was dry and she felt lightheaded. Supposing he was asleep or had company? Her heart dropped a little at that thought. Then, before she knew it, she could hear his voice.

'Hello? Who is this? Is that you, Maura?'

His voice was soft and as he said her name she could hear the yearning that she was experiencing herself.

She swallowed heavily.

'Terry.'

She heard the relief in his voice. 'It *is* you.'

The line went quiet as each tried to think what to say.

'I want to see you, Maura.' Terry sounded unsure of himself. 'I mean, if you want to see me, of course.'

'I was just going home. To my house. I just got the message.'

'Can I come to your house, Maura?' His voice was pleading.

'I'll give you the address.' She could barely talk.

'I know the address. I'll meet you there soon!' His voice had a jubilant ring to it that made her heart lurch in her chest.

She laughed. The ice had broken into a thousand pieces.

'Of course. You're a policeman – you would know my address.'

'Naturally.' She could practically see his little lopsided grin, could hear it in his voice.

'See you soon then.' She replaced the receiver and shivered with delight. She was hungry again. Only this time it wasn't for food.

Terry Petherick was staring at the telephone in his hand. She had rung! He wasn't wrong. She still wanted him as much as he still wanted her! He picked up his car keys and jacket and literally ran from his flat. He leapt into his car, a Ford Escort, and began the journey to Rainham. To Maura's house.

He had found himself driving to Dean Street earlier that evening, hoping for a glimpse of Maura. That was all. He had experienced an all-consuming passion for weeks just to look at her. Ever since he had seen her the night of the bombing, it had been like stepping back through a doorway, into another world. There had been women over the years but never any who affected him like Maura Ryan.

Every warning bell in his body was clanging and jangling at this moment, but he did not care. All he was really sure of was the fact that he had to see her. Touch her. Feel her. Even knowing what she had done – that she had been an accessory to murder. The attraction that had been between them from the start was still there like a shining beacon. He put his foot on the accelerator and whizzed through the icy streets towards her and all that she promised. For once in his life he was acting on impulse, and he was loving every moment of it. He felt alive. Really alive. And it felt good.

Maura pulled into her drive and sat in the car for a few minutes. She could feel her own nervousness and savoured every second of it. She looked at the large house sitting in ghostly darkness and for the very first time was glad to be home . . . and glad that Carla was not there. She had never been with a man since Terry, had gradually suppressed all her feelings, both sexual and romantic, concentrating on her work and Carla. And now her senses were filling her up, overflowing from her body, like the bursting of a great dam.

She got out of her car and went into her house. Her daily woman, Mrs MacMullen, had been in and as usual had left the central heating on low. The house was warm and inviting. Maura ran up the stairs like a young schoolgirl getting ready for her first date. She threw off her clothes and stepped into the shower, scrubbing her body until it glowed pink.

When she finally heard Terry's car she was in her lounge in a white silk dressing gown, sipping a glass of red wine. As she heard his footsteps crunch on the gravelled driveway she felt an intense euphoria flood her body. He had come. He had really come for her. She went into her hall and opened the front door.

She noticed that he was breathing as heavily as she. And then, without a word spoken, she was being kissed. And it was all so natural, as it should have been. How it once had been. He was kissing her face, her eyes, her neck. Taking his hand, she led him slowly up the stairs and into her bedroom.

They faced one another in the soft light from bedside lamps. She stared deeply into his eyes and saw mirrored in them her own feelings of love and desire. She began to unbutton his shirt and as she pulled it from him saw the broad shoulders, the tightly muscled arms, and felt new again, as she had the first time they had made love. He opened his trousers and showed her he was hard. She traced the outline of his erection with her fingers, softly and tantalisingly. She was feeling the woman heat between her legs and the tightening of her nipples. He was naked and she watched him, fascinated, as he stood before her, proud and strong. He opened the cord of her dressing gown and she stood, quivering with excitement and longing.

She saw his eyes roaming over her body and wanted him then, more than she had ever wanted anyone or anything in her life. He pushed her backwards gently on to the bed and kissed her body, little biting kisses that were hurtful and so erotic. He tasted the muskiness of her and felt the heady delight that he had thought was gone for ever. He pushed her legs up to her shoulders until she was full open to him – like a ripe pink peach. She watched him enter her with one deep thrust, and she groaned like an animal. Together they moved in perfect unison.

She matched his strokes with hard thrusts of her hips against him. She could feel the mounting excitement as she reached her orgasm and heard herself moaning and panting, begging him to thrust deeper. She could feel the droplets of sweat from his body dripping on to hers and gripped him with her legs, drawing him inside her, deeper and deeper, until she thought that she would die of pleasure. Their slippery bodies thrashed wildly as they reached orgasm. She could feel his hand squeezing her breast so hard that she cried out.

Then they lay, spent and replete, their hearts thudding against each other's chests. They lay tangled together for long quiet minutes, savouring the familiar feel of one another after so long an absence. Finally Terry leant on his elbow and kissed her gently on her swollen lips, and she looked at his face – the face that had alternately haunted and drawn her for nearly nine years – and smiled.

'It's been so long.' Her voice was so low as to be virtually inaudible.

'Too long, Maura. Much too long.'

They lay together until their bodies became still and the passion that had encompassed them had drained away. He kissed her again, staring down at her as if he wanted to devour her. His eyes drank in every feature and his brain filed them away, never to be forgotten. And she did the same, lying there. They were both aware that it was only a temporary love affair. That in the cold light of day they would have to part, each going back to their different world which neither would ever be able to leave. But this was never said. What they had at this moment was enough for them. And if they had to part, they would at least have had this night.

Terry gathered her to him and locked her into his embrace. 'I never meant to hurt you, you know. I swear.'

Maura spoke softly. 'I know, Terry.' She should tell him about the baby now. It was the perfect opening. But she could not. She would never, ever tell him about it. A lone tear slipped from her eye as she looked at him and he licked it away with his tongue. She would not tell him about their child as he would not talk about what Michael had had done to him. It was like a silent agreement, an unspoken treaty. So they lay together, speaking the love words that came so naturally to their lips. And then they loved again. Not the wild thrashings of before but a long, slow, leisurely loving that left them both breathless and satiated. Then all too soon it was the morning and they could delay their parting no longer.

'Come on. I'll make you some breakfast.' She pulled on her dressing gown and went to the kitchen. The birds were singing in the early morning light and Maura wished that the day would never come. That they could keep the night for ever. She heard him whistling as he showered and felt an urge to cry out. Against God. Against fate. And against injustice.

She took a loaf of bread from her freezer and made toast. She had just finished scrambling the eggs when he came into the kitchen, his hair still wet from the shower. She gave him a cup of coffee and placed his breakfast in front of him.

'You never cooked me breakfast before.'

'I was never allowed to stay out all night in those days.' She made her voice light.

He smiled. 'What are we going to do, Maura?' The words were like a physical blow. They both knew that there was nothing they could do.

She sat at the table opposite him.

'What happened last night was beautiful, Terry, but we must accept it for what it was – a beautiful interlude from our lives. Our real lives. Tomorrow is a new year . . . 1976 . . . and you will go back to your policing while I will go back to being Maura Ryan.' She smiled sadly. 'Please don't let's spoil it with might have beens and halfhearted promises. We live in different worlds, you and I. Worlds that can never be united.' Her voice broke.

Terry knew that she was right, and he loved her all the more for her honesty. Too much had happened over the years. And she was more of a woman in his eyes for what she had just said than any so-called Earth Mother would ever be.

They ate breakfast together, both acutely aware of the sky gradually becoming lighter outside the kitchen window. They chatted about nothing, little inconsequential things that stopped them thinking or talking about the big things. The real things. The real world. Finally Terry got up from his chair, and Maura knew that the parting had come.

'Can't we meet sometimes, Maura?'

She shook her head sadly. 'No, Terry. It's best we leave things as they are. There's no future for us.'

'Will you come to the door with me?' She could hear the tears in his voice. She shook her head.

'No. You go. I'll sit here. I don't want to see you driving away from me.'

'Oh, Maws.' He was kneeling in front of her, holding her so tight she could barely breathe. 'I can't go, Maura. I can't leave you like this.'

She kissed the top of his head. 'Go. Go on. Don't make this harder than it already is.' She cupped his face in her hands for the last time.

'I love you, Terry Petherick. God help me, I'll always love you.'

'I know. I love you too.'

She pushed him away from her. She had read so many times the phrase 'their hearts were breaking', and now she found out that it was true. Your heart could break and it was an intense physical pain that made you want to scream out, a deep roaring scream, from the depths of your body.

She sat at the table and it was as if her senses had been magnified a thousand million times. She heard his footfalls on the thick carpet. The sound of the front door closing behind him was like a deafening crash. And finally she heard his car start up. Then she listened to it driving away.

Away from her . . . and back to his real life.

It was over. The night was finished and real life had begun again. But she would carry the memory of it with her to her grave. She cried, a loud, noisy cry that was all the more wrenching because it sounded so lonely.

Terry drove home to his flat in Hampstead. He drove slowly, not in the reckless way he had driven the night before. Leaving Maura had been the hardest thing he had ever done in his life, but he knew that she was right. That she was stronger than him. Much stronger. And he guessed, correctly, that she was much lonelier. But whatever she was, he loved her.

Chapter Twenty-One

It was the third of January and Maura and Michael were driving to Lord Templeton's office. Maura still had the glow of love-making on her, despite the tears afterwards. In the last few days she had somehow resigned herself to being without Terry, to being without any man, though the thrill of the sexual encounter was still vivid in her mind and body. Michael was discussing what had happened between Maura and Janine.

'Calm down, Maws, for Christ's sake. After what happened to Benny, you can't blame her for getting a bit shirty. Janine's what's known as a shitter. And there's plenty of them about, believe me.'

'It's not that, Mickey. But the fact that Roy was a Ryan is what attracted her in the first place. She was after a bit of rough and then she came unstuck. Look at how she dumped Carla! Now Roy, who's turned out to be a bloody good provider, is in a bit of schtuck, she wants him to become a bloody bank clerk or something! It's laughable.'

'Then laugh! I know that our Roy would no more

leave this firm than he would cut his own throat. Stick him back in the bookies, that should shut Madam up for a while.' He grinned. 'I wonder what she'll say when she finds our Roy wants us to be godparents? That should go down about as well as a pork chop in a synagogue!'

Maura laughed, a harsh bitter laugh.

'What a start to the New Year. Benny dead. Mother treating us as if we've contracted bubonic plague, the old man permanently pissed . . .'

'Stop talking crap, Maura.' Michael's voice was sharp as glass. 'What happened to Benny was an occupational hazard. It could have been any of us. You, me, any of us. That's the chance we take in our line of . . .'

He paused as if looking for a word. Maura finished the sentence for him.

'Business!'

He grinned. 'That's it, Maws! Business. All we can do now is go on from here. We can't bring Benny back no more than we could Antney. Concentrate on Templeton. He's the goose that's gonna lay our golden eggs. Only he don't know that yet!' He laughed again.

'You were dead right about the docklands, I can see that now, Maws. He offered Dopolis the East End bait. What Lord Willy was after was the warehouses and the old Dockers' Mansions.

'I know this much, girl. He's gonna need muscle. Plenty of muscle. And we have that in abundance. That's our strength.'

She nodded absently.

'I'm telling you, Maura, 1976 is going to be *our* year.'

She looked out at the cold, dirty London streets and sighed. 'I hope so. God, I hope so.'

*

Lord Templeton stepped out of his limousine. His chauffeur held the door open for him and Templeton walked past him as if he was invisible, as he did every day. He walked with his confident stride up the flight of steps that led into the main reception area of his building in Park Lane. His liveried doorman saluted him and he acknowledged the man with a minute nod of his head. His personal secretary, David Manners, followed him, practically running to keep up. He had a detailed list of Templeton's appointments for the day.

Templeton strode purposefully into the large reception area and, just for a second, his step faltered. Standing beside his personal lift were Michael and Maura Ryan. Swallowing deeply, he glanced around him. The staff milling about were staring at him curiously. Pulling himself together, he plastered a broad smile on to his face and carried on walking to his lift.

He concentrated his attention on Maura. He was surprised at how lovely she was. She looked like a deb in her light beige Chanel suit with its black piping. Her hair, freshly washed, glistened in the artificial light. He took in everything about her from the kidskin boots to the silk scarf wrapped carelessly across her shoulders and held there with a gold and diamond tiger brooch. Against his will he was impressed. She was exquisite.

As for the man standing beside her, he was probably the most outstandingly handsome man Templeton was ever likely to see. Michael also was dressed in impeccable taste. Templeton felt that sickening feeling that precedes a fall from a high place. Never in all his life had he been intimidated. Now that he was experiencing it, he decided he did not like it one bit. He carried on walking towards them, and with every step that took him closer felt more scared, more nervous.

Maura smiled as he approached them and held out her hand. 'So pleased to meet you at last, Lord William. My brother and I have been so looking forward to it.' Her voice held no trace of its usual cockney accent.

Her words reassured Templeton slightly and he smiled back at her, showing perfect white teeth.

'Delighted, my dear. If I had known how lovely you were, I would have made sure we met much sooner.'

He turned his attention to Michael, amazed at just how big he was – almost a foot taller than himself. Michael shook his hand without speaking, his hard eyes telling Templeton exactly how the land lay.

His lift door opened and he ushered them both inside, waving David Manners away imperiously.

'I'll send for you, David, when I need you.'

Manners nodded. There was something funny going on here, he knew that much.

The old man who worked the lift gave Maura an appraising stare.

They made their brief journey in silence. Maura watched Templeton's face. She knew that he was frightened but had to admit to herself that for all that she liked the look of him. He was angular-looking: pointed nose, pointed cheekbones, and even pointed ears. He had a mass of sandy brown hair that, she guessed, was difficult to tame. It seemed to give him a slight air of vulnerability. He had very deep brown eyes, and thin sparse eyebrows like most sandy-haired people. It was his mouth that attracted her. It was not very big for a man, but it was strong. It could have been due to his very angular jawline. Whatever it was, she liked it. She only hoped they could all come out of this place today with a degree of accord.

The lift doors opened and they all stepped out into a wealth of mahogany. The walls were panelled, the only furniture a large mahogany desk and two leather-covered wing chairs. Behind the desk sat a young woman, the standard secretary to a rich man. She was very attractive in a subdued way. Maura could picture her unpinning her luxuriant black hair one day and turning into a femme fatale. She put her hand to her mouth to stop herself giggling. She had to try to control the weird things that kept invading her mind.

By the secretary's desk were two large double doors. Templeton opened these and led them into his office. Michael looked around him contemptuously. Like the room outside this also was a shrine to wood. Once more it had panelled walls, but in here they were adorned with a few well-chosen and, Michael guessed, very expensive sporting paintings. He was not aware that the largest, of a beautiful dark horse, was in fact a Stubbs. The floor was covered in the same deep grey carpet as the ante room. There was another, much larger mahogany desk. Along the right- and left-hand walls were two large Chesterfields, black and gleaming, as if just taken from their protective wrappings and never yet sat upon. In front of the desk were two more wing armchairs. Maura sat in one and Michael in the other.

Templeton went to the double doors and told his secretary to bring in some refreshments. He then walked nervously to his own chair behind the desk. As he reached it he stumbled and had to grab the desk to right himself. Eventually he sat down. His chair was much higher than the two opposite; an American designer had once told him that it would give him a psychological advantage.

Obviously the designer had never met anyone like the Ryans. He put his hands together as if in prayer.

'What can I do for you?' He was embarrassed to find that his voice sounded cracked and high. It was Maura who answered him.

'I think you already know the answer to that, Lord William.' She made his name sound ridiculous. Her voice had hardened now they were alone and once again he was reminded of how dangerous these people were. He was saved from answering by his secretary who came in wheeling a trolley, also mahogany. Michael was beginning to wonder if the man was a wood fetishist. The trolley held not only coffee and tea but also toast, muffins, jam and honey.

'Would you like me to serve, sir?' The girl smiled, watching Michael from the corner of her eye.

'Just leave it, Marie.' Templeton's voice was brisk. The girl nodded and slowly left the room, shutting the double doors behind her.

Maura pulled off her kidskin gloves and placed them on the floor with her bag.

'Fancy a cuppa, Mickey?'

Michael nodded and Maura poured three cups of tea, as if they were at a tea party. She handed one to Michael who spoke for the first time, his voice as rough as concrete.

'Well, this is nice, I must say. My little brother Benny used to love a cup of Rosie in the mornings. Said it made him crap.' He looked directly at Templeton, causing the hairs on the back of his neck to rise.

'Crapped regular did our Benny. Seven o'clock every morning. Did he crap himself while he was being murdered? I understand you know all about it.' Michael's voice was matter-of-fact.

William Templeton felt sick. The cup of tea that Maura had handed him was rattling in its saucer. He was shaking from head to foot. Maura put down her own cup and, going to him, removed the cup and saucer from his grasp.

'What do you want?'

Michael sipped his tea and said: 'What we want is a little bastard called Dopolis. I think that you know where we can find him. I want to question him personally about my brother's death.' He smiled at Templeton. 'The police are looking for Benny's murderer as well, you know. Why don't you give them a ring? Ask them about me, Michael Ryan. Ask them about my temper.' He was talking in a conversational way, and somehow it made his words more frightening. 'My temper's a legend in London, ain't it, Maws?' She nodded. 'I once rammed a Rolls-Royce because I thought the driver had given me a dirty look. Wrote off a brand new Merc doing it. But, you see, my temper is atrocious.' He leant towards Templeton. 'It's just like the wrath of God. Only in London, I *am* God.'

'I had nothing to do with your brother's death. I swear it!' Templeton was aware that he was babbling.

'Then you won't mind telling us where Dopolis is, will you?'

'I have no idea.'

Maura shook her head as if looking at a naughty child. 'I don't think you realise what you're dealing with here. We . . .' she gestured with her hand towards Michael '. . . are like terminal cancer. We'll get you in the end, so you might as well save yourself unnecessary grief. You've already made us very angry and that's dangerous. Now, I'll give you one last chance. Where can we find Dopolis?'

Templeton was rooted to his chair. His eyes darted around the room as if looking for some kind of divine intervention from behind the panelling. He had thought he was dealing with illiterate fools. But no. The so-called fools had tracked him down and cornered him on his own territory. All he could do now was extricate himself as best he could.

'He lives in Surrey.' He scribbled the address on to the pad in front of him and practically threw it across the table at Michael. Please God, he prayed, make them go away now. If you do this for me, I swear that I will be a good man from now on. Like many a man before him, he was praying as a last resort.

Michael picked up the scrap of paper and stood up. 'Right then, I'm off. I'll leave you in my sister's capable hands. She can explain to you all about the partnership.'

'Partnership?' Templeton was flabbergasted.

Michael laughed. 'Catches on quick, does old Willy. The partnership between us. Me, her, and lastly you.' He pointed towards Templeton. 'Oh, and before I forget, I'll be calling you Willy. Lord William's a bit too much of a gobful, ain't it? You, though, will call me Mr Ryan. If – but only if, mind – I get to like you, I might let you call me Mickey.' He laughed again. 'Give you something to look forward to, won't it?'

'There's just one last thing before I go. Don't get Harry Dash – that's flash to you – with my sister here. Whatever she says, you do it. Get that?'

Templeton stared at him.

Michael shouted: 'I said, GET IT?'

'Yes!'

'There's a good boy. Well, cheery bye, or whatever you big nobs say.'

Kissing Maura on the cheek, he left the room. Templeton stared at the doorway as if he had never seen it before.

Maura poured herself another cup of tea. 'Right then, shall we get down to business?'

She felt a bit sorry for the man in front of her. After her night with Terry and the hurt she felt at their parting, she found room in her heart for pity. She took a deep breath and started on what had long been her favourite subject: docklands.

'We know you were really after our properties in Tobacco Dock and similar areas. I happen to know you also have properties there. The idea is that we pool resources. I realise that you have more of an insider's knowledge of what's going on there. Between us we could sew that place up. Once the work starts, we can guarantee the labour and that there will be no delays of any kind. We "own" just about every major contractor in the South East. If push ever came to shove we could stop work there from ever beginning, and I know you wouldn't want that to happen. We're willing to let our brother's death go as far as you are concerned. Dopolis will pay for that. You can either come in with us or sink. It's your choice.'

She picked up her cup and drank her tea. William Templeton was dumbfounded. He was being threatened by a woman! And a working-class woman at that. And these yobs wanted to go into partnership with *him*! If it wasn't so scary he would laugh. He was all for cads and bounders – as long as one kept to one's own class. But to be associated with Michael Ryan! It was unbelievable.

Dopolis had turned out to be a bigger mistake than he had first thought. Now he would *have* to get involved with the Ryans, whether he liked it or not. His idea of getting the Greek to start a gang war seemed stupid now that he had met the real McCoy. He admitted to himself that he had been a damn' fool. His belief that the working class was a bunch of mindless dunderheads had proved fatally wrong. It seemed he was the dunderhead at this moment.

'Well, what's it to be? I haven't got all day.'

Templeton grimaced. 'I don't really seem to have much choice, do I?'

Maura smiled at him. A real smile that made her look very young and very pretty.

'Believe me, Lord William, when I say that you saw the nice side of Michael today. Unless you'd lived our kind of life, you could not hope for one minute to be able to understand us. I would ask you, though, to treat us with the same respect as you would any business associates. You will find that you deal mainly with me. I run the property side of our businesses. What I'm hoping to learn from you is the redevelopment business. It is my fervent wish that my family should find a good respectable outlet to channel money into.'

Grudgingly, Templeton admitted that he could like this girl. She was at least sincere. He shrugged his shoulders at the inevitable. He knew that he had to deal with the Ryans whether he liked it or not. There was no way out. He was caught up in a spider's web, and like the fly knew he would eventually give up struggling.

'The development business is not really respectable, Miss Ryan. In fact, it can be very dirty.'

Maura interrupted him, laughing.

'I think you misunderstand me, Lord William! What I mean by respectable is that, although it may be illegal and at times dirty, it is socially acceptable. Like adultery. If you want my honest opinion, I think you and your kind are the biggest bunch of hypocrites I have ever had the misfortune to come across.' She took a cigarette from the packet she had placed in front of her and lit it, blowing the smoke across the desk into his face.

'You frown on Mr Working Class for having a little flutter. Yet the Stock Exchange gambles daily with millions of pounds. Banks do it, and building societies. And let's face it, it's not even their money they're using. But there you are. The double standard prevails. One set of rules for the Hooray Henrys and another for Mr Joe Public. Well, let me tell you something. I may not have a family tree like yours, or be that articulate in my grammar, but there's one thing I *have* got going for me – I have money. Plenty of it. And with the kind of money I have, every door can be opened. Even the Royal Enclosure at Ascot. That's how we found you out. You broke the golden rule of villainy, Lord William. You let the world in on what you were doing. A fatal mistake.'

A light seemed to go on behind Templeton's eyes and Maura could not help grinning at him.

'Let me guess. You couldn't resist showing off to him, am I right? Well, that little faux pas on your part led us straight to your door. Whereas me and my brothers – Michael especially – our faces are slapped across the *News of the World* at least once a month, but they can't prove anything. It's all supposition. Now you,' she pointed at him with her cigarette, 'are going to be our Mr Legit. I want you to tell me exactly what's going to happen to the old docks.'

Templeton stared at Maura for a few seconds. He knew that all she had said was right.

'Maura . . . may I call you Maura?'

'Of course.'

'I think that you and I could do business together. I have a feeling we could even be friends.'

She smiled at him and breathed a sigh of relief. She made a conscious decision to prove to him that she was as good as, if not better than, anyone he had done business with before.

'Seeing as we have you by the bollocks, as my brother would term it, I don't see why we can't be friends. Now, about the docks.'

She was being deliberately crude. She wanted his friendship, but she also wanted his co-operation and until she was certain she had that, she would continue to remind him just who he was dealing with.

Templeton pressed the button of the intercom on his desk.

'Yes, sir?' The sweet voice of Marie crackled into the room.

'Hold all my calls and bring in some fresh tea.'

'But, sir! You have an appointment in ten minutes to see the Secretary of State for the Environment!'

'Then you'll just have to tell him that I am in an urgent meeting.' He cut off the connection.

Maura raised her eyebrows at him and he was amazed to hear himself laugh. He had taken rather a fancy to the girl. Opening a drawer in his desk, he brought out a folder. He opened it and took out some papers and a map. He passed this to Maura. While she studied it, Marie brought in some more tea and removed the large trolley. Her face was set in a frown. This time she banged the door shut behind her.

'Well, Maura, I will tell you all that I know. This,' he swept his hand across the papers in front of him, 'has been discussed behind closed doors for some time. As you so astutely pointed out, there's a lot of money to be made there. In 1967 the East India Dock closed. In '68 the

London Docks. In '69 Katherine Dock, and in '70 Surrey Docks. All we are waiting for is the eventual closure of Millwall, and the Royal Victoria and Albert. That is when it will all start to happen.'

'So the other docks will eventually close?' Maura kept her voice neutral. In fact, she was flabbergasted.

'Oh, yes. Within the next five years. That's why no money's going in there. The more rundown and depressed the area gets, the more we can justify reclaiming the land. Job creation et cetera.' He smiled at her. 'I am afraid that we live in a world where the masses are spoonfed bullshit, if you will forgive the expression. The average man on the street buys the *Sun* to look at a pair of breasts. In reality, he's reading Tory propaganda. Whoever is in office at the time all this begins, be it Tory, Labour or, God help us, Screaming Lord Sutch, will be jumping on the band-wagon. Funding it, giving out grants. "We'll give you money to make money" . . . that's every government's policy. Personally, I think it will be the Conservatives, but I'm not worried either way. This has been sewn up for a long time. Now, drink your tea while it's hot and I'll explain to you more fully. I think you will find it fascinating.'

She and William Templeton smiled at one another. Maura shook her head slowly and said, 'And they have the nerve to call *us* villains!'

In 1976 the Docklands Joint Committee published the London Dockland Strategic Plan. The Ryans and Lord Templeton were on their way.

Book Three

THE DOWNFALL

It is a strange desire to seek power and to lose liberty

– Francis Bacon, 1561–1626

What will you give me, and I will deliver him unto you?
And they convenanted with him for thirty pieces of silver

– Matthew, 26:15

Chapter Twenty-Two

12 February 1985

Geoffrey Ryan parked outside Le Buxom. It was not yet nine o'clock in the morning. He picked up his briefcase from the passenger seat of his dark blue BMW, locked up his car and went into the club. The cleaners all greeted him. In 1980, a restaurant had been opened in what had been the basement. This meant that the club was open nearly twenty-four hours of the day. He went down there to discuss the day's menu with Peter Petrillo, the head chef, who had finished a ten-year stretch in Parkhurst then been given the job by Michael Ryan.

Geoffrey looked over the menu briefly and nodded his head, as he did every day. Then he ordered coffee and went up to his offices. He lit a cigarette and, settling himself into his chair, began his work for the day, going over the figures for the clubs and wine bars – a new acquisition of Maura's to cash in on the yuppie boom. When he opened a drawer to get his calculator, he saw it was missing: Michael had been in and taken it again.

Putting his cigarette out, he pulled himself from his seat and made his way to Michael's office next door.

Although Geoffrey had the larger office, most of the business was done by Michael and Maura from the smaller office. He knew deep inside that they had given him the larger office to placate him. Also, the smaller office was always referred to as Michael's office when in reality it was Michael's and Maura's.

He frowned as he walked through the door. He never came in here unless he absolutely had to. The room was empty. He looked on the large desk for his calculator, moving papers and files haphazardly. As he turned away he noticed that the small filing cabinet was unlocked, the keys still in the lock but the top drawer slightly open. He shook his head. Walking to it he pushed the drawer shut and was about to lock it when he stopped dead. Biting his lip he pulled the drawer back open. This was the one place he and the others were barred from. Only Michael and Maura had access to it. Now by some twist of fate it was open to him and he was torn between a desire to know what was in there that was so private and fear that he'd be caught looking. He decided to take his chances. Checking the corridor outside, he shut the door quietly and went back to the filing cabinet. He pulled out one of the files and began to read it. After a few minutes he forgot his fear of Michael and Maura, and took the file back to his office. A deep rage grew inside him as he realised just what he had stumbled across.

Maura and Leslie were in Brixton. They pulled up outside a block of flats. Leslie got out of the car and opened the door to let Maura out. Having locked the car, he followed her up the filthy stairs that led into the block of flats. They were low rise flats, only two storeys. Maura walked along the balcony until she came to No. 28. She knocked on the front door, which was opened by a little girl of about eight. The child was half caste and, Maura noticed, extremely thin and emaciated.

'We're looking for Jackie Traverna's house. Is this it?' Maura's voice was friendly and kind.

'Yeah. But she's in bed.'

'I think she will see me. Just take me to her, my love.' Maura's voice sounded false, even to her own ears. She had lost the knack of talking to children.

The child shrugged her skinny shoulders. As if to say, who cares? Maura followed her up a dark narrow hallway and into a small bedroom. The place was messy, the bedroom entirely taken up by a large double bed, though Maura guessed that when Jackie was on her feet she kept it clean and tidy. In the giant bed lay Jackie herself. Her coffee-coloured skin was shining with a film of sweat.

Maura gasped when she saw her. 'Leslie! Get in here.'

He ran in the room thinking that Maura had come across some kind of trouble.

'Fucking hell!' His voice was shocked.

In the bed lay Jackie, recognisable only by her wiry Afro hair. Her face was so swollen she looked as if she had been attacked by bees. On each of her cheeks was a large stripe which went from the corner of her mouth to rise up until it disappeared into her hairline. Jackie looked up with sad eyes.

'Maura.' Her voice was muffled.

'All right, Jackie. All right, mate. Who did this? Was it Rubens . . . Danny Rubens?'

Jackie nodded her head, fear in her eyes.

'Don't worry now. I'm going to see you're looked after.'

'Thanks. Can't . . . speak.' The woman could barely move.

'I know. I know. I'll be back later. All right?'

She smiled at Jackie, but inside she was fuming. 'Come on, Leslie. Get your arse in gear.'

Once they were back inside the car, Maura lit herself a cigarette and said, 'Pick up Lee and Garry. We're going to pay Rubens a little visit.'

Geoffrey had been reading the file for about an hour. He was still reading it when Michael came into his office. Geoffrey looked up at him, the hurt in his eyes almost a tangible thing. Michael saw the green folder and tried to play for time.

'Any more coffee going, Geoff?'

Geoffrey ignored him. Picking up the folder, he threw it across the desk.

'Thanks a lot, Bruv.' His voice was flat.

Michael sighed. 'For Christ's sake, Geoff. You're not my keeper, you know.'

Geoffrey lit another cigarette, his hands trembling.

'That's just it, though, ain't it, Mickey? I ain't nothing.'

'Look, Geoff, you know what they say. What you don't know, don't hurt you.'

Geoffrey pulled on his cigarette and let out the smoke through his nose, looking like a belligerent bull.

'You've mugged me off, ain't you?'

Mickey laughed. 'Come on, Geoff. I would have told you eventually. Why are you making such a big deal?'

Michael's voice was getting tight. He did not feel like all this today.

'I'll tell you why I'm making such a big deal, shall I? I've just read this crap.' He pointed to the green folder.

'And I realise just what I am in this firm. I run the clubs, sort of. I run the wine bars, sort of. I watch over the bookies and the cab ranks. While you and Maura – marvellous fucking Maura – do the *real* work.'

'Leave her out of this.' Michael's voice was hard and low.

Geoffrey stubbed out his cigarette. 'No, I won't leave her out of all this. She's the cause of it all. Since the day she came into this firm you've pushed me out.'

Geoffrey's voice was high and he knew it sounded hysterical, but he did not care. He had to get this thing sorted out, once and for all.

'You're talking crap and you know it, Geoffrey. Now give it a rest, for fuck's sake.'

Geoffrey began shouting, all caution gone now. 'No, I will not give it a rest! I read, by accident, that you are about to embark on the biggest gold robbery this country's ever known, and you have the nerve to stand there and tell me I would have been told eventually! And when was that gonna be? When it was in the papers or on the news? Just what kind of cunt do you take me for? What else has been going on behind my back, eh? Well, answer me then.'

Geoffrey had risen from his seat and stood in front of Michael who was a good three inches taller and at least two stone heavier. Both knew that if it came to blows, Michael would win hands down. Geoffrey did not care.

Michael tried once more to pacify him. 'Keep your voice down, Geoff. There's no need to let everyone know, is there?'

'I bet everyone *does* bloody know! Everyone except me, that is.' He prodded his chest. '*I've* stood by you through thick and thin, from day one. But since that fucking leech

Maura came on the scene, I've been pushed out. It's been you and Maura . . . Maura and Michael . . . the dynamic duo. Batman and Robin's got nothing on you two. She was shagging an old Bill and yet you treat her like visiting royalty.'

Michael's hand went up to Geoffrey's throat. He slipped his other hand around his brother's neck and squeezed.

'Let's get the violins out, shall we? Geoffrey's little heart is broken! You ponce! You disgust me.'

He hurled Geoffrey away from him and went to the window, running his hands through his hair.

Turning back, he thrust out a finger. 'I'll tell you why Maura has taken your so-called place, shall I? Because she's got more bollocks than you will ever have! You've been like a bloody albatross hanging around my neck all my life. I've had to carry you ever since we were kids.' Michael wiped his hand across his face, agitated and annoyed. 'If you'd been left to your own devices, you'd have been banged up years ago. And *you're* jealous of your own bloody sister because she has what it takes. She sussed all this out.' He gestured around him wildly. 'You couldn't organise the proverbial piss up, mate. You could never have figured half of what she has. You fucking wind me up! You always have done.'

He pointed at Geoffrey again, his face contorted with temper. 'Shall I tell you something? You're working here because Maura suggested it. If it had been left to me, I'd have had Gerry Jackson running this show, mate. I'd have dumped you years ago. But, no, Maura said: "Family first." I swallowed, but deep down in my heart I didn't give a toss.

'Now if you don't like it, you can piss off. But I tell you

this now. If you ever . . . ever . . . speak about her like that again, I'll bury you. Now do me a favour and fuck off before I really lose me rag.'

Geoffrey stared at Michael, dumbstruck. He could feel the waves of resentment coming out of every pore in Michael's body. He realised something he had known secretly for years, something he had never dared admit to himself before: he irritated Mickey. And yet he would have died for him. He was the only brother left who was not married or living with a girl. Even Michael had a regular boyfriend. He had lived his life for Michael.

He straightened himself up slowly and, picking up his jacket and car keys, walked from the office. As he came down the stairs into the foyer he realised that the cleaners had all stopped work. They had been listening to everything. He could feel his face burning with humiliation. He left the club and got into his car as if in a daze. That Michael could have spoken like that to him! He felt sick with the realisation of what had just happened. And with the fact that nothing could ever be the same between them again.

Maura and the three boys were at Danny Rubens' gaff, a terraced house in Tulse Hill. Lee banged on the front door hard. It was opened by a young girl who looked about seventeen. Though knowing Ruben's taste, Maura thought she was probably about fifteen, top whack.

'Is Danny about?' They pushed past the girl into the house.

'He ain't up yet. He don't get up before twelve.'

Garry smiled at her. 'Well, it'll be a nice change for him then, won't it?' They all began to walk up the stairs.

'Who is it, Estelle?' A deep brown voice bellowed the

words down the stairs. The four walked in its direction.

Maura and her brothers noticed that the house was very well decorated and very clean. Inside Danny's bedroom, Maura smiled at him.

'Well, well. You are a big boy, aren't you?' Danny Rubens was lying in bed naked. He pulled the duvet over himself. He was still half stoned from the previous evening but alert enough to know he had invited big trouble to his house.

'Shut the door, Garry. We don't want everyone hearing Danny's screams.'

Danny's big black face was sweating and his eyes were like dark brown pools in his head. His head was shaved and Maura could see a vein pulsing, just below his right eyebrow. He was scared, very scared, and that was just what she wanted. Danny Rubens had taken to body building while doing a three-year stretch for aggravated assault. He was enormous and that usually gave him the edge.

'What you want?'

Maura laughed. 'Cut the coon talk, Rubens, you've never been out of London in your life.'

Garry, Leslie and Lee guffawed at this. They knew how to play the game. Maura pulled the duvet from his body, leaving him naked and exposed.

'I'm here about a girl of mine – Jackie Traverna.'

'Ain't never heard of her.'

Maura opened her bag and lit one of her cigarettes. Every action was watched closely by Rubens. She puffed on her cigarette until the end glowed.

'I've been hearing stories about you, Rubens.' Maura pointed to her brothers. 'Hold him.'

Leslie and Lee went to the bed and, after a struggle,

held Danny Rubens down on it. Maura gestured to Garry. 'Hold his legs open for me.'

She drew the cigarette smoke into her lungs and watched impassively as Rubens tried to fight his way out of the situation. Finally he was lying spreadeagled on the bed. 'Now I want you to tell me why you striped up one of my girls.'

Rubens was absolutely terrified. His eyes were stretched to their utmost, showing all the yellow whiteness.

'I tell you, sis, I ain't never done no harm to no black chick.'

Garry punched him in the face.

'If you ain't never heard of her, how do you know what colour she is?'

'I guessed, man. I guessed.'

'Oh, shut up, you black ponce.' This was Leslie. 'Let my sister speak.' His voice was slow and bored-sounding. Rubens thought he would wet himself with fright.

'I have heard, Mr Rubens,' Maura stressed the Mr, 'that you have some rather big ambitions. One being to become the Pimp Extraordinaire of the West End. I also hear that you are after some of my girls.'

She sat on the bed and opened her bag. Rubens was holding his head off the bed, straining his neck to see what was going on. He was naked and vulnerable and did not like it.

Maura took a snub-nosed .38 special from her handbag. Rubens' eyes were now like flying saucers.

'What you want with that!' He was nearly crying.

'My sister is going to blow your balls off, Danny. One by one.'

Leslie's voice was jocular.

Maura held the gun against Rubens' genitals. He could

feel the hard coldness of the steel against his skin. She rubbed it gently along the length of his penis and under his testicles. Rubbed it slowly, dreamily, as if she was enjoying it. Then she took another long drag of her cigarette. Rubens, who had been 'The Daddy' while he was in Durham jail, who had been working the streets nearly all his adult life and who could instil fear into most people, burst into tears. They ran from his eyes and down his face. Great bubbles of snot billowed out of his nose and his gigantic shoulders heaved.

'Please . . . don't shoot my cock off!' He sounded like a small boy.

Garry, Leslie and Lee were laughing again.

Maura put her cigarette butt on Rubens' stomach. He felt the burning through his tears. Maura left the cigarette on his belly, so the embers would scorch the skin slowly and painfully. He was howling in pain.

'Where's your Stanley knife, Danny?' Maura's voice was soft and gentle, as if they were lovers on a picnic.

'I swear . . . I swear to you I ain't got no Stanley knife.'

'Pain is a terrible thing, isn't it? Jackie Traverna was in pain, Danny, she was in such terrible pain.' Her voice hardened. 'Now it's your turn.' She nodded at Leslie who took a Stanley knife from the pocket of his jacket. He held it glinting over the man's face.

'What's it to be, Danny boy? Cheek or cock? It's up to you. But make your mind up quickly or I might just do both.'

Danny was staring at Leslie's face and knew he was not joking. He saw, even through his fear and his tears, that he had met with a will much stronger than his own.

'Please, man. Please.' His voice was just a croaky whisper.

'Face it is then!' Leslie grinned and pulled the Stanley knife from Danny's eye down to his mouth. He cut deeply and confidently. The blood came out slowly, as if not sure what it wanted to do as the layers of skin gradually unfolded. By the time he had repeated the action on the other side of the man's face, the blood was pumping out with each of his heartbeats. They all stood up as if of one mind. As his hands were released, Danny brought them up to his face. When he took them away, his palms were stained with deep crimson blood.

He screamed loudly, painfully, like a hare caught in a trap.

'Don't ever get ambitious for anything or anyone that belongs to me, Danny. Next time you might not be so lucky.'

'Oh, God, I'm bleeding! Help me somebody!' The white satin sheets on his bed were slowly being dyed red.

'Come on, boys. We've got a lot of work to do.'

As they left the room the young girl Estelle ran inside. When they left the house, her screams were even louder than Danny's.

Geoffrey was sitting in his flat. He had poured himself a large Scotch and was sitting on the sofa remembering every detail of his life with Michael. One memory stood out like a shining beacon. He gulped his Scotch as he remembered a day almost forty years earlier.

He had been just coming up eight, Michael nearly ten. It was during the war, and their father had dropped them both through a hole in the remains of a bombed-out house. Mickey, as usual, had no fear. He just put his torch on and shone it around the debris-strewn cellar. The occupants of the house were lying around like lumps of bloody red meat. The stench had been unbearable. Geoffrey could still remember the way he'd felt that day, rooted to the spot with fear. His father's voice had been coming from above, urging them to hurry up. Looting bombed houses was a serious criminal offence.

Michael dragged the body of a little girl off a tin petty cash box. She had been blown across it in the blast. He then passed this up to their father and quickly began collecting up anything that was useful, edible or saleable. He had gone about his work silently and quickly, calling softly to Geoffrey to help him move the body of a man. He had known it was a man by the clothes. The face had completely gone.

Geoffrey had found it impossible to move. Michael had gone to him and punched him in the stomach, winding him, urging him to hurry up and help him. Between them they dragged the man's heavy body on to the floor. Geoffrey had been crying by this time. Michael had stripped the man of his wallet and watch. Then he had gone to the woman who had been grotesquely thrown to the floor. Her legs were wide open and her arms and neck lay in positions that would have been impossible had she been alive. Michael took her brooch and her wedding ring. Geoffrey had heard the crunching click of her bone as he had broken her bent finger to remove it. Then their father had pulled them both out of the hole. He could still feel the sting of his father's belt later that night as he had been strapped for 'being a baby'.

From that day on he had tried to emulate his brother. He had joined him in beating people, robbing the bomb-sites, everything. In all truth, Geoffrey admitted to himself, he had hated every minute of it. And it dawned on him now that Michael knew this, had always known it, and that's why he despised him. In Maura, Michael had found a kindred spirit. Another loner. Another warped version of their father. He finished his glass of Scotch and sat back in his seat.

He couldn't join Mickey now, that much was obvious, but he would sure as hell beat him. And that bitch of a sister! He had the knowledge and he would sit and wait, and then one day he would use it. He saw once more the looks that had been on the cleaners' faces, and felt an urge to murder the pair of them.

Still, as his old dad used to say when they were small: 'Don't get mad. Get even.' That's just what he intended to do.

Maura and Michael were eating a late dinner in The Greek Revolution in Beauchamp Place. They had been discussing their day. They made a stunning pair. Even at thirty-five Maura was still as young-looking as ever. She dressed down, never wearing clothes that were in fashion but choosing plain and expensive classics, as only the very rich can. Her blond hair was longer now, cut into a long bob. It hung just below her jawline, framing her finely boned face. With her lightness, and Michael's dark good looks, they were the perfect foil for one another.

Even in his fifties, Michael was still a very attractive man. He dressed conservatively but well, sticking as he had always done to greys and blacks. Occasionally he wore something he termed 'ostentatious', but those times were few and far between.

'Well, I think Geoffrey's probably over his tantrum by now.' Maura sounded worried.

'Quite frankly, Maws, I don't give a shit. He winds me up.'

Maura was quiet for a moment. She had felt the tension building up between them for months. It truly amazed her that Michael, who was usually so perceptive about everything, failed to notice what was in front of his eyes. Geoffrey was jealous of her and she knew it. But now he was also jealous of Michael, and she had a gut feeling that Geoffrey could turn out to be quite dangerous.

Michael wiped his pitta bread around the plate, picking up the last of the tsatsiki, and popped the bread into his mouth. 'So, tell me. What are you going to do for Jackie Traverna?'

'Oh, I don't know, Michael. The poor bitch is in a terrible state. Give her some money, I suppose.'

Michael laughed. 'You're like a fucking social worker! I'd better keep a close eye on you, girl. Next thing I know you'll be giving all our cash away to the starving millions!'

Maura smiled, knowing that Michael was deliberately steering the conversation away from Geoffrey.

'Before I forget, Maws. Willy Templeton wants in on the gold plan. I said yeah. What do you reckon?'

'Why not?' She shrugged. 'He seems to be in on everything else.'

She picked up a prawn and pulled its head off. 'If that's what you want, Mickey. I'm easy.'

'He's doing a great job down at St Martin's Wharf. It's a funny thing, Maws, but having a lord on your side certainly helps matters along. Don't you think?'

His voice was cold and calculating.

'Of course it helps. It's like going to parties with famous people. Everyone's a starfucker at heart. Stars included. They love us because we're rough diamonds. Personally, I don't give a monkey's either way. I like Willy, though.'

And she did. She liked him very much and it was strange, because she knew that without him Benny would still be alive. Even knowing that, she still could not help liking and admiring him. He was what she had learned to term an 'educated villain'. Through William Templeton she had met many more like him – rich, educated men who pulled off brilliant scams. Scams that were never allowed to get into the newspapers or come to prosecution because the firms involved would lose their credibility on the Stock Market with disastrous economic and political results. Instead the wrongdoers were given enormous golden handshakes and a big party as a leaving present. And their pictures appeared in the papers with the sob story: 'Ill health brings the head of So and So corporation's career to an end.' 'I want to spend more time with my wife and family' was another favourite excuse. It was not only the big businessmen who were involved in these things, but politicians, judges . . . just about every profession had its fair share of con men. Gradually, through William Templeton, Maura and Michael were finding out exactly who they were. And they were learning a whole new ballgame.

The waiter brought their main course, kleftiko, and refilled their wine glasses. When he left them, Maura spoke.

'I want an early start tomorrow. I've finally sorted out the last few wrinkles in the gold plan. If everything looks OK to you, we can begin to set it all up.'

'I'll drink to that, Maws.' Michael picked up his glass of Chablis.

'Cheers.'

They touched glasses. If you did not know them you would think they were planning a party, not the biggest bullion robbery England had ever known.

*

While they were sitting in the restaurant, Danny Rubens was lying in hospital. He had been sedated heavily, but one of the nurses was intrigued. Because, although he was in a deep, drug-induced sleep, his hand was still holding on tightly to his genitals.

Chapter Twenty-Three

14 February 1985

Maura knocked on the door of Geoffrey's flat. He lived not far from Michael in Knightsbridge. She had been there only twice before. Even though they had worked together and were brother and sister, they had an accepted and unspoken agreement: I don't like you, so keep your distance. Up till now Maura had respected this.

Geoffrey opened the door. He seemed surprised to see her standing there. He looked terrible. He had not shaved for a couple of days, and being so dark-haired now had dark stubble around his jaw. Maura was shocked to see that it was tinged with grey.

He and Michael had been so alike all their lives, Geoffrey was like a watered-down version of his brother. He looked great, he was handsome, but when people saw Michael they seemed to overlook Geoffrey afterwards. Today he looked old and ill and Maura felt sorry for him. The lines around his eyes, so sexy on Michael, made Geoffrey look jaded and debauched. His dark hair, normally washed and gleaming, was greasy and lank. She watched him look her over from head to toe. It was a sneering look as if she was so much dirt.

'And what do you want?' His voice was belligerent. His face was close to hers and she could smell the sourness of the vast amount of Scotch he had been consuming since his fight with Michael.

'May I come in?' Her voice was neutral.

He held the door open and watched her pass. For the first time in her life she was a bit frightened of him. He slammed the door shut behind her and walked into his lounge. Maura followed, unsure if she was doing the right thing. The room was in a state of chaos. The curtains were still pulled even though it was nearly lunchtime. She went to his oak bookcase and studied the titles for something to do. Her mind was trying to think of a way to defuse the situation.

Geoffrey pulled open the heavy curtains and the weak February sunshine lit the room. She carried on looking at the books, waiting for him to open the conversation. Give her some kind of inkling of how to go about pacifying him over what had happened.

'Thinking of taking up reading? How about *Crime and Punishment*? You can borrow it if you like.' His voice was sarcastic.

She faced him.

'Why didn't you turn in for work yesterday?' She tried to sound ignorant of what had taken place between the two brothers, but as soon as she spoke knew she had said the wrong thing.

Geoffrey laughed.

'Are you telling me that Big Brother didn't tell you all about our little fight? Mickey even tells you when he gives his boyfriend one up the jacksey. I'm sure a good row with his brother would have been worth mentioning.'

Maura stared at Geoffrey for a few seconds before answering him. She decided to come clean with him. It was obvious that he was not going to make this easy.

'Look, Geoff, he did tell me about it. And he really is cut up about it. You took it too much to heart . . .'

Geoffrey sat in a chair and began to laugh at her.

'Oh, get stuffed, Maura. Cut up? He'd be more cut up if that mangy old dog of Benny's died. He don't give a toss about me, and from now on I ain't gonna give a toss about him.'

'But where will you work? What will you do?' She went to him and knelt in front of his chair.

'Oh, don't you worry, I'll still be working for you all.' He stressed the you. 'But I tell you now, and you can tell Mickey this if you like, I'll not be at his beck and call twenty-four hours a day. When I've done my stint of work I'm off. And I won't do any "heavy" work. If you or him want anyone roughed up or threatened, then you'll have to get one of the others to do it.'

'That's fair enough, Geoff. I was thinking, how about you take over the docklands? I think you and Willy would work well together, and me and Mickey . . . well, we have other irons in the fire.'

Geoffrey grinned, a horrible smelly grin that made her feel sick.

'So little sister has come to pour oil on troubled waters? You're offering me the docklands because you think that it will make me toe the line. Be a good boy.'

'No, Geoffrey. You could have had it before.'

He cut her off, his voice low and serious. 'Do you realise that I am over fifty years old? I have never married or even lived with a woman. I just worked that business with Michael. And then you came and you took it all from me. You inveigled your way into his pocket and you've been resident there ever since.' He was looking at her with a hatred that was tangible. Maura sat back on her heels and stared into a wrinkled, hate-filled face. In the grey sunlight he looked like a gargoyle come to life. But he had hurt her. Hurt and annoyed her.

'Do you know your trouble, Geoffrey? You don't know how to live a life. You act like a leech sucking everyone else's glory. You lived in Mickey's shadow, mate. You didn't have to, it was your own choice. You could have married if you'd wanted to, but you didn't. Not because of Michael, but because you knew deep in your boots that you weren't fit to mate with anyone. Mother called me and Michael neuters years ago, and maybe she was right, but I think that you're one as well.'

'You bitch! How dare you come here spouting your crap?'

Maura stood up and smoothed out the creases in her skirt. Slowly and deliberately, she leaned towards him. 'Just because you've read a few books don't make you Magnus fucking Magnusson you know. You're full of old shit, mate. You want to put down Herman Hesse and Tolstoy and go out of this flat and get yourself a bird. A real bird, not one of the high-heeled call girls you normally knock around with. A real woman, with a mind of her own.

'You make me sick, Geoff. You're always moaning about something. Everything in your life is analysed and picked over until you find a slight to *you* somewhere in it. Whether it's a chance remark or a frigging so-called conspiracy, like the folder you read the other day. You're paranoid, that's your trouble. Now if you want to come back to work tomorrow, go to the offices at St Martin's Wharf. If not, then that's up to you.'

She started to walk from the room. His voice stayed her. 'I hate you, Maura. I hate you so much I can taste it in my mouth. It's like gall. Mother said to me once you weren't like a normal woman. You didn't have the normal feelings any woman has. And now I know it's true. You even killed your own baby.'

She turned on him like a tiger. Her voice bitter, she said, 'That's Mother's opinion, is it? Well, next time you two are chatting about me ask her this. Ask her who held me down on the table that day when a dirty old man scraped my baby away. Ask her that. And while you're about it, ask her why she accepts money from Michael every week, yet won't even acknowledge his existence. Ask her why she drove poor Carla into marrying that bloody Malcolm. Why she kept her and never tried to reunite her with her mother. I know what everyone thinks about Janine but I'll tell you this much . . . once Mother got Carla into her house and had another little girl to dress up and take to mass, she would never *let* her go back home. You an' Mother are like two peas in a pod. You're both manipulators but neither of you could ever manipulate me or Michael. That's what gets up your noses!'

Before he could speak again she had left the flat, slamming the door behind her.

Geoffrey sat in the chair for a while, thinking. All his instincts told him to forget Maura and Michael for ever. But his devious brain told him that if he did not work for them he could not gather his information. And he would gather it. And he would use it. He would swallow his pride and go into work in the morning. But he would be biding his time . . .

*

Maura drove to Jackie Traverna's house. She was fuming inside. Geoffrey was a pain in the neck. He always had been, and she had a feeling he always would be. She parked her Mercedes Sports outside Jackie's block of flats. Locking it carefully, she went up the small flight of stairs.

As she walked along the landing towards Jackie's flat she was aware of the attention she commanded. Women were standing on the landing chatting, children of all colours and creeds were playing both on the landing and on the concrete forecourt of the flats. Everywhere was the flaking paint and crumbling brickwork that denoted the conditions of poverty these people lived in. The women who were chatting looked at her burgundy Jasper Conran dress and quite obviously real fur coat, and were quiet and hostile. Maura had to turn her body sideways to pass them.

In their crumpled velour tracksuits and shapeless dresses they looked like old women, yet Maura could see from the tight skin on their faces that they were much younger than her. If her life had been different she could quite easily have been one of them. Then her mind rebelled against that thought.

No. She would never have allowed herself to look like these women. Most of them had given up hope at a very early age. No matter what had happened to her, she knew she would always have kept her self-respect.

Jackie's front door was ajar and she walked inside, hesitantly. If those women who had looked at her with naked envy knew that she carried a gun in her bag, they might have had different feelings.

'Jackie? Jackie love?' Her voice was soft. She heard a noise from the bedroom and went inside. Jackie was lying on the bed. Her face had lost some of its puffiness and she looked better. Not much better but better than she had on Maura's last visit.

'Oh, Maura . . .' Jackie tried to speak.

Maura sat on her bed. 'I just popped by to see you, Jackie. Shall I make you a cup of tea?'

Jackie's deep brown eyes opened in surprise. Maura Ryan making her tea? It was like expecting the Queen to wash your kitchen floor.

Maura smiled at her, guessing her thoughts. She found the kitchen and made a pot of tea. The room was tiny but relatively tidy. She noticed that there was hardly anything in the cupboards. Leaving the tea to draw she walked back out on to the landing. The women were still there and Maura guessed that they had been discussing her arrival. She strode purposefully towards them.

'Do any of you happen to be friends with Jackie Traverna?'

A fat woman with long straggly brown hair answered her. 'I am. Why?' Her voice was hard and flat.

'I suppose you know that she's had an accident.'

The fat woman sighed loudly. 'I've been taking her Debbie to school for her. Why?'

'If I gave you the money, would you get her in some shopping?' Maura saw the women exchange looks. 'I'll pay you to do it, of course.'

The fat woman shrugged. 'All right.'

She followed Maura back into the flat. Maura was gratified at the friendly way in which she went into Jackie's room. Maura picked her bag up from where she had placed it on the bed. Opening it, she took out five twenty-pound notes. 'Do you have a freezer, Jackie?' The woman nodded her head.

'Good. There's a hundred pounds there and I want you to fill her freezer and cupboards up. I'll give you a score for your trouble. OK?'

The fat woman stared at the money in astonishment. Then she took it from Maura. She guessed from Maura's voice that she was not Social Services or Probation. When the woman went she would find out about her from Jackie.

When the neighbour was gone, Maura poured Jackie and herself out some tea. Taking it into the bedroom, she placed Jackie's cup into her hands. She had managed to pull herself up in the bed and Maura could see the purple bruises on her arms and shoulders. Damn Danny Rubens!

Opening her bag again, she lit two cigarettes and gave one to Jackie. Maura studied her face. She had about thirty stitches in each cheek and would carry the scars for the rest of her life. She pulled out a building society book and gave it to the woman.

'Inside there is five thousand pounds, Jackie. I want you to use it for a holiday or whatever. When you're feeling better I want you to take over the job of head girl at the Crackerjack, our new club.'

It took Maura a minute to realise that Jackie was crying. She took the tea from her and placed it on the floor by the bed. Then she put an arm around her shoulders.

'Hey . . . hey. Calm down, Jackie.'

She spoke with difficulty. 'You've been so good. I was so worried. I thought I'd end up at King's Cross with the pervies.'

Maura looked into her eyes. 'No way. You're a good girl, Jackie. And the head girl's job is a bloody good earner. You'll be fine. Absolutely fine.'

She picked Jackie's tea up from the floor and passed it

to her. 'Now you drink this while I get you and me an ashtray!'

When the fat woman got back from shopping she was amazed to find the 'rich bird', as she had termed Maura in her head, washing the kitchen floor. When Maura left a little later she was sure she had pushed up Jackie Traverna's street credibility a hundredfold, and only wished Jackie had not had to go through all that pain and suffering to achieve it.

When Maura got to her own house a bunch of white roses had been left in the glass porch. Intrigued, she opened the card. It said: 'Happy Valentine's Day. Mickey.'

She smiled to herself, but deep inside a little voice was asking her why she never got flowers from any 'real' men. Men who were not related to her. Inside the front door was a pile of letters. Picking them up, she went through to her kitchen. She placed the roses on the draining board and flicked through the letters. Bills and circulars. Then she noticed a thick cream-coloured envelope. Opening it, she brought out a beautiful card. It had real velvet flowers on it, arranged in a basket made of gold thread. This was definitely not a Woolworth's special. She smiled. Michael again. She opened the card and nearly died of shock.

'Will you be my Valentine? Have dinner with me tonight. 7.30 at the Savoy. Willy.'

For a few sweet seconds she felt that powerful excitement that a new love affair can bring. Then she glanced at her watch. It was past five now! She ran up the stairs to get ready. She was gonna knock his eyes out!

William Templeton sat at his table. He sneaked a glance at his watch. It was twenty to eight. She wasn't coming. He felt his heart sink. Maybe he should have rung her. Then she could have cold-shouldered him over the phone and that would have been the end of it. But he had seen that card in Harrods and had felt a foolish urge to buy it for her. He almost laughed. At his age? On the wrong side of fifty . . .

He had that terrible feeling people get when they have been stood up. That feeling that makes them think that everyone knows what's happened to them. That everyone is smiling at them behind their hands. He felt a shadow fall across him as he stared at the menu for the hundredth time and waved his hand imperiously.

'I'm not ready to order yet, thank you.'

'I should hope not. The least I'd expect is that you would wait for me to arrive!'

His eyes lifted and she was standing there, looking lovelier than he had ever seen her before. She had on a grey fitted dress of watered silk. As with all her clothes, it was perfectly plain. But with her breasts and slim waist, she did not need any of the frippery that most women wore. In her ears she had perfect pearl earrings and around her neck a small single strand of the same grade. Her pale white skin brought them to shining life. Her silky white-blond hair looked immaculate, as always. William took pleasure in the admiring glances that were coming their way.

He stood up awkwardly. 'I thought you weren't going to come.'

Maura sat down and smiled at the waiter who held her chair.

'Well, I didn't get your card until after five o'clock so I had to rush a bit.'

'You look exquisite, my dear, like a very beautiful painting. Now then, some champagne, I think.' He smiled. 'Real champagne, not the dishwater that's served in your clubs!'

Maura laughed. Really laughed, for the first time in years. It felt good to be pursued. Wanted. And this man certainly wanted her . . . She relaxed back into her chair and let good feelings wash over her.

Chapter Twenty-Four

19 March 1985

'Where did you get the numberplates from?' Michael was keyed up.

Leslie grinned. 'I got the numbers from a motorway service station car park. I had the actual plates made up by Jimmy Charlton. He owes us a favour.'

'Good. Are the Range Rovers ready to go? And the bikes?'

Leslie nodded. 'Yep. They've been serviced and valeted. They're as clean as a nun's knickers.'

Garry grinned. 'I've sorted out all the guns. They're cleaned and ready to go.'

'Good. Very good. You realise this is a big undertaking, don't you? This ain't like a normal blag. Every Filth in the country is going to be looking for that gold. It will be the biggest chance of promotion since Ronnie Biggs had it on his toes.'

'Well, they ain't caught him yet.' Maura's voice was jocular. Everyone laughed except Mickey.

'There's still time for that. Whatever happens, don't get too cocky, lads. Just keep to the ground rules I laid down and we'll be OK.'

Maura stood up and looked around at her brothers' faces. 'What about the hole?'

'All done. Ready and waiting.' This from Lee.

'Then all that's left is to sort out the alibis. I'll leave that to you lot. Whatever it is, make sure it's tighter than a duck's behind. OK?'

Everyone nodded.

'See you in the morning then.' Michael smiled at the faces around him. 'Unless there's any questions?'

'I've got a question.'

'It would be you, wouldn't it, brain box?' Maura's voice was light.

The chances were that if Garry asked a question it would be a good one.

He adjusted his glasses. 'What happens to the Filth?'

Michael and Maura had been half expecting someone to ask this.

Michael answered. 'I wasn't going to tell you till the morning. But as you ask . . .'

He paused for effect and swept his gaze around all his brothers.

'You waste them. Every one of them. The fewer people to identify us, the better.'

Roy coughed. 'What about the old Bill though, Mickey? They're in on it, ain't they?'

'Yep. Right up to their shitty little necks. All the more reason to get rid of them. People get jumpy.' He shrugged his shoulders as if to finish his sentence.

'Righty ho. Now who fancies a few pints?'

The four younger brothers all got up from their seats.

'No pissing it up tonight!' Michael's voice was stern. 'And, Garry, contact lenses tomorrow.'

'Don't worry, Mickey. Everything will be fine. As sweet as a nut.'

When the boys left, Maura turned to Michael. 'I ain't happy about knocking everyone off, Mickey.'

Michael sighed heavily. In his dark handmade suit and pristine white shirt he looked like a banker. Which was exactly the impression he wanted to create. In the small Portakabin they both looked out of place.

'Look, Maws, you can never leave anything to chance.' He went to her and put his arm around her shoulder, pulling her so close she could feel his breath fan her face. 'You just let me do all the worrying now. You've done your bit.'

'Once the killing starts, Mickey, we lose the protection of all our plants. You realise that, don't you?'

'Yeah, I realise that, Maws. But that Tory MP, the one soliciting in King's Cross . . . well, he's gonna be our scapegoat. The day after tomorrow the pictures we've got of him will be on their way to the gutter press. That should take most people's minds off the actual robbery for a while. Until the main shock wears off anyway.'

Maura was quiet and he took it as a sign of acquiescence. 'Come on, girl, let's get off home. We're all a bit jumpy.'

Driving home Maura was more than jumpy. She was positively terror-stricken. As she drove into her driveway she saw that all the lights were on and her heart lifted a little. Carla was here. She jumped out of the car with delight. That meant that little Joey was with her as well. She let herself into the house.

'Auntie Maura! Auntie Maura!' Four-year-old Joey ran towards her, his chubby arms outstretched.

Maura picked him up in a big hug.

'Hello, Tiger.'

She saw Carla watching them from the kitchen doorway. As always when she saw her she was overwhelmed with a feeling of love and affection. Carla looked like a young Janine, with her red-brown hair and slim figure, except Carla had something more – she had a womanly aura that Janine had never had.

'I've just made some dinner. You couldn't have timed it better.'

'What brought you here? I didn't expect you until the weekend. Not that I mind. You could move in if you wanted to, you know that.' Maura sounded almost her old self. She could kiss Carla for taking her mind off what was happening tomorrow.

Carla went quiet. Her face closed up in the way that Maura knew so well. Something wasn't right.

'What's happened?'

Carla ran her hands through her long hair in her old familiar gesture.

'Come and have dinner, Maws. I'll tell you while we eat.'

Maura followed her into the kitchen. She was frowning now. Joey was holding her tightly around the neck. In the kitchen she could smell a chicken casserole, and realised that she was in fact quite hungry. She sat at the large kitchen table and watched Carla while she worked. This was Carla all over. She would not tell Maura anything until she was good and ready. She guessed that the trouble was with Malcolm, Carla's husband. After Benny's death and Carla's rejection of Maura and Michael, they had not seen her for nearly a year. Then one day Maura had come home to find Carla sitting on her doorstep. She had had a big row with her Nana, as she called Maura's mother. Maura had immediately installed her back in her own room and all had been forgiven between them.

Then, six years ago, Carla had married Malcolm Spencer. He had been two years older than Carla at twenty-six, and for Maura at least it had been loathing on first sight. He was an architect, he was middle class, and he was the most pompous ass that Maura had ever come across. But Carla had loved him, so she had swallowed her own reservations and countenanced the match. When Joey had been born she had nearly liked the man who was married to the most important girl in her life. She could see how pleased he was with his son and it had made him seem human somehow. Until the christening.

This had been a strained affair as her mother was there, naturally. Sarah had studiously ignored her eldest son and only daughter. That was bad enough, but then Malcolm had upset everyone there. Carla was holding the baby next to the font, everyone standing respectfully around. Carla had handed the infant to the priest and had lost her grip, only slightly. The priest had instantly taken a firm hold on the child and no harm was done. It was the kind of thing that in most families would have been considered an excuse for a joke. Brought up every now and then in family gatherings with a bit added on.

Instead, Malcolm had snatched the child from his wife, causing Carla to lose her own balance. Maura and all her brothers had stood tight-lipped until the service was finally over. There had been no enjoyment after that. Everyone had just stood patiently waiting for it to end. After the service, outside the church, there had been murder. Michael had told Malcolm in no uncertain terms that if he ever as much as raised his voice to his niece, or dragged her over again, he would bury him underneath the new motorway currently being built.

Maura was sure that the incident had finally shown Malcolm what he had inadvertently married into. Since then there had been a strained truce between all parties concerned. Now here was Carla and little Joey and she would bet her last pound there was something seriously up.

She played with Joey, who had recently learnt to sing 'The Wheels on the Bus', until such time as Carla finished preparing the meal. Finally, they were all seated and eating the chicken casserole. Carla had also made duchesse potatoes and broccoli and Maura was enjoying it until Carla started telling her what had happened.

Carla and Joey were supposed to be going to the zoo with his playgroup. When Carla had driven him there, with a packed lunch and his mackintosh because the spring weather had been so uncertain, she had been told that one of the minibus drivers was ill so the trip had been cancelled. Joey was heartbroken and had refused to stay at the playgroup. So Carla had put him back in the car and instead of going to the zoo as planned, decided to take him home with her and catch up on some household chores. She guessed that Malcolm would not be too happy as he worked from home the days that Joey went to the playgroup, especially today as they were not due to come home until five o'clock.

When she had reached her house she had noticed a pink Fiesta in the drive. She had parked her own car outside on the road, thinking that someone from Malcolm's work had come round to see him. Getting Joey out of the car, she had gone around the side of the house and in the back door, reasoning that if she opened the porch door, and then the front door, she would more than likely disturb Malcolm and his guest. Inside the kitchen, she pulled off Joey's coat and wellingtons and made him a drink of orange. He sat at the table drinking it, for once quiet and still.

Putting on the kettle Carla decided to ask Malcolm and his visitor if they wanted a cup of tea. She left the kitchen, crossed the large entrance hall and went to the door of the room that was Malcolm's office when he was home. She tapped on it and walked inside. Her mind registered the fact that the heavy brocade curtains were drawn. She had not noticed this from the front of the house as this room backed on to the rear garden. Although the room was quite dark she could see well enough. She could see that Malcolm was sitting on his office chair, and that sitting on top of him, with her blouse open exposing her breasts and her skirt pulled up to her waist, showing anyone who cared to look that she was knickerless, was Miss Bradley-Hume, Malcolm's secretary. They were unaware of her for a few seconds and Carla stood rooted to the spot watching the rise and fall of Miss Bradley-Hume's buttocks. Then Malcolm had put his head forward to kiss the woman and had seen Carla standing there. In his fright he stood upright, dropping the prim and proper Miss Bradley-Hume on to the floor. Carla was mainly aware of the fact that Miss Bradley-Hume had large, rather baggy breasts.

Then she had the woman's long mousy hair and was pulling her by it across the carpet. She could see the woman trying to free herself, clawing at Carla's hands that had her hair in a vice-like grip. Malcolm was staring at Carla absolutely shell shocked.

Giving Miss Bradley-Hume a hard kick in her stomach,

she turned her attention to her husband. Seeing him standing as he was with his underpants and jeans (his designer jeans that he thought made him look so macho) around his ankles, she was finally convinced that she had married a complete and utter fool. His little skinny legs with their sparse hairs looked like a chicken's. She noticed that his member, which had never been that big to begin with, had now shrunk into a small wrinkled sausage and she had the urge to laugh. If only he could see himself! Mr Important!

Miss Bradley-Hume had picked herself up off the floor and retrieved her knickers, which were on the drawing board. She stood now, fully attired, in front of Carla.

'This is not what it looks like.' Her refined twang sent shivers of diabolical hatred through Carla's body.

'Get out of my house, you slut. You fucking filthy dirty slut!'

Miss Bradley-Hume's long horsey face dropped with shock. Carla laughed, her eyes wild.

'Oh, have I shocked you with a naughty word? Fuck . . . don't you like that word? Well, that's what you were doing, you upper-class whore. You were fucking my husband. Fucking, fucking, fucking . . .'

Malcolm shuffled across to her as quickly as his trousers would allow. She felt the stinging blow as he slapped her across the face. Then she was calm. She watched Malcolm pull up his ridiculous jeans.

'Get out of *my* house now. Both of you.'

Miss Bradley-Hume went quickly. The change in Carla's voice was enough to send her running to her car. On her way out of the door she knocked Joey to the floor. His shocked crying penetrated Carla's rage. Going to him, she picked him up.

'All right, baby. It's nothing. Just a little accident, that's all.'

She turned back to her husband. 'I meant what I said, Malcolm. I want you out of *my* home.'

He tried to bluff his way out, his domineering personality coming to the fore.

'I will not leave this house. You're overwrought. I admit I've been a naughty boy . . .'

'Naughty boy!' Carla's voice was incredulous. 'You're a fucking cretin, Malcolm, that's what you are. And you're getting out of this house, or I'll get my uncles to move you for me!'

It was the first time she had ever threatened him with anything, let alone her uncles. Malcolm was aware that his hold over Carla was not as tight as usual. He tried a different tack.

'Will you stop using that F word! You really are showing your working-class lineage today, aren't you?'

Carla was patting Joey's back. His sobs were quieting now as he listened to his parents' quarrel.

'I am going to Maura's, Malcolm, and when I get back from there in a few days I want you out.' Her words had a finality about them that frightened him.

'Oh, baby, I know what I've done is wrong. But she was asking for it.' His voice was wheedling. Cajoling. He needed her.

Carla laughed harshly. 'I should think she *was* asking for it. No one else but you would fuck something so ugly. Only you. We're finished, Malcolm. Finished.'

'What about Joey? I'm his father!' Malcolm was self-righteous now.

'If you do what I tell you, and get out of my life and *my* house, I may let you see him from time to time.' She was enjoying herself. Now that the initial shock had worn off, she realised that she finally had a bona fide reason to get rid of him.

'Carla, please. For all the love we've shared . . .'

'Drop dead, Malcolm.' Her voice was flat and hard. 'Come on, Joey, let's go to Auntie Maura's, shall we?'

She went from the room, across the large entrance hall and finally out of the house. Settling Joey into his car seat, she went back into the house and collected her bag and a few things. As she left for the last time Malcolm tried again.

'Please, Carla.' His voice was desperate now.

Standing on the driveway, she placed the middle finger of her right hand in the air then, gathering as much air into her lungs as possible, shouted at him: 'Rotate on it gently, arsehole!'

Then, getting into the car, she drove to Maura's.

Maura listened to Carla in amazement. She could not help picturing her dragging the woman across the carpet by her hair.

'Oh, Carla love, I'm so sorry. It must have been terrible.'

Carla smiled sheepishly.

'Stop spitting the meat out, Joey.' She looked back at Maura. 'Actually, Maws, I enjoyed every minute of it! I think I finally saw him as you all see him.'

'We've never seen him with his cacks down!'

Both women laughed. 'You know what I mean. He's a prat, Maws. A prize prat.'

Maura was serious. 'But you did love him, didn't you?'

Carla looked at little Joey. 'Yeah. I did love him in the beginning. But not any more.'

Maura carried on eating. The food was tasteless now. She was consumed with a feeling of hatred for Malcolm that made her want to go and kill him.

'Can you imagine Nana's face when she finds out I've left my lawful husband?'

Maura was cavalier. 'Oh, sod her, Carla. Let her think what she likes. You can stay here with me until we get you sorted out.'

Carla put her hand gently over Maura's.

'I know that. I'm like a bad penny, ain't I? Always turning up. My mum didn't want me. Nor my dad. And now even my husband's done the dirty on me. Maybe I do something wrong.'

'Don't be so silly!' Maura's voice was sharp. 'I'll tell you something, shall I? Once, a long time ago, I was in a similar state to you. I went to Marge's. Well, she said something that I'll never forget. She said that self-pity was a luxury none of us could afford. Those weren't her exact words, but that was what she meant. You must pick yourself up, brush yourself down . . .'

'And start all over again.' Carla sang the last sentence and they both laughed again.

'Yeah, well. That's about the strength of it.'

'In a funny way I feel free. Like I've been let out of prison after a long stretch.'

'That's good, Carla. Try to keep that feeling. It will help you over the next few weeks. And there's one other good thing. My mother won't ring you here so you can put off talking to her for as long as you want.'

Joey upset his beaker of milk and both women jumped up to get a cloth. Even though Carla's being there was because of trouble, Maura was glad to have her and Joey anyway. It took her mind off what was going to happen the next day. And she could not rule out the fact that it would give her a cast-iron alibi if, by any chance, the police did decide to interview her.

Chapter Twenty-Five

It was 4am on 20 March 1985. Maura and Michael were sitting in a Portakabin in a yard owned by Michael's friend, Jim Dickenson. Jim was an old lag. Throughout his life he had been put into prison for various offences, ranging from bank robbery (he got only eight years because his gun was not loaded) to extortion. He had tried to blackmail a high-powered executive who was a transvestite. On leaving jail he had approached Michael. They were friends from the Notting Hill days of Joe the Fish. He was a big powerful man and Michael had set him up in a plant hire business in Cranford. He had bought the business as a going concern and it had been put into Jim Dickenson's name. To all intents and purposes, Michael Ryan had nothing whatsoever to do with it.

The yard consisted of over four acres of land, surrounded by ten-foot fence panels and guarded by three Dobermans and a Rottweiler. This morning, though, it was empty of any life other than Michael and Maura. The dogs were shut into a pen kept especially for them. Their barking and howling was already getting on Maura's nerves.

Michael glanced at his watch. It was four minutes past the hour.

'Another ten minutes, Maws, and it will all be over.'

Maura lit yet another cigarette and tried to concentrate her mind on Carla and Joey.

Roy and Gerry were waiting at the roundabout on the Bath Road. Both were on 650cc Kawasaki motorbikes. They were dressed in black from head to foot. Gerry could feel the sweat pouring from his forehead. He was frightened, really frightened. He wished he had the guts just to start the engine and go . . . go anywhere away from here.

Roy was thinking about Janine, and Benny who was nearly ten. Where his wife had completely disowned Carla, she tried to possess the boy. He closed his eyes, trying to concentrate on the job in hand. If they went wrong now, that would be the end of them. Banged up good and proper. He felt the loose feeling in his bowels and hoped that he would not have to empty them at the roadside. He reassured himself with the fact that this robbery had been planned down to the minutest detail. What he would not give for a fag! Just to be doing something other than waiting for the lights of the articulated lorry. He could sense the nervousness of Gerry Jackson and it made him feel worse. He breathed deeply, trying to control his heartbeats.

Garry, Leslie and Lee were in a dark blue Range Rover. All three were already wearing black balaclavas with just slits for eyeholes. Garry kept up a stream of low chatter. Leslie and Lee just grunted replies. All were nervous. Garry caressed the shotgun that he was holding. At four minutes past four they all started counting down.

There were just ten minutes until the off.

*

Davie Muldoon drove the container lorry with its cargo of gold towards Heathrow airport. His mind was miles away on an argument that he'd had with his wife the night before. She was a pain in the bloody neck. First she informs him that her mother's coming, yet again. Then she drops the real bombshell. She's pregnant again. Four bloody kids in five years.

She looked like something from a Hammer horror film already. She tipped the scales at just over sixteen stone! When he had first met her she had been eight stone with the best set of bristols he had ever seen. Nowadays, what with the rolls of fat and the stretch marks, it was like mounting Red Rum. But true to form she went by her old ruse. Attack was the best form of defence. Before he could comment on the fact that they could barely meet the mortgage payments as it was, without another baby to feed and clothe, she had started on about his drinking. Well, if she had a good look in the mirror she might get an inkling as to why he drank so much.

He needed at least eight pints of Hurlimans even to consider kissing the ugly bitch. He shook his head sadly as he drove along. He had been well and truly caught there. All his mates had warned him: 'Look at the mother and see the daughter, twenty years on.' He was well gutted.

The house looked like a council tip. She never cleaned up. Last night she had stood before him in all her glory. With her bleached yellow hair with the roots grown out nearly two inches she looked like a candidate for the black and white minstrel show. He grinned to himself. Her outsize nightdress had been stained with everything from baby puke to tea. Even her teeth were going rotten in her head. She said it was because of having the kids so quick, but he had already made a shrewd guess that not cleaning them was also a large contributory factor. The dirty bitch! He shuddered. She was only twenty-four! What would she be like in another five years?

Joey Granger had been watching the changing expressions on his friend's face with fascination. He also had an idea what had put them there. He had met Davie's wife Leona only once and that had been enough. She had reminded him of a Rottweiler in drag. Poor old Davie, he had to be the most easy-going bloke in the world. Which was probably why she got away with so much. If she had been his wife he would have given her a good slap a long time ago.

'Light me a fag, Joey?' Davie's voice was soft.

'We're not really supposed to, you know.'

'Of course I know, but it's never stopped us before!'

Joey lit two cigarettes and passed one to Davie.

'I hate these big pulls, they make me nervous.'

Joey laughed lightly.

'Smoke your fag and calm down. There's more old Bill out there than on the Masonic Lodge's annual beano!'

Davie smiled despite himself.

In front of the articulated lorry was a white Granada. Inside were Detective Inspector Tomlinson and three younger men, DS Milton, DC Johns and DC Llewelyn. DC Johns was what was commonly termed a chatterbox.

'So, sir, if no one knows that this gold is going to Heathrow, why so many police?' His voice was very young and very naïve and DI Tomlinson was sorry for him. Just for a second though. He had too much else on his mind.

'DC Johns?' His voice was stern.

'Yes, sir?'

'Shut your bloody trap for five minutes, and give your arse a chance!'

Llewelyn and Milton laughed softly. Johns sat silent and embarrassed. How were you to find out anything if you never asked? he reasoned.

Tomlinson was nervous, very nervous, and the younger men put it down to the seriousness of what they were doing. In fact, he was more aware of what was going on than they were or even than the Bank of England was. He had always had a passion for the horses. Over the last few years it had become an expensive passion. A passion that Michael Ryan had encouraged wholeheartedly. At this moment he could not make his mortgage payments, his car payments or, God help him, his maintenance. He was also into Michael Ryan for so much money he felt faint if he thought about the actual amount. It was his job to see that these three imbeciles bodged their job. Then he was home and dry, with all his debts paid.

The guns were still locked in the special armouries built into the dashboard in the front of the armrest in the back. He had the keys, and would take as long as he could before arming the three young cowboys in the car with him. He sneaked a look at his watch. Four minutes till the off. He was surprised to find that he was not even sweating.

Behind the articulated lorry was another unmarked car. This time it was a Sierra. A dirty brown-coloured Sierra 1600E.

Inside were DI Becton and another three young plain-clothes, DS Bronte, DS Marker and WDC Williams. Becton was annoyed. He did not like the thought of a WDC in this thing at all. He also held the magic keys that would arm what were in effect little more than children. Becton, too, had to make sure that his end of the operation went wrong.

After twenty years in the police force he had finally been found out. He was married with three teenage children, a lovely wife Jeanette whom he honestly loved with all his heart, and a nice detached house in Chiswick, nearly paid for. He had only one problem and it was a big one. He had discovered many years ago that he had a penchant for very young boys. Up until now it had never interfered with what he termed his 'real life', his family and his career. Then a week ago he had been sent certain pictures of himself through the post in a plain brown envelope. There was no mistaking that it was him in the pictures. They were in glorious colour. They were also very explicit.

He had been standing in the hallway, clutching the pictures to his chest, when Jeanette had walked out there. She had looked as pretty as a picture in the early morning light, not at all like the mother of three teenaged children or like the wife of a sexual pervert, because when he had seen himself in those pictures he had realised exactly what he was. And the thought of her knowing and his children knowing had nearly brought on a heart attack.

He had telephoned the number enclosed with the picture and now sat in this car, with two young men and a lovely young lady, waiting to do something that would be a blot on their career files all their life. He glanced in the mirror and saw the meatwagon full of uniforms driving behind him. He looked at the clock on the dashboard of the Sierra. Three minutes to the off. He was trembling.

*

As the meatwagon passed them, Gerry and Roy started up their bikes. Gerry's took three good kicks before it roared into life. They pulled their visors down on their helmets and nodded to one another, then they roared off behind the meatwagon. It was about two hundred yards from the roundabout. Inside the meatwagon were ten armed officers, most of them dozing. Only two were alert. One was the driver, DS Raymond Paine, and the other the controller of the radio, DS Martin Fuller. Both were unaware that they were going to be blown off the road within seconds. Outside the window, Paine could hear the dull drone of the police helicopter that was following them above. He yawned. He hated these special assignments.

Roy had already cocked his .357 Magnum. He drove parallel with the meatwagon and with one shot completely disabled the vehicle. The back tyre blew out with a ferocious bang that woke up all the sleeping officers. They woke up just in time to feel the van mounting the grass verge at the side of the road and then turn over twice before it finally came to rest on its right side, on the opposite side of the carriageway.

'Jesus Christ! Did you see that?'

Up above in the helicopter Officer Watts and Officer Harper had seen in the dim light a bright blue flash.

'Calling all units in the vicinity of the roundabout on the Bath Road. We have reason to believe a robbery is in progress . . .'

As the helicopter message came over the radio in Becton's car, WDC Williams answered the call. Becton and the two young men were already out of the car and going to the aid of their colleagues. WDC Williams was aware in the pandemonium that Becton had not unlocked the small arms cache. She punched the dashboard in frustration. There had been the definite sound of a shot, officers were undoubtedly injured, and they did not have so much as a lolly stick between them. It was pathetic!

She picked up the radio handset and began to call for the fire brigade and ambulances.

DI Tomlinson had done his job properly. At least from the Ryans' point of view. As soon as the shot had been fired he had pulled the white Granada on to the side of the road. The articulated lorry had had to swerve to avoid him. It had wheezed to a stop, only to find its way immediately blocked by a Range Rover that seemed to appear from thin air.

'It's a robbery!' DC Johns' voice was incredulous.

Before they had even had time to answer him, two sawn-off shotguns had been pointed at the windows of the car. Within seconds, the doors had been opened and they were all lying on the damp road with their hands handcuffed behind their backs.

Davie and Joey were sitting in the articulated lorry, dumbstruck. Then a big man in a black balaclava motioned with a large gun for them to open their doors. Before the trip they had been told not to open the specially constructed doors even if Jesus himself appeared and asked for a lift. This was all forgotten in their panic. They opened the doors and jumped from the cab.

Davie watched his lorry being driven away by two masked men.

*

Gerry, Leslie and Lee jumped into the Range Rover and as they screeched off saw that the police helicopter was hovering just above their heads. Leaning dangerously out of the front window, Garry, always the most adventurous of the boys, opened fire on it with his M16 rifle. He had brought it with him deliberately for this job. In the distance, on the M4, they could hear the wailing of the police and ambulance sirens. Garry's hair caught fire beneath his balaclava as the helicopter exploded. Leslie dragged him back inside the window, then helped him to put his hair out. They were laughing hysterically now. It was all over.

Back at the yard, Maura and Michael were in a state of nervous agitation. It was four-twenty-five. As if of one mind, they both left the Portakabin and stood in the yard. Just to the right of them was an enormous black hole. It was twenty-five feet deep and almost forty long. It had been dug vertically as if it was a sloping runway, which in effect it was. It was fifteen feet wide. Brother and sister walked across the gravel and opened the large iron gates.

'Mickey, I'm so scared.' Maura's voice was barely a croak.

'Ain't we all, darling?'

He smiled at her in the darkness. She could not see it but she could hear it in his voice.

Fifteen minutes later the articulated lorry drove through the gates followed by the Range Rover. The bikes had been left at the scene of the robbery.

Roy drove the lorry straight into the hole. Getting out, he and Gerry scrambled up the sloping floor.

On either side of the hole were gigantic mounds of dirt. The hole itself had been dug by a large drag line crane. It had taken nearly five hours.

Leslie, Lee, Garry and Roy all got into giant Caterpillar 'dozers. In less than an hour, they had filled the hole back in. The lorry was gone. It had disappeared off the face of the earth. It would sit under the ground for a few years until it was safe to try to shift the gold. Michael watched his brothers parking different types of plant over the burial place. It was covered with everything from dumper trucks, low loaders for cranes and the Caterpillar 'dozers.

At the scene of the robbery, pandemonium was breaking out. Becton and Tomlinson were both receiving the sharp edge of Chief Superintendent Liversey's tongue. He was absolutely fuming.

'The bloody lorry has disappeared off the face of the earth. You two didn't even have the sense to arm your men!' He was spitting with temper as he spoke. 'How the hell am I supposed to explain this one away? That's what I'd like to know. If I didn't know better I'd think you were communists! You bloody fools!'

He was interrupted by an ambulanceman. 'Excuse me, sir, but there were no fatalities. I thought you would like to know. Only one major casualty and that was a gunshot wound. I gather that in the course of the van crashing, one of the men in the back inadvertently shot the fellow sitting opposite.'

'What about the helicopter pilots?'

'Burnt to death, I'm afraid.'

'Then how can you say there were no fatalities? You're all bloody fools!'

Liversey stomped away from the men. He knew this much – heads were going to roll over this and he had a feeling that his would be one of them. He would have been even more galled if he'd known that the articulated lorry that had been carrying nearly twenty million in gold bullion was buried, with the engine still hot, not two miles away.

At eight o'clock that morning, Jim Dickenson opened his yard. By eight-fifteen it was a hive of activity. He loved his plant hire firm. He loved Michael Ryan for letting him have it. By five that afternoon the newly filled-in hole was just part of the usual landscape. Not one of the men who worked there even guessed that they were walking and driving over twenty million pounds' worth of gold. Yet the robbery was to be their only topic of conversation for ages.

At six-fifteen, Maura and Michael were driving along the M4 back into London. Leslie and Garry had driven off earlier, as had Roy. Lee was to dump the Range Rover in Langley, Slough, where he had left his car. Everyone agreed it had been a good night's work. Gerry Jackson had left earlier than everyone else as he had to open the main betting shop in Wandsworth. After all, life had to go on.

Maura walked into her house in Rainham at nearly nine in the morning. She was tired out. Little Joey was there to greet her and she kissed and cuddled him for a while before going up to bed. She noticed that Carla did not enquire where she had been all night. After a warm bath, she slipped naked into her bed. The coolness of the sheets was reassuring to her somehow. She had managed to talk Michael out of a killing spree, but he had still allowed Garry to shoot at the helicopter. She burrowed into her pillow. She had heard on the news that the men had been burnt to death. Both were married with children. The radio announcer's voice had been so matter-of-fact about it.

She turned over again in bed and attempted once more to get comfortable and empty her mind of all the bad things. She had too many bad things filed away. She heard Joey's joyful laughter float up the stairs and into her bedroom and the thought of the helicopter pilot's children rose up in front of her. They were small and helpless in her mind's eye. And faceless. Like her own baby which still wandered into her thinking sometimes, especially when she was done like now. The robbery itself bothered her not one iota. It was the killing. She did not think for a moment that what she had told Leslie to do to Danny Rubens counted. He was scum. He had cut up one of the girls who worked for them and he had paid the price. She could not look on the police as her brothers did, as the enemy. An omnipotent force that had to be thwarted at every turn. She did not really care about the police much, one way or the other.

Except for Terry Petherick . . . She sat up in bed and rearranged her pillows, sinking back into their coolness. If she started to think about him she would never get any sleep. She heard the bedroom door creak open.

'Are you asleep?'

Carla's voice was soft.

'No, love. Come on in.'

Carla walked into the bedroom with a glass of brandy. She went to Maura and put it on the bedside table. 'I thought you could possibly do with this. I left Joey watching a Postman Pat video, so I have a few minutes to myself.'

Maura sat up in the bed. She knew that Carla was offering her an opening, if she wanted to talk to her. And she did want to talk; she wanted to tell her how unhappy she was about all that had happened in the last twenty-four hours. But she couldn't. She picked up the glass of brandy and sipped it. Carla tried again.

'William Templeton rang last night. He wants you to call him as soon as you can. I forgot to tell you.'

'Thanks. I'll ring him later.'

'I was listening to the news just now. It seems that two of the policemen who were guarding some gold that got stolen were shot dead about half an hour ago. The police think that the raiders may have thought they could identify them.'

She watched Maura's face closely and was not surprised to see her blanch.

'A Vecton I think it was, and a Tomlinson.' Her voice trailed off as she watched Maura's features. Her aunt's mouth was moving but she seemed unable to speak.

Maura's mind was whirling. Not Vecton . . . Becton and Tomlinson. The two who were being blackmailed. She put the brandy on the bedside table and, pushing Carla away roughly, jumped out of the bed.

She practically ran to the wardrobes that covered one entire wall. They were mirrored and Maura could see the reflection of her breasts, bouncing as she ran to them. Pulling one of the doors open she started to dress herself, dragging the clothes on to her body in her haste. She pulled on a pair of jeans and a cashmere sweater, and then, pushing her bare feet into some leather moccasins, ran out of the room and down the stairs, Carla following her.

'For goodness' sake, Maura. What's up?' Carla's voice was troubled. She knew that Maura was upset over what she had said. She felt responsible.

'Nothing. I just have to see Michael, that's all.' She picked up her car keys and ran from the house to her car.

Carla went into the lounge where Joey was sitting in front of the television set, watching Postman Pat and Jess. She sat on the sofa and stared at the screen, wishing that she had kept her mouth shut.

Michael was asleep when he heard the pounding on his door. He immediately thought it was the police, and jumped out of his bed naked. Then he heard Maura calling through the letterbox.

'It's me. Let me in now!'

Thinking that something had happened he rushed to the front door and let her in. As he opened up she almost fell into his hall. Her hair was dishevelled, her face streaked with mascara. He shut the door quickly and tried to grasp hold of her. She pushed him away roughly.

'You bastard! You rotten stinking bastard!'

Michael's mouth dropped open with shock. 'What? What have I done?'

'You had those two policemen shot after you promised me . . .'

Michael yawned. 'Oh, is that all? I thought it was something important.'

His voice was low and full of sleep.

Maura stared at him in astonishment. Is that all? she thought. That is the extent of his morality.

'I thought something had happened. Something terrible.' He walked into his bedroom and pulled on a dressing gown. She followed him and, as he turned to face her, tying the belt, launched herself at him, hair and nails flying. Her right hand dug into his face and she felt the skin tear as she scratched him deeply.

'You rotten bastard! You stinking lousy bastard!'

Within seconds he had grabbed her arms and thrown

her on the bed. He held her there, with her arms pinned to her sides, while she fought him like a wildcat. Using every ounce of her strength she tried to get away from him, so she could carry on her fighting. She could hear herself spitting obscenities at him, all the bad things that she had carefully locked away over the years bubbling out of her body. Spewing out from between her lips. And still Michael held her down on the bed, his face placid and closed. Finally, after what seemed to Maura to be an eternity but was only about five minutes, the tears came. Hot gushing tears that soaked her face and hair in seconds with their salty residue. She felt the fight leave her body as if it had been exorcised.

Then Michael had her in his arms. He was stroking her hair and murmuring calming words and phrases. And Maura was aware that she was letting him. She needed him. His arms were circling her like steel bands and she knew she would forgive him anything. Had, in fact, already forgiven him for what he had done. It was herself, Maura Ryan, she would never forgive.

Michael held her until she was calm again and her crying just little hiccups. Then, pushing her away from him so he could see into her face, he spoke.

'Listen, Maws. Those police were on the take. One was a child molester. He hung around the train stations looking for little rent boys. Now I'm queer, Maws. Or gay, whatever you want to call it. But most gay men would no more touch them little boys than they would cut their own arms off. That's pervert country, Maws, where all the nice Mr Respectables in their city suits and briefcases get a quick blow job off some poor little bugger, before going home to the wife and kids and their dinner.' His voice was low and sure and hypnotic.

'As for the other one, he was more bent than a nine-bob note. His wife suffered because he was a violent wife-beater. And when he began to take his temper out on the kids, she went on the trot and divorced him. He still had an injunction order out on him, to stop him going around her house and belting her.' He watched her face for any sign that she was weakening. He did not like this Maura. A frightened, beaten Maura. She sniffed loudly and looked into his eyes.

'What . . . what . . . about the heli-helicopter pilots?' She still could not control the little heaving sobs.

'They were nothing to do with you, Maws. That was down to me and the others. All you did was help us plan it. Don't go to pieces on me, Maws. Not you. Think of them as you would a scumbag like Danny Rubens. It's Us and Them; girl, and up until now you've lived by that rule. Don't go soft on me now. You've run this firm with me for years. You've been the mainstay of it. But I could do without you, Maws, if you really wanted out.'

His soft voice had an underlying threat in it that did not go unnoticed. She swallowed deeply.

'I don't want out, Mickey.' And she didn't. It was all that she knew.

He smiled. One of his best smiles that seemed to light his face up from within.

'That's my girl.' He enfolded her in his arms again and she relaxed against him. Michael was right. In all the years she had worked for him and with him it had never seemed to bother her before. But deep, deep down in the bottom of her being she knew that the killing had always bothered her. She still woke up at nights with her body bathed in sweat, thinking about Sammy Goldbaum. She opened the little filing cabinet in her brain and once more filed all the bad things away. Until the next time she broke down.

Michael held her close and stared at the wall over her shoulder. Of all the things he had expected to come from the gold robbery, this was not one of them. He had only seen her like this once before, after Benny's death, when Sammy and Jonny had been put away. Well, he would do now what he had done then. Keep her by him. Watch over her. And hopefully snap her out of it. He kissed the top of her white-blond head. He did love her. He loved her very much.

The Gold Bullion Robbery hit every front page, as did the killing of the policemen. Everyone was blamed from the IRA to an Italian terrorist organisation, the latter in the *Sun*'s leader, three days after the robbery. The *Guardian* called for a Government Inquiry into how such a top secret operation could have been leaked to a person or persons unknown.

The police kept a low profile. They had their suspicions as usual, but no solid evidence of any kind. Chief Superintendent Liversey was given early retirement, as were two prominent members of the board at the Bank of England. If the police had held an Internal Inquiry they might have been given to wonder how so many high-ranking officers could afford holidays in the Seychelles and the Bahamas.

The robbery was finally knocked off the front pages by a Member of Parliament. He had been secretly photographed propositioning a prostitute who worked King's Cross 'rough trade'. As usual the British public much preferred to read about a good sex scandal rather than a robbery with violence and murder. The *Daily Mirror* called for another Government Inquiry, this time into the sex lives of prominent Tory MPs. The particular MP involved remained a favourite of Michael Ryan's for some time.

Geoffrey Ryan wrote out all he had read about the robbery in the green folder. He then placed it with the file he was gathering on Maura and Michael. One day, though he did not know when that day would be, he would use it against them.

Chapter Twenty-Six

12 October 1986

Michael Ryan walked along the Embankment. He turned up his coat collar to try to warm himself. People were hurrying by. A man walked up behind him and fell into step with him.

'Mr Ryan, you're very late.' He had the soft Southern Irish drawl.

'I know. I was caught up in some last-minute work. You know how it is.'

The man, although a full head shorter than Michael, was very powerfully built. His small dark eyes continuously scanned the crowds of people as if on the look out for something or someone.

'We need to know if you can deliver, Mr Ryan. We have been waiting this last two weeks for word. That's why I arranged this meet today. Every Garda from Belfast to Liverpool is looking for me. It's only for yourself that I came out of me hiding.'

Michael took a deep breath. He was as good looking as

ever and more than one woman gave him an admiring glance as they passed.

'Look, Mr O'Loughlin, these things take time. Especially now. As you just said yourself, everyone is looking for you, and the people you are likely to be dealing with as well. Christ Almighty, I'm taking as big a chance as you are! All I can tell you is what I have been telling you for days. I am doing the best that I can. Everything is shitting hot bricks at the moment.'

Patrick O'Loughlin's face hardened and he grabbed Michael's arm.

'Look here, Ryan, you have more than enough police and judges in your pocket. Rumour has it that you have more than your fair share of politicians as well. All I want is a few passports, that's all. Jesus knows, we have enough guns and Semtex to rearm the bloody British Army. But it's not guns or Semtex we're after these days. It's passports.'

'Give me another couple of days. I have a big job going on in St Martin's Wharf. I have Germans, Micks, the lot on it. I'll get you passports and perfect watertight covers. Now let's leave it there, shall we? I'll be in touch in a few days. OK?'

'I don't seem to have much choice, do I?'

O'Loughlin nodded at Michael and, turning away from him, disappeared back into the crowd. As he walked away from Michael two men approached on either side of him. Too late he realised their intent. As his hand went inside his jacket for his weapon, he felt a gun being pushed into his side.

'If you try anything, Pat, I'll drop you here in the street.'

Then he was bundled into a waiting Daimler at the

kerbside. As he was relieved of his gun one of the men spoke to him.

'You've been grassed, Pat, me old mate. Well and truly grassed.'

Pat O'Loughlin sat back in the seat with a show of careless indifference. Inside he was like a seething cauldron. He stared out at the passing buildings. Michael Ryan had double crossed him. Only he could have fingered him. Involuntarily he clenched his fists. Michael Ryan would pay.

Maura got out of bed still half asleep. The low buzzing of her alarm had woken her too early, or at least that was how it felt. She stood by her bed and stretched. Pulling on a robe she went downstairs to her kitchen, picking up her mail and the daily paper as she went through her hall.

She made a pot of tea and, lighting one of the sixty cigarettes she would smoke that day, unfolded the paper. Staring out at her from the front page of the *Daily Mail* was Patrick O'Loughlin. She studied the picture, stunned. Then she looked at the headlines: IRA KILLER ARRESTED. Forcing her mind to work, she read the story.

'Due to information received, Patrick O'Loughlin, wanted for the bombing of a military base in Surrey where four soldiers died, was picked up by the police as he walked on the Embankment yesterday. He is also an escaped prisoner. He was given four life sentences for sectarian killings in Belfast. The man he was seen with yesterday is still being sought by the police . . .'

Maura's mind was racing. O'Loughlin had met Mickey yesterday and any policeman worth his salt would have recognised Michael Ryan. The ones who were not in their pay tried to make their careers by nicking him. She pulled deeply on her cigarette, got up from her seat and went to the telephone on the kitchen wall. She rang Michael's number. It was answered almost immediately by his boyfriend.

'Get Mickey, now!'

'But he's in the shower . . .'

'Well, get him out then!' Her voice was harsh.

Richard Salter pursed his lips. He did not like Maura and she did not like him. Placing the receiver on the small coffee table he went into the bathroom. Michael waved him away, soap running down his body as he washed his hair.

'Mickey love, your sister's on the phone. She says she must speak to you now.'

Michael stood under the water for a couple of seconds to get rid of most of the soap. Then pulling a towel from the rail he put it around his waist, knocking Richard flying as he hurried out of the bathroom. He picked up the phone, dripping water everywhere.

'What is it, Maws?'

Richard watched as Michael's face changed from undisguished shock to seething rage. He ran back to the kitchen to finish making the breakfast. Whatever that sister of his was saying had certainly given Michael the hump! Still, he reflected as he scrambled eggs, at least *he* had not done anything wrong.

Ten minutes later, as he placed breakfast on the table, he heard the front door slam. Michael had gone without even kissing him goodbye! Richard sat at the table with his face set in a frown. Damn that bloody bitch! He looked at Michael's fluffy scrambled eggs and, smiling, picked it up and scraped it on to this own plate. Waste not, want not, that was his motto.

Michael got into his car, his mind working overtime. As he made his way through the busy morning traffic his rage subsided. Maura had said that they had to think this thing through calmly, and she was right. He had a niggling suspicion in the back of his mind about who had grassed him up. His face set into a hard frown. From what Maura had told him the paper had more or less said that whoever had been with O'Loughlin had been responsible for his being picked up. Joe Public didn't know who that was but the IRA did. And that could mean big trouble. He had been dealing with them for years.

He carried on driving out of London towards Essex. He could not understand why Maura lived in that great big house out in the sticks. He pulled into her drive and got out of the car. She already had the front door open. He kissed her on the cheek. She put her finger to her lips and he followed her through the house to her kitchen, where her daily woman, Mrs MacMullen, was pulling on her coat.

'You'll be paid for today, Mrs Mac, but I need the house to myself.'

'Oh, that's all right, lovie. I don't mind.' She smiled at the pair of them and walked out of the kitchen. They both stood silently until they heard the front door slam.

'She let herself in while I was in the shower. Sorry about that. Coffee?'

Michael nodded.

'Look, Maws, whoever fingered me was very close to home. The only ones who knew about the meet were me, you and Geoffrey.'

Maura shrugged, not taking in what he was saying. 'It could have been someone from O'Loughlin's end.'

Michael sat at the table. 'Why would one of the Micks want to set me up?'

She turned to face him. 'Well, it certainly wasn't me!' Her voice was cold.

'I know that, Princess. That leaves only one other person . . .'

When Maura realised what he was saying she began to shake her head in disbelief.

'No. Not Geoffrey. For Christ's sake, Mickey, he's our brother.'

She poured out the coffee with trembling hands.

'I think that Geoffrey has tucked me up, Maws. It's a gut feeling. He ain't been right for a long time now. Whoever grassed to the old Bill knew exactly where we were meeting, everything. I only knew an hour beforehand myself. You know I have the phones swept once a month. They're cleaner than the Russian Embassy's. No, whoever it was, was close to home. There's no doubt about that.'

'It could have come from O'Loughlin's end.' Her voice was sad. Even as she spoke she knew that Michael was right. She sat down heavily, as if very weary. 'So, Mickey, what are you going to do?'

He sipped his tea. 'What do you think? I can't let this go.'

Maura bit on her thumbnail. 'You don't know for sure yet, Mickey.'

'Listen, Maws, there's a few things that have been bothering me for a while. He asked to be put back into the clubs, didn't he? He didn't want to work with William any more. Right?'

Maura nodded her head slowly.

'Well, the takings were right down. I asked him about it and he said that all the clubs were in the same boat. Then I find out that the New Rockingham Club and the Pink Pussycat have nearly doubled their takings. So I know that he has his hand in the till. He was also seen with Old Billy Bootnose, a known nark. Richard saw them.'

Maura flapped her hand at him. 'I'm sorry, Mickey. For all Geoff's faults he ain't a grass. As for your Richard . . .'

Michael bellowed at her, 'Oh, Maws, grow up for fuck's sake! It's staring us in the face. Richard works in and around London, picking up garbage for the gossip columns. There ain't nothing that he don't know or can't find out. You might not like him but that don't alter the facts. Geoff is selling us out. Not just me. I bet you any money you like, it's you as well.'

'So what's the next step?' Her voice was small.

'Let's just say he won't be going home to dinner with that snot-nosed bird he's got himself.'

Maura gave Michael a level stare, then shook her head, 'No, Mickey. You can't! Not your own flesh and blood. For me, Mickey. For Mum. Don't do it.'

Michael placed his hand over her smaller soft one and squeezed it.

'I can't let this go, Maws.' His voice was quiet now. Final. Maura looked at him wildly, trying to think of a solution to the problem.

'Mickey, please. I'll sort this out.' She forced conviction into her voice. 'I'll get rid of him to another country. He can go to Spain, look after our holdings there. I'll sort it out with him, I swear. He'll toe the line. He must know that you've tumbled him. I'll be responsible for him.'

'All right. All right.' Michael's voice was annoyed. 'You've got twenty-four hours to get rid of him. If he's still around after that, then he's dead. You can tell him that from me. Now I have got to go and square it all with Kelly. You can bet your life they all think it was me fingered O'Loughlin.'

He stood up abruptly and Maura was reminded just how big and dangerous he could be. He kissed her on the forehead and left the house. She sat for a few minutes letting all he had said sink in. Then, lighting another cigarette, she went to the phone and called Geoffrey. Her heart was so heavy, she felt physically sick at the turn of events. If Geoffrey refused to leave the country he was a dead man.

Michael drove to Le Buxom. Although they had offices all over London, the club would always be his favourite place. He had built an empire from these tiny offices and always felt safe here. He had never enjoyed working on the building projects, always feeling more at home with the seedier businesses. To all intents and purposes they were legitimate, valid excuses for spending money. They paid tax, they paid VAT. But deep in Michael's heart it would always be the clubs, the betting offices and the robberies that were his forte. Unlike Maura, he had never lost touch with his poverty-stricken roots. He only had to close his eyes to see once more the cockroaches, the bare floors, and his mother's ever-swollen belly.

Michael wanted money that would astound the senses, money that would be a never ending pit to draw from. He wanted to be like the educated villains he had met through Templeton. He wanted to wear his riches like a cloak, he wanted to be able to buy anyone and anything that he desired. And with the gold heist and the docklands' holdings he would be able to do that. He knew that they had pulled off one of the biggest scams in the history of English crime. That the police were no nearer solving the case of the stolen gold than they were to solving the murders of Jack the Ripper. He had been secretly pleased with himself. Now Geoffrey was going to ruin that.

He had an insight into himself that would have amazed and confused his sister. He knew in his heart that Geoffrey was his Achilles heel. If he ever got caught or called in for questioning, he knew that it would be because of Geoffrey. None of the other boys would ever dream of trying to implicate him or Maura. But Geoffrey would.

In 1980 Garry had been identified at the scene of a robbery. He had appeared at the Old Bailey, accused of armed robbery. Michael had retained the best barrister in London, Douglas Denby QC. Garry had walked free, but Michael knew that if he could have been persuaded to chat to the police about his eldest brother, the boy would never even have had to go to court. Yet Michael had not been worried. He knew that even if Garry got fifteen years, he still would not open his mouth to anyone. Not so Geoffrey. Geoffrey reminded him of a snake, fooling its quarry into a false sense of security, before pouncing on it and destroying it. He had a viper in his camp and his sister could not see it. And the sad part was, Geoffrey wanted to destroy her more than he did Michael.

He parked his car. After carefully scanning the road for anything suspicious, he got out and went into the club. Gerry Jackson was there.

'Hello, Mickey!' Michael heard the pleasure in his friend's voice and was gratified. Gerry was wearing his toupee. On the night of the club bombing his hair had been burnt off and it had never grown back. During the day Gerry wore his hairpiece. He had also lost an ear, and part of his face and neck was still raised and mauve all these years later. Michael cared for Gerry as much as he did his younger brothers.

'All right, Gerry? Anyone been asking for me?' He kept his voice light.

Gerry shook his head.

'The Irish looks better. Is it a new one?' Gerry laughed at the reference to his wig. He was very good-natured despite his ferocious looks.

'Yeah. Cost me nearly two hundred quid. Real hair, see.' He took the toupee off his head and handed it to Michael who took it from him. He did not know what else to do.

'Yeah. It's lovely.' They both laughed together. For the first time in years Michael remembered them as children, playing together. Gerry's dad had been killed in the war and his mum had worked the Bayswater Road. She had brought up her six children on the proceeds of the game and National Assistance. She lived out in Enfield now, a respectable old lady who doted on her grandchildren.

Michael had a terrible feeling of foreboding as he stood with Gerry. He threw the wig back to his friend and, smiling, went up to the offices.

It took him a while to get through to Kelly. When he finally did he was not surprised to find that he was treated with the utmost suspicion.

'Look, Kelly, I was set up. I take oath on that.'

Kelly's thick Northern Irish accent crackled over the wire. 'Pat O'Loughlin was a bad man to cross, Ryan. Once they ship him back to the Maze he'll be back in the driving seat. You're a dead man.'

Kelly's voice was matter-of-fact, as if he was discussing the weather.

Michael was having difficulty in controlling his temper. The famous temper that could instil fear into the most hardened of criminals.

'I told you, it was a set up. What more do you want from me? I've been associated with your bloody organisation for nearly thirty years, mate. I was giving contributions before you was even born.'

If he told them about Geoffrey they would never trust him again, and then his brother would be dead and his mother would be heartbroken.

Kelly broke into his racing thoughts.

'We think, Mr Ryan, that you have done a deal. An hour ago Sean Murphy and Liam McNamara were picked up at another of your so-called safe houses. You're a dead man, Ryan.'

The phone went dead.

Michael sat staring at it in amazement. Murphy and McNamara! He put the phone back in its cradle. A cold sweat had broken out on his forehead. He got up from his chair and went to the drinks cabinet in the corner of the room. He poured himself a large brandy and drank it straight back. Geoffrey had done him up like a kipper. Well, he would wipe Geoffrey Ryan off the face of the earth. Sod Maura, and sod his bloody mother! He would get the word out that Geoffrey had grassed the Irishman up. That way, if the IRA got to him first, all well and good. If not, then Michael himself would blast the bastard through his guts. He could do without the Irish anyway. He phoned Maura's house. He had to let her know what was going on.

Templeton answered the phone.

'Willy?'

'Why, hello, Michael.' His voice was warm.

'Is Maws there?'

'No. She's gone to your mother's to see Geoffrey. Can I help? I said I would man the phones for her. I wanted to take her out to lunch, but you know your sister. Business first!' His tone was jocular and friendly.

Michael forced himself to laugh.

'If she comes back before I see her, will you give her a message for me? Tell her that I *must*, absolutely must, get rid of the employee we were discussing. Tell her that Kelly insisted. Got that?'

'Yes. Don't worry, I've written it down.'

'See you later then, Willy.'

' 'Bye, Mickey.'

So Maura had swallowed her pride and gone to their mother's house. Obviously that was where she'd tracked the little bastard down to. He must think he was safe there. The slag!

Michael pulled on his coat and left the club. It was now early afternoon and the traffic was thick. He finally drove into Lancaster Road, seething with anger. Geoffrey had tucked him up and Geoffrey would pay. He would try to get his brother to leave his mother's house, but if he wouldn't then he would drag the bastard out if need be. Fuck his mother! Fuck the lot of them! He wasn't going under for the toe rag. In his temper Michael did not notice the black Granada Scorpio that was parked opposite.

Maura had finally located Geoffrey at their mother's house. Garry had answered the telephone and she had told him not to say she had called. She had a feeling that if Geoffrey knew, he would try and get away. She had to see him before Michael did. She told Garry to keep him there until she arrived. She had parked her car in Bletchedon Street and walked around to her mother's house, in case Geoffrey had been scanning the road from the window. As she had walked up the familiar steps her heart had been hammering dangerously. She had not been to this house in over ten years. Not since the fight after Benny had been murdered. She shuddered. She did not want to see her mother and open all the old wounds, but she had to. She only hoped Geoffrey would realise that she was trying to help him.

She plucked up her courage and knocked on the door. She could hear the dull taps of her mother's shoes across the linoleum and guessed that she had come from the kitchen. The door opened and the two women came face to face for the first time in eleven years.

Maura was shocked at the sight before her. Her mother was nothing more than a fat little old lady. Her face was wrinkled up like a walnut and her hair, still in the scraped bun of old, was completely grey. Only the eyes were as she remembered them, alive with malice and triumph.

Maura realised her mother thought that she had come to beg some kind of forgiveness. Well, that was all right with her. She would play any kind of game she had to today. She knew, though, that seeing her mother meant nothing to her now.

'Hello, Mum.' She was amazed to find that her voice was normal.

Sarah's eyes swept her from head to foot. Maura was wearing a black trouser suit with a white cashmere jumper underneath. She could practically hear her mother counting up the cost in her head.

'What do you want?' Sarah's voice was flat. It was obvious to Maura that she was going to make it as hard as possible for her.

Maura walked into the house without being asked. She had to push past her mother, and was made aware of just how tiny she was.

'Is our Geoffrey here?'

As Maura spoke she walked through to the kitchen. Sarah followed her. Her mettle was up but she kept silent. There was something funny going on here. Geoffrey was like a scalded cat. Every time the phone rang or someone knocked, he nearly had a seizure. Well, she had a feeling that her daughter held the key to a mystery and for that reason, and that reason only, would stomach her presence in her house.

Maura entered the kitchen. Geoffrey and Garry were sitting at the kitchen table. Garry smiled at her, but Geoffrey looked as if he had been struck by a thunderbolt.

'Hello, Geoffrey.' She looked straight at him. The kitchen looked and felt familiar. It had not changed one iota in the last ten years.

'Can I speak to you? Alone, please.'

She saw Geoffrey's eyes go to his mother who was standing behind her. Maura nodded at Garry. Getting up from the table, he went to where his mother was standing.

'Come on, Muvver. Let's leave the lovebirds alone for a minute.'

Sarah pushed at him roughly. 'Get your bleeding hands off me! What's going on here?'

Maura turned to her mother and, grabbing her shoulders, bundled her none too gently out of the kitchen door.

'Let go of me, you bloody lanky bitch!'

'Garry, take her into the front room. Her statues are probably lonely.' Maura's voice was sarcastic. She looked closely into her mother's face. 'Keep your nose out, Mum. It doesn't concern you.'

She shut the kitchen door firmly, blocking out her mother's raised voice. She could hear Garry trying to pacify her. Geoffrey was watching her warily. Maura could feel the fear emanating from him.

'Michael knows everything.'

Geoffrey dropped his gaze.

'Let's face it, Geoff, it wouldn't take long to sniff out something so putrid, would it? I've come to help you, though looking at you, I don't know why I bothered. You've got twenty-four hours to get out of the country.'

Geoffrey's head shot up. There was a peculiar light in his eyes, as scared as he was.

'I ain't going nowhere. You don't scare me.'

Maura laughed out loud. 'Oh, but I do. I scare you shitless, and so does Michael. And the mood I left him in, he'd scare the devil.'

As she spoke, she heard four loud bangs, then Geoffrey began to laugh hysterically.

Michael screeched to a halt outside his mother's house. Fiona Dalgleesh was walking her young son to the shops and was startled by the squealing of wheels. She grabbed her son's hand. Bloody lunatic drivers! She saw a large, good-looking man get out of the offending car. It was about fifteen feet away. Then, in the weak October sunshine, she saw a distinct gleam. She looked across the road to where a black car was parked and opened her eyes wide with shock. A man was sitting in the passenger seat of the car, and he had a gun! Without thinking she threw her son to the pavement and lay on top of him. A piercing cry escaped from her lips.

Michael got out of the car still seething with rage. He heard the girl scream and looked in her direction. He saw her throw herself on top of a little boy. It was the last thing he was to see. A moment later a bullet entered the side of his head and splattered his brains all over the pavement.

The girl saw him crumple and fall, a bewildered expression on his face. The man with the gun then got out of his car and shot the victim three more times. Even in her shock and fear, Fiona Dalgleesh knew that those shots were unnecessary. The big, good-looking man was already dead.

As the car drove away, the road became once more quiet and residential. Only Michael's blood, running along the pavement in crimson rivulets, showed that anything was wrong.

When Maura and Garry heard the shots they both rushed from the house. Sarah followed them. Geoffrey stayed in the kitchen alone.

Suddenly the street was full of people, emerging from all the houses like ghouls. Maura ran down the steps to the pavement. She raised Michael's head and cradled it in her arms, too shocked even to cry.

Geoffrey, her mother, her brothers . . . everything was wiped from her mind. When the police and ambulance arrived they had forcibly to pull Maura from her brother's body. Her white cashmere jumper was stained with blood and particles of brain and skull. Garry stood beside her, silent and shocked. Sarah had taken one look at her eldest son lying sprawled across her daughter's lap and walked back into her house. She felt nothing.

Maura and Garry were taken to hospital suffering from shock. Maura had to be sedated. The next morning she left the hospital with William Templeton. The newspapers were in attendance. All the nationals had pictures of Maura with Templeton's arms around her. She was aware, even in her grief, that he had burnt his boats for her and she was grateful to him. He took her to her house and kept the world away from her.

She refused to speak to anyone, not even Carla or Marge or her brothers. Roy took over the reins of the business and though nothing was ever said, all the brothers wondered what had happened with Geoffrey and why, as the eldest after Michael, he had not taken over the businesses himself.

Maura had three separate interviews with the police. She told each of them the same thing. She had no idea who had been behind her brother's murder.

But she did know and she concentrated all her energy into that fact. After two weeks of seclusion Maura felt ready to face the world again. She emerged from her grief, tougher and harder than ever before. She had hatred inside her now, a great big sour-smelling hatred. And she was going to use it to her advantage. Michael was dead, but the Ryans would go on. She owed him that much.

Chapter Twenty-Seven

Maura walked into the club at nine-thirty, exactly fourteen days after Michael was murdered. Gerry Jackson went to her and put his hand on her shoulder gently.

'If you need me, Maura, just call.'

She nodded at him and walked up the stairs into the offices. The music in the club was loud and harsh. She could hear the chatter of the customers and the clink of glasses above the din.

Roy was obviously shocked to see her.

'Maws?'

'I had to get back into the world, mate. Thanks for taking over everything. I promise you won't lose by it.'

He got up from the desk, embarrassed to be caught sitting in what had been Michael's seat.

Maura waved him back. 'You don't have to move, Roy.'

He sat down again. He was shocked at the change in her. She looked old. The years had piled on her in the short time since Mickey's death. She also had a steely glint in her eyes that had not been there before. If he did not know better he would think it was Michael come back in female form.

'I've kept everything going here as best I can, like. I know that's what Mickey would have wanted.'

Maura could hear the sadness and loss in his voice. Going to where he sat, she slipped her arms around his neck.

'I miss him, Roy. It's like a physical pain at times. As if a crucial part of me is missing.'

'I know, Maws. I know.' He held her hands in his own, surprised at the gentleness in her. 'We'll find out who set him up, Maws. Don't you worry, girl.'

She sighed. She knew exactly who had set him up. She straightened up, running her hands through her hair.

'What's been happening here?'

'Oh, nothing for you to worry about, Maws.' Although she could not see Roy's face, she knew that something was up by the sound of his voice. She walked around to face him and sat opposite him on the chair by the desk.

'What's up?' Her voice was hard.

'Look, I'll tell you about it another time. You're in no fit state . . .'

'Cut the crap, Roy. I'm a big girl now, in case you haven't noticed. I also run this firm. I have done for nearly twenty years.' Her voice softened at the look on his face. 'You have no need to try to protect me, Roy. I can do that myself.'

'We've had aggro out on the streets. Every firm with dreams of the big time has been showing its face.'

Maura sighed heavily.

'I should have guessed that the tomb robbers would be out in force.'

'Look, Maws, it's nothing I can't handle.'

She picked up the pack of Benson and Hedges from the desk and lit one.

'I want to know what's been going on, and I want to know NOW!'

Roy just sat staring at her. Maura knew that he wanted to help her, that he wanted to do what Michael would have done. But he would never be Michael in a million years. *She* was the nearest thing to Michael Ryan. In fact, she felt as if he had entered her body and was looking out of her eyes, so strongly did she feel his presence at this moment.

'Look, Roy, I need to get back to normal. I know you all loved him, but me and Mickey . . . it was special.' Her voice was low and charged with emotion.

Roy felt choked. He looked into her ravaged face, so skilfully made up, and knew that all that she said was true. Maura and Michael had been closer than any two people he had ever known. He spoke and his words had the effect of a bomb blast on her, so great was her rage when she heard them.

'A black crew have been muscling in on the hot dogs. Yardies. They swooped on three prime sites the night Mickey died.'

Maura's voice when she finally spoke was dripping with malevolence.

'Yardies? YARDIES? I ain't trashed at the Scotland Yardies so a bunch of bloody coons won't give me any grief. I'll sort the buggers out myself. Get Gerry from downstairs and get on the phone to the other boys. We're going to have a sort out on the street. Starting with the bloody "macaroons". Now tell me *everything* that's been going on since Mickey died.'

Roy began to speak, glad in his heart that Maura had

come to take over the reins. He had not done a very good job, he knew. He had wanted to but had no idea how everything was run. Maura, Mickey and Geoffrey had always been the thinkers of the family. The rest of the boys had been the heavies. He had been impressed with Maura's acumen in the past, now he was impressed by her dogged determination to sort out all the trouble that Michael's passing had created.

Barrington Dennison was thirty years old. He stood five foot ten and, as a body builder, his shoulders and arms were huge. His biceps measured over twenty-eight inches. Barrington Dennison was proud of his physique and proud to be black. His hair, which was grown into long, fat, spiralling dreadlocks, was tied in a pony tail with a piece of spearmint green leather. The leather was the same shade as his tracksuit.

He walked with a strutting cockiness away from his BMW car. In Brixton, where he was born, the letters stood for 'Black Man's Wheels'. His current girlfriend, an eighteen-year-old blonde, was sitting in the car, smoking a joint. She was waiting for Barrington to conclude his business.

Barrington was a Yardie. He told everyone who asked that he was one. He loved it. Within hours of the news of Michael Ryan's death hitting the streets, he had taken over three sites that he had been after for a long time, believing, as many people did, that with Michael's death the streets were once more open territory. He also dealt in grass and ecstasy. And lately crack.

He looked at his watch, a brand new Rolex. It was just on eleven-fifteen and time for a pull. A 'pull' was the term used for clearing the tills on the pitches. This was done every few hours. That way, if the pitch was robbed, whoever did it would not get too big a 'wallet'.

He was unaware as he walked towards the busy pitch that he was being watched.

Maura called to him: 'Are you Barrington Dennison?' Her voice was friendly and soft.

Barrington glanced in the direction of the voice and saw a good-looking white woman standing by a Mercedes Sports. He smiled at her and was pleased to see her smiling back. 'Yo, Momma. You wantin' me, baby?'

He walked over to her, his strut even more emphasised as he realised that all the people on the hot dog pitch were watching him. A rich white bitch could only do his street credibility good. He stood in front of her, pleased as punch that he was in full view of the people on his pitch. He watched her lick her lips.

He grinned at her, showing perfect white teeth.

'I have something for you, Barrington.' Her voice was caressing.

She was opening her bag, a large leather shoulderbag.

'Do I know you? You sure look familiar.' He stopped talking as he saw her take a length of lead piping from the enormous white leather bag. He heard her laugh.

'I'm Maura Ryan, you big, fat, bastard.'

As his mind registered her words he was held from behind. He could feel himself being dragged on to the dirty pavement, and for a second wondered if he could still be seen. Then he was being held by two large white men, and suddenly he was frightened. It had all happened too fast for his brain to react. They had got him exactly where they wanted him. He could have wept.

He saw Maura Ryan raise the piping over her head and bring it down with considerable force on his knees. The piping was twelve inches long and three inches thick. It shattered his kneecaps. He screamed. Then he felt the piping come down again and shrieked again. White hot pain was flashing behind his eyes, coming in sickening waves. He felt the arms that held him loosen their grip. Then Maura was kneeling beside him. She pulled his head up by its dreadlocks and stared into his face.

'Don't ever get ambitions again, prick. Do you hear me? Next time I'll leave you in the same state I left Danny Rubens in. Michael Ryan is dead, but I am alive and kicking and don't you ever forget that. You pass the message on to your Yardie friends.'

Barrington nodded through his agony.

Maura and the men stood up and he watched through a haze of pain as they approached the pitch. It was deserted. The two young black boys working it had run off. They had no intentions of getting involved with that type of violence. Maura and Roy secured it and left.

As Maura went to her Mercedes she passed Barrington Dennison again. She looked at his twisted legs and pain-ravaged face, and felt herself begin to buzz with excitement. She had handled that exactly as Michael would have done. He would be proud of her!

When they arrived at the other pitches, they were already deserted. Bad news travels fast on the streets.

Barrington's girlfriend was so stoned she did not even realise that anything out of the ordinary had happened until the ambulance arrived. She had been too busy listening to Bob Marley singing 'Redemption Song'.

Back at the club, Maura and the boys discussed the measures they would have to take to re-establish their superiority in London. Within a week it was done. Maura had proved herself a shrewd woman and slipped on Michael's mantle easily. When she was sure she was firmly entrenched, she turned her attention to the Irish problem and her brother Geoffrey.

Kelly was waiting for Maura in a small bedsit in Kilburn. The owner of the house was a sympathiser. There were many of them in London.

Kelly heard a car drive into the deserted street and glanced at his watch. It was just after two-fifteen. This must be Maura Ryan. He got up from his seat and went to the window. Pulling back a grubby net curtain, he watched her as she locked up her car and walked into the house. The front door was already open. He could hear her soft steps on the stairs.

He carried on looking out of the window to make certain there was no one else about. He was still not sure exactly what kind of meet this was going to be. The death of Michael Ryan must have hit her badly; he knew himself how close they had been. For his own part, Kelly had always liked and respected Maura, and enjoyed doing business with her. In the IRA there was no discrimination; women were blooded along with the men. He had met women in the cause who were much, much harder and shrewder than many of the men. He knew women who would not think twice about blowing up a school bus or shooting a pregnant woman, something that most of the so-called hard men would baulk at. But above everything else he trusted Maura Ryan, and it was for that reason, and that reason only, that he had agreed to meet her tonight.

He turned from the window as she tapped lightly on the door of the room, and let her in.

'Hello, Kelly.' Her voice was neutral.

'Maura. Please take a seat.'

As always, he was courteous. It came naturally to him where women were concerned.

Maura sat on the tiny PVC sofa and took the glass of Bushmills that Kelly offered her. He sat opposite her and smiled. He was quick to notice in the light of the naked light bulb that she smiled with her mouth but not her eyes. She was obviously still grieving. As she opened her black bag to get her cigarettes, Kelly felt a small twinge of uneasiness. Maura sensed it.

'Don't worry, Kelly, this isn't revenge time. I know exactly what happened and I want to explain it to you.'

He picked up a book of matches from the small coffee table between them and lit her cigarette for her.

'Go ahead. I'm listening.'

Maura pulled on the cigarette and blew the smoke out through her nose.

Kelly grimaced. He could stomach many things from women, but smoking was not one of them.

Maura breathed in deeply. When she spoke her words were hesitant and sad.

'It wasn't Mickey who grassed up O'Loughlin and the others.'

'Well, who was it then?' His voice was brisk.

Maura took a gulp of the Bushmills, its peaty tang giving her courage.

'It was my brother Geoffrey.'

Kelly digested this bit of information.

'Mickey was good to you over the years.' Her voice was full of the pain of losing him.

'Listen, Maura.' Kelly's voice was gentle. 'There was one thing Michael could never understand. In London, the Ryans are big. You own the majority of the police force. You run the main clubs. Your businesses include gambling, drinking, sex, all the things that are big money spinners. You're also involved in the building and construction games. But, you see, to us and the likes of us, you're small fry really. We're an international organisation, known and feared all over the world. We're given money by Gadaffi, Baader Meinhof, the PLO. The list is endless. All we ever gave you was our trust. And that trust was broken.'

Maura was angry. 'For God's sake, Kelly, why do you think that I'm here tonight? I want to clear Michael's name. He'd been paying into your cause since 1960. He helped you over the years more than he had to. He hid people. Got arms, Semtex. He gathered information on Members of Parliament and members of the armed forces. People whom you then blew up and killed or maimed.'

Kelly interrupted her.

'I'm not disputing all that. Michael was a good business asset over the years. Holy Jesus, we never wanted to harm him but it was the logical step to take after what happened.

'What exactly do you want here tonight? Tell me that, Maura. Michael's death is done, over with. I'm sorry we got the wrong man though that can soon be remedied. But I think that you came here tonight to ask for something. Not just to tell me that your brother Geoffrey is for the chop.'

'What I want is us all back on our old footing.'

Kelly laughed. Really laughed.

'Sure, you're a funny lass. Three of our best men are on their way to the Maze and you want us to forget all about it! Are you demented, woman?' He laughed again, wiping his eyes with the back of his hand.

Maura lit another cigarette from the butt of the previous one. She looked solemn and annoyed.

'I'm glad to think that you had such a high regard for Michael.' Her voice dripped sarcasm. 'That he was so indispensable to you. But you see, Kelly, Michael meant everything to me. Everything. His death was not a "logical step" in my eyes. It was a brutal killing that was unnecessary. If you had waited and let us inform you of the circumstances, it could have been avoided.'

Kelly was sorry for his laughter. In his first flush of joviality he had forgotten that he was talking about this woman's kin. In the IRA you had no allegiance to family or friends. Only to the cause.

'I'm sorry. Sorry to the heart for laughing. But you do understand what I was saying?' He looked into her sad white face and was sad himself. There were many women like her who had lost their loved ones to the cause. Husbands and sons who would never be coming home again, or were rotting in the bloody Maze. He tried again.

'You realise that Geoffrey is a dead man now, don't you?'

She nodded.

'Look, Maura, I'll tell you what I'll try to do, but I can't promise anything. I'll talk to a few people for you . . . explain the situation like . . . put them straight. The fact that you sacrificed Geoffrey should tell them that you're trying to re-establish your old footing. But that's all I can do. I can't personally guarantee anything. You must understand that.'

It was all she had expected. She had at least seen the back of Geoffrey. That was her main reason for coming here. She smiled at Kelly wistfully.

'Well, I for one won't hold a grudge. I remember when

my brother Benny was murdered, Michael said it was an occupational hazard. He said it could have been any one of us, and he was right. It's the price we pay for the life we lead, I suppose.'

'It's the same with us, Maura. Sure, isn't that fecking Geoffrey the foolish one? Biting the hand that feeds him. Well, in a family the size of yours, there has to be one bad apple. It's the law of averages.'

Maura shrugged.

'I suppose so. Still, he won't be around much longer.'

Kelly smiled and poured them both out another drink.

'I can guarantee that. Now drink up. You look as if you need it.'

Chapter Twenty-Eight

November 1986

Michael's body was being lowered into the ground. It was a freezing cold day. A fine rain had been falling all morning and overhead dark clouds were gathering for the storm that would erupt later in the afternoon. Maura was not crying. Her eyes scanned the crowd of people; over a hundred had turned out for Michael's funeral. She noticed that the hostesses were out in force. Some of them had stopped working over twenty years previously but stood now with their younger counterparts, in their smart coats and brightly made-up faces, looking genuinely sad. It pleased Maura to see them there. They remembered the strong, vibrant Michael of his youth.

Her eyes wandered to Geoffrey who was standing to the right of the grave. Maura could see he was crying, tears streaming down his face. He stood beside their mother, who was stony-faced and dry-eyed. Maura felt an urge to walk around the open grave and throw him in on top of the brother he had helped to murder. If it had not been for him, no one need be here today. Michael would be in his office as he always was, bright and early, no matter what time he had got to bed the night before. She only hoped that wherever Michael was he would see Geoffrey's death. She smiled to herself. It was to be the typical IRA assassination for informers. Kneecapped first and then a single shot to the back of the head. Ten days after the funeral, Kelly had said.

Geoffrey raised his gaze from his brother's coffin and locked eyes with his sister. He thought for one moment that she was smiling at him and smiled back at her tremulously. Then, when she dropped her eyes, he realised that the breach with Maura would never be healed. Geoffrey knew that he had opened up a can of worms that was going to be the finish of him. All his years of planning and watching and listening had been to no avail. When he had set the ball rolling for Michael's death he had regretted it almost immediately. He would give his own life now to have him back.

Maura stared into the gaping hole. Michael was down there in a wooden box and he would never be coming home. She hated Geoffrey with a vengeance now. If she had let Michael finish him when he had wanted to, maybe it could all have been avoided. If someone had told her a month ago that she would be the instigator of one of her own brothers' deaths, she would have protested vehemently. Now she could not wait for it to happen.

She saw that people were watching Geoffrey pityingly as he cried and that only made her anger more intense. She was disgusted. She turned her face away and buried it in William Templeton's coat. He held her tightly to him, murmuring into her hair.

'It's all right. Everything will be all right.'

Sarah Ryan was watching her daughter. She noticed that Carla was as usual close by her. Sarah herself had Geoffrey on the left of her and her grandson Benny on her right. She reached out her arm and placed it across her grandson's shoulders. He shrugged her off. At almost eleven years of age he thought that he was too old to be cuddled, thought that he was a man. He wished he had been allowed to stand with his father and his uncles. He had loved his Uncle Michael, and although he did not know it, was the double of him as a child. He had the same features, expressions, everything. He also had the same quirk to his nature that Michael had had. Sarah and Janine both doted on him and did not realise that he was turning into a greater misogynist by the day.

Sarah concentrated on her only daughter. She wished that she was burying *her* today. As bad as Michael had been she had preferred him to her daughter. In Sarah's mind men were a violent breed. It was a fact of life. While women should be strong but never violent.

She'd watched women brawling in the street – 'old shawlies' as the olden day Irish women had been called. Her own mother had been known as the most argumentative woman in Shepherd's Bush. But Sarah could never condone her daughter's way of life. She could not see what should have been staring her in the face: that Michael and Maura were as one, twins born years apart. She could not see that her daughter had loved her brother wholly and desperately. She could not see that Maura had been slowly dying inside since she was sixteen and had experienced the pain of rejection by Terry Petherick and the agony of having her baby scraped from her body. That all the pain and hurt had had to come out at some time. In some way Sarah herself had pushed the memory of the abortion into the back of her mind. If she ever did think about it she soothed her own guilt by telling herself that a child from her daughter's body should never have been allowed to walk the earth.

Terry Petherick and two other policemen were sitting in an unmarked car by the funeral cortège, jotting down the names and car numbers of everyone at the funeral that they recognised or were unsure of. From another car a police photographer was taking photos. In spite of everything, all the policemen were impressed by the number of influential people who had turned up to pay their last respects. It showed them also that Michael Ryan had had a lot of pull to get such a turn out.

The Shakespeare Set, also known as the Dear and Dahling Brigade, were all there: so-called respectable actors and actresses who lived on the fringes of the London gangster scene. There was the usual smattering of over-the-hill models, hoping to get their faces into the nationals once more and then sell their 'my nights of love with gangland murderer' story to the *News of the World*. Even though Michael Ryan was the best-known shirtlifter in the South East! Even after his death the sycophants and hangers-on were still after a little bit of reflected glory.

Terry Petherick smiled to himself. He had noticed a few back-benchers looking solemn and nervous. I wonder how much they owe? he thought to himself, and carried on scanning the mourners. A good few boxers and sports promoters were there along with some big name gangsters from Liverpool and Birmingham. They had travelled down to show their faces and offer their condolences, and also to see how the land lay. Whether there would be an opening for them now. See if the Ryan family was as strong as before. Terry counted three QCs and two judges, one of whom had been drummed out of his profession because of a penchant for rent boys and child pornography. Quite a little cache, he mused. There were the usual blaggers, mainly small-time, in catalogue suits and nervous twitches, who would relive Michael's funeral for years as the highlight of their criminal career. Give them a bit of pull if they ever got banged up again.

Then Terry saw that the funeral was now over and people were making their way to their cars. That's when he saw Maura. He felt the familiar tightening in his guts that she caused whenever he laid eyes on her. She was as lovely as ever and he relived in his mind the last night they had spent together. He was still unmarried, and it was because of this tall, stately, and utterly unscrupulous woman. He wound down the window of the car and the damp cold whipped at his face. He knew that she had seen him.

Maura was walking towards her funeral car when she saw the face of the man she had alternately loved and hated watching her. William had his arm round her waist and felt her body stiffen. He held her tighter but she pulled away from him and walked to Terry's car.

'Bloody hell! They won't do nothing to us, will they?'

Terry could have laughed at the fear in the young PC's voice, but was too busy watching Maura approach him. She spoke and her husky voice sent his pulses racing.

'Hello, Terry. It's been a long time.'

'Hello, Maura. Too long.' They stared at each other as if devouring one another with their eyes. The policemen and William Templeton were well aware of the spark that was flaring between them.

'I'm sorry about your brother's death.'

As Terry spoke, Garry and Leslie came over to the car,

accompanied by a drunken Lee. They were all incensed at the police and press being there. Outside the graveyard was a film crew who were recording all the famous people who had turned up. Michael dead was as newsworthy as he had been alive.

Garry leaned in at Terry's open window.

'Why don't you fuck off? Mickey's dead and you lot still won't leave him alone.'

Leslie and Lee stood aggressively behind him. The atmosphere was charged with malice.

'Leave it, Garry!' Maura's voice was clipped and as hard as steel.

He faced her angrily.

'They're plainclothes Filth, Maws.'

'Just shut it. I won't have any aggravation today. Now get moving. People are beginning to stare at us.'

Her voice dripped ice and Garry, Leslie and Lee were nonplussed for a moment. Lee, who was well away, did not grasp the warning in her voice. He lurched towards the car, belching loudly.

'You wankers!'

Maura grabbed his arm. Her hand was like a steel band. She spoke through gritted teeth.

'Garry, you'd better take him away from me before I get really annoyed.' She shoved Lee towards Garry and Leslie. 'I'll deal with you lot later. Now, take him and get out of my sight.'

The two men took Lee away from the car hurriedly. Maura was watching the people around her. She knew that the confrontation had not gone unnoticed. She nodded her head to Terry and walked to her own car. She was fuming inside at Lee and Garry but her own brain was telling her that she had been a fool to stop and talk to

Terry in the first place. But she could not help herself. Seeing him sitting there had brought it all back, the longing and the wanting that she had suppressed for nearly all her adult life.

Sarah had witnessed Maura's talk with the police and had taken a long hard look at Terry Petherick.

He sat in the car watching Maura walk away from him. The other two policemen were terrified.

'I thought we was all goners there, sir.'

Terry dragged his eyes from Maura's retreating back and looked at the younger man.

'No. You were quite safe, son. Even the Ryans wouldn't murder in broad daylight.'

His friend, DS Cranmer, walked over from the other police car. Opening the back door of Terry's Sierra, he got inside. 'I see your old bird stopped for a chat then?'

Terry laughed. 'Get stuffed, Cranmer.'

As Cranmer chatted on Terry was wondering if he would ever live it down. It was the first thing any new officer was told when he came to Vine Street. And the funny thing was, nearly all of them were impressed by it. He shook his head at the double standards in his world.

Maura reached her waiting car amid condolences and offers of help for the future. She noticed that William had disappeared somewhere in the crowd. When she finally stepped into her car Roy was waiting inside for her as she had asked him. She settled herself and tapped on the glass screen that separated them from the driver.

He spoke to her over a microphone.

'Yes, madam.'

'Could you please take me to the Bramley Arms? We will not be going back to the house just yet.'

The driver nodded and started up the limousine, leaving St Mary's RC cemetery behind. When they arrived at the Bramley Arms a few minutes later they got out of the car and went straight into the back bar.

On the table was a bottle of Remy Martin and two glasses. Maura slipped off her black coat and gloves. Sitting at the table, she poured out two stiff drinks.

Roy sat beside her. He accepted the proffered drink and waited for her to speak.

Maura gulped at the brandy. Getting out her ever-present cigarettes she lit one, drawing the smoke deep into her lungs. Roy noticed that her hands were trembling.

'Did you notice Anthony's and Benny's graves? They look tatty. Remind me to get on to the cemetery officials.'

Roy nodded at her. He could see that she was wound up to fever pitch.

Maura looked into Roy's open face. She realised how like Michael he looked. How all the boys looked like Michael. She felt an urge to cry. Really cry. She gulped at her drink again. Seeing Terry had re-opened old wounds.

'I wanted to talk to you, Roy, as the next in line in age.'

He looked shocked. 'What about our Geoff?'

Maura took a deep breath and slowly and precisely told Roy everything, glad of something to take her mind off Terry Petherick. Glad to be able to share her problem with someone . . . to be planning ahead. When she finished telling him he was white-faced and tight-lipped.

'He tucked Mickey up? That's what you're telling me, ain't it?'

Maura nodded.

'I'll kill him, Maws! I'll kill the bastard!' He raised himself out of his seat as if he was going to do it immediately. Maura grabbed his arm.

'Don't worry. As I told you just now Kelly's going to sort it out. He owes Michael that much.'

Roy sat back in his seat and wiped his hand over his face. 'I knew that something wasn't right, Maws, but I could never find out what it was. To think that Geoffrey's been waiting and planning this for years. The dirty sod!'

'Well, the only people who know about it, Roy, are you and me. And it's got to stay that way. Especially now with Mickey dying. We're going to be in the frontline.'

Roy nodded slowly.

'Why did you never tell me this before?'

Maura sighed heavily. 'When Mickey was alive we thought we had it all under control. Geoff was working for us. The friction that had occurred over the years seemed to have died down. Oh, there's lots of reasons. I never wanted Geoffrey dead. Never. Not until Michael was murdered. Christ, I even tried to save him!' Her voice broke.

Roy poured out another stiff brandy and put the glass into her hands. She took a large swallow to steady her nerves.

'So what's going to happen with the businesses now?'

'Firstly I'm going to hand over the docklands to Willy and the accountants. Willy's a partner and he's trustworthy. Then I'm going to extend all our other operations. I'm going to try to get rid of the gold bullion as well. Michael and I had a contact in the Channel Islands. He can offload the majority of it. But I'll need a number two, Roy, and that's why I am asking you. What do you say?'

'You know the answer to that, Maws.' He took her hand gently in his. 'I'll do whatever you say. I know you're the brainy one. Janine's always calling me a thicko.' He grinned.

Maura was annoyed.

'Listen, Roy, you might not have a degree but you're cute enough. Janine should watch her trap. She's got too bloody much of it.'

'Don't worry, Maws. She don't get it all her own way. She just thinks she does.' He raised his thick black eyebrows and smiled. Maura found herself smiling with him.

Roy picked up his glass. 'Well then, girl. Here's to us!'

'To the Ryans!'

They both drank deeply, then Maura stood up unsteadily. 'We'd better get to the wake. Good grief, I'm pissed!'

'On a day like today, Maws, it's the only way to be.'

They laughed softly together. Except Maura's laughter was tinged with hysteria.

Back at Michael's flat the atmosphere was tense. Michael's boyfriend Richard was red-eyed and nervous. He had taken the death badly. About forty people had been invited back to the flat, mostly family and close friends. When Maura and Roy arrived, the first person she saw was Gerry Jackson. She went to him, the brandy making her more open than she usually was.

'You'll miss him more than anyone, Gerry. You went back a long time.'

He nodded sadly.

'Yeah, Maws. I will. You know that me mum's here? She always liked Mickey. Say hello to her for me. It would mean a lot to her.'

'I will, Gerry. She's a good woman.'

'I remember once when we was all small . . . you weren't even born then . . . me and Mickey was only about twelve. Just after the war. Well, me mum was on the "bash" then, down the Bayswater Road. I'm not ashamed of it. She fed and clothed the lot of us from her earnings. Anyway, me and Mickey was out playing and this gang of older boys came into Kensington Gardens and started taunting me about me mum. They were about sixteen and I was scared, Maws. Bloody terrified! And then Mickey started to punch the biggest one. He went garrity. And the other boys, they were frightened, see. Because even then Michael had something about him that scared people.'

His voice was low and charged with emotion. 'Did you know that he sent my old mum a ton every Christmas? Never forgot her once. A nice card and a hundred quid. I loved that man, Maura. Loved the bones of him. Whatever people might say about him.'

Maura was touched by his devotion. 'He loved you, Gerry. I know he did.'

Gerry brought out a large white handkerchief and blew his nose. His scarred face and missing ear were more noticeable than usual.

'He loved *you*, Maws. Loved you to death.'

She felt the large ball of tears in her throat and hurriedly excused herself. She made her way to the kitchen and got herself a drink. The kitchen worktops were piled with alcohol of every kind. Michael's boyfriend followed her in there. Looking at his white face, Maura felt sorry for him. She had never liked Richard, had never liked any of Michael's boyfriends, but seeing the grief on the man's face, she was sorry for him.

'I'll miss him, Maura. I know that people frowned on us but we loved each other in our own way.' She could see the tears shining in his eyes and suddenly wanted to escape from the flat. Run away somewhere where Michael was unknown. She fought down the feeling of panic. She was drunk, that's what was wrong with her. From the lounge she heard her father's voice starting to sing.

She patted Richard's shoulder and walked back into the lounge, holding on to her glass of brandy tightly. Her father was singing an old Irish ballad and it sounded funny with his cockney accent. She leaned against the wall and listened to the words of 'The Wild Colonial Boy'.

Maura studied her father's shrunken form. Thanks to her mother's dominance, she had hardly seen him over the years, and, looking at him as he sang, she was suddenly lonely for him. For his cuddles and his kind words. Everyone in the packed room, full of cigarette smoke and perfume, stood silently while he sang an ode to his dead boys.

Maura, along with many people in that room, blinked away tears. She decided that Michael would have approved of his father singing. Would have enjoyed it, had he been here. She sipped at her drink.

When Benjamin finished singing everyone called for another and Maura's voice was the loudest. Drinking his beer and clearing his throat, Benjamin began singing once more.

As Maura listened to the sad words of 'Down In The Valley', she felt the grief inside her gradually ebbing away. She knew these songs back to front. They were songs that had been sung at countless funerals over the years. Then her Auntie Nellie, an old lady now, began to sing a song that had all the older people joining in. It was an old Irish rebel song and it made Maura feel sick. The people they were singing about had murdered the man they had all come to bury, if only they knew it.

Maura looked at Geoffrey, standing by their mother, and knew by his face that he was thinking the same thing as herself. Well, the same people would be getting rid of him soon and she thanked God for it.

She swallowed back the rest of the brandy, then made a decision. She was going to get Willy Templeton and she was going to take him to her house. Then she was going to have mad and passionate sex. It was the only way, to her mind, to end a day like today.

She lurched away from the wall and went to find him.

Chapter Twenty-Nine

Maura had been teaching Roy the ropes slowly over the last few months, until now, in January, he was finally getting an understanding of all the different aspects of the businesses. She had handed the docklands over to William Templeton. All she had to do there now was turn up for monthly meetings. She had found herself concentrating more and more on the family businesses as time went on – the clubs, betting shops, and the newer borderline businesses, such as the Mortgage and Investment Corporation that Michael had set up in 1984. Today she was trying to explain all this to Roy, as she wanted him to come in and take a large amount of the donkey work from her.

'The rub is, Roy, we give mortgages through our own lending company. Now the company itself has no actual investors, so we sell our clients to other companies, such as the Bank of Kuwait, et cetera. It's pretty simple really. That way we make a quick profit, and if the client gets into difficulties with their payments, then *they* can foreclose. That way *we* never have to take anyone to court. It's all out of our hands.'

'Sounds simple enough.' Roy's voice was worried and Maura guessed that he had not really grasped what she was saying.

'It is. That's the beauty of it. We advertise in the local papers, offering everything from small personal loans to remortgages. You'd be surprised at the number of people out there who want to "unlock their capital", as the advertisers put it. We offer from five to a hundred grand, secured against their properties. Even bought council houses. Literally anything. Our main aim, though, is to get the first-time buyers. We're already renting office space with a series of estate agents. That way, when people see the property they want, we're there waiting for the poor buggers. It's a doddle, Roy. You'll soon pick it up, mate.'

Roy frowned as he listened to her speak.

'And this is legal, Maws?'

His voice was sceptical and she laughed. 'Yeah, it's legal, all right. Hard as that is to believe.'

'What if they can't afford the place they want?'

'That's easily remedied. You can borrow three times your earnings, so if a youngster comes in and he earns, say, twelve grand a year, for argument's sake, then the borrower will tell him to bring in some "moody" pay slips, say one for a week when he did a load of overtime, so it looks like he earns sixteen grand a year. So instead of giving him a mortgage for thirty-six grand he gets one for forty-eight grand. I know it sounds bent, but believe me, Roy, banks and building societies do it all the time.'

'I see.'

Maura lit a cigarette and continued. 'Now about the council estates. I've extended the areas for the tally men. And that's another misnomer. The way that the law works, you can lend people money providing they buy goods from you. You can't under any circumstances offer them money straight off. What the tally men do is, they knock on someone's door and then offer them a continental quilt set at, say, two quid a week. The quilt set costs a score so you know that you have five weeks to get them to borrow off you.

'After a few weeks, the tally man then offers them a loan of maybe fifty quid, to be paid back at a fiver a week. The person takes up the offer and they get the money on the spot. They then pay back eighty quid. A clear profit of thirty quid. I know it doesn't sound much like that, but when you consider we make about three thousand loans a week it soon mounts up. Then they're offered a ton. The tally man holds out the hundred pounds and nine times out of ten the temptation is too strong. They go for it.'

'But what if they can't afford to pay the money back, Maws?'

'Then we send the big boys round. Some of the larger council estates are into us for a small fortune. And before you ask, it's perfectly legal. Getting into debt is now socially acceptable. You want that TV or video, you get it on the never-never. Big stores offer credit, everyone offers credit, it's like a public service these days. Even the social security has jumped on the band wagon. They borrow money now as well!'

Roy grinned but his big moon face was bewildered by it all. 'Can I take these files home and study them?'

'Of course you can. The sooner you learn the better.'

He picked up the files and put them into his briefcase.

'The bloke from Jersey is just about ready to shift the gold.'

'Don't you think that it's a bit quick, Maws? Michael was looking at leaving it for five or six years.'

'Well, Michael ain't here now, is he? I make the decisions and I want shot of it. The bloke's popping over at the weekend. I want you at the meet with me, OK?'

'Sure, Maws. Whatever you say.'

She went to the coffee percolator and replenished their cups. Passing one to Roy, she smiled at him sadly.

'Have you seen anything of Mother?'

Roy sipped the lukewarm liquid and shrugged.

'She was pretty cut up about Geoffrey.'

'I guessed as much.'

'Why didn't you go to the funeral, Maws?'

'Because I'm not a hypocrite, that's why. I would have spat on his grave.'

'Have the old Bill been in touch?'

Maura shook her head vigorously, sending her hair rioting around her face.

'Not so much as a hello, kiss me arse or anything. And that's just how I like it!'

'But don't you think that's strange?'

'Not really. They know that we do business with the Irish. They probably think he double crossed them or something. To be honest, I don't give a damn. If they had anything they'd be battering the door down, but I'm too wily for the old Bill. I have more plants in the police stations in London than there are in the Royal Botanical Gardens! If they walked in here now they'd find nothing. Nothing that they could nick me for. Me and Mickey only ever made one mistake and that was Geoffrey. Only you and I know the score now. Without one of us talking they ain't got nothing. So relax.'

'Well, you ain't got any worries where I'm concerned.'

'I know that, Bruv. That's why I'm trusting you with all this.'

Roy smiled at her, pleased to be so well thought of.

'Right then, Roy.' Maura checked her watch. 'I've got a meet with a firm of "blaggers" from Liverpool. I'd better get on me way. It's ten-thirty now. If I don't leave soon I'll catch the lunchtime traffic.'

Roy stood up and stretched. 'Okey doke. Sure you don't want me to come with you?'

'No, thanks. I've been dealing with this little firm for about eight years now. They're kosher. See you later, mate.'

Roy left the house and Maura lit herself another cigarette. Roy was working out all right. He couldn't express himself very well, but he was shrewd enough. He was getting the hang of everything. She had given Leslie the betting shops for a while. He was doing a good job. Garry and Lee were finally getting their act together. They had got a bit lairy after Michael's funeral but she had nipped that in the bud. All in all, considering what had happened, things were going quite well.

She finished her cigarette and got ready for the meet with Tommy Rifkind. It would be the first with him since Michael's death. He had come to the funeral to pay his respects, but now Maura had to deal with him alone. For a few seconds she wondered if it was all worth it. But as usual she pushed the thought away. The least she could do was carry on, for Michael's sake. He had built this little empire up from nothing, from being a bookie's runner at barely ten to a breaker in his teens. She owed her brother this. As she owed him everything. And if he was watching over her, as she sometimes fancied that he was, she hoped that he was pleased with how she was carrying on without him.

*

When Maura got to the club in Dean Street, Tommy Rifkind was already inside waiting for her. She showed him up to her office immediately. Like herself he was a busy person. He had his number two with him, Joss Campion, a six feet six inch rugby player with the ugliest face Maura had ever seen. Tommy, on the other hand, was five foot eight with a slim, lithe build. He also had the darkest brown eyes that Maura had ever seen on a light-skinned man. Michael had always said that he had a touch of the tarbrush in him. Inside the office the men sat down and Maura smiled at them.

'Sorry to keep you. Get yourselves comfortable and I'll organise some coffee.'

A little while later they were all drinking hot coffee laced with brandy, Tommy's favourite. Joss Campion had poured his into his saucer and after blowing on the hot liquid loudly was now slurping it from the saucer. He was completely unaware of all the noise he was making. Maura had to bite her lip as Tommy rolled his eyes at her.

'Joss, would you rather I put the saucer on the floor for you?'

Joss hung his enormous head like a child.

'Sorry.'

'I apologise, Maura. Joss's mother never quite managed to get him completely house trained, you see.'

She laughed. 'That's all right. My brother Benny was much the same.'

'I'm glad you understand. My wife won't have him in the house.' Tommy smiled. 'Well, Maura, down to business. I have a little proposition to put to you.' She nodded. 'I've acquired some information on a bank in South London. The pull from it will be around two hundred thousand. As usual we'll give you twenty per cent, on the usual terms.'

Maura licked her lips as she thought.

'How many cars would you want?'

'Two. One a high-powered vehicle, the other a nondescript Volvo estate. You know the type of thing, a family car.'

Maura nodded. 'OK. I'll put the word out on the street. I can supply "shooters" if you need them.' Tommy shook his head. 'In that case, all I'll need is the times and the date. And I do ask that you keep the violence to a minimum. It's not just you, Tommy. I tell all "blaggers" the same thing.'

He smiled.

'This will be as sweet as a nut, as you cockneys say. You'll be given the information seven days before the off.'

'Great. That was short and sweet!'

'I try to please. By the way, I'm so sorry about Geoffrey, Maura. So soon after Michael.' He opened his arms in a gesture of helplessness.

'Yeah, well. These things happen. I'm in full control now and nothing has changed really. I'll run the streets as they've always been run. I won't take any nonsense.'

Tommy was quite aware of the underlying threat and nodded as if he was answering a question.

'I respect that, Maura, and you have nothing to worry about from me and mine.'

She laughed heartily, but when she spoke, her voice was icy cold.

'I know.'

Tommy felt a prickle of fear on the back of his neck. In Liverpool he was the Daddy. What he said invariably went. He prided himself on not being frightened of any man, yet this tall, beautiful and intelligent woman sitting opposite scared the life out of him.

He had never wondered, like many people, why Maura was not married. There were rumours that she was a lesbian, but he knew different. It was simply that the man who would take her on, her and all that she entailed, had not been born yet.

He cleared his throat.

'Did you receive the wreaths I sent?'

'Yes. Michael would have appreciated it. He always liked you, Tommy.'

'I expect you miss him.'

'Oh, yeah, I miss him.' She stood up abruptly to let him know that the meeting was over. She held out her hand and he shook it gently.

'I'll be in touch then.'

'OK.'

Joss smiled at Maura as he left and she forced herself to smile back. When they had left the office she lit herself a cigarette and, opening the drawer in her desk, took out a photo of Michael and herself. They had been having a drink in the club downstairs and Leslie had snapped them laughing together. It turned out to be a beautiful photograph and she had had it enlarged. She sat staring at Michael's handsome face. Oh, she missed him all right. Desperately.

Sarah Ryan sat at her kitchen table sipping a cup of steaming hot tea. In front of her, spread out on the table, were the papers from a file she had found in Geoffrey's old bedroom. He must have hidden them there at some point before he died. She knew that she had been meant to find them. Written in them, in Geoffrey's large bold script, was all the information he had gathered about Michael and Maura over the years. As Sarah read them a seething rage gathered inside her. Now she knew why Geoffrey was dead. Four sons she had buried, Anthony when he was no more than a baby. What was she to do with the information in front of her? She could take it to the police now and get it over with, but it incriminated all her sons, both living and dead. She had heard through the grapevine that Roy was now Maura's number two, whatever that meant. Janine had told her all about it a few days ago. She sighed. If she did take this little lot to the police, the whole family would be put behind bars.

She picked up the papers and took them upstairs to her bedroom. She hid them in her wardrobe. She would leave it for a while until she had thought it all through.

She looked out of her bedroom window and down on to the street. She saw Margaret walking along with her mother. If only Maura had turned out like her, Sarah would be a happy woman. If only she had not met up with that bloody policeman, that Terry Petherick. If she had got herself pregnant by anyone else, it would all have blown over. Then a thought struck her. That's who she could take the papers to if the day ever came when she decided to make them known to someone. She smiled to herself nastily. That would keep it in the family, so to speak. If she was going to expose her daughter, then that's who she would expose her to!

She clasped her hands together in a gesture of prayer and whispered: 'Oh, Jesus in Heaven, in the Kingdom of goodness and light, help me to make the right decision.'

There was one thing that Sarah was sure of: Maura was capable of anything, even capable of hurting her own mother if she had to . . .

*

Janine was sitting drinking coffee with Roy. The years had not been kind to her. She looked much older than forty-eight and her face held a permanent frown. Benny Anthony burst into the kitchen.

'Hello, Dad!' He was surprised to find his father at home and it showed in his voice.

'Hello, son.' Roy's voice was warm. 'No school then?'

'Nah. There's a teachers' strike on.'

Janine butted in to their conversation.

'Get upstairs and do some of your homework. Your dad's busy.'

Benny's face dropped.

'Oh, Mum!' He was whining. 'I hardly ever see me dad.'

Janine's voice rose in a screech. 'You do what I tell you!'

Roy cut her off. 'For crying out loud, Janine! Keep your hair on.'

She leapt from her seat. 'Oh, that's right! Shout at me in front of Benny. Go on, Roy. Turn him into an animal like you and that stinking sister of yours.'

He sighed. 'You're beginning to sound like a broken record. Do you know that? The same old shit is dug up and pulled out, day after day.'

Janine was standing in front of him. Her face was a mask of hatred.

'You won't get your claws into him.' She pointed to where Benny was standing watching the fight between his parents. 'Oh, no. Not you or that whore of a sister of yours. She's already turned my Carla against me. I'll see you both dead first!' She ended on another screech.

'Calm yourself down, you dozy bitch. You're frightening the boy.'

Janine began to laugh.

'Me! Me frighten him? That's a laugh. His father's working for the biggest whoremonger and murderess in London and you accuse *me* of frightening the boy! Are you sleeping with her, Roy? I heard that Mickey was.'

He got up from his seat and slapped her across the kitchen. She fell to the floor, a large red mark already appearing on her face. She put her hand to her cheek silently, afraid now of a Roy she did not know.

'You stinking bitch! That's the last time you badmouth me or my family. Do you hear me? How the hell have I stood you all these years, with your miserable face and your slutty ways? Well, you've ballsed yourself right up now because I'm going. I'm gonna leave you to pickle in your own juices, Janine, and I'm taking the boy with me.

'As for our Carla . . . you dumped her, darling. You dumped her on me mother. So where you got your information from I don't know. And Carla left my mother's because my mother is like you. She wants to own people and Carla won't be owned. Neither will I from now on.'

Janine slowly pulled herself up from the floor.

'You'll take my son nowhere, Roy. I mean it. I'll go to the police . . . I swear it, Roy. I'll do for you.'

He stared at her, disgusted.

'You would and all, wouldn't you?' His voice was quiet.

'Yes, I would. You'll never turn my son into a Ryan. Not in a million years. I'd see you dead first.'

Roy picked up his briefcase and walked to his son. 'Don't worry. I'll be back to see you in a few days.'

Benny was crying and threw himself at his father. 'Oh, please don't go, Dad! Don't leave me here with Mum and Nanny Ryan. I hate them . . . I hate them!'

Roy pulled the boy close and looked at his wife. 'See

what you've caused, you bitch. SEE WHAT YOU'VE CAUSED!'

Janine was staring at her son as if he had grown another head. Then, forcing herself to move, she went to him and tried to pull him from his father's arms.

'No, Dad. Please! Don't leave me here with her. I want to go with you. Please, Dad. Please don't leave me here.'

As Janine tried to pull her son away from his father, Roy turned and punched her as hard as he could in the face.

'Get your bloody hands off him!' Roy was shouting again.

Janine had been knocked backwards by the force of the blow, grabbing the edge of the kitchen table to save herself from falling. Her nose was bleeding profusely and she could feel her eye beginning to swell.

'Son.' Roy shook the hysterical boy. 'I promise you that I'm not going to go anywhere. I'm gonna stay.'

Janine opened her mouth and Roy pointed at her. 'One more word out of you and I'll commit a fucking murder. Yours! I'm staying here. This is MY house! Get it? I can't leave this boy here alone with you, he hates you as much as I do. You're nothing but a silly, vindictive bitch. You move to the spare room as from tonight, and if I ever get wind that you've tried to take this boy away from me, or this house, I'll bury you.

'I should have put a stop to your gallop years ago, with your sluttish ways and your delusions of grandeur. I'm sick to death of you! So now you know.'

Roy held his son tightly. He should have put his foot down years ago. Instead he had let her have it all her own way, just to keep the peace. Well, no more.

'Come on, son. We'll go and get a McDonald's, shall we?'

Roy knew that Benny lived for McDonald's. At this

moment he would have given his son anything to stop the racking sobs that were shaking his body.

He put his arm across his son's shoulders and walked from the room. Janine's face hardened. If it took her the rest of her life she would get even with him for this.

In the car, Roy let Benny's sobs subside before he spoke to him.

'I'm sorry that I hit your mum, son. I lost me temper.'

'I ha . . . hate her. I hate . . . her and Nanny Ryan.'

Roy sighed. What a state of affairs! That would teach him to break his usual habits. He had gone home for a quick coffee and five minutes' peace. Instead he had opened up a complete hornets' nest. His son hated not only his mother but his grandmother as well.

Benny sniffed and wiped his nose on his sleeve. 'I do, Dad. They never leave me alone. You're never there so you don't see them. They're both at me all the time.'

'Well, I can promise you this much, son. I'll be there for you in the future.'

Benny tried to smile. 'When I grow up, I want to be just like you, Dad.'

Roy bit his lip. Good job Janine couldn't hear him. He grinned.

'We'll see, son. We'll see.'

Chapter Thirty

'I'm telling you, Sarah, that's what happened.' Janine wiped her eyes with the back of her hand. 'He walked out with little Benny and they didn't come in till late.'

'And Roy actually raised his hand to you?'

'Yeah. Look at my face. Then when they finally came in he said that if I didn't toe the line he would take Benny and move into Maura's.' Janine was crying again.

Sarah put her arm around her shoulders. 'He didn't mean it, love.'

Janine pushed her away. 'Oh yes he did! I know he did.' She put her face into her hands. 'I have to get my Benny away from him otherwise Maura will get her claws into him and that will be that. Benny already thinks that the sun shines out of her . . .'

'Listen, Janine. For all Maura's faults, and God knows there are many, she wouldn't harm the child.'

'Not now maybe. But in the years to come, she will. She'll have him in the family business. And I couldn't stand that, Sarah. Not my Benny. My baby. He's eleven now, but what about when he's seventeen or eighteen?

That's not far away, is it? First he'll go on the protection rackets. Then she'll have him in the betting shops. Then the hostess clubs. Where will it all end? I don't want my son shot like yours. Can't you see that? I don't want to be taken to the morgue to identify my son's remains.'

'Calm yourself down, Janine, that's not going to happen.'

'How do you know? You've already buried four sons!'

Sarah was silent as she digested the logic of Janine's argument. And she had to admit to herself that the girl was right. If little Benny went the same way as his father and uncles . . . And aunt. Oh, yes, she mustn't forget his aunt . . . that is what would happen.

The other boys were all living with girls. Only Leslie had married his. They would all have children, the Lord willing, and what would be the end result? They would eventually take over where their fathers left off.

'Listen, Janine. I promise you now that that will never happen to Benny. Not if I have anything to do with it.'

She made another of her famous pots of tea and finally, after calming Janine down, sent her back to her own house. Alone, Sarah thought about what Janine had said. It was odds on that Benny would eventually go into the so-called 'business'. All the grandchildren would, unless Maura and the others were stopped.

Her husband had had control of the boys when they were younger. He had taught them how to lie, cheat and steal. How to be 'hard men'. Now look where it had got them. Four of her sons had been brutally murdered. Not a day went by but she thought of them all. Even Michael, as a small boy. In her mind's eye she saw him when he was a child, when Benjamin used to take him to the bombed-out houses.

She looked around her kitchen. It was nice. Nice and clean and modern. A far cry from the days of cockroaches and squalor, when they had coats on the bed to keep them warm and only a thin stew to fill up their ever-empty bellies. Oh, they had come a long way since then, and in her own fashion she had been proud of Michael's determination to lift himself out of the slums. Until the killing had started. When Anthony had died, she had died a little bit herself. And Benny's death, her lovely, good-natured Benny who was always in trouble of some kind but always laughing . . . his death had broken her more than any of them. Then Michael, then Geoffrey. She could never allow that to happen to any of her children again. Or her grandchildren.

She got up from the table and glanced at the clock. It was just on one. She had plenty of time. Benjamin was drinking in the Kensington Park Hotel and would not be back for hours. She went to the phone in her hall and dialled the number she had taken down after Michael's funeral. She had got the number from Directory Inquiries, and now she knew why. She had taken it down for just such an occasion as this. It was the number of Vine Street Police Station.

'Good afternoon, Vine Street.' The clipped impersonal voice crackled in her ears.

'Can I speak to Detective Inspector Terry Petherick, please?' Sarah's voice was quavery and nervous.

'Who's calling?'

'I . . . I would rather not say. I . . . I have some information for him.'

'Hold the line, madam, and I'll see if he can take your call.'

The line went silent, and Sarah was beginning to

wonder if she was doing the right thing when a deep male voice asked how he could help her.

Terry Petherick was putting on his sports jacket, ready to go to lunch. His friend and colleague Cranmer called to him as he was leaving the office.

'Hang on, Tel. There's a call for you. Some woman. She won't leave her name.'

Cranmer held the phone out. Terry walked across the crowded office, his heart beating fast. Surely it could not be Maura? The sensible part of his brain pooh-poohed such an idea but the illogical part hoped and prayed that it was her.

'Hello, Petherick here.'

'This is Sarah Ryan.' The second name was barely audible.

'Who?'

'Maura Ryan's mother.'

It was a Ryan but not the one he wanted.

'What can I do for you?'

'I want to see you, in private like. I have some information. You must keep this secret, though. Some of your men are on my daughter's payroll.'

Terry frowned.

'That's a very serious allegation.'

Sarah swallowed deeply and closed her eyes.

'I have certain papers in my possession that I think you would be interested in.'

'I see. So you want to meet me, is that it?'

'Yes, that's it. But you mustn't let anyone know what you're doing. Believe me when I tell you these papers could incriminate a lot of people. Do you know Regent's Park?'

'Of course.'

'I'll meet you there Saturday. In the Zoological Gardens, outside the cafeteria, at three.' Sarah replaced the receiver before he could answer. She was sweating profusely.

Terry stared at the telephone.

'Who was it?'

'Mind your own business, Cranmer!' He tried to make his voice jocular. 'I'm off for my lunch. See you later.'

As Terry left the police station and went to his car he was intrigued. What could Sarah Ryan, the well-known matriarch of the Ryan family, want with him? He knew that Geoffrey Ryan's murder was not even really under investigation. How they managed to get away with all they did was a mystery in itself . . . or was it? He had often thought that one or two of his colleagues were on the take. Not just because they had plenty of money, though that was one sign, but because the Ryans always seemed to be one step ahead of the police. He knew from experience that knowing someone was guilty was one thing, proving it a different thing altogether. He was sure that the Ryans had inside information. Well, he would know when he met Sarah Ryan . . .

If only he was meeting Maura! But she had come a long, long way since the last time they had met. She was into the Ryan businesses up to her pretty little neck. They were further apart now than ever before. The word on the street was that Maura had taken over from Mickey with all guns blazing.

Suddenly he was not very hungry. All he really wanted was something that he had tasted many years ago. Like Adam and Eve, he preferred forbidden fruit.

*

Sarah put down the telephone and went back to her kitchen. Her heart was beating a tattoo inside her body. She had started the ball rolling, and she was glad. She would end her daughter's reign of terror. As she set about making her husband a meal, she thought again about what Janine had said and hardened her resolve. She would sacrifice her sons and her daughter if it saved at least one person from being destroyed. And if little Benny was to be saved, then she was the only one to do it.

It wasn't until much later that she remembered that the reading of Michael's will was to take place the next day, Friday.

Sarah sat in the solicitor's office with her husband. She sat well away from her only daughter and four remaining sons, as if they carried a fatal disease.

The solicitor, Derek Hattersley, was more nervous than the people in front of him. He kept having to blow his nose. This was a very difficult will. In his experience each member of a family regarded himself as the rightful chief beneficiary. He cleared his throat and began to speak.

'I must tell you all beforehand that the bulk of Mr Ryan's estate goes to just one person. He had, however, made some very substantial bequests to you all.' He smiled, trying to bring a note of lightness to the occasion. The only person to smile back was Benjamin Ryan and Derek Hattersley was aware that the man was slightly drunk.

'I'll start then.' He cleared his throat again noisily and began to read. ' "I, Michael David Ryan, being of sound mind, leave everything I own, other than the few bequests I have detailed, to my sister, Maura Ryan." '

Derek Hattersley glanced around the assembled family and was surprised to find that not one person had changed expression. All were as blank-faced as they had been when they arrived. But he reminded himself that these people were also criminals. They would not be the type to show their emotions anyway. He took a deep breath. If they wanted to fight about it, they could do it amongst themselves. He would not get involved.

'"I leave her all my properties and holdings. I also leave her two thirds of the monies in my bank account. The rest is to be shared between my mother and father and my brothers. I leave twenty thousand pounds each to my niece Carla Ryan and my nephew Benjamin Anthony Ryan. This is to be put in trust for Benjamin Anthony until he is twenty-one. Carla Ryan may have access to her money immediately. I also leave fifteen thousand pounds to my great-nephew Joseph Michael Spencer, also to be held in trust until he is twenty-one, and twenty thousand pounds to Gerry Jackson my closest friend."' Derek Hattersley blew his nose again and looked at the people in his office.

'Mr Ryan was adamant that the will be as short as possible and in his own words. He wrote the will himself and I drafted it for him. He also left two letters to be given out on this day. I have no knowledge whatsoever of their contents.' He relaxed, feeling he had extricated himself from any tricky situation that might arise. 'The letters are addressed to his mother and his sister.' He nodded at each woman as he spoke.

Still nobody said a word. Then Sarah asked in a shaky voice, 'Where's my letter?'

'I have it here, Mrs Ryan.' He passed the long white envelope to her, and Sarah stared at her dead son's small close-knit writing.

'I want my share of his money to go to the police widows' fund.'

Roy was stunned.

'You can't do that!'

'Oh yes I can, Roy Ryan. I want none of his blood money.' She picked up her handbag and, jerking her head at her husband to follow, left the office.

Derek Hattersley blew his nose again. It was now red and shiny. He passed Maura's letter to her and she thanked him politely.

'If you would be so kind as to sign some documents . . .'

'Certainly.' Maura smiled at him.

Twenty minutes later they all left the office.

'Well, that's that then, Maws. Mickey's last will and testament.'

'Yeah, Garry. It's the final parting, ain't it?'

Leslie put his arm around her. 'Cheer up, girl. Mickey wouldn't want you moping.'

Maura tried to laugh. Leslie trying to be tactful was not a very pretty sight.

'Let's all go and have a good drink!' This from Lee.

'Sounds good to me. What about you, Maws?'

'All right then, Roy. Let's go back to the club. There we can drink for free!'

Sarah and Benjamin were in the back of a black cab. Benjamin was annoyed.

'You've got too bloody much of it, Sarah. They're your own flesh and blood, yet thanks to you I hardly ever see them nowadays.'

She crossed her arms over her chest.

'You should think yourself lucky! They're nothing but bloody criminals. Mind you, that shouldn't worry you, should it?' Her voice was sarcastic. 'You're no better. I've been on this earth for seventy years, and I've spent over fifty of them years with you. Eighteen I was when you got me pregnant, Benjamin Ryan. Eighteen! And I stuck by you, no matter what you did. I stuck by you. And for what? What? To bring a crowd of bloody hooligans into the world, that's all.'

She looked out of the taxi window at the passing people, all living lives that did not touch hers.

Benjamin scowled, his leathery old face more wrinkled than usual.

'You make me laugh with all your "holy joeing". When you was eighteen, Sarah Ryan, you was what would be termed today "a right little raver"!'

'I was not!' Sarah's voice was incredulous.

The London cabbie was listening avidly to the old people in the back of his taxi and had difficulty in keeping his face straight.

'Were so!' Benjamin's voice had the truculent note that grated on Sarah's nerves.

'Oi, mate!'

'Yeah.' The cabbie's voice was full of laughter.

'Do you know the Bramley Arms?'

'You hum it, son, and I'll play it.'

Benjamin scowled deeply at the cabbie. 'None of your sauce. Just drop me off there. You can dump her where you like.' He pointed at Sarah with his thumb, leaving her silent and tight-lipped all the way back to Notting Hill.

Once back inside her house Sarah made herself a pot of tea. Taking it into the lounge, as she now called her front room, she poured herself out a cup. Then sitting in her chair by the fire, she opened Michael's letter. Trust Benjamin not to be interested in his eldest son's last communication. All he was interested in was the money the boy left. She began to read.

Dear Mum,

I am writing this letter to you because I feel that there are many things that have to be said. I know that my life was not what you wanted for me, but it was the path that I chose and I do not regret one day. The only regret I have is that I loved you, Mum, and it hurt me when we fell out with one another. I understood how you felt about Benny, as I loved him as well. If you are reading this then I am with him and Anthony, and gone from your world. I want you to know that I will miss you more than anyone.

I want to ask you something, Mum. I want you to look out for our Maura. She needs you. She always has done. Since that trouble with the policeman, she has been hurting inside. I know this is true, Mum, because I have watched her. I have done all that I can for her. I now ask you to try and take her back into the arms that held her as a baby. Maura needs her mother. Please tell Dad that I loved him very much.

I will always love you, Mum, no matter what.

Michael

Sarah felt the scalding tears behind her eyelids and squeezed her eyes tightly shut to block them out. The letter in front of her was from the old Michael, the young tearaway, not the hard, embittered, bloodthirsty man that he became. She saw him as he had been the night that Maura was born, tall and strong and with his whole life in front of him.

'Oh, God. Oh, son.' She put her hand to her mouth and held it there tightly. Now the tears did break through, like a dam bursting.

'My beautiful son. Oh, God help me, I loved him so much.'

In the club Maura and her brothers were getting drunk. Good and drunk. Maura could feel the first waves of euphoria coursing through her veins, knowing that it would soon turn to maudlin sentiment.

It was a 'Michael' day. He was in the forefront of everyone's mind. Gerry Jackson had joined them and Lee was acting as bartender. Sitting in the meat seats they all drank steadily and seriously, as if by the sheer act of getting drunk they would all feel the pain of Michael's death less.

'I can remember when Mickey was working for Joe the Fish. Handsome bleeder he was then and all.'

'That's a long time ago, Gerry.' Roy's voice was unsteady.

Gerry gulped at his gin and tonic. 'Your old mum used to be really hard up them days. Everyone was. All the birds was after him but he never spent his money on them. Took it straight home to his muvver. Do you know, Maura, that he bought your communion dress from the proceeds of a robbery?'

'No, Gerry.' She smiled at him, glad to be talking about her brother.

'Oh, yeah. I remember it as clear as day. Me and him ripped off a betting shop. He was a crafty sod! Even then he was streets ahead of everyone. Joe the Fish tried to keep him in line but he couldn't. He was "ducking and diving" all the time he worked for the old git.' Gerry's voice was hard now. 'I hated that old bastard.'

'Well, Mickey didn't, did he?' Leslie was well and truly drunk otherwise he would have chosen his words more carefully. 'Mickey was knocking him off, weren't he?'

Garry turned on him. 'Shut your bloody gob!'

'Well, Mickey was queer. Mickey was as queer as a nine-bob note. As for Joe the Fish . . . that's where he got the bloody nickname! From "queer as a fish" . . .'

Leslie didn't finish because Garry punched him in the face, knocking him off his chair.

'You just shut your bloody trap up!'

'All right. Calm down.' Lee tried to pour oil on troubled waters.

'Bollocks, you! You're always sticking up for him.' Garry was belligerent when he was sober. Drunk he would fight his own fingernails.

'Shut up.' Maura's voice was low. She could not get up the enthusiasm to stop the argument.

'Look, Garry, we're here to honour Michael's name. So sit down and wrap up. If you can't take your drink, you shouldn't get drunk.'

Roy's voice was stern and authoritative. Everyone stared at him in awe. Leslie pulled himself from the floor and slumped back into his seat. Maura, through her drink-hazed mind, realised that Roy had really begun to get confidence in himself. He would be a good number two.

'When you gonna read your letter, Maws?' This from Lee, trying to change the subject.

'When I feel up to it.' She got up from her seat and made her way out to the reception area. Picking up the phone, she rang Willy at his office on St Martin's Wharf. He answered himself, which was a godsend as Maura was aware that she was having difficulty forming her words.

'Ish that you, Willy?'

'Hello, Maura.' His tone was cool. She had been seeing him less and less since the night of Michael's funeral and he didn't like it one bit. In spite of himself he thought a lot of her and it galled him that she could take him or leave him as the fancy took her.

'I'm pissed.'

'What do you want me for? I'm very busy . . .'

'I've just been to the reading of Michael's will and I'm lonely and depressed.' And drunk, she thought.

'Really? So you want to see me, I take it?'

'Yeah . . . What I need at this moment is a good hard shag!'

William smiled. She certainly had a way with words. But if he went running now she would just carry on using him. On the other hand, he had finished most of his business for today and she did sound lonely and desolate. He couldn't bring himself to say 'desperate' but that's what he really meant, and deep inside he wanted Maura on any terms.

'Where can I meet you?'

'Come and get me from the club. I'll be waiting for you.'

She replaced the receiver and went back to the meat seats. The men were all friends again, talking about Michael, each trying to outdo the others with funny anecdotes. Maura sat back in her seat and picked up her replenished glass. She raised it in a silent toast to her brother.

Her last thought before she passed out was that Michael would have approved of this drinking session in his honour. When William turned up an hour later he had practically to carry her to his car.

He took her home, silently annoyed at the condition she was in. She lay across the back seat of his car snoring softly, her large breasts straining against the thin silk blouse she was wearing. He had to admit that even drunk and dishevelled she was still the sexiest woman he had ever known.

Maura woke at eleven-thirty that evening with a violent headache. She noticed that she was naked in her own bed. Slowly the events of earlier in the day came into her mind. She turned over in bed and felt someone lying beside her. It was William. She could feel that her body had been roughly mauled and guessed that he had taken advantage of her drunken state. Well, she had asked for it really. She lifted herself up gently and felt the waves of sickness assail her. She stepped gingerly from the bed, placing one foot firmly on the floor before attempting to walk in the semi-darkness to the bathroom. She could hear William's loud snores coming from the bed.

In the bathroom she looked into the mirror above the wash basin. She looked terrible. Her make-up was all over her face and her eyes were more lined than usual. She looked old. Older than her thirty-six years. She washed her face, splashing the cold liquid over her face and neck to try and bring some life back to her brain. Then she remembered the letter.

She pulled on an old bathrobe that was hanging behind the bathroom door and went down to the lounge. Her bag was on the coffee table where Willy had obviously left it. Picking it up, she turned on one of the lamps by her reading chair. She settled herself down with her feet tucked up underneath her, opened the bag and took out the white envelope. She stared at Michael's closely written script for a while before she carefully ripped open the envelope and took out a single page of writing.

Hello, Maws,
If you're reading this then I'm brown bread! [He had drawn a little smiley to let her know that it was a joke.] You will already know I have left everything to you. You deserve it. It amounts to well over a million pounds. The docklands will bring in much more eventually. You have it all now. Everything.

I am writing this letter as I wanted to tell you some things that I may never have told you while I lived.

Firstly, I am heartily sorry for what happened all those years ago. I know that you loved that old Bill with all your heart and I ballsed it all up for you. I have tried to repay you for that, Maura.

Secondly, I think that you should try and marry old Templeton. If you did you would become a lady. Though you always have been in my eyes.

I love you more than you would ever think. Don't end up like me, Maws, with no home life to speak of.

I admit that is the price I pay for being a homosexual.

Thirdly, try and make it up with Mother. You were very close once, and I think that deep down you both miss one another. Try and heal the breach, that's all I ask of you.

Lastly, I don't trust our Geoffrey as far as I can chuck him. He's not kosher, Maws. Put our Roy in as your number two. He's got more savvy than people give him credit for. Also try and keep an eye on the old man. Whatever happens with Mother, you was always his favourite and I know from talking to the boys that he misses you very much.

Well, that's about it, my darling. Keep this letter

private as I don't want everyone knowing that I am really as soft as shit! [Another smiley.]

Look after the boys for me, and look after yourself. There's a codicil to my will that I asked old Hattersley to keep private. I have left my flat and personal belongings to Richard. We have a good relationship and I want to leave him provided for.

I also left fifty grand to Save the Children. That is not to be made public in any way. I have a feeling, Maws, that I will never make 'Old Bones', as Auntie Nellie used to say, so I write new letters every year to be on the safe side.

Look after yourself, Maws.

Your loving brother,

Michael

P.S. Hattersley is as bent as a two-bob clock. I have left some papers for you that he will be holding until you have read this letter. Go and see him on the sly. It's stocks, bonds and other papers. There's also the number of my Swiss bank. They will be notified on my death that you are the new executor.

Maura stared at the letter. Trust Michael to cover all his bets. Only he would leave letters that were updated every year. She looked at the date at the top. It was written on 5 August 1986, before all the trouble with Geoffrey. She sighed. Fifty grand to Save the Children. Her eyes were misty. When they had seen pictures of the starving children on the news he had not said a word about it. Yet it had moved him enough for him to leave them fifty grand. That was the kind of gesture he would make. The papers always had him as a shady, murdering villain, and that was just how he liked it.

He knew about Geoffrey, had always known. If only she had let Michael sack him when he had wanted to maybe all this would have been avoided. She closed her eyes to stop the tears. She had done enough crying and it would not bring him back.

She opened her eyes and saw William standing in the doorway.

'My dear girl, you look absolutely scrumptious.'

She put the letter into her bag and smiled at him, a hard cynical smile that did not reach her eyes. She let her gaze roam over his body.

'You took advantage of me earlier, didn't you?' Her voice was low and husky. He nodded. 'Well, now I'm going to take advantage of you!'

William laughed, trying to imitate a cockney accent. 'Does that mean I'm gonna get a good hard shag?'

Maura placed her bag on the floor and stood up. 'Only if you're a very good boy.'

As they went back to bed together Maura prayed that William would be enough to take her mind off her troubles. Even as she thought it she knew it wouldn't happen. There was only one person who could do that, and he was as far from her grasp as the Milky Way.

Chapter Thirty-One

Saturday was cold and bleak, with a flurry of snow in the air. While Maura and William were eating a leisurely late lunch together, Sarah was sitting on a bench waiting for Terry Petherick. He arrived just after three. He smiled at her as she sat stony-faced and silent. Looking at him, she was reminded that he had fathered her first grandchild and was made aware of just how beautiful that child would have been.

'Mrs Ryan?'

Sarah nodded and he sat down beside her.

'It's cold today, isn't it?'

She nodded again.

'Would you rather we went and got a cup of coffee? Had our little chat in the warm?'

'Yes. That would be better. I'm frozen to the marrow.'

Terry took her arm and led her into the cafeteria. Sitting in the warm drinking a cup of hot sweet tea, Sarah was plagued by doubts. She knew that what she was about to do would cause no end of trouble, not only for Maura but all her children.

She took a deep breath. 'If I give you the information, could you make it easier on my sons?'

'The information is mostly about Maura, I take it?'

Sarah nodded her head.

'Well, I could try. It really depends on what kind of information you give to me.'

Looking at Sarah, Terry felt like a snake in the grass. She was an old woman. She was Maura's mother. If things had worked out differently, she could have been his mother-in-law. He sipped his coffee. Her sons had beaten him nearly to death. He wondered if she knew that.

'I know many things about my daughter. My son Geoffrey, he kept names, dates, papers, that sort of thing. Going back years. I think that it was Maura who had him . . .' Her voice trailed off.

'Is that why you wanted to see me?'

Sarah gazed deeply into his eyes.

'You knew my daughter before . . . Well, before she went into the business with Michael.'

'You know about that then?'

'I knew everything. Maura was pregnant.'

Terry's eyes opened wide.

'That's impossible!'

'No, son. She was pregnant all right. That's why Michael had you so badly beaten. I took her to a back-street abortionist. She nearly died from what that bastard did to her. She was ill for a long time. It was because of the abortion that they sterilised her.' Sarah had no idea why she was telling him all this. Perhaps in her own way she wanted to make some sort of allowance for her daughter's actions. Give him some of the blame.

'I never knew. I swear to you that I never knew.'

'Oh, I know that, son. Maura told me that herself. She had gone to your flat to tell you when you finished with her. By then Michael had found out about the two of you, and the rest's history.'

Terry was reeling. Maura pregnant by him!

Sarah sipped her tea and began to talk again. Telling him everything.

'She changed then. I'm not saying it was all your fault but when she came out of the hospital she was hard. As the years went on she seemed to get harder. As if she was taking all her hurt out on the world. Whatever she may be now, before that happened to her she was a good girl. A kind girl.'

'I don't know if this will make any difference, Mrs Ryan, but I loved her.'

'I believe you did.'

'I just can't take it all in. If I had known, I would have stood by her.'

Sarah shook her head.

'You wouldn't have, son. Michael would never have let you. Even if you had left the police force, he would have hated you until the day you died. That's why I wanted to see you. In a way you're caught up in this as well. I want my grandchildren to grow up away from the taint of the Ryan name. I want them to be factory workers, road sweepers, anything! Anything but villains.'

'I understand. But you must realise that once you start something like this, it can't be stopped. There'll be no going back.'

'I know that. I've made up me mind. My children have got to be put right. Only I can do that. I made them, now I must destroy them. It's simple really. I want your help. If needs be, I'll go in the witness box.'

'No! That won't be necessary.'

'Listen, you, if you're worried that something might happen to me – don't be. I'm seventy years old and in all those years I've never been frightened of anything that came out of me own body.'

Sarah opened her bag and took out the file of papers that Geoffrey had left. She handed them to Terry.

'These are all that Geoffrey left. My phone number is on the outside of the file. Get in touch whenever you need me. The only thing I ask is, please try and help my boys. I know they must go away but the main one you should be after is Maura.'

She got up from her chair. Holding out her hand, she shook his. Then, nodding at him, she left.

Terry sat alone, thinking about all that had been said. Maura pregnant with his baby. He saw her as she had been that first night they had made love. Her willingness to learn from him. Her trusting eyes and soft body. He felt the burning of tears in his throat. She had been so soft then. He realised that having an abortion must have destroyed her. She loved children, they had discussed them enough times. Then he thought of the last night he had spent with her. That coming together of adults. The frenzied thrashing of their bodies. The cool musky smell of her. And she had not told him even then about the baby.

Neither of them had married. Both were put on this earth for one another, and one another only. He knew that now. He put his head into his hands.

A voice broke into his thoughts. 'Are you all right?' A short dumpy waitress stood beside him.

'Yes, thank you.'

She looked concerned about him. 'You look terrible.'

Terry stood up and threw three pound coins on to the table.

'It's nothing. Just a bit of bad news, that's all.'

He walked out into the freezing air, putting the file that Sarah had given him under his arm. He would read it later. At the moment all he wanted to do was walk and think.

Maura and William had gone back to bed. They were snuggled up together. Maura smiled at him, her first real smile for days. At last she had found someone to care for her. And he did care for her, she knew that. She would put all the bad behind her and just concentrate on the good.

She was still quite young and Michael's letter had shown her that time could run out quickly. She thought fleetingly of Terry Petherick, as she always did when she was feeling solemn. Terry Petherick was standing in Regent's Park thinking about her at the same moment.

Both began to make plans. And although Maura did not know it, both her plans and his would one day merge with explosive consequences.

Terry was in a quandary. A week had passed since Sarah had given him the papers. He had no doubt that what Geoffrey had recorded was true. The names and dates coincided perfectly. What was worrying him was that not only were most of his colleagues on Maura's payroll, but a few of the higher ups too. His Chief Inspector for one. Armed with all this information, he was not sure who to confide in. This wasn't a case of a few bent coppers. This was more a case of a few honest men against a veritable army of policemen on the take! Whatever happened, it would burst wide open not only his friends but the whole of London's police force.

He now had documented evidence that Maura and Michael Ryan were behind the bullion robbery of '85. Geoffrey Ryan had even procured the route map that had been used. Terry was in no doubt that it was probably full of prints. He even knew who was warehousing the gold. All well and good, except how in all honesty could he break this news without letting on that the police were also involved right up to their shitty little necks?

He could have cried. In the last seven days he had looked at his friends with new eyes. Had listened to their accounts of arrests made and known deep in his heart that they were deliberately looking the other way where the Ryans were concerned. No wonder Mickey and Maura had got away with so much. They owned not only Vine Street but West End Central as well. He couldn't believe it. They had 'tags' in Brixton, Kilburn, Barking. In fact, there was not one station where they didn't have an 'ear' on the payroll.

Now he, Terry Petherick, had all the information he needed to put them away. Even the full co-operation of their mother. And his hands were tied because when the Ryan ship finally went down it would take the police force with it. It was bloody laughable! As for this Templeton . . . he was up to his neck in skulduggery of one sort or another and his family connections had kept him out of jail for years! Terry wasn't up against a few big villains, he was up against the whole bloody establishment.

He picked up the phone on his desk and dialled the number of the Special Investigations team. He would give the lot over to them. Let them have the honour of sorting it all out. He was sick to the stomach with the lot of it.

While the phone rang he doodled on his pad. It wasn't till later in the day he saw that he had drawn a heart with a dagger in it.

Superintendent Marsh was sitting staring out at the city skyline. It was dark and the lights were shining like beacons across the Thames. He had been sitting like that for nearly three hours. The information that the young DI had brought in had completely destroyed his equilibrium. He had been waiting for something like this for ten years. Now it was dropped, literally, into his lap he wasn't sure exactly what to do with it. He was waiting for his superior, who thankfully was not on the bent list, to come and talk with him. If all this information was true, and he had a sneaking suspicion that it was, all hell would be let loose and the West End police would be running on a skeleton crew. He shook his head at the enormity of what he was about to unleash, the sad part being that DI Petherick had unwittingly dug his own grave. If this hit the tabloids, no one would work with him ever again. Policemen were like doctors. They never shit on their own, no matter who the patients might be.

Terry was called at home at midnight. He was told to get dressed and meet Marsh at twelve-forty-five. As he got in his car he realised that he had started something that would have repercussions for years to come. Maura Ryan would finally be put away, but he wasn't sure it was a fair price to pay for all the trouble it was going to cause. He was even less sure an hour later when he found out exactly what was to happen.

He was sitting in a small back room in a terraced house in Wimbledon. Superintendent Marsh had been talking steadily for nearly an hour. While Marsh paused to light his cigar, Terry jumped in.

'What you're trying to say is that the people in authority will be getting off scot free?'

Marsh inhaled smoke into his lungs and coughed. Holding his hand across his mouth, he tried to explain.

'Look, son, I know how it must seem. The thing is, some of these men have been with the force for twenty years. They will retire quietly . . .'

'And get their pensions and their early retirement bonuses!' Terry's voice was disgusted. 'I can't believe my ears, Marsh. I bring you evidence of corruption on a bigger scale than anyone could ever dream of and you have the gall to sit there and tell me that the majority will be walking away completely exonerated.'

Marsh nodded.

'I know how you feel, son.'

'No, you don't! You have no idea what I am feeling at this moment. I am bitter and disgusted. These people have been collecting money from known criminals for years and they are not going to be brought to account. Whereas the little fish like Dobin will be crucified for them.'

'Listen, son . . .'

'Stop calling me fucking SON!' Terry smashed his fist on to the table in front of him. 'We're creeping around in the middle of the night like burglars. I can't believe this is happening. You tell me that bent coppers are going to walk out of their jobs without even a slap on the wrist. We are carrying on like guilty criminals, meeting in dingy little houses in the middle of the night, and the actual scumbags that we're here on account of are walking away from it all. It's not bloody on, mate.'

'Listen, Petherick. If this hits the streets we're fucked.

If you want it plain then I'll give it to you plain. Can you imagine the outrage this would cause if it ever hit the tabloids? Have you thought? Our street credibility would be lower than a fucking gas meter bandit's! Think about it. We'd never live this thing down. The only way we can even begin to sort this out is internally.

'They know that they've been collared. They're leaving the force. That's all that we can do! When you get older you'll realise the sense in what I'm saying. Else all the toe rags they've put away, the rapists, muggers, murderers, would be screaming for retrials as soon as their arresting officers were nicked. We're talking too many people to let this ever get out. I know that what they're getting seems a small price to pay for their misdeeds, but believe me the other way would cost us more.'

Terry was stunned.

'What about Maura Ryan? Or is she to walk away too?'

'Don't you worry about her, we have her bang to rights.'

'Of course, let's get our priorities right, shall we? Get the real villains. Well, let me tell you something, Marsh, I think that Maura Ryan, as bad as she and her family are, is as nothing compared to the Filth you're letting off so lightly. In my book a bent copper is worse than any villain.'

Marsh walked around the table and put his hand on Terry's shoulder.

'I know . . . I feel the same. I'm following orders the same as you. But the sheer magnitude of what you found out is what's stopping us making this public. Can't you see that? The force would be crucified in hours. Top men in key jobs on the take? Come on, son. It's too much.'

Terry listened to Marsh and had to agree with what he

was saying. It just seemed unfair to him that so many people would walk away without so much as a stain on their character when, by rights, they should have been made to take the consequences of their actions.

'I'm still not happy. Even if this does cause trouble, surely it would be worth it? Joe Public isn't as stupid as you seem to think. I for one would much rather see justice being done than take part in something that I know is wrong.'

Marsh puffed on his cigar. His shiny bald head had a fine layer of perspiration over it. This young man was beginning to get on his nerves. The last thing the force needed at this time was a cop as honest as this one. Terry Petherick wanted to stir up a hornets' nest, and there was no way he would ever be allowed to get away with it.

'Look, go home. Sleep on it. Once you've had a chance to think about this logically you'll see it from our perspective.'

Terry got up slowly from his chair and looked into Marsh's eyes.

'Now I know why we're nicknamed the "Filth".'

When Terry had left, Marsh sat back down at the table. If only everything was as easy as Petherick seemed to think it was. The nice policeman gets the naughty villains. Only in this world, most of the police were villains! Marsh let out a long drawn-out sigh. It was his job to keep Petherick's mouth shut. And that was just what he intended to do.

Terry drove home in a temper. The streets were deserted and he had an urge to drive to Fleet Street and shout his mouth off about the lot of it. He knew he wouldn't, though. He hadn't come this far in his career to blow it now. He realised that for the second time in his life he'd had to make an important decision between the force and Maura Ryan. And that for the second time the force had won.

Chapter Thirty-Two

Janine put Roy's breakfast in front of him. He began to eat. She poured herself a cup of coffee, walked out of the kitchen into the lounge and laced it with vodka. As she turned from the drinks cabinet she jumped. Standing in the doorway watching her was Roy.

'I thought you were eating your breakfast.'

He finished chewing his mouthful of food and pointed to the cup Janine had in her hand.

'Bit early even for you, ain't it?'

Janine dropped her eyes. She felt herself blushing. 'It's my life, Roy . . .'

'Well, in future, if I ain't here, you get Benny a cab to school. I don't want you wrapping your car round a lamp post with my son in it. Pissed out of your nut!'

Janine's voice rose. 'I'm not pissed!'

Roy sniffed and wiped his nose with the back of his hand. 'Not yet. You just do what I tell you. Get it?'

Janine stared at him, her face twisted with anger.

Roy bellowed at her: 'I SAID . . . GET IT?'

'Yes. I get it. I'm not deaf, you know.'

'No, darlin', not deaf. Just half pissed as usual.'

Roy walked back to the kitchen to finish his breakfast. Standing on the bottom stair in the hall watching him was Benny.

'You dropping me off at school, Dad?'

Roy nodded.

'Great. Mum's driving is getting worse.'

'In future, son, you do not get in any car with your mother, right?'

Benny shrugged his shoulders.

'Suits me, Dad.'

Janine, listening to all they said, swallowed her coffee and vodka down in two gulps and refilled her cup. Sitting on the settee she sipped the neat spirit. Slowly the tears came. Roy had taken everything away from her over the years, her self-respect and now her child. The tears came, tears of self-pity. A little while later she heard them leave the house. Benny had not even bothered to say goodbye to her.

Roy and Maura were driving out to Essex. She had an appointment with a goldsmith, Lenny Isaacs. Roy pulled up at some traffic lights and looked across at her.

'You're in a good mood today, Maws.'

She smiled at him. 'Yeah, I am actually.'

'What's brought all this fun and laughter on?'

'Nothing, you cheeky bugger. You better go, the lights have changed!'

'Oh, shit!'

A van behind started blowing its horn.

'All right. All right, I'm going. So what's the secret then, Maws. A bloke?'

'Maybe.' Maura thought of William Templeton.

'It *is* a bloke!' Roy's voice showed his surprise.

'Listen, dickhead, I'm in a good mood because I just am. That's all.'

'Women's bloody logic amazes me!'

Maura laughed at him.

'Talking of women, what's the score with Janine?'

Roy scowled.

'I thought we were talking about women. Not the monster from the black lagoon.'

'Nasty, nasty.' Maura grinned.

'Listen, Maws, Janine is getting on my nerves. She drinks like a fish.'

'Janine? She was always a teetotaller.' Maura sounded sceptical.

'Not any more. The marriage is going down the pan. Correction, *is* down the pan. We haven't slept together for over four years. If it wasn't for Benny I'd have had it on me toes ages ago.'

'How long has she been drinking?'

'The last year or so, I think. But the last few months she's been drinking quite heavily.'

'She always was a funny bird. I never liked her, I admit that. But all the same, she is your wife.'

'I tell you now, Maws, if it wasn't for Mother I'd dump the bitch. But Mother thinks the sun shines out of her arse.'

'That's a fact. Well, Roy, you know your own mind. Myself, though, I'd get shot of her, whatever the old woman thinks. Let's face it, you're the one who's got to live with her, not Mother.'

Roy nodded.

'What's the score with this Isaacs bloke?'

'Apparently he knows the big boys in Jersey. Reckons

he can get rid of the gold over there, and gradually it will be put on the market again. That means that the market will be flooded and the price of gold will drop, but by then we'll have made a mint, if you'll excuse the pun, and some prat will be running all over Europe counting the gold reserves. Eventually some bright spark will suss out that the missing bullion is being sold legally and it will all be hushed up. As usual. So if you want to buy any gold in the next few years, stick to South African Krugerrands!'

Roy burst out laughing.

'You're bloody mad!'

'I know . . . I know. I'm happy mad, though, that makes a difference!'

'I hope this Isaacs bloke ain't going to waffle all day. Front wheels never seem to know when to shut up. Sammy Goldbaum used to chew my ears off!'

At the mention of Sammy's name Maura felt herself go cold. She hadn't thought about him for a long time.

'Here! You all right, girl? You've gone pale.'

Maura lit a cigarette.

'Yes, I'm OK. Just felt a bit funny for a second.'

Roy realised that he shouldn't have mentioned Sammy Goldbaum. He could have kicked himself.

'I tell you what, Maws, before we go on this meet, what do you say we find a nice little pub and have a bite to eat and a drink?'

Maura knew Roy was trying to make amends and smiled at him. 'That would be great.'

Terry Petherick was called in to see Marsh. He took the seat offered to him and waited silently for his boss to tell him what was going down.

Marsh lit himself a cigar, his only extravagance.

Blowing smoke across his desk, he began: 'Have you thought over what we were talking about?'

Terry nodded.

'I take it you are more amenable today?'

Terry nodded again.

'Good . . . good. We've decided that the collaring of the Ryans will be given to you. I'm sure you already know that whoever gets them has his career made. Unless, of course, you get knobbled by them first.'

Terry stared at him. He could see nothing to laugh about.

'We know that you're as straight as a die, and in view of all the information you've gathered we feel it is only fair . . .'

Terry interrupted him.

'All right. Cut the crap. What exactly's going down?'

Marsh had an overwhelming urge to put his cigar out in Petherick's face. Who the hell did this little shit think he was? Instead he took a deep breath and tried to control his temper.

'Yesterday Maura and Roy Ryan had a meet with a goldsmith . . . Lenny Isaacs. I had her tailed. Obviously they're going to be shifting the bullion soon. That's when we're going to pounce. Once she's nicked for that we can pile on the other charges as and when we feel like it. As I told you the other night, we have her bang to rights. We swoop when they make the exchange. It's as simple as that.

'About the other business . . . the Complaints Investigation Bureau are dealing with it internally. We're not going to approach anyone until the Ryans have been collared. That way they won't get any warnings. You and I will be working together closely on this one. You mustn't mention it to anyone. I'll see you in a few days when I have more to tell you.'

'Sarah Ryan asked me if it was possible to get the boys lighter sentences?'

Marsh smiled nastily. 'Well, there's no harm in asking, I suppose.'

When Terry had left the office Marsh sat for a while smoking his cigar. It would not do to tell Petherick that none of the Ryans could be allowed to go to prison. The Ryans were going to be wiped out. They had bought themselves too many friends in the force to be allowed to live. They had to be shut up, and shut up permanently. As Petherick would be finding out all too soon . . .

Sarah was making Benjamin's dinner. He had come in from the pub and gone straight up to bed. Said he felt tired today. Sarah was annoyed. Felt drunk more like. As she was peeling the potatoes she heard a crash from above her head and looked up at the ceiling. Nothing. She listened again. Then putting down the potato peeler, made her way up the stairs to their bedroom.

Benjamin Ryan was lying on the floor clutching his chest. One look at his face, grey and drawn, told Sarah he was very ill. She went to him and tried to lift his head from the floor.

'Benjamin!'

He opened his eyes. Sarah noticed the blue tinge around his lips.

'It's me chest, Sar. Get me a doctor. I've gotta pain in me chest . . .'

Sarah ran down the stairs and phoned an ambulance. Then she rang Janine and told her to tell the boys what had happened. Slamming down the phone, she went back upstairs and sat on the floor with her husband until the ambulance arrived.

*

Sarah sat in the Cardiac Care Unit with her husband until he lost consciousness. She was praying over him all day. At seven in the evening Maura and Roy turned up, both pale and worried. Janine had not thought to try to contact the other boys. Roy took his tiny mother into his arms.

'What happened, Mum?' His voice was gentle.

'It was terrible. He collapsed in the bedroom. I found him on the floor.'

'Do they know what caused it?'

'Yes. He had a coronary. He's never been ill in his life.'

'We would have been here sooner but we was out all day. You should have rung one of the other boys, not Janine. They'll be here soon.'

He was going to murder that drunken bitch when he got home. His father ill in hospital and she'd left a message at the club for him to call! Not even telling Gerry Jackson what it was all about.

'I was too scared to call anyone. I didn't want to leave your father. Look at him. He looks terrible.'

She sounded so old that Maura and Roy were suddenly reminded of the fact that their parents could die soon. That their father could be dying now.

Roy sat his mother in the chair by the bed then looked at his father's wasted body.

'I'm going to find a doctor. Maws. Look after Muvver. I'll find out what's going on.'

Maura automatically put her arm around the woman she had hardly spoken to for years. Both forgot their animosity in the light of Benjamin's illness. They were just a mother and daughter, united in their grief.

'Everything will be all right, Mum . . . I promise you.'

Sarah held Maura's hand in her own.

'Oh, Maws, he's so ill. What will I do without him?'

'Don't you worry, Mum, he'll be all right.' Maura's voice sounded much more confident than she felt.

Leslie, Garry and Lee turned up a little while later. All were sober, looking worried about their father.

Maura and Sarah stood by Benjamin's bed, the two women supporting each other as best they could. It was too soon after Michael's and Geoffrey's deaths to face another one. Though they had all treated Benjamin with scant respect and only haphazard affection over the years, now he lay ill they were all reminded of the fact that he was their father. Even a bad parent was entitled to respect on his death bed.

Carla rushed into the hospital at ten-thirty. Her long red-brown hair was blown all over the place and she had on an old coat. Even untidy, she looked lovely. She went straight to Roy. Her father held her while she cried. She was the living image of Janine, and for a second he remembered the vital woman he had married.

'How's Grandad Ryan? I was out all day with Joey. I only got the message when I came home.'

'He's very ill, Carla. But they think he could pull through.'

'Come on, Carla. Sit here beside me.'

Garry's voice was soft. Carla was like the family mascot. She sat down in the chair and he gave her a cup of coffee. Inside the room Maura and Sarah stood either side of Benjamin's bed. At ten-forty-two he opened his eyes and looked at them.

'Me two best girls. I suppose I've missed the pub?'

Looking at their anxious faces, he tried to grin.

Sarah and Maura laughed through their tears.

'Yes, Dad, you missed the pub.'

'Remember what I've always said . . . when I die, I want me ashes put in the Bramley Arms.' He closed his eyes.

Maura and Sarah finished the sentence for him: 'So you'll always be there for opening time.'

It was a saying of his they had heard all their lives.

'That's it, girls. I think I'll have another sleep now.'

He closed his eyes. When he was asleep the two women hugged one another.

'I reckon he'll be all right now, Mum.'

The nurse who was in the room and heard the exchange smiled at them.

'Why don't you all get home and get some rest? He's stable now.'

'Come on, Mum. I'll run you home.'

'No, I can't stay in that house on me own. I've never spent a night there alone since before the war.'

Maura could hear the fear in her mother's voice. 'I'll stay there with you. Don't worry. Come on, let's get you home.'

Both women kissed Benjamin and left the room.

Maura drove Sarah home a little later, amazed at the way events had brought them together as Michael had wanted.

'Sleep in my bed with me, Maws.'

'All right then, Mum.' They went up to the bedroom, both quiet and sad.

As they undressed they were both aware of the truce that had been drawn up between them. Maura knew that for the first time in years her mother needed her. She was sorry that it had taken her father's near death to achieve it.

Sarah got into her bed and watched Maura folding her

clothes. She looked at her daughter's unblemished body and beautiful profile. She would have been a fit mate for that Terry Petherick. He was one of the few men she had seen who towered over her daughter. Maura took off her bra and Sarah looked at her large firm breasts and pulled her eyes away quickly, feeling that spark of jealousy many women feel when they see their daughters' strong, taut bodies. Maura slipped into the bed beside her mother, feeling strange at the turn of events. She had rung William earlier and told him what had happened, and that she was staying the night with her mother. She knew he was miffed as he wanted her with him. They were now a real couple, making plans with each other. She had decided to give herself to him as he wanted her too. Seriously and for always.

'I'm frightened, Maws.' Sarah's voice sounded hopelessly old and tired. Maura patted her hand.

'He'll be fine, Mum.'

'I was eighteen when I married your father. My father, God rest him, had gone around to Ben's house and given him the hiding of his life. Then he had arranged the wedding. That was over fifty years ago now. And Michael had been that child. My first born son. 1935 that was. Then I had child after child. Your father. He used to joke that he only had to walk past me to get pregnant. You were me last one. Me daughter for me old age. I never really loved your father, you know, but when you spend all that time with someone, it's hard to imagine being without them. Even when they're a waster, like your father.'

'I can understand that, Mum. It's a long time.'

'It's good of you to stay with me, Maws. I know we haven't exactly seen eye to eye.'

'Look, forget that, Mum,' Maura interrupted her

mother. 'We're together now. That's all that matters. That's what families are all about. Pulling together in the bad times and sharing the good.'

Not that we ever did that, Maura thought to herself.

Sarah stared into Maura's face. In the light of the bedside lamps, she looked very young and Sarah was reminded that she was the tool that was going to destroy her daughter. Whatever happened she was going to have to do that. Maura smiled at her sadly.

'Do you remember when I was a kid and I used to sleep with you when the old man was in prison? We used to have chats. That's what you always used to call them . . . chats. I wish we could turn the clock back to those days. Be like we were then.'

'So do I. But nothing can ever be the same as it was.' Sarah sounded as if she was holding back tears and Maura assumed they were for her father. She never dreamt they could be for her.

'I wish I had kept my baby, Mum. I still think about it sometimes.' Maura's voice was wistful.

'I wish you'd kept it and all. I wish I'd never taken you to that flat in Peckham.'

'That's all water under the bridge now, Mum. I went of my own accord.'

'No, Maws, it was me. I was scared that you'd be tied to someone you didn't love, like I was. Then, when I met Terry . . .'

'You met him? When?' Maura's voice was sharp, and Sarah realised her mistake.

'Oh, it was at the funeral. Michael's funeral. I spoke to him there.'

Maura relaxed. 'Oh, then. Yeah, our Garry had a go at him.'

Sarah swallowed deeply.

'I know. I was watching. Along with many other people.'

They were quiet for a while, both occupied with their own thoughts. Then Maura spoke softly.

'Look, Mum, let's just concentrate on getting me dad out of hospital and back home. Everything else is done. Over with.'

She nearly told her mother about William Templeton but stopped herself. She knew that her mother didn't really like him.

'Mum?' Maura's voice was quiet.

'Yes.'

'You don't regret having all us kids, do you?' Suddenly it was important that she knew the answer.

Sarah was silent for a while before answering.

'Of course not, Maws.'

As she spoke, she asked God to forgive her for lying.

Chapter Thirty-Three

February 1987

Leslie and Garry were collecting the protection money. As they pulled up outside a Greek restaurant in Ilford, Garry noticed a blue Granada parked a few cars away from them.

'Les . . . see that blue Granny? I'm sure it's been following us.'

Leslie looked at the car.

'I haven't noticed it.'

Garry got out and walked to the Granada. He tapped on the window. As it opened he leant down and looked into the car.

'What you doin' here?'

The blond man inside looked puzzled.

'I beg your pardon?'

'I said . . . what you doin' here?'

'I've come to have a meal in the restaurant. Why?'

'Nothing.'

Garry walked away from the car, still not sure what was going on. He got back in his own car beside Leslie.

'Let's sit here a minute and see if that bloke goes in the restaurant.' Sure enough, the man got out of his car and locked it up. Then he went into the restaurant.

'You wait here, Les.'

'OK.'

Garry went into the restaurant. The man from the Granada was studying a menu. Leslie walked through to the kitchen, picked up the envelope with the 'rent' in and walked back out again. As he passed the man's table he said, 'Have a nice meal.'

The blond man watched him leave. After a quick moussaka and a brandy, he paid his bill and left. He drove to the nearest phone box. He had to let Marsh know that Garry Ryan had tumbled him.

Maura and William were visiting Benjamin. He had been home from the hospital for ten days and was not taking kindly to his new regime. Not drinking, no smoking, no fats.

'Seems bloody silly living if you can't enjoy yourself.'

William smiled.

'Really, Mr Ryan, once you get used to the changes they won't seem so bad.'

'I dunno about that. It's easy for you to say, ain't it? You ain't been told you can't enjoy yourself no more.'

William shook his head. Benjamin Ryan was not only ignorant but stubborn. He had absolutely refused to conform to any advice that the doctors had given him.

'Nuffink but a load of bleeding foreigners. Can't understand half of wot they're waffling about. Bloody macaroons, eye ties and sodding krauts telling *me* wot to do!'

Maura laughed.

'Oh, Dad, Doctor Hummelbrunner isn't German. He's Austrian.'

'All the bleeding same if you asks me.'

'Leave him, Maura. I'll make sure he follows the doctor's orders. Now shut your trap, Benjamin Ryan, when we've got visitors. Would you like another cup of tea, Lord William?'

'I really wish you wouldn't call me that, Mrs Ryan. Willy will be quite adequate.'

Sarah smiled uneasily. She didn't like having a lord in her house. It made her uncomfortable. Where her daughter was concerned, there seemed to be nothing but trouble. Sarah had read about this Templeton in Geoffrey's papers. He was a villain. Only in Sarah's eyes he was worse than her children, because he had been given a good start in life which was more than her brood had ever had. It wasn't right . . .

Sarah was beginning to regret her newfound friendship with her daughter. She should have kept it as it was. Kept her away from the house. The trouble being she was the apple of her father's eye. She waited every day for that Petherick to call her about the papers she had given him and up till now she had heard nothing. She was beginning to wonder if she had done the right thing.

'You all right, Mum?'

Sarah looked at Maura.

'Tired, Maws, that's all. I think you two had better make a move in a minute. I want to settle your father for a nap.'

'Okey doke. I've got to meet Leslie and Garry anyway.'

William Templeton got up and placed his cup and saucer on the coffee table.

Maura went to the bed that had been put in the lounge and kissed her father goodbye.

'Take it easy, Dad, and do what Mum tells you.'

'I will, girl. See you tomorrow then.'

'Goodbye, Mr Ryan.'

'Tata, son. See you again.' He winked at William. 'Bring me a medicinal brandy next time.'

'Oh, Dad. Give it a rest, will you!'

When Maura and William had left Sarah settled Benjamin for his nap. 'Our Maura's done well for herself there, Sar. Looks like he's got a couple of bob.'

'Well, money isn't everything and I don't think our Maura's exactly hard up.'

Benjamin caught hold of her hand. 'I never give you much, did I, gel?'

She looked into his rheumy eyes.

'Well, you did your best. Now try and get yourself off to sleep. I'll call you at nine o'clock for your tablets and we'll watch a bit of telly. How's that?'

'All right, love.'

Sarah collected the used cups together and carried them out to the kitchen. As she filled the sink with hot water she looked around her, remembering the cockroaches, the empty bellies, and the years of hardship she had experienced within these walls. And she remembered Maura with her long blond hair flying behind her as she played out in the street . . . Leslie's permanently running nose. 'Silversleeves' the others had called him . . . She could almost hear Mickey's voice floating up from the basement . . .

She turned off the tap and began to wash up. In her mind's eye she could see Geoffrey on the day Maura had made her first Holy Communion. Geoffrey had been so proud of her. All the boys had been scrubbed up and taken to the church. Garry and Lee had been irritating her all that morning. Geoffrey had thumped the pair of them.

She had felt so proud of them that day. She had walked, head high, with her nine children all clean and shining.

She smiled to herself. If only you had an idea what was in store for your children! All those years ago she had thought Maura would grow up, marry, and give her grandchildren. Instead, she had grown up and done the complete opposite. First thing in the morning she would phone that Petherick and see what was going on. If she had to wait much longer she'd have a heart attack herself! Once Maura was arrested she would be able to breathe freely. Whatever happened, she had to get her away from the boys. Benjamin's heart attack had shown her that they weren't getting any younger. If she was to sort her family out before she herself died, she had to do it now.

Maura and William were in Le Buxom by ten o'clock. Gerry Jackson had been in the act of throwing out a prominent Member of Parliament who had a penchant for trying to dance with the strippers when Roy had arrived. Recognising the man, Roy had taken him down to the restaurant to try to sober him up before the place got packed. He left him with one of the waitresses and went back into the club.

'That old bastard gets worse, Gerry.'

He nodded.

'He gets on my bloody nerves. He'll be on telly tomorrow or the next day telling everyone to listen to their consciences and vote for the Tory Party.'

'Mickey had the right idea, you know. He used to keep records on all the prominent citizens and use them to his advantage.'

'Yeah, I know. The West End's full of bloody Arabs at the moment. That'll cause hag, it always does. They won't go near the black birds and so the blondes will be "going case" two or three times a night, which means permanent bitching. By the way, that coon Rubber was in here earlier, selling coke. I slung him out but I thought I'd let you know. All the hostesses are as high as kites.'

'Thanks for telling me, Ger. That's all we need. Well, keep your eye on them. I don't want them fighting with the punters. They can do what they like to one another.'

Roy went back up to the offices to see Maura.

'All right, Roy?'

'Yeah, not too bad. We've got the Right Honourable Dickhead in again tonight and that bloody Rubber's been in and sold the hostesses coke. Other than that, everything's fine!'

Maura laughed.

'Send Leslie round to have a word with him. I heard through the grapevine he got a good hiding outside the Pink Pussycat last week for selling bad stuff. Tell Leslie to make it plain that this is his last warning. I don't want this place raided for drugs.'

'Okey doke. Leslie and Garry are due in shortly anyway. Actually, Garry rang in earlier. Reckons he was being followed by a bloke in a blue Granada.'

Maura rolled her eyes to the ceiling and took a deep breath. 'I don't believe him! He is so paranoid it's a joke!'

William Templeton looked at her, puzzled. 'What do you mean?'

'Oh, Will, it would take all night to explain it.'

Roy started to chuckle.

'He thinks that he's being followed all the time. We all wind him up about it. He's really paranoid.'

'Has he always been like this?'

'Since he was a kid. He told me once that when he gets really wound up he hears voices!' Roy laughed.

'Good God!'

Maura put her hand over her mouth to stifle her giggles. 'No, not God . . . more like the devil!'

William smiled but in fact he was disturbed.

'What did you say to him?'

'Not a lot, Maws, just the usual. That I'd phone around the Bill shops and see if they had any information. I'll tell him later it was just a mistake on his part.'

'Good. Humour him. That's the best way.'

'If you want to shoot off, Maws, I'll pick up the rents. I'm staying on here for a while anyway.'

'Thanks, Roy. That would be great. Once Les has been sent to sort out Rubber, would you ask him to pick up some parcels for me? The addresses are on this piece of paper.

'We're meeting Isaacs again on Sunday night to complete the deal, so I want you, the boys and Gerry Jackson with me. Tooled up. Sawn-offs, not handguns. OK?'

'What time?'

'We'll meet here at about five-thirty. Right then, Will, let's get going.'

He stood up.

'Would you like to go out to eat?'

'Why not?'

'See you's later then.'

When Maura and William left, Roy started going through the papers. Sunday was two days away, and he was going to wish that he had listened to Garry's story. Although none of them knew it, the net was closing.

*

Lenny Isaacs was sitting in his hotel room, shaking like a leaf. Terry Petherick and Superintendent Marsh were sitting opposite him.

'I swear on my mother's grave, I don't know what you're talking about!'

Terry flicked the ash from his cigarette onto the carpet.

'Listen, Lenny, we know everything. We know about the gold, about the robbery, and we also know about you. So why don't you save yourself some trouble and just tell us what we want to hear?'

Lenny was biting his lip. His short stubby fingers were trembling and he was trying as hard as he could to stop himself crying.

Marsh looked at him pityingly.

'I can promise you, Lenny, that the Ryans will not know where we got our information from. All we want to know is when the meet will be. We'll do the rest.'

'I'm sorry. I know nothing. I'm over here on holiday.'

Terry lost his temper.

'Cut the crap, Isaacs! You're over here to buy illegal gold. How about we pull you in now? Leak your name to the papers. Say that you're helping us with our enquiries. Then leave you on remand in funky Brixton where you can sit and wait for the Ryans to waste you!'

Lenny paled.

'You wouldn't do that to me!'

Terry smiled.

'Just try us and see.'

Lenny looked down at his hands. Terry could see his shiny pate through his thinning hair.

'It's on Sunday. We all meet on Sunday. You realise that I'm a dead man?'

Marsh stopped chewing his thumbnail and said, 'We'll

see about that, Lenny. Don't worry. Now tell us nice and slowly what's supposed to be going down.'

Lenny cleared his throat and took a sip of his wine. 'We're meeting at a place called Fenn Farm.'

'We know all about Fenn Farm. What we're more interested in is times.'

'Seven-thirty on Sunday evening.'

Terry looked at Marsh.

'That only gives us thirty-six hours.'

'Don't worry, Petherick. We'll be more than ready for them.'

Lenny Isaacs wiped a stray tear from his eye. Maura Ryan would have his nuts for this. He was already dead.

Maura had just put a chicken in the oven and was preparing the vegetables for Sunday lunch. She wanted to eat at twelve so she and William could have the afternoon free. When she had finished scraping the carrots, the telephone rang. It was Margaret.

'Hello, Marge.' Maura's voice was warm.

'Hiya! I thought I'd give you a quick ring and see how you was getting on.'

'Terrific. I was just starting the dinner actually.'

Margaret's voice was incredulous. 'Maura Ryan cooking! Now I've heard everything!'

'Ha, ha, Marge!'

'This William must be some guy. If he can domesticate you, he must be the business.'

'He has not domesticated me . . . I often cook.'

'Pull the other one, Maws, it plays "Hard Day's Night"! Seriously, I'm just pleased you're so happy. It's about time.'

'Oh, Marge, it's great! I wish to God I'd got myself in

a relationship years ago. I don't think I'm in love exactly . . . but I just want to be with him all the time. In fact, I *am* with him all the time.'

'I can remember when me and Den were like that!'

'Come off it, Marge, you and Den are still like lovebirds. You two even embarrass your own kids with all your kissing and cuddling.'

'Don't talk to me about my kids . . .'

Margaret's voice was sad.

'Why, what's happened?'

'It's Penny. She's got herself a bloke.'

'What's wrong with that? You can't keep them tied to your apron strings for ever.'

'It's not that, Maws. He's a bloody Sikh.'

'You're joking!'

'I wish I was. He even wears a turban. Mind you, I had to laugh. Little Dennis saw them together in the High Street and went up and asked him when his head was gonna get better. That's how we found out. Penny and him had a big fight about it and when I tried to sort it all out, Dennis dropped the bombshell.'

Maura was laughing so hard she had an ache in her ribs.

'I wish *I* could see the funny side of it all.'

'You bloody hypocrite, Marge! You're the one who brought them up with liberal ideas. Everyone's the same, no matter what colour they are or what religion. Now poor old Penny's got herself a coloured bloke, you're doing your nut!'

'Well, I never thought they'd want to go out with one, did I?'

Maura was still chuckling.

'What's big Den got to say?'

'Oh, him! He's about as much good as an ashtray on a

motorbike. "Leave her alone, Marge. Let her find her own way . . ." I said, "You won't be saying that when she's walking round with a red spot on her forehead and a gold lamé sari." '

'Oh, Marge, stop it. You're making me guts ache. Can you see her in a sari with all that ginger hair of hers?'

'Oh, I don't know what to do.'

'Well, if you want my advice, I wouldn't protest too much. Remember what we were like at that age. The more people try and tell you what to do, the more you're inclined to go against them!'

'Yeah. I've thought of that.'

'Let her get it out of her system.'

Maura heard William get out of bed. 'I've gotta go, Marge. I'll try and get over to you tomorrow. Say about lunchtime, how's that?'

'All right, Maws. I'll make us a nice quiche.'

'How about a curry? You'd better start practising Indian cookery.'

'Piss off, Maura!'

'And you! 'Bye, Marge.'

Maura put the phone down and leant against the wall, laughing. Poor old Marge!

'What are you laughing about?'

Maura went to William and kissed him.

'I'll tell you all about it later. I've started the dinner, we're eating early today. I thought we could go out this afternoon for a walk or something. I have to leave at four to meet Roy and the others.'

William looked down into Maura's bright blue eyes.

'Tell you what. Scrub the walk, we'll go back to bed. How's that?'

Maura kissed his mouth hard.

'I was kinda hoping you'd say that!'

Terry and Marsh were in the Special Operations room at Scotland Yard, going over the final details with a hand-picked bunch of men. Marsh had recruited them from the SPG. All had licences to use firearms.

'So we swoop at precisely seven-forty-five. That gives them fifteen minutes to negotiate with Isaacs. We've put a man with him so he doesn't lose his nerve. He'll introduce him to Maura Ryan as his partner. You all understand what you are to do?'

All the men nodded.

'Good.'

Terry stood up and faced them.

'The main aim is to bring the Ryans in. All of them. This is going to be one of the biggest busts this country has ever seen. Nothing is to go wrong. You only fire if it is absolutely necessary and then you aim only to wound if possible.'

The men nodded and looked at one another. Unknown to Terry they had all been told to open fire immediately they entered the barn. Not one person was to be allowed to leave that place alive, Lenny Isaacs included. No one knew why this young DI was being kept in the dark. They were just following orders.

4.00

Sarah was sitting with Benjamin watching a Doris Day film on TV. She was trying to knit and finding it increasingly difficult to concentrate. She had left message after message for that young man Petherick and he had not been in touch. She was worried that one of the people who worked for Maura had found out what she had done. If Maura knew she would kill her, she knew that. For all her talk of never being frightened of anything that came out of her own body, she was increasingly nervous. Today for some reason she had had a terrible feeling of foreboding. It had been weighing down on her like a lump of concrete in her breast since she had got out of bed this morning. She put her knitting down and rubbed her eyes.

'How about a nice cuppa, Sar?'

Benjamin spoke without taking his eyes off the television. Sarah stood up, glad of something to do. She made her way out to her kitchen and put the kettle on. She had been going to visit the boys' graves today. Mainly Anthony's, Benny's and Geoffrey's, she only ever paid Mickey's a flying visit. But for some reason she did not want to leave the house.

As she set about making the tea, a deep coldness came over her and she had to sit down at the kitchen table. She had only felt like this twice in her life before and that was when Benny had died and Geoffrey had gone missing. She had had a feeling similar to this the day the police had reported to her Geoffrey's body had been found. She closed her eyes to blot out the picture of him in the mortuary. He had been shot in the back of the head and the bullet had come out just under his jawline. He had had a surprised expression on his face. Now she had that feeling again. She was convinced that something was going to happen today. Something bad.

When she finally took the tray of tea in to Benjamin he was asleep. She turned the sound down on the TV and sat and drank her own tea. Waiting for a knock on the door or the phone to ring.

4.30

Maura was driving to Le Buxom to meet the boys. She had not felt so happy for a long time. William had tried to persuade her to let Roy deal with the business today and she had been very tempted to stay in bed with him. After all these years she was finally having a relationship with a man, and loving every second of it. She only wished she had let herself go before now. She found herself smiling at complete strangers at traffic lights and laughed to herself. If this was love she was enjoying every moment of it. She decided that she would pass more of the business over to Roy. He was doing so well now. She wished he could get rid of Janine but knew that concern for Benny kept him with her.

She could understand that. If she had become a mother she knew she would have done anything for the good of her children. She wished again she had kept her baby. It would have been grown up now with a life of its own.

She pushed the thought from her mind. She was happy today and nothing was going to interfere with that! She turned her thoughts to Marge, determined that nothing was going to spoil her happiness. All she wanted to do was get the meet over and get back to William.

She was humming a little tune as she pulled into Dean Street.

4.45

Lenny Isaacs had dosed himself up with brandy. The policeman assigned to keep him from bolting was Detective Sergeant Paul Johnson. He had been given his orders two hours ago. Once the shooting started he was to push his gun into Isaacs' side and blast him. There was something definitely fishy about all this but as his old dad used to say: 'Ours is not to reason why.' If it got him a promotion he didn't give a toss. The likes of Lenny Isaacs were scum anyway. He'd be doing a public service.

Lenny sat in the barn. It was freezing and he shoved his hands into the pocket of his sheepskin. He was praying for the first time in thirty years. DS Johnson sat opposite staring at him. Lenny wished to Christ the copper wasn't such a big bastard. He would have tried to make an escape. The trouble was he had never been the hero type. More the 'I'll scratch your back' class of villain. He hadn't slept all night and had been jittery all day. Maura Ryan, whether she was nicked or not, would make sure he disappeared. Oh, God in heaven, help him, for fuck's sake!

Chapter Thirty-Four

4.50

Fenn Farm was derelict. It had not been worked for years. Maura had bought it for a song at an auction a few years previously and was going to sell it eventually, subject to planning permission for a housing estate. Green belt land was not classed as sacrosanct any more. If you had the money and the contacts you could build just about anywhere you wanted to. Arable land that was worth only a few hundred pounds an acre could become, overnight, prime building land worth millions. This was the Thatcher era, when anything that was commercially viable and cost the government nothing was encouraged wholeheartedly. Even building estates on old power stations was acceptable, provided you filled the land in with plenty of concrete first. Then the people who bought the houses were given lists of trees they could plant, trees with very shallow roots that would not disturb the sludge and radioactive waste lying beneath the houses. It was a developer's dream, and Maura Ryan had had the foresight to cash in when land was still at nominal prices. The days when the working-class men dreamt of winning fifty thousand pounds on the pools were long over. You could not buy a flat for that amount now, let alone live for the rest of your life on it. England was the epitome of the consumer society.

Today Terry Petherick was watching from the sidelines as the farm was being set up ready for the arrival of the Ryans. Everywhere he looked there were men with high velocity rifles, all taking up position in and around the barn. The light was fast fading, and Terry was reminded of an old World War Two movie, seeing the men dressed in black spiriting around with faces covered in camouflage make-up and guns glinting in the half-light. He fingered his own gun and prayed that he would not have to use it. Especially not on Maura Ryan.

He was sitting on an oil drum watching the activity around him when a man standing near him answered a call on his walkie talkie. Terry had not been issued with one and until this moment had not thought it strange. When he heard what was being said on the man's radio, it became crystal clear to him just why he had been overlooked in that department.

The voice crackled over the radio and into Terry's brain. 'Remember, not one Ryan is to leave the farm alive. You cut them down as they arrive.'

'Understood. Over and out.'

The man began to walk towards the barn door, and Terry realised through his reeling thoughts that the man had not noticed him. In the twilight and with the camouflage make-up he was indistinguishable. He sat for a while on the oil drum, letting what he had heard sink in.

Maura and her brothers were going to die. They were

being led here, to this farm, like lambs to the slaughter. And it was his fault. He had taken the files to his superiors and then had listened to their excuses as to why none of the judges and policemen on the Ryans' payroll would be brought to justice. Now it was revealed to him with shocking clarity why the Ryans had to die. While they held knowledge that could rock the country, they were dead men. And women. He must not forget Maura, the mastermind behind it all. It was she who was the biggest target: Maura who was the fly in an otherwise perfect ointment. He could have kicked himself. Here he was, with his ideals about justice – good and bad, law and order – and there was no such thing. Not in this country, or indeed the world.

He looked at his watch. The luminous dial showed that it was just five o'clock. Looking around him surreptitiously, he began to move slowly towards one of the last remaining cars outside the farm. He was praying that the keys were still in it.

He slipped behind the wheel of the Sierra Estate and felt a surge of thankfulness that was almost sexual. The keys were in the ignition. He swallowed deeply, feeling the momentary hesitation that always precedes an act of wrong doing. Only what he was doing was not wrong. He had sworn an oath to uphold the law in this country, and as far as he was concerned that was just what he was doing. Stopping the wanton murder of a whole family. No matter what they had done, nothing warranted what was to happen at this farm tonight. He had two hours before the Ryans were supposed to arrive and he would try to stop them if it was the last thing he did.

He started the car up and drove cautiously away from the farm house and the barn. He drove as if he was supposed to be driving the car away, neither too fast nor too slow. He remembered that on their way to the farm today he had seen a phone box in the lane about a hundred yards from the farm's exit. He drove there, his breath barely entering his lungs in his state of nervous tension. If somebody tried to stop him, he would use his gun. Whatever happened, Maura Ryan was not going to die, not in a barn on a cold February evening, mown down like a dog.

5.05

'Right then. Is everyone happy with what they are to do?'

Roy, Leslie, Garry and Lee nodded at Maura.

'Good. We'll have a quick coffee and then make tracks. It'll take over an hour to get there.'

'I still think we're being watched.' Garry's voice was low.

Maura sighed.

'Oh, for Christ's sake, Gal. If we were being watched, one of our plants would have let us know before now. You're so paranoid lately.'

'I'm telling you now, that bloke I saw in the blue Granny was definitely waiting for us.'

'Give it a rest, Garry. You're like an old woman sometimes.'

Garry looked at Roy. 'Well, when we're all fucking nicked, don't say I never warned you.'

Lee laughed, then said in a girlish voice, 'All right then, Garry. I promise you with all my heart.'

Garry looked at him, frowning.

'I'm glad you think it's funny. I hope you find it as amusing when you're sitting in Parkhurst or Durham doing a twelve stretch.'

Leslie pulled on his cigarette.

'Only twelve years? I'd have thought we warranted at least a thirty.' He looked at Lee. 'Remind me to nail someone's leg to a table. We can't have the Krays outdoing us at the last moment.'

Everyone laughed but Garry would not be silenced.

'Yeah. And the Krays are still inside, remember that. In fact if you –' he pointed at Leslie viciously – 'get put on the "Island", you might get banged in a cell with one of them. Reggie, that is.'

Lee grinned.

'Not you though, Garry, you'll be put in Broadmoor with Ronnie. That's where all the nutters go.'

'Oh, shut up, for Christ's sake. No one's going anywhere.' Maura was getting annoyed.

Garry flicked his hair from his eyes. 'Well, there's one thing I can guarantee. You won't be in Cookham Wood with the other long-timers like Hindley. You'll be top security, girl. We'll all be A grade. Like terrorists.'

Before Maura could retort, Lee spoke. His voice was soft as silk. 'Have you been reading that book again? *How to Win Friends and Influence People*?'

Everyone laughed.

'Oh, piss off, the lot of you! The last book you's read was *Fluff and Nip*.'

Then the phone rang and Maura picked it up, chuckling as she did so.

Terry went into the phone box and dialled directory enquiries. He asked them for the number of Le Buxom. When they gave it to him, he dialled the operator for a reverse charge call. He did not have a single coin on him. He stood in the cold with bated breath as the operator tried to connect him. Le Buxom was the only place he could think of where someone would know the whereabouts of Maura Ryan.

He was literally praying as he heard the distant clicking and whirring of the telephone exchange.

Maura picked up the phone. 'Hello?' Her voice was calm and happy.

'I have a reverse charge call from a call box in Essex. Will you accept the charges?'

The operator's clipped tones were bored and efficient.

Who on earth could be ringing her from a call box? Maura racked her brains.

'Of course.'

'You're through, caller.'

'Hello, can I speak to Maura Ryan?'

She felt her heart stop in her chest. She would know that voice anywhere. All around her the boys were good-naturedly ragging Garry as they drank their coffee. In Maura's head there was only one sound: Terry Petherick's voice.

'Is there anyone there?' He sounded desperate. 'I must speak to Maura Ryan or someone who can contact her.'

'This is Maura Ryan.' She was amazed at how calm her voice sounded.

'Maura, this is Terry . . . Terry Petherick. Please don't put the phone down.'

'What do you want?' Even as she spoke so normally she could feel the almost adolescent longing and excitement he had always created in her.

'You mustn't go near Fenn Farm. The Special Investigations Branch are waiting for you. They're armed and ready.'

'What!' The sound of her voice silenced her brothers. They all looked at her.

'I know it sounds crazy, but believe me, Maura, you're in big trouble. We know everything about you. Everything.' He stressed the last word.

'But how?' She sounded very young in panic.

'Look, can we meet? I can't stand here explaining it all. They're looking for me . . . or will be when they realise I've gone.'

'What are you talking about?' Maura's voice was scared.

'Look, Maura, is there anywhere we can meet? It must be somewhere the police don't know about. Have you a secret hideaway?'

Maura was thinking out loud. 'Marge's house . . . Carla's . . .' Then it struck her. 'Do you know Mickey's old place?'

'Yes. I know it.'

'I'll meet you there.'

'OK.' Terry put the phone down and went to the car.

'What's happened, Maws?'

'You were right, Garry. The old Bill have tumbled us. Isaacs must have grassed.'

Garry stood up from his seat and threw his coffee cup at the wall.

'I knew it! I bloody knew it! You wouldn't listen, would you?'

'Calm down. Calm down. Shouting and hollering ain't gonna help us.'

Roy looked at his sister.

'What's the score?'

'I'm not sure yet. I want you all to lie low for a while. I'm meeting somebody who knows what's going on. Fenn

Farm is well and truly out of the question. I'll be at Mickey's old flat. I want you all to ring in there from wherever you decide to go. All right?'

'Who was that on the dog and bone?'

'Just a friend, Les. A good friend.'

'Well, I'm off to Muvver's. Who wants to come?'

Leslie nodded at Lee. 'I'll go with you. At least she'll guarantee some decent grub with an alibi.'

'Well, wherever you all go, don't forget to ring me at Michael's.'

'What about Richard? He might not like you just turning up at his drum.'

Maura picked up her bag and scowled at Lee.

'Fuck Richard!'

'No, thanks. He's not my type.'

Maura laughed despite herself. 'Come on, you lot. Let's get a move on.'

Richard was asleep in bed with a Filipino man he'd picked up the night before. They had only emerged from the bedroom once to have some sandwiches before they went back to bed for another session. Richard was cuddling into the man's back when he heard the hammering on his front door. He hoped it was not that bitch Denzil again. Since Michael had died he had practically haunted him. Richard's most oft repeated statement was: 'Straight I may not be . . . choosy I most definitely am!' And he had not sunk as low as Denzil. Not yet anyway.

He walked naked into the hallway.

'Who is it?' His voice was high and cracked.

'It's me. Maura Ryan.'

'Oh!' Richard opened the front door and let her in. Since Michael's death he had added a mortice lock to the door which was why Maura's key was not enough to gain her access.

'I never expected you!'

Maura could hear the surprise in his voice.

'Well, you've got me, Richy baby. Until I say otherwise.'

She walked into the lounge and threw her bag on the sofa. Going to the drinks cabinet, she poured herself a large Remy Martin.

Richard was in a quandary. He most definitely did not want Maura Ryan in his flat. And it *was* his flat. Michael had left it to him. But he was not brave enough to ask her to leave. He just stood in the doorway watching her. She was wearing a deep red trouser suit that perfectly complemented her white-blond hair. Her large breasts were just covered by a white silk shirt. Richard could see that she was braless. He had envied her her breasts from the first time they had met. He had also been jealous of the way Michael worshipped her. The fact that he knew she did not like him had not helped matters very much either.

He heard a stirring in the bedroom and felt faint with fright. He had completely forgotten about his Filipino friend! He saw Maura's puzzled expression and tried to smile.

'It's a friend of mine.' As he spoke the man came out of the bedroom and Maura could not help but stare at him. He was tiny and slim, like most Filipinos, but he had the largest organ Maura had ever seen in her life. It was like a baseball bat. She made a conscious effort not to let her mouth fall open with shock.

'This is my friend, his name's Weykok.' Richard's voice trailed off as Maura began to guffaw with laughter.

'Well, it would be, wouldn't it?'

Weykok stood with his thin bony shoulders pulled back, as if trying to emphasise his enormous member. He seemed to enjoy the stir that he was creating. Richard turned to him and bundled him back into the bedroom. Maura sat on the sofa laughing her head off. She had needed something to lighten the situation and it had come in the shape of a man called Weykok.

Richard came back into the lounge; he was wearing a silk dressing-gown. 'He's leaving now.'

As he spoke the little man came into the room, fully dressed. He held out a tiny hand.

'Money, please.'

Maura saw Richard flush. Enjoying herself, she said innocently, 'Does he charge by the inch or the centimetre? After all, we're in the common market now.'

She started to laugh again and Weykok laughed with her good-naturedly. Maura went to her bag and opened it.

'Have him on me, Richard. How much?'

Weykok seemed to understand this as he said politely, 'Eighty-five pounds, madam, please.'

Maura pulled out two fifty-pound notes and gave them to him, saying, 'Keep the change.'

The little man bowed to her, and after a mumbled conversation with Richard in the hallway, left the flat.

'Well, Richard, I'm afraid I'll be invading your space for a while. Let's try and get on, shall we?' Her voice was friendly.

'Are you in some kind of trouble, Maura?' Richard was serious.

'Sort of.'

'In that case I'll do all I can to help. Not for you but for Michael. I know that's what he would have wanted me to do.'

He said the words simply and with an innate sincerity that made her feel guilty for her earlier jokes at his expense. She was reminded that she needed him. Needed him badly.

'Someone will be coming here soon to see me.'

She saw his face fall and hastily reassured him. 'Don't worry, Richard, there'll be no violence or anything like that.'

She saw him relax and for a second felt sorry for him. She sat back down on the sofa and patted the seat beside her.

'Come and sit here, Richard. We need to talk.'

Terry Petherick was in Dagenham. He parked the car he was using in the car park of the Ship and Shovel public house. Leaving it there, he went out on to the A13 and flagged down a passing mini cab.

'Bloody hell! You in the TA?'

As Terry sat beside the minicab driver, he remembered that he was still blacked up.

'Yes, actually. I've been on manoeuvres and my car broke down.'

'Oh, I see.' The man's voice was gravelly as if he needed to clear his throat. 'Where you want droppin' off?'

'Could you take me to Knightsbridge, please?'

'Yeah. Course, I was in the TA, you know. Went to Germany once . . .'

Terry closed his eyes. This was all he needed, a 'weekend warrior' for a cab driver.

Maura was chatting to Richard, trying to make friends with him. She knew that she needed him, desperately. She could not help noticing that all around the room were pictures of Michael and Richard, laughing and with their arms around one another. It was only Richard's association with her brother, and his fear of her, that was keeping him from throwing her out, she knew that.

'I needed somewhere to meet someone important. Where no one would think of looking for me. I know this is a cheek, Richard, but it was the only place I could think of.'

He shrugged.

'Well, it's yours for as long as you want to use it. Now, can I make you something? Tea? Coffee?'

Maura smiled. 'Coffee would be great.'

She looked at the large cuckoo clock on the wall. It was nearly a quarter to seven. She bit her lip. Where was Terry?

Roy was sitting at home with little Benny. He was nervous and worried. He would ring in to Maura at seven. Give her a chance to sort herself out. He looked at Janine. She was lying on the couch half drunk. He suddenly felt a tightening sensation in his bowels. For the first time in years he was scared.

Sarah was watching the three boys surreptitiously. They had all turned up together to visit their father, but they were not right somehow. They were all taut as bowstrings, as if waiting for something to happen. Garry got out of his chair.

'Can I use your phone, Mum?'

'Of course you can.'

He went out into the hallway and rang Maura. While he was doing it, Leslie and Lee kept Sarah in the front room chatting. Both were nervous under the plaster gaze of the holy family and the various saints that stood around the room. It seemed every time they visited her a new statue had been added to the collection.

Sarah sat with them while they chatted to her and Benjamin, but still had the bad feeling in her side. The dragging feeling that seemed to be increasing as the day wore on.

At six-thirty Marsh realised that Terry Petherick had gone missing. Busy as he was getting everything set up, he had not given him a thought till then. Although Terry did not know it, he was going to be silenced along with the Ryans. Oh, they would not kill him. Not unless they had to . . . He was going to be named as the person who had shot Maura Ryan on her entry into the barn.

Now Marsh knew that somehow Terry had cottoned on to what was going to happen and had driven one of the unmarked cars out of the farmyard. He was fuming. There had been two cars outside, both to be driven away before the Ryans were due to arrive. In the commotion, as everyone got ready and set up the barn for the meeting, Terry had just got into one of them and driven off. God knew where. Personally Marsh hoped it was not to the newspapers. While Maura Ryan was alive and kicking they dared not touch her. She could open her mouth about things that would smash open the Metropolitan Police force and West Midlands Serious Crime Squad, and she also knew things about docklands and other prime areas of development that could bring down the government. He shivered. She had them literally by the bollocks.

Now there was another thing that he knew for definite. Maura Ryan was not coming anywhere near this barn or even this county. Terry Petherick had jumped fences today.

In either camp, whether it was the police's or the Ryans', Petherick was a dangerous man.

Terry knocked on the door of Michael's flat and Maura let him in almost immediately. They stood in the hallway staring at one another for long moments, both drinking in the other as if they were dying of thirst.

Maura was the first to speak.

'Come through, Terry.'

He followed her into the lounge.

'This is Richard, an old friend of my brother Michael's. He lives here now.'

Terry held out his hand and Richard shook it.

'I'll make some more coffee, shall I?'

'I could certainly do with some.'

Richard smiled at Terry and went to the kitchen.

'Sit down.'

They sat on the sofa together, nearly touching, and Maura felt the heady sensation of being close to him for the first time in years. She savoured it for a few moments to try to commit it to memory. Terry was doing exactly the same.

Finally Maura spoke. 'So, what's going on?'

'You're not going to like what I have to tell you, Maura.'

'I know that, Terry. But I still have to know the score.'

He took a deep breath.

'Your brother Geoffrey kept a file on you and Michael.' He watched her large blue eyes open wider. 'When he died it came into your mother's possession. It had details of the gold bullion robbery, even the route map – which incidentally had your prints all over it. It had the names of every high-ranking official in the government, police and law courts, how much you paid them and what you paid them for. Maura, it had everything.'

She was absolutely dumbstruck.

'Your mother rang me and asked me to meet her. I did.' He swallowed deeply. 'She gave the file to me and I passed it on to the SIB.'

Maura shook her head in disbelief. 'The Special Investigations Branch? I see.' Her voice was small. 'So between my mother and yourself, I was well and truly . . .'

'No, Maura. No. I know how it sounds but we wanted to help you.'

Even as he spoke he knew it sounded lame.

'Come off it, Terry! I'm not as daft as you seem to think. You and my mother wanted me put away. Neither of you thought about all the so-called "goody two-shoes" wankers on my payroll. It never occurred to either of you that *they* were abusing *their* positions. Oh, no! You two just wanted me sent down, out of harm's way. Well, let me tell you something. If it hadn't have been me and Michael buying them bastards off it would have been someone else. This bloody country is rotten to the core, mate. Everything has its price, whether it's a small backhander to get a bit of planning permission or a large donation to the appropriate political party for a development. Like docklands . . .'

'I know now that what you're saying is right.'

'Oh, shut up! Shut up!' Maura was shouting now and Richard was listening to everything that was being said.

'You was always an idealist, Terry . . . like some sort of bloody knight errant. Always wanted to get the bad guys, didn't you? Well, let me ask you something. What's happening to the people we've been buying off? I bet they aren't being given a twelve-gun send-off, are they? Are they? Of course not. They'll walk away as they always have done with an OBE or a golden handshake. No one must ever know that Sir Godly Goodly, who just happened to go to Cambridge with most of the other scum from the higher echelons of British Society, is on the fucking take!'

Her mouth was flecked with spittle and she ran her hand through her hair in agitation. 'Why aren't they after the real criminals? The rich and pampered criminals. Why must we take the fall for them? You answer me that.'

Terry stared at her, knowing that all she said was true. He was aware from the day that Marsh had told him what was going to happen to the men on Maura's payroll, that it was unfair. That the Ryans were going to carry the can for them so that Joe Public never knew what was really going on. He felt a fool. He had betrayed her. After all he had done to her in the past, he had betrayed her again because he'd thought that what he was doing was right. And now he knew that there was no such thing as 'right' and 'wrong' any more. Was it right that judges could sit on a bench and put away men for being a danger to society at large and then acquit other men who were a much bigger danger, just because they were being paid to do so? Was it right for the top police who were financing their gambling or other hobbies to be retired when in reality they should be doing time? No, it was wrong. Maura Ryan was a criminal but she had never pretended to be anything else. She did not shield herself with the mantle of a good education and a law degree. If what she did was wrong, at least she did it without pretending to benefit the nation.

Richard walked into the room with a tray of coffee and sandwiches. He placed it on the coffee table and spoke. 'I couldn't help hearing your conversation.'

Maura and Terry both looked at him as if they didn't know who he was. They'd forgotten him.

'I work for the papers. You know that, Maura. From what I've just heard, I think that while you have access to journalists you're safe as houses.' He looked from one to the other. 'Think about it. Maura knows all the people who are on her payroll. While you're alive, Maura, the police dare not touch you.'

'They were going to kill them all. Every one of them. At Fenn Farm tonight.' Terry's voice was flat.

'If you'll forgive me, I guessed as much for myself. What you must do, Maura, is leave the country. Go somewhere where they can't get to you.'

'They would!'

'No, let me finish. You must write down everything you know about the people who are on your payroll then you must leave it with someone, to be opened only on your death. That way you will live a very long time, believe me.'

Maura and Terry stared at him. As fantastic as it sounded, it held the ring of truth.

'I know plenty of journos who'd commit murder for a story like this. It's got everything a journalist needs.'

'He's got a point, you know.' Terry's voice was excited.

Richard spoke again. 'Honestly, Maura, I know what I'm talking about. Look at Profumo. Christ, that still gets dragged up every so often. People like to think that the rich people who run big businesses and the people in government are in cahoots with shadier people. It makes them feel better about their own lives. There's nothing the British like more than to tear someone apart, preferably someone they created or voted in in the first place. The gutter press makes its money doing it, whether it's the Westland affair, the Profumo scandal or a judge who's into pornography. As long as it's someone with plenty of money or a high profile, the British Public loves it.'

The more Richard spoke, the more sense he made to Maura.

'But where could I go?'

'Anywhere you wanted to, really. While you're alive and kicking and able to open your mouth, you and your brothers are as safe as houses.'

She slumped back on to the settee. 'Let me think about it. I can't concentrate . . .'

'Drink your coffee and have a sandwich. We'll think of something, don't you worry.'

Maura was beginning to understand what. Michael had seen in Richard. He wasn't just a pretty face.

Chapter Thirty-Five

Marsh was worried. Very worried. It seemed that Maura Ryan had gone on the missing list. From information he had received, it seemed the only person at her house was William Templeton. Lord Templeton. Three of her brothers were at their mother's and the other brother, Roy, was at his own house in Chigwell. Maura Ryan had not appeared at any of her clubs or other businesses. He had put a call out to watch for her car but didn't hold out much hope there. He was dealing with a dangerous lady, a woman with the means of destroying numerous people, himself included. And to top it all, she now had the championship of Terry Petherick!

He sighed and lit one of his cigars, looking up as the door of his office opened.

It was Superintendent Ackland of the Special Investigations Branch. Ackland was notorious in the force for his violent and disruptive personality. He was one of those men who should by rights have chosen a life of crime. Brought up in the Gorbals, he had an animal cunning and an empathy with the criminal mind that was out of place in the world of the police. Or so Marsh had thought until he had read the names of seemingly respectable men on Maura Ryan's payroll.

Like many Scotsmen, James Ackland was quite small, with a muscular body and the high forehead and erratic hair of his ancestors. He had tiny blue eyes that seemed to be permanently on the move, darting around his head as if he was frightened that by the act of relaxing his gaze he would miss something important. Even after twenty years in London, his Scottish accent was as pronounced as ever.

'You've read the files, I take it?' Marsh's voice was low.

'Aye. I have that.' Ackland laughed. 'Well, there's one thing for sure . . . she's a canny lass. The way I see it, there's not a lot we can do to her. Or her family, come to that.'

His face seemed to straighten, as if wiped clean with a blackboard rubber. 'But I'll think of something. Though myself, I think the people on the take should be brought to book. But you know and I know they won't be.'

Marsh nodded and puffed on his cigar.

Ackland picked his rather bulbous nose, making Marsh feel sick.

'The only way out is to annihilate the bitch. Usual code of conduct, of course. We find her, then we have what the papers euphemistically call a "shoot out". It's odds on that she's carrying a firearm. Christ, man, from what I read in the file, I wouldn't be surprised if she was carrying a tactical nuclear missile!'

His voice was jocular again. 'I don't like covering up for people, especially people who should know better, but there you are. We're all under orders.'

Ackland helped himself from the bottle of Famous Grouse that Marsh had on his desk, pouring the dregs from a coffee cup into a waste paper basket and filling it nearly full.

'We have to find her first.' Marsh's voice sounded as if that would be an impossible task.

Ackland sniffed. 'No one can hide for ever, Marsh.'

Maura was writing furiously. She was making a document which, if it got into the wrong hands, would bring the country to its knees. Her brain was working overtime, remembering every little detail she could about the people she had dealt with. Unknown to her there were people named in her account who had not appeared in Geoffrey's. She was concentrating on the 'biggies', as Richard had called the cabinet ministers and the Bank officials. She also listed every large developer and industry chairman who had at one time or another dealt with either herself or Michael.

Terry watched her as she worked, reading each page as she finished it and realising with each word just how corrupt and evil the establishment had become.

William Templeton was worried. Very worried. Like Marsh he was wondering where on earth Maura had got to. He glanced at his watch. It was nearly two in the morning and still no word. He looked around Maura's lounge at the family pictures that abounded. On top of the television cabinet were photographs of Carla. From a small child to a grown woman, her life was lovingly documented. On the occasional tables were photos of Maura and her brothers, mainly Michael.

He got up from his chair and went to the kitchen to make himself yet another coffee. As he poured hot water over the coffee granules there was a knock on the door.

Banging the kettle down on the worktop he answered it, his heart in his mouth.

A man was standing outside the porch. He was holding a police badge in his hand. Slowly, William opened the door.

'Sorry to disturb you at this time of night, sir.' The man had a pronounced Scottish accent. 'I am Superintendent Ackland of the Special Investigations Branch. Could I please talk to you for a moment?'

The man smiled and William saw that he had tobacco-stained teeth. He held the door open and gestured for the man to come inside.

Please God, don't let her be dead. William was convinced that it was bad news of some kind. It was not until Ackland told him that he was going to be arrested and charged with certain offences, including conspiracy to murder and armed robbery, that he realised just how bad.

'Do you realise who I am?' His voice was outraged.

'Aye, I do. But you see, Lord William, I couldn't care less if you were the Prince Regent himself. If you don't do what I tell you, I'll drag you to the police station so fast you'll burn a hole in the pavement! Outside this house is an army of policemen, with guns, just waiting for a word from me. You're going to be the bait that tempts the big fish. The big fish being Maura Ryan.'

'I have no idea where she is.'

'Maybe not, but it's odds on you'll be able to find out. Now, shall we have a nice cup of tea and a chat?'

Ackland's voice was friendly and for some reason this worried William more than anything.

Maura was in deep trouble and he guessed that he was going to be asked to double cross her. This Scottish lout had as good as already said that. What was worrying

William was the fact that, as much as he cared about Maura, his own skin would always come first. It always had.

At two-thirty Maura took a rest from her writing to have a cup of coffee. Richard had produced a photocopier that he kept for when he worked from home. He was busy in the bedroom copying all that Maura had written so far. Richard had wanted to be a 'real' journalist all his adult life. He realised that in his hands he had the scoop of the century and that he could never use it. As he read what Maura had written his eyes goggled. He would bet his last pound that the Secretary of State for the Environment was probably sitting at home and sweating like a pig. He must have been told all that was going on. The same could be said for the Home Secretary.

As he read, Richard had the beginnings of a plan forming in his mind.

In the lounge Terry and Maura drank their coffee in silence.

'What do you think the outcome will be?' she asked.

Terry shook his head.

'I really don't know, Maura. I feel responsible for it all.'

'That's not surprising, is it? Considering you are! You and my mother.' Her voice was bitter.

'I don't blame you for being upset with me but I am trying to help you now. Surely that says something?' Terry was desperate to reassure her of his backing.

'You're trying to help me now because the people that you worked for . . . the people that you revered and tried to emulate . . . turned out to be more bent than I am. *That's* why you're trying to help now. You said yourself that you knew before you even went to Fenn Farm that the so-called "biggies" who were on the take would walk. I don't need you, Terry Petherick. I never needed you.'

'You did need me once, Maura.' His voice was quiet and earnest.

She lit a cigarette and looked into his face.

'Oh, yeah? And when was that?'

'When you were pregnant. When you had the abortion. When you were lying in hospital desperately ill. Your mother told me all about it.'

He sounded calm and caring.

Maura snorted. 'So, mouth almighty told you that as well, did she? What else did she tell you? Did she tell you that she once accused me of sleeping with Michael? Did she tell you that? Did she tell you that for all our faults, real and imagined, she took the money that was sent to her every week?' She was quiet for a few seconds. Then, her voice low, she spoke again.

'I never needed you then, Terry, so don't flatter yourself. I was young and naïve and the only mistake I made, as I see it, was getting involved with someone like you. Even then you wanted to change the world. Michael told me what happened to you. We had enough plants in the force, even then. You were pulled over the carpet for your association with Michael Ryan's sister and you dumped me. You had a choice, me or the force, and your precious police force won. Then, when my mother gave you Geoffrey's papers, you couldn't wait to run to your superiors with them. Terry Petherick, the Vine Street Marvel, uncovers the biggest case of corruption this century. Only you didn't realise then that what you actually had was something the government and the police would rather hush up than expose. You struck out, mate.'

'I've lost everything. My job . . .'

'Oh, sod your job!' Maura was shouting. 'I don't give a toss about you or your stupid job!'

'Whatever you think now, Maura, I loved you. But we were so young then. What about the night we spent together after Benny died? You told me then that you still loved me.' He pointed at her. 'You told me to go the next morning. It was your decision.'

He felt an urge to weep. He had inadvertently brought her nothing but grief from the day they met.

'I sent you away because I wanted to.'

'Oh no you didn't! I won't have you saying that. You sent me away because you were in too deep with Michael. It was for that reason and that reason only.'

Maura watched his handsome face and admitted the truth of what he was saying to herself.

'Shall I tell you something? Shall I tell you the real truth of my life?'

'Yes. Please tell me.'

'When I met you in 1966, I felt something I had never felt before. Or since.' She stared at a spot on the carpet, afraid to look at his face. 'I wanted you so badly I could taste it. Do you remember when you told me you were a policeman? I nearly had a heart attack!'

She laughed softly. 'I sneaked around for months to meet you, lying to my mother and father and my brothers. Then, when I got pregnant and went to your flat to tell you, you finished with me. I had that baby scraped out of me by a dirty little Paki. I can still smell that flat sometimes. I can still see the baby lying in the bottom of a washing up bowl. Perfectly formed and dead.

'And do you know what the ironic part of it is? I never wanted to be anything other than a wife and mother. I know that the feminists would crucify me if they heard me speaking like this but it was all I ever wanted: a husband, a home, and children. A houseful of children. Then when I had the abortion and it went wrong, I came out of the hospital and all that had been taken away from me. I had nothing to give to a husband or a lover. I was empty inside. I nearly died, you know. And for a long time that's exactly what I prayed for. Then I had the idea of working for Michael. He never really wanted me to work in the family business but I forced him. I knew that he felt responsible for what had happened to me and I used that to get the ice cream and hot dogs from him. After that, I gradually took over from poor Geoffrey.

'If I hadn't gone into the business then, Geoffrey and Michael would have stayed together as a team. Though Michael never really had a lot of time for him, I must admit that. And somehow, all that happened over the years built up and built up . . . until this. I'm the most wanted woman in England now and all I ever wanted was to be Mrs Average. That child would be twenty-one now. Grown up and going out into the world. Instead it was flushed down a toilet in a multi-storey tower block in Peckham, and I'm being hunted by armed police . . .'

Her voice trailed away and Terry knew that silent tears were falling from her eyes. For the first time he realised just how much he had really hurt this woman. He asked himself for the hundredth time since Mrs Ryan had told him about the abortion, whether he would have stayed with her had he known. And being an honest person he knew that he could not answer that question so many years later. All he was sure of was that he had wrecked Maura's life. That she had always been inside him somewhere, like a piece of a puzzle that was gradually being put together.

He put an arm around her hesitantly, afraid that she would push him away, but she didn't. Instead she held on to him tightly, pulling his body against her own as if trying to crawl under his skin. And he held her while she cried and was not surprised to feel his own tears fall as they both healed a breach that spanned twenty years.

Richard had heard what had been said and being a tactful person coughed loudly before he went into the lounge. Maura and Terry pulled away from one another and Richard acted as if he could not see they were both very upset. Instead he smiled brightly and sat on the floor in front of them.

'I have the most amazing idea. I think that you'll love it.'

Maura wiped her eyes, grateful for the intervention. He was going up more in her estimation with every hour that passed.

'What is it?'

'I've been reading what you've written down and I think that you have more than enough to do a deal.'

'What kind of deal?' Maura's voice was more alert now.

'I think that if our friend here . . .' he pointed at Terry . . . 'goes to see his superiors with a copy of what you have written, and tells them that there are numerous other copies in the hands of unscrupulous people, then they'll be more than ready to come across.'

'They'll never do a deal.'

'How can you be so sure, Terry? I think that the Secretary of State for the Environment will have the last say on what happens. After all, there are some pretty heavy heads on the chopping block.'

'But who will we give the copies to?'

'Let me worry about that, Maura.'

'I know one person who would be glad to help us.'

'And who's that?'

Maura looked at Terry. 'Patrick Kelly.'

'What, the IRA man?' Terry's voice was shocked.

'Yeah. He's an old friend of mine. We go back years. Plus he owes me one.' She thought of Michael as she spoke.

'Wouldn't he use it, though?'

'Only to his own advantage. The British Government are in closer contact with the Irish than people think. They trade information with each other when necessary. The government know who the real leaders behind Sinn Fein are. Gerry Adams is just the media go-between. The real leaders are never mentioned.'

'Rich and important men, I suppose?'

'No, Terry, not all of them. I know that the IRA get a bad press but the majority of them are fighting for a cause that they believe in. Like any society they have all sorts, from the lower end of the scale to the top of it. Kelly is at the top of the scale and I know I can trust him.'

'So that's one person. Can you think of any more?' Richard was loving every second of this now. It was the most exciting night of his life. For the first time he was involved in something that was really important, and even though he would never be able to boast about it, he would know inside that he had been a part of it. Had helped to mastermind it.

Maura frowned. 'The only other person I can think of is Derek Lane.'

'But no one knows where he is.' Terry's voice was puzzled.

Maura couldn't help laughing. 'Terry, Derek Lane and people like him are easy to find if you have the right connections. Michael and I were in partnership with him out in Spain. He owns the monopoly on the timeshares out there. I have the full partnership with him now that Michael's dead. I could fly out to Marbella and explain the situation to him.'

Terry was flabbergasted. Even though he knew that Maura and Michael were heavyweights as far as the British gangland scene were concerned, he never dreamt for a second that they were in league with people like Derek Lane. Yet he should have guessed. After all, they were birds of a feather really. Derek Lane had gone on the trot in 1977 and not been seen or heard from since. He was wanted for countless murders and other serious crimes. He had been the Birmingham equivalent of Michael Ryan, only unlike Michael had not tried to work within the law as well as outside it. In the end England had got too hot for him and he had disappeared.

'Well, that's two good people. They'll do for the moment. Now then, Terry, are you willing to be negotiator? Will you go and see Marsh?' It was the least he could do for Maura.

'Yes. I'll go.'

Richard smiled.

'Good! Now all we have to do is work out what terms we want and everything will be underway.'

Maura laughed softly. 'You're really enjoying this, aren't you, Richard?'

He nodded his head at her. 'Yes, actually, I am. Now who wants more coffee?'

Roy heard the phone ring through a fitful sleep. He sat up in the chair, not sure for a moment exactly where he was. He looked at the clock on the mantelpiece. Four-fifteen.

The television showed an old black and white film. He dragged himself over to the phone.

'Yeah?'

'Roy? Roy Ryan?'

The clipped voice was familiar.

'Yeah. Who's this?'

'It's Jackson. DI Jackson.'

'Well, what do you want?' Roy had never liked Jackson.

'William Templeton was brought in earlier and he's shouting his mouth off about your sister and other things. I thought you ought to know.'

The line went dead and Roy stared at it for a few moments, letting the words sink in. Then he dialled Michael's flat.

Maura answered.

'Maws? I just had a call from Jackson. Willy's been nicked and he's telling them anything they want to know.'

'OK, Roy. Thanks.'

'What's happening, Maws?'

'At the moment you're as safe as you possibly can be. After eight o'clock this morning, everything will be fine, I promise you.'

'But what . . .'

'Roy, I'm sorry, mate, but I have to go. Get some sleep. I promise that you'll be fine. Tell the other boys for me.' She put the phone down, leaving Roy for the second time in five minutes with a dead phone in his hand.

'They've dragged in William Templeton.' Maura's voice was flat. She had hardly thought about him since the trouble had started and yet, not twenty-four hours ago, she had been making love to him.

'Does he know much?' Terry was concerned.

'No. Nothing that they don't already know. If I know Willy, he'll be trying to save his own neck. They must have picked him up from my house.'

'Well, let's forget him then and concentrate on what the terms are going to be. We haven't got long now.' Maura stretched and both men watched the rise and fall of her breasts. She yawned loudly.

'Right. Where were we?'

Chapter Thirty-Six

Marsh and Ackland were already sick to death of William Templeton and the Home Secretary had been on the phone twice in the last hour. Like everyone else he wanted this 'little business', as he put it, cleared up once and for all. Marsh had wondered fleetingly whether the Home Secretary had been up all night as well, because by the annoyed note in his voice Marsh got the impression that the man was tired. Sick and tired, by the sounds of it. As they all were.

The phone on his desk rang and he answered it.

'What!' He had lost any remnants of civility at about four in the morning. Now, at eight-fifteen, he had had just about enough.

'Detective Inspector Petherick is here to see you, sir. I told him that you were not to be disturbed but he insisted that you would see him.'

The WPC's voice was petrified. She had already been bawled out twice by Marsh already, and she had only come on duty at seven o'clock.

'Send him up, girl! Send the bugger up!'

Marsh slammed the phone into its cradle.

'It's Petherick . . . the little scumbag!'

William Templeton stared at the two policemen. Marsh snapped at him, 'Go into the other office, you. And keep your mouth shut!'

William walked through the connecting door and sat down. He was tired and hungry and scared. From what he could gather, they knew all about him and his royal connections were not going to help him at all. He sat in the uncomfortable chair and put his head in his hands.

Terry walked into Marsh's office with his head held high and a confident stride. Under his arm was a blue cardboard folder. He could feel Ackland measuring him up.

'Well, well, well . . . if it isn't the laughing policeman.' Marsh's voice dripped sarcasm.

Terry sat in the chair vacated by Templeton.

'It seems to me that I'm the only policeman in England who actually has something to laugh at. I know for a fact that you don't.'

Marsh screwed up his eyes. This was not the man he had seen previously. This was a man with a secret, an important secret, and one who knew how to use it.

'What happened to you? Where did you go?'

Terry looked at Ackland.

'I can't tell you that. What I can tell you is, Maura Ryan is willing to do a deal.'

'A what?' Marsh's voice bounced off the plasterboard walls.

'A deal.' Terry threw the folder on to the desk. 'In there is information. More than was in Geoffrey Ryan's file, I might add. There are copies of this information with numerous different people. I am here to talk business with you, gentlemen. And the Home Secretary, if he hasn't already been informed.'

Terry relaxed into his chair. He was enjoying this which was the last thing he'd expected. He watched Ackland pick up the file and flick through the papers.

'And what kind of a deal were you looking for?' Ackland's voice was resigned, as if he had expected something like this.

'Maura Ryan wants to be left alone. She and her brothers. She wants to keep her holdings in docklands, which are perfectly legal, and to run her clubs as before.'

'And what will she give us in return?'

Terry smiled at Ackland. 'In return she won't open her mouth about any of this.' He pointed to the file that Ackland was holding. 'And she will return the gold bullion that went missing in eighty-five. She also gives you her word that she will only deal with legitimate operations in all her future business investments.'

'And you honestly think she'll get away with this?' Marsh was practically foaming at the mouth.

Terry nodded. 'Yeah, I do.'

'Your career is finished, my boy!'

Terry laughed. 'Oh, shut up, Marsh, for God's sake. You sound like something from "Dixon of Dock Green". This whole place . . .' he waved his arm '. . . is rotten, mate. Rotten to the bloody core. Of course my career is over. It was over before it began. Because if you read those files carefully, Maura's and Geoffrey's, the only people to get any kind of real promotion were those on the bloody take!'

Ackland sighed.

'So you know where Maura Ryan is, I take it?'

'Yeah, I know. And I'll never tell you, so you'd better

think again if you're going to try and kick it out of me.'

Terry stood up. 'I'm warning you both now. Copies of those files have been faxed to two other countries. They were sent hours ago to reliable people. If so much as one hair of Maura Ryan's head is harmed they go straight to the tabloids. The Ryans own a bit more than you think. They own journalists and newspaper editors, with more than a few television newspeople thrown in. Not just in England but in the States and in Europe. Maura Ryan is willing to retire gracefully and just carry on with her legitimate holdings. Think about it carefully, gentlemen. She is not a woman to cross, believe me.'

Ackland raised his hand to silence Marsh who looked as if he was going to have a coronary at any moment.

'I'll have to speak to my superiors before anything can be decided.'

'Fair enough.' Terry glanced at his watch. 'I'll be in contact in four hours. At twelve-thirty.'

'You won't get away with this, Petherick. I'll get you personally.' Marsh's voice dripped with venom.

Terry leant on the desk, both palms flat, and looked into Marsh's sharp-featured face.

'You'll get me, will you? Funny how you don't want to get the others, the ones on the take. The big developers and the MPs and the Chief Super that you work for. Does he know that he's been tumbled yet? That his holidays in Kenya and the Maldives are over? That his little scams have all been found out? Does he know that the Ryans even have the name of the prostitute he visits every Wednesday night? The one who ties him up and spanks him?

'Don't say you're getting me, Marsh! Go and get some real villains for once in your life.'

Terry straightened his back and stared defiantly at the

silent and grim-faced man before him. 'One last thing. Would you tell the Chief Super that I have a bit of news that might interest him?'

'What's that?' Marsh spat the words out.

'Tell him that the girl he sees every Wednesday, Samantha Golding, was diagnosed as having Aids. Tell him the Ryans even knew that before him. Before any of you. And don't you dare act the outraged policeman with me! You were willing to take part in the murder of an entire family. If you had done you would have kidded yourself it was for your country. Well, you know and I know it would not have been. It would just have saved a load of fat bastards' arses. If you loved your country so much you should have pissed off to the Falklands, Marsh. And from what's in that file,' he pointed to the folder Ackland was holding, 'that was another complete cover up and shambles!

'Now, I'm leaving. I'll be back in touch at half-past twelve.'

He stormed out of the office, leaving a white-faced Marsh and a quiet and subdued Ackland.

'You asked for that, Marsh. I have to take my hat off to the man. What he said was true.'

Marsh was in such a monumental temper he forgot his fear of Ackland. He picked up his cigar and said, 'Oh, fuck off, you Scottish turd!'

In the office next door William Templeton began to laugh.

Terry did not go back to Michael's flat. It had been arranged that he would go back to his own place, in case he was followed.

He drove there on a high. At least he had told Marsh

exactly what he thought of him. Inside his flat he made himself some coffee and sat reading the paper. He had lost the urge to sleep, was in the state of overtiredness that seems to make a person more alert and mentally agile.

He sat at the table and thought about Maura. Nothing he did would get her out of his mind for even five minutes. Once again the words on the page in front of him were replaced by a vision of her face. She was flying to Marbella today. Although he had told Marsh that the file had been faxed through to two different countries, it was not true. Maura was going to take copies to the people concerned herself. She was flying to Marbella at five-thirty from Gatwick.

He sipped his coffee. He had lost everything now. His job, his way of life. And he had sacrificed it all for Maura Ryan. He looked around his kitchen, and then, as if he had been jolted from his chair, went to the phone. He knew what he had to do.

Sarah was enjoying having the three boys home. The feeling of foreboding that had plagued her the whole day before lifted off her as she cooked breakfast for them. She prepared what had long been known in the family as a 'Benny Special': two eggs, five slices of bacon, black pudding, tomatoes, beans, mushrooms, and even fried liver sausage, along with huge amounts of toast and a good strong pot of tea to wash it down with. She had felt sorry for Benjamin, eating his poached egg while they wolfed down his favourite meal, but consoled herself with the fact that he would thank her for it one day.

Just after breakfast the phone rang and Garry ran to answer it. Sarah was not sure what was said but the boys all looked a lot happier. She left them all in the kitchen while she gave Benjamin a blanket bath. He still couldn't get out of bed.

As she washed her husband's face, he grabbed her arm gently. 'All right, Sar?'

'Yeah, why?' She looked at him, puzzled.

'You're enjoying having the boys home again, ain't you?'

She smiled. 'Yeah. I miss them all.'

'I never gave you much, did I, girl? Except the back of my hand. It makes you think, you know, being stuck in bed.'

Sarah looked down at her husband's rapidly wasting body. Just for a split second she saw the eighteen-year-old boy who had whistled at her one bright summer evening in 1934. He had been tall, dark and handsome, wearing a bowler hat that night which had somehow set him apart from his contemporaries. Sarah felt an enormous lump in her throat for the man he had been.

'I know I never tell you very often, Sar, but you was always my girl. You know that, don't you? I always loved you.'

She nodded at him. It was one of those rare moments that occur in everyone's life. One of those times when there really isn't anything to say.

Ackland had spoken to the Home Secretary at length, and was now waiting for Terry Petherick to ring through to his office. Marsh had already left, as had William Templeton. Whereas Marsh had been disgusted by the turn of events, Templeton had been relieved – though Ackland was quick to guess that Templeton knew he had lost Maura Ryan's friendship.

He sighed heavily as he waited for Terry to call. The file

that Petherick had left was, even at this moment, winging its way across London to be studied and talked over with the Secretary of State for the Environment amongst others. Ackland, unlike Marsh, knew when he was beaten and deep in his heart was glad that Maura Ryan had eventually outwitted them. His own conscience said to him: Why should she be a scapegoat for the real criminals?

He was glad when the phone finally rang. Lack of sleep was catching up with him.

Maura picked up the phone at twelve-forty. It was Terry and she knew even before he spoke what had happened. She could feel his euphoria coming over the telephone line.

'They've agreed! Agreed to everything!'

'Oh, thank God!'

Maura took her first really deep breath for what seemed like days.

'They didn't argue about any of it?'

'No, Maws, not a thing. It's perfectly acceptable. Tell Richard he did a good job. We all did a good job.'

'What about my brothers?'

'Fine. Everything's hunky-dory.'

'Thanks for all your help, Terry. I promise you won't lose by it.'

Maura's voice was humble and sounded strange to Terry's ears.

'So you're off to warmer climes then?'

'Yeah. I suppose we won't see each other again.'

'Well . . . you never know what's going to happen, do you? I'd better let you go. You have a lot to do before you fly out.'

'Goodbye then, Terry. And thanks again.'

'You're welcome.' His voice was soft. 'Goodbye, Maura.'

He put down the phone and Maura stood in Michael's flat feeling more desolate and alone than she had ever done before. She had beaten the police and the establishment and yet she felt nothing. Nothing except an overwhelming loneliness.

Richard came into the room.

'We won then?' He sounded happy.

'Yeah. We won.'

He was sad to hear Maura's flat and broken voice. 'You'd better get a move on, you know. You have to be at Gatwick by three-thirty.'

'I know.'

Richard put his arm around her. She was much taller than him and he had to look up into her face.

'Michael used to say to me when I was down: "Ricky, remember that today is the first day of the rest of your life." I know it's an old cliché, but it's also a very true one.'

'Oh, Richard. What would I have done without you?'

She kissed him full on the mouth then said, 'I'd better phone Roy, tell him the good news.'

Maura sat on the Monarch Flight to Gibraltar. It was five-twenty-nine and the plane was due to take off at any time. She was sitting in a window seat. The seat next to her was unoccupied and she was glad – she was not up to making conversation with strangers. Plus she was shattered. She had been awake for nearly twenty-eight hours.

She closed her eyes, willing the plane to take off. Terry Petherick came straight to mind . . . She admitted to herself that she still had all the old feelings for him. The feelings that had assailed her on and off for over twenty years. When she had spoken to him on the telephone and he had said goodbye, she had felt as if her heart had been ripped from her chest. What was it about the man? Why did he make her feel like this? Even when she had learned that William, who was supposed to love her, had been willing to trade her to the police, she had not felt the intensity of feeling as when she had heard that single word from Terry: 'Goodbye'.

When she had told him the night before about the baby and what had happened, she had hoped, deep down, that it would bring them closer together. And it had, for a little while. But only for a little while. She supposed he thought that by doing the negotiating for her with the police he had repaid any debt that he owed her. She bit her lip.

In the seat in front of her were two little boys, both excited to be going on holiday. The bigger of the two, a boy of about ten with light brown hair and mischievous brown eyes, kept looking through the gap in the seats at her. As they jumped around in excitement Maura knew that she would not have a lot of peace on the flight.

She closed her eyes tighter, willing the plane to take off so she could at least have a cigarette. She felt someone sit down in the seat beside her and pretended she was asleep. She was too overwrought to start making small talk with anyone.

'Maura Ryan, I arrest you.'

Her eyes flew open and she looked at the man beside her, dumbstruck.

'But . . . but . . .' Her voice was locked inside her throat.

'I hope you're pleased to see me?' Terry's voice was

deep and husky. He was smiling that little lopsided grin that had captured her heart so many years before.

'But I don't understand. When I spoke to you . . .'

'I was still trying to get on this flight then. They held the place for me, you know. One of the last perks of being a policeman. My final abuse of my position.'

He smiled at her again. 'I don't know if you want me, Maura. But I want you more than ever. I think deep in my heart I've always known that one day I would come and claim you as my own.'

She was still staring at him in absolute amazement. Terry was frightened now. If she pushed him away this time it would be for good and he did not think he could live with that.

The plane began to taxi down the runway, building up speed. As its nose left the tarmac, Maura smiled at him.

'Oh, Terry. I'm so glad you came. So very, very glad.'

He kissed her then, a long lingering kiss that was witnessed by the two boys in the seat in front. It was their giggling that broke them apart.

'Do you mind?' Terry's voice was jocular and the two little faces disappeared from sight.

He looked at Maura's radiant face and thanked God she still wanted him.

'So you're arresting me, are you?' Her voice was full of love.

He nodded at her, drinking in every feature and contour of her face.

'Yes, I'm arresting you . . . and I'm afraid that you're going to get a life sentence. The whole of it to be spent with me.'

Maura looked at him seriously. 'I'll still be running the clubs and . . .'

Terry put his finger to her lips.

'I don't care, Maura. All I want from now on is you.'

They smiled at one another as the plane gradually flew higher into the sky.

Read on for a preview of
Martina Cole's compulsive and
thrilling new novel . . .

REVENGE

Available autumn 2013.

Prologue

The Lord shall smite thee with madness

Deuteronomy 28:28

2012

'Hello! Are you not listening to me? My little girl has been missing for three *fucking* days. I think that might be worth your attention, don't you?'

Michael Flynn was so angry he was almost spitting his words down the phone. Over six feet tall and with a heavy build he was a big man and, as everyone in the room knew, he was more than capable of great violence. He was paying them for their expertise, which they currently seemed to be lacking in. In fact, they were irritating the arse off him with their stupidity.

'Her mother is giving me serious grief, and that alone is a fucking bugbear. I need to know where she is, people! So I think you lot had better get me the information I need before I start to think you're all mugging me off. I know she isn't exactly what you might call a wilting fucking violet and, believe me, when I locate her I will personally launch her into outer space for this. But I want her found. You are the *Filth* – this is what you fucking do! You locate errant fuckers. So you had better start doing it quickly. I am not a man who is known for his patience, and I have a very low threshold for idiocy.' He slammed down the telephone.

Jamie Gore listened to his boss rant at the policemen in his employ. Everyone knew that Jessie Flynn, Michael Flynn's daughter, was about as dependable as a Nigerian marriage broker; therefore, she held no importance whatsoever to anyone, especially to the police. She could get away with anything – from possession of any substance, including a bomb, should she ever purchase one, and that was all thanks to her father's influence. He'd paid the Old Bill handsomely to *ignore* her over the years; now suddenly he wanted them to make her a priority? Bit of a turnaround there. He spoke up. 'Look, Michael, with all due respect, you know your daughter as well as we do, she could be fucking anywhere. She goes on the missing list regularly . . .'

Michael Flynn was dark-haired and dark-skinned, he had the Irish gypsy in him there was no doubt about that. He was a handsome fuck, and his good looks were part and parcel of his persona. Both men and women were attracted to him, and he had always used that to his advantage. His startling blue eyes were now trained on Jamie Gore, and the man felt the first prickle of uneasiness at the intensity of his gaze.

'You having a fucking laugh, Jamie? You think I brought you lot here for nothing? My old woman is like a fucking lunatic! My little Jessie is on the missing list! No one, and I mean *no one*, has seen her for *three fucking days*! I know she is a lazy mare, I know she lives on her own fucking time-zone, and I know she is the biggest pain in the rectum since records began. But she is still my baby girl. So my advice would be to fucking well find her! Track her down, let me know where she is so I can deliver her back to her mother and then we can go home.'

Michael looked around the room, and he knew that every bloke in there was thinking the same thing: Jessie Flynn was probably tucked up in bed with another lowlife, another fucking no-mark she had picked up on her travels. She was a trollop of the first water, having been sleeping with the enemy since she was fourteen years old. He wondered how many of his workforce had serviced her at one time or another. She was a beautiful-looking girl, with the morals of a fucking alley cat. It didn't matter – he still wanted to know where she was. More to the point, her mother *needed* to know. Josephine was deeply concerned for her daughter's whereabouts.

Jessie was not a girl you could lose sleep worrying about all the time – she stumbled from one disaster to the next (usually the disaster was a man), but she always seemed to come out on top. He made sure of that. She came home at some point and then her mum would be so pleased to see her there would be no retribution of any kind. That was the trouble. Michael personally believed that his daughter needed a fucking good slap, but his wife would never agree. If Jessie murdered the neighbours with an axe and it was caught on CCTV, his wife would say, 'Well, they must have upset her.' Jessie could do no wrong in her eyes.

He too had indulged her once, when she had been small and still lovable, but that had changed the moment she discovered the power of her sexuality and the harm it could bring to her father who she had once adored. He had given up trying to force any kind of fatherly rules or regulations on her. Jessie wouldn't listen to him anyway – she was a girl after his own heart in many respects. She did exactly what she wanted, and she did that with the maximum amount of energy she could muster. But she was a whore, and that fact broke his heart. Not that he could ever let that be known – in his game that would be seen as a weakness.

He sighed heavily. The men in this room were some of the hardest men in the south east; they *all* worked for him and were pleased to do so. He was a hard man, everyone knew that, but he prided himself on being a fair man, a decent man in some respects. These were men who were at the top of their particular games, and he used their nous and their instincts for his own ends – and made sure that they earned a good fucking wedge at the end of the day. Michael Flynn was a one-off; in his world he was a man who was not only feared, but who had also earned the respect of his peers, and who had managed to rise to the top without treading on too many people's toes. He had embraced his partners in crime, and made sure that they earned enough to prevent them coveting what he had. Now he had the partnership and the major earn from every Face in the country – well, in Europe, if truth be told. And the men he dealt with owed him, respected him for his achievements, and did not begrudge him his percentage because, without him, most of them would never have got as far as they had. He had worked his way up the ladder, realising early on that to keep on top you had to have a loyal and willing workforce, and that if you wanted to earn a place of importance in the criminal world, you also needed a very lucrative and honestly run legitimate business, as well as the wherewithal to not only invest heavily in other people's businesses, but to also be able to offer them a modicum of protection should Lily Law decide to investigate them at any time.

Well, Michael basically owned Lily Law, and it was not fucking cheap. He paid out a serious fucking wedge to the Old Bill, and they, for their part, did fuck-all the majority of the time to earn their crusts. It was one of the things that really irritated him, but they were what his old partner Patrick Costello used to call a 'necessary evil'. He had worked hard to get them in his pocket, and many of them had *him* to thank for their additional wages, nice cars, and kids' educations. Because of that, he held all the major cards: he could negotiate a prison sentence, he could make certain charges disappear, he could fit up anyone who he felt was getting a bit too big for their boots. It was a win-win situation. No one had ever had that much power over the law before. He had orchestrated that by himself, and now he was a man who was settled at the top. No one in his game would ever feel the urge, or indeed the need, to try and take his place and run his businesses. He was too shrewd for all that old fanny. His legit businesses were huge earners as well – he could explain away everything he owned. In short, Michael Flynn was virtually untouchable.

But now he was looking out at the men he knew as friends, not just as business associates, and he felt the prickle of shame wash over him. His daughter going AWOL was not something they saw as in their remit to sort but, as they were on his payroll, they had no option but to listen to him and offer their help in any way they could.

His Jessie's reputation had preceded her as always. They all assumed she was drugged and/or drunk out of her head some-where, because that was what she was famous for. Twenty-two years old, and she was already a legend in her own lunchtime. She had been excluded from every school he sent her to, and instead she had embraced the underworld from an early age – from the drug dealers, to the scumbags who hung around the council estates, the burglars, gas-meter bandits with homemade tattoos – she spent her time in filthy squats until he brought her back home to her mother time and again. After cracking open a few heads, of course.

Michael had given up on her completely by the time she was sixteen. Once he had found her naked on a filthy mattress in a condemned house in Hackney with a junkie three times her age, who had given her not only a black eye but a dose of gonorrhoea as well. He had known then that he had no choice but to step away from her emotionally. He loved her, but he could not get through to her. Nevertheless, he had gone back and almost kicked the man to death for doing that to his baby. He had vented his anger, looking around at how she had been living. She was available to any man who tipped her the wink and who she thought would anger her father, and bring him shame.

He didn't understand it. She had had a home that was not only full of love for her, but was beautiful. She had everything she could have desired: the chance to go to a good school, and a good life ahead of her. But, from fourteen years of age, she had made it her business to find the lowest of the low, and make a home there for herself with them, and she had broken her mother's heart in the process. Unlike her father, her mother still felt her daughter could turn her life around, redeem herself. But Michael refused to get involved any more; she was his Achilles heel, his only real weakness. Her antics were common knowledge in his world, and it was only his status that stopped people from gossiping openly about her.

He had tried everything, and she had fought him every

step of the way. She was his daughter, and he would protect her as much as he could but, in his darkest moments, when he heard about her latest escapades, or the police informed him she had been arrested once more, he had wished her dead, and he hated himself for that.

Seeing the suffering she caused his wife made him resent Jessie. Jessie had broken her mother early on. She still cared what happened to her daughter; she hoped that she would come home one day, and it would be forgotten, and they would live a normal life together, like everyone else. Michael knew better. He just provided Jessie with the means to live her life, but at least her need of money allowed him to police her in some ways.

Jessie had given birth to a child at sixteen, but the child was no more to her than a doll she dressed up on special occasions. She left him to be brought up by her own mother. Michael loved the bones of his handsome little grandson, who had more of the Flynn family in him than whoever had been the fucking piece-of-dirt culprit. Not that Jessie had any fucking idea of her son's parentage of course; the poor child had been no more than a who-dunnit and, with Jessie, that meant it could have been literally *anyone*. Oh, he'd accepted the reality of his Jessie a long time ago. He loved her, but he didn't *like* her one bit.

Now her mother was worried about her and, if he was really honest with himself, so was he. He understood her much more than she had ever realised; she was a ponce of Olympian standards, but she had never missed an opportunity to pick up her allowance. She should have been at his offices the night before to pick up the money, but she had been a no-show. That was not like his daughter at all – she craved money like a junkie craved a fix. She spent like a woman with no fucking arms – on clothes, shoes and, unfortunately, men. His Jessie never missed her cash payment; she had her credit cards as well, but he could monitor them, so she knew the value of a pound. Jessie was a druggie, a drunk and a waste of space, but she was never late for her allowance. He made sure that it was far too lucrative for her to turn down.

So where the fuck was she?

Jessie Flynn opened her eyes, and fear enveloped her.

It was pitch dark, and she was aware that she was bound, both her hands and her feet tied. For all her exploits, she had never found herself in a predicament like this. She was racking her brains to work out not only who the fuck she had upset recently, but who would have the guts to do this to her knowing who her father was. She knew, on one level, she was in serious trouble, but she was still having a problem accepting that.

She was Jessie *Flynn*, for fuck's sake! Her dad was the biggest Face in town. That had always meant she was immune to aggravation of any kind – even when she caused outrageous problems for herself, those problems were automatically negated by her father's timely intervention.

She strained her eyes to see where she was being held captive, but the darkness was total. There was nothing to see at all – just a pure blackness. She was actually truly frightened, and that shocked her. She had never felt real fear before – it was an alien concept – and she swallowed down the scream that she could feel building inside her throat. She would never let anyone know that she was scared or worried about anything. All her life she had lived behind a mask of defiance, and she was not going to let this situation freak her out.

She took a few deep breaths to calm herself; her heart was hammering in her ears, and she could hear it so loudly it was like a drum beating in the room. It bothered her more than she liked to admit. It was too quiet, that was the problem; there was no sound other than her own breathing, her own heartbeat.

Instinctively, she knew that was not a good sign. This was not a situation that she could interpret or make any sense of. She was not unused to waking up somewhere strange, without any memory whatsoever of how she had arrived there. She would often see a man asleep beside her and have no idea who he was or where she had come across him. But she would find out eventually; she would talk to them and gradually she would get the gist of how she had arrived in their bed and, somewhere in the back of her mind, she would dredge up something to explain the events of the night in question.

This was different. She was tied up and she was in pain. Her arms felt like they were being wrenched from their sockets, and her ankles were tied so tightly she couldn't feel her feet.

She felt the fear rising inside her once again, and she fought it down; whoever had done this to her would never get the satisfaction of hearing her cry out into the darkness, or calling for help. She was shrewd enough to know that, wherever she was, crying out for help would be futile. If there was any chance of being heard her mouth would have been taped shut. The silence around her was complete, like the darkness; she was not somewhere random passers-by would stumble across, let alone somewhere that noise would cause people to panic or phone the Filth. She was being held captive for some reason – she just hoped that the reason would be explained to her sooner rather than later.

She was cold, and she could smell the mustiness of the mattress she was lying on – the place was damp, so she could even be underground. The silence and the stench made her think that might be the case. She knew, deep in her guts, that she was not here for any reason that might benefit her.

She closed her eyes tightly because, once more, she was feeling the urge to shout her lungs out, however futile. She needed to use the toilet, she felt a sudden urge to open her bowels; she was coming down fast, and she could feel it. She had not eaten properly for a few days and, now that she was sobering up, she was becoming even more afraid of the dangerous predicament she found herself in. She tried to bring her hands out from behind her back, but she couldn't. They were tied together so tightly, every movement caused a burning pain. It occurred to her suddenly that she was still fully clothed, so whoever had done this to her did not seem to have touched her in a sexual way. She was not sure that was a good thing either – that would have been something she could understand, could even control. Everything in her life until now had been about using her feminine wiles to get what she wanted.

She took a few more deep breaths, but the panic lingered close to the surface. She closed her eyes tightly and tried to relax her body, but it was hard. Her arms were screaming now; she had probably been tied up for a good few hours, and her trying to move around was causing the pain. She tried to wiggle her fingers – a voice in her head was telling her to keep the circulation going. Tears formed in her eyes, and she blinked them away furiously. She was not going to show her fear to anyone, that was simply not in her make up.

This had to be a kidnapping. The thought gave her a

thrill of anticipation – if that was the case then her dad would pay them and that would be it. Though she also knew her dad would never rest till he had tracked them down – not for taking her hostage, of course, but for trying to have him over. She suspected he wouldn't actually bother to pay them if it was left up to him – it was her mum who would insist. Her mum was all he cared about really, and his grandson, of course. Her son was the only saving grace Jessie had; her dad couldn't control her life, so he was determined to control his grandson's. He loved him though. She saw that, and it hurt her.

She managed to turn over on to her belly, and that eased the pain in her shoulders. She had never in her life felt so vulnerable or so alone, and she was craving a drink. Not water – though even that would be welcome. No, she was craving a real drink. She needed a large vodka or a Scotch, just something to take the edge off. Valium at least would help her relax and work out what she was going to do. It occurred to her that for the first time in years she was stone-cold sober, without the crutch of either chemicals or alcohol.

She heard the scraping sound of a heavy door opening somewhere in the distance outside the room where she was tied up like a kipper, and she felt the unmistakable prickle of genuine terror.

Detective Inspector Timothy Branch of the serious crime squad was annoyed even though he had always known that this day would come. He was not a fool – no matter what Michael Flynn might think. He had been aware from the first moment he had taken the man's money that he was, to all intents and purposes, now owned by him. He would be called on at some point to repay the favour; he had just not expected it to come so fucking soon. In fairness, this actually was a police matter – a missing daughter was not something to take lightly. He shouldn't feel so angry about being summoned into his offices by Flynn, or about the man demanding, in a loud and threatening manner, that he wanted results.

'Take the opportunity to earn your fucking keep, you useless fucking ponce!'

That hurt. Timothy knew when he was being taken for a cunt, and the man he was dealing with was not someone who could be palmed off with legal jargon, more's the pity. He knew he had to deliver, and deliver sooner rather than later.

Michael Flynn was like a man demented. 'She disappeared three days ago, Branch, and I have it on good authority that she was last seen in a pub in Upney. She scored some coke and grass, and she left around midnight, and no one has seen her since.'

Timothy Branch nodded, as if he was in full accord with everything he was hearing. His carefully modulated pseudo-posh voice was like a red rag to a bull, though he wasn't aware of that just yet. He was a snob, and a social-climbing arsewipe who had no qualms about taking money on the side to bankroll his wife's pretentious upper-middle-class lifestyle, and who had believed that his expertise would never be compromised by his association with a known villain. His stupidity and his arrogance were exactly the reasons why he was on Michael's payroll in the first place; without someone like Flynn on his side, he had no chance of hitting the big time.

'I will put out a missing persons report, Michael, but, in all honesty, she will probably turn up as per usual, we both know that.'

Michael looked at the man he had been paying handsomely for so long, and it occurred to him that he had been paying out a decent wedge to a complete fucking moron. Timothy to have known that at some point he would be called on to deliver, that the day would come when he would be asked to do a favour of some description. Now he was being asked to do something that he should be doing *anyway* – look for a missing girl – but he was not really demonstrating the level of motivation that Michael's regular payments should have guaranteed. In fact, he was not showing the least bit of willing, and that alone was irritating. He was showing no consideration of how much he had pocketed over the last few years, or how his rise through the ranks of the police force had been orchestrated by the same man he was now attempting to mug off.

Michael Flynn was not in the mood for this kind of aggravation; the last few hours had been a revelation to him as to how deeply his daughter and her fucking lifestyle had impacted on him personally. He was now being treated like a fucking tourist by a no-mark who relied on him for a second wage, and that was not something he could allow. 'You useless fucking cunt! All the money I have slipped your way, and you treat me like a fucking greebo! Like a fucking no one!' He dragged the terrified man from his chair, savouring his fear, and his dawning comprehension of exactly who he was dealing with. 'I expect the best, because that is what I have paid for over the years, and you are two seconds away from making me regret my decision to put you on my payroll. A decision that I can easily rectify – and that, my friend, would of course mean that you would have to return every penny I fucking shoved your way over the years. You avaricious useless fucking ponce! I hate dishonest Old Bill more than anything. If I ever get a capture it had better be from one I couldn't buy off. That's an honest nicking, you see, and I could swallow that. But Filth like you are only there to do what I fucking request of them.'

Timothy Branch lay on the floor of his own office, with his arms over his head to protect himself from another onslaught from Michael Flynn. He was well aware that everyone in the station could hear the conversation and would know exactly what was going on. He was waiting for the beating that he was convinced was going to come. He had made a mistake of Olympian standards, and he could not rectify the situation because he had brought it on himself. He had honestly believed that being a policeman, a *senior* policeman, would have guaranteed him immunity from this sort of behaviour. He had assumed that Flynn, for all his money and reputation, would have thought long and hard before he raised his hand to a member of the police force. But he had been very wrong. Flynn's power went far deeper than he had ever anticipated. The fact that no one had come to his aid was a real lesson for Timothy Branch. The outer offices were now deathly quiet; everyone out there was listening to this exchange and he knew his humiliation was now complete.

Then the office door opened with a bang, and Chief Superintendent Dennis Farthing came into the room like an avenging angel, all cigarette smoke and false teeth. Timothy Branch felt relief washing over him, until he heard the man say with mock sincerity, 'A sorry business this, Michael, but don't you worry, my friend – I will have my best men on it, of that you can be assured. Jessie is a priority, I guarantee.'

Michael Flynn felt the anger seeping out of him. This

was what he wanted – a promise that everything that could be done to find his daughter was being done. His wife needed that, she needed to know that Jessie was being treated as a priority, that he was using his considerable power to locate her child. But, deep down in his gut, he knew that something was not right, that this was far more serious than anyone really thought. Jessie never missed a pay day, and she never went twenty-four hours without ringing her mother. Even drugged out of her brains, she still rang her mum for a chat, because she knew that if she didn't get in touch Josephine would worry herself sick. Jessie knew that her mum needed to hear from her, that she wasn't a well woman in her own way. It was Jessie's only real saving grace that she rarely let a day go by without a call to her mum.

Now it was almost four days since anyone had seen or heard from her. If Michael was honest, he was feeling more uneasy by the hour.

Josephine Flynn was having trouble breathing. It was a warning before she got one of her panic attacks, so she sat down in her chair and tried to regulate her breaths. She hated herself for her weakness, but she had always suffered with her nerves. She could feel her heartbeat slowing down, and she closed her eyes in relief.

She savoured the calmness that washed over her, the feeling of normality and the knowledge that she had conquered her demons, if only for a little while. She opened her eyes slowly, and looked around sadly; she knew she should motivate herself, tidy up, *do* something constructive. But she wouldn't because she never did. No matter how many times she convinced herself that she was ready to finally do it, to finally take control of her life and her surroundings, when it came to the crunch, she *never* did anything that made a real difference.

She noticed that the curtains were open; Michael must have snuck in and opened them while she was sleeping. She knew that if he had not opened them she wouldn't have bothered. She liked them closed, she liked to shut out the world, the *real* world. Michael always argued that they had such wonderful views – all farmland and no other houses in sight. He thought that would make her feel better, make her feel easier in herself. But he didn't understand that the view outside the windows was irrelevant, she had no interest in it whatsoever. She had no real interest in anything other than her immediate surroundings.

She got up slowly, and went to her dressing table. Michael had left her a pitcher of fresh water, and she smiled at his kindness. She poured a glass out for herself, and then she meticulously counted out her medication. She swallowed the pills quickly, comforted by the feel of them in her mouth as she forced them inside her with huge gulps of the fresh water her husband knew she needed. She felt better immediately; she had taken her first step into the day, a day that was as fraught for her as every other day in her life.

She went back to her chair, and settled herself down again. Everywhere she looked was cluttered – piles of photographs, newspapers, or used jars. Shoes were piled in the corners, and her clothes were strewn all over the floor. Rubbish was kept in bin bags, and she had placed them lovingly against the walls. The clutter was her armour against the world – it made her feel safe. She could look at something that she had kept for reasons known only to herself, and she could smile in remembrance of a memory long gone – a memory no one cared about but her.

Now her Jessie was gone. No word at all, and Josephine knew in her gut that something bad had happened to her daughter.

She opened up her make-up bags which were never far from her side and, pulling a large mirror towards her, she began the long and painstaking artistry she used to create the image that allowed her to face the world as best she could.

Michael Flynn was tired. He had not slept properly for two days and, even though he had not believed it possible, he was deeply concerned for his daughter's safety. She was selfish, greedy, manipulative and devoid of any real morals, and that was exactly why she never failed to turn up for her allowance. She had very expensive tastes, and she liked to be able to indulge herself; she wasn't as low rent as she made out.

She was never off his radar no matter what anyone else might think or what he might let them think. She was always going to be his baby. She was a girl who made it very difficult to love her, who knew exactly how to rattle his cage. It was something she had made her mission in life; hurting him was something she enjoyed so much she had even left her own son behind in her pursuit of his unhappiness. He had taken on responsibility for the child along with his wife though, to his daughter's chagrin, it had not been a chore for them. In fact, it had been almost like a rebirth for them both, inasmuch as they had adored their grandson from the moment he had entered the world. Jessie, on the other hand, had not been miraculously changed by giving birth to her own flesh and blood, as her mother had been convinced would be the case. Instead she had abandoned her little son at the first available opportunity, and she had drifted in and out of his life ever since. Michael hated her for that, even more than he hated her for how much she had hurt her poor mother.

Jessie thought she herself was the only person worth a day's interest. But that was his daughter – an arrogant fucker, who had no moral compass whatsoever. She saw everyone around her as someone to be used for her own ends, and that included her own child, her own flesh and blood. Michael had been forced to accept that about her over the last few years and it had not been as easy as everyone had believed. It had been very hard for him. Because he had loved her with a vengeance. She was his baby girl, his only child. She was also a selfish, vicious, bitter, manipulative, avaricious, devious, two-faced ponce, whose only interest in life seemed to be getting drunk, drugged, laid, or a combination of all three. She had been the apple of his eye once, and now she was someone he had to live down on a daily basis. It was only his standing that stopped him from hearing the real gossip concerning her, and he knew that was a good thing because if she pushed him too far, he knew he might finally do something to get himself nicked.

He was staring at the phones in his office, hoping that whoever had her would just ring him up and let him know she was OK. Then, once he had paid them off, and his Jessie was accounted for, he would hunt the bastards down like the fucking rabid dogs they were, and personally make sure that they never again put any other parents through such agony. He would take great pleasure in ensuring they disappeared from the world around them in as much pain and terror as physically possible.

He was taking his daughter's disappearance personally; whoever was behind it was trying to prove a point. This was about him. It had to be. Inside his head, he could not help wondering if his daughter was a part of it all. She was capable of anything, as he knew better than anyone. But he hoped that he was wrong. For all that had happened, he hated to think she was capable of trying to rip him off and, if she *was* trying to do that, he would personally make sure that everyone involved would be made aware of how irritated their actions had made him, his Jessie especially. If she was involved, that would be the last straw, and he would have to take drastic action against her.

There were some things that could never be forgiven. Some things that could finally cause a body to turn on their own.

Jessie woke up once more, and she was immediately aware that there was somebody else in the room with her.

It was still pitch dark. Still cold and damp. She knew that she couldn't be the first to speak – her dad had always told her: when in doubt, shut your trap. If you kept your own counsel, eventually the others would feel the need to explain themselves, and he had been right. She had learnt that the hard way. So she didn't say a word.

She could hear the shallow breathing of whoever was now in the room with her and, more to the point, she knew that they could also hear her breathing. They would know that she wasn't asleep any more. She was very much awake. It was a terrifying experience. She had never once, in her whole life, needed to worry about someone else's reactions to her or her antics. No matter what had happened to her, no matter what she had said or done, she had always known that her father would be in the background, and the reason why she would ultimately be safe no matter what she did. No one was willing to confront her because that would mean they would have to deal with *him*. That was something no one in their right mind would even consider. It was her get-out-of-jail-free card, the reason she pushed everything as far as she could. It was why she had been able to fuck her father over again and again. He had always made sure that she was untouchable. She had thought she was invincible because of her father – it was something she relied on. No matter what she did, no matter how much trouble she had landed herself in, her father had always made sure that it had all gone away. It was something she had seen as another of his weaknesses, as another reason to do whatever she wanted. After all, no matter what she did, he bailed her out. He made sure that her actions did not infringe on his lifestyle in any way and that was what it was all about. She knew his reputation was everything to him. Well, she was his daughter, his only child, and she had made damn sure that his reputation as a parent was worth nothing. She had enjoyed that, enjoyed the knowledge that her actions had undermined him, and made him see that he was not worth anything really.

But now she didn't know what to think. She would have to play this one by ear. She was in serious trouble. Whoever was behind this was not someone who cared about her or her family name.

She was so scared. She wasn't alone in this darkness, and she knew that she wasn't going anywhere anytime soon.

Josephine Flynn looked at her little grandson and smiled. He was beautiful – dark-haired and blue-eyed – his grandfather's double. He even had Michael's mannerisms. It was uncanny considering Jessie had no idea who had fathered him. Josephine believed that Michael's genes were so strong they had cancelled out any that the culprit contributed. She hoped so, for the child's sake; his father could be anybody – that was the honest truth. Jessie had only had the child because an abortion was out of the question as far as her father was concerned. It was also the only thing that would make her mother turn against her daughter. Still, Josephine liked to think, in her lighter moments, that her daughter wouldn't have been capable of doing something so heinous.

Jessie knew how she had struggled to have *her*. She had lost all her other children – some even after Jessie's birth. A child, Josephine believed, was God's gift, and to refuse such a wonderful offering was beyond forgiveness. So Jessie had calmed down, stopped her drinking and drug-taking for a while, and she had brought this handsome gorgeous boy into the world. Jessie had then walked out of her own child's world when he was two days old; she had given him over to her parents without a backward glance. That had hurt Josephine more than anything else her daughter had done, even if she was happy to take him on. Jessie had only been sixteen, and Josephine had hoped that giving birth might have made her daughter grow up, start to understand that all actions had their own set of consequences. But she had been wrong, very wrong – if anything, it had just made her daughter worse.

Jessie had not even bothered to name her own child, and that, for Josephine, summed up the whole situation. So she had named him herself – Jake – and Jessie had not voiced an opinion either way.

Jake was six years old now, but he wore clothes for an eight year old. He was bright as a button, already reading and writing well beyond his years, and showing every sign of being academic. Well, he had not inherited that from his mother! Jessie had always been a poor student – not because she wasn't clever, but because she was lazy. Jessie had always taken the path of least resistance. Josephine blamed herself; they had waited so long for Jessie to come along, and she had ruined her from day one. She regretted that now. Her mother had been right all those years ago. She had warned her that Jessie was a girl who needed to be chastised, who had a strong will that needed to be curbed.

Michael, in fairness, had allowed her free rein with Jessie's upbringing. He had never forced his own opinions on her where the child was concerned, even when she had known he had every right to call the shots. Michael loved her too much – he always conceded to her and her wants. He adored her, and she loved him all the more for that, because she knew that her problems would have made a lesser man run away as fast as his legs would carry him. But her Michael had never once made her feel anything other than cared for and cherished.

She watched as her grandson looked around her cluttered bedroom, and she waited for what she knew was coming.

'It's very dark in here, Nana. Why don't you come into the garden with me? You could push me on my swing if you liked.' The hope was in his voice, as always.

Josephine smiled sadly. 'That's what we have Dana for, Jake. She's much younger than Nana and she can run after you. How about after your swing, we have dinner with Granddad, and then we can all play a game together?'

Jake Flynn shrugged; it was no more than he had expected. 'OK. Will my mummy be coming to see me soon?'

It was a loaded question, and one he asked occasionally

when he remembered he had a mummy. Josephine swallowed down the sadness inside her as she answered him brightly, 'You'll see her soon. You know that she is *very* busy. But as soon as she gets some time off from work, she will come straight here to see you.'

Dana O'Carroll was a good nanny – she knew when to intervene and, grabbing the child's hand, she said loudly in her thick Irish brogue, 'Come on now, Jake, let's go and play, shall we? Your nana needs to sort out a few things.'

Josephine watched them as they left the room, and she closed her eyes in distress. Pulling herself from her chair, she looked at herself in the full-length mirror that Michael had bought for her all the way from France. It was very old, and had cost a small fortune. She loved it. She saw a very beautiful woman, well dressed with perfect make-up, and sad green eyes. She didn't look her age, and her figure was still to be envied. Her thick blond hair had to be coloured now; a girl came every month and saw to that, her nails, and her waxing. She had always been a woman who had looked after herself in that respect. She suspected she could still turn a few heads – that's if she ever left the house, of course – and she knew that Michael was proud of her. He had always made her feel like the only woman in the world, and he still treated her like a queen.

If only Jessie had tried to understand him, meet him halfway even, she knew they would not be in this situation. But Jessie always had to have the last word, and had understood that, because of her mother's problems, she had the upper hand. Jessie hated that her mother's world was so small, and she blamed her father for everything that had happened. No matter how hard Josephine had tried to explain the truth, Jessie had not believed her. Now she was terrified that her daughter had taken up with someone who had harmed her, hurt her little girl in some way.

Jessie had a knack for finding that type of person – men who used her, who treated her like she was nothing and discarded her without a backward glance. Men who she sought out, and who she paid for, bankrolled with her father's money, and who she knew would make him angry because she was throwing her life away just to hurt him. Now, it seemed she had finally picked the wrong one – a man who she couldn't control.

It had been too long. Her Jessie never went a day without talking to her – whatever she thought about her father, she loved her mother. They were very close, and it was only the knowledge that she would find it hard if she didn't see or hear from her little girl, that had stopped Michael from sidelining his Jessie for good. He felt it would do her good to have to earn her own keep, and see what the world was like without his name to protect her; Josephine had argued that if he did that she would be in danger of losing her altogether. Her real fear was that Jessie would end up on the streets, selling herself to whoever for enough money to get stoned. Now she wondered if he had been right all along, and a short, sharp shock, as he put it, might have done Jessie some good.

She picked up her favourite rosary. It had been a present from Michael on their wedding day – it was not expensive, it was very plain, made from olive wood, but it meant the world to her.

She kissed the Cross of Christ, and blessed herself quickly. Then she walked from her bedroom into her large sitting room. There she knelt down before the crucifix that dominated the room, and she began the first decade of the rosary. She normally enjoyed the Joyful Mysteries but, since Jessie's disappearance, she was now concentrating on the Sorrowful Mysteries. She could feel the despair that Mary, the Mother of Jesus, must have felt when her son had been taken from her. All she wanted, all she was praying for, was a phone call. Just something to let her know her daughter was safe.

'Is he fucking sure? How are we supposed to plot his daughter's last movements? I mean, in all honesty, where would we start? She could have been literally anywhere.' Marcus Dewer was genuinely perplexed. He was also feeling worried – like many of Michael's workforce, he was guilty of having known Jessie Flynn in a biblical sense. If he was honest, on more than one occasion. Now she was on the missing list, and he was terrified that Michael would find that out. Like most people, he believed she was on the nest somewhere, drugged out of her brains and oblivious to all the aggro she was causing.

Jamie Gore shrugged. 'It is what it is, Marcus. She likes this part of Brixton because she can score here. So let's get parked, and start asking round.'

Marcus sighed, and parked the BMW neatly. He looked at the photo of Jessie; she was a pretty girl, there was no doubt about that.

'This is fucking stupid! Everyone knows there's a price for information on her. The whole of the Metropolitan Police are scouring the Smoke. So what we are supposed to find out I don't know.'

Jamie Gore secretly agreed with his friend, but he was too shrewd to say that. 'Marcus, do me a favour, will you? Shut the fuck up, and do what the man is paying us for. Who knows – we might stumble on to something accidentally. In fact, I think we should poke our heads into a few skag houses. You know what junkies are like – the fucking Third World War could erupt and they wouldn't even notice until they ran out of heroin. So there's a chance, albeit a very slim one, that they might not know about her being missing. And don't forget, Marcus, if we find out something important, we will be greatly rewarded.'

Marcus nodded, but he wasn't convinced. He was more worried that they would be the ones to find her, overdosed and dead as a doornail. *That* wasn't the kind of news he would relish giving Michael. It was what the majority of people believed had happened to Jessie Flynn – they were waiting for her body to turn up, and no one wanted to be the one who found it.

Jessie was weak. The man who was holding her only gave her the minimum of water; she was always thirsty, although the hunger wasn't so acute any more. She couldn't work out how long she had been down here in the darkness. She seemed to sleep a lot, so she guessed that he was putting something in the water to keep her sedated. At least he had untied her hands although she was still manacled around her ankles, and the chain was attached to an iron hoop on the wall behind the mattress. She was still in darkness – the only time there was any light was when he brought her water. He had a torch, but it blinded her, so she covered her eyes. She had a feeling he wasn't interested in her seeing him anyway. She played the game – that was all she could do.

He had still not spoken to her, and that frightened her more than anything else. She had threatened him, abused him, told him that her father would be searching for her, and he had not reacted in any way. He had shone the torch and shown her an old chamber pot where he expected her to do her business. She had railed at him, cursed him, but there had been no reaction.

She had woken up earlier because she could hear him moving around outside the door. She swallowed down the rising panic that was getting harder and harder to control. She didn't know what she was supposed to do, what he wanted from her. She could smell her own faeces, could feel the dirtiness of her body and clothes. She had waited for him to rape her, or assault her, but he had done nothing. He brought her some water at regular intervals, and he emptied the chamber pot at some point, and he had also left her a blanket. She could only assume he had kidnapped her, and he was waiting for her father to pay the money. He would pay it – her mother would make sure of that. But why was it taking so long?

She kept thinking of every serial-killer film she had ever watched, every book she had ever read about men who abducted young women, and tortured and raped them. Only in the books and the films, there was always a detective on their trail who you knew would eventually save the girl and kill the maniac; you knew that because the detective *always* solved his case no matter how obscure the clues. The maniac would also often be in direct contact with the police, would be taunting them and, as the reader or viewer, you would be cheering on the detective, knowing all along that he or she would eventually work it out. But that was not real life. She worried that he was going to come in at some point and really hurt her, and she was so terrified about that.

Her initial arrogance was gone; she was not only stone cold sober for the first time in years, she was also acutely aware that she wasn't ready to die. She loved her son in her own way, and she wanted to see him again, see her mum, be hugged by her once more. She had to wonder if this was something to do with her dad – he had stepped on a lot of people's toes. Surely she should have been out by now if it was about money? What if this man was holding her as a grudge against her father? Or what if he was a serial killer and her father's name and reputation meant nothing to him?

She pushed her fist into her mouth to stop herself from screaming; she still had enough strength left to make sure she didn't show him her fear. She wouldn't show him how scared she was until she absolutely had to. She would beg him on her knees if that was what he wanted, she would do whatever she needed to try and get herself out of this situation.

She pulled the blanket around her, and she forced herself to try and think rationally. But it was hard to concentrate – the darkness was so intimidating, so final. And the man who held her was still an enigma. Until he spoke to her or acknowledged her presence in some way, she knew she couldn't even begin to understand exactly what she was dealing with. She felt the tears running down her face, and she didn't even try to stop them.

'Come on, Jake, eat your dinner up.'

Michael winked at his grandson, as always amazed at the love the child could engender in him. Considering the circumstances of his birth, Michael had always been in awe of the feelings he had for this child.

'I'm eating my dinner, Granddad, so I can grow up big and strong like you.'

Michael sighed. He remembered when his Jessie had been like this little lad, innocent, trusting and eager for her parents' company. All that had changed when she was thirteen. Overnight she had become a different person – difficult, awkward, full of hate. Everyone said it was teenage angst, that she would grow out of it. But she hadn't, she had gradually got worse, and she had become out of control. Now she was missing, and he didn't know what more he could do.

Have you read all of Martina Cole's phenomenal bestsellers? Available now in paperback and ebook

DANGEROUS LADY

No one thinks a seventeen-year-old girl can take on the hard men of London's gangland, but it's a mistake to underestimate Maura Ryan: she's one very dangerous lady . . .

THE LADYKILLER

George Markham has a nasty little hobby, which erupts into an orgy of vicious sexual depravity. In charge of the case, DI Kate Burrows fears losing everything she cares about to . . . the ladykiller.

GOODNIGHT LADY

In the sixties Briony Cavanagh ran a string of notorious brothels in the East End. But her business brought her into contact with the violent heart of London's gangland . . .

THE JUMP

Donna Brunos is devastated when her husband is jailed for armed robbery. Implementing his escape plan takes her into a brutal and violent world which threatens everything she believes in.

THE RUNAWAY

Cathy Connor's life as a prostitute's child changes for ever when she is forced into care. When she crosses paths with ruthless Eamonn Docherty nothing's going to make her run away . . .

TWO WOMEN

Brutalised throughout her marriage, Sue Dalston smashes her husband's skull with a claw hammer in a final act of desperation. Celled up with murderess Matilda Enderby, their fates become inextricably linked . . .

BROKEN

One by one, children are being abandoned. Thankfully, they're rescued from harm. Then one victim is not so lucky, and DI Kate Burrows knows she's in a race against time to save lives . . .

FACELESS

Eleven years ago Marie Carter was convicted of killing her two best friends. Now she's being released from prison and Marie Carter wants retribution.

MAURA'S GAME

Maura Ryan was once the queen of the criminal underworld. The enemies from her past are about to learn that the dangerous lady is back and she's as lethal as ever . . .

THE KNOW

When her eleven-year-old daughter Kira disappears, Joanie Brewer's darkest fears are realised, and her obsession to uncover the truth threatens to destroy her entire family.

THE GRAFT

Nick Leary couldn't say what kept him awake that night. When he heard footsteps downstairs, his instinct was to fight. But what happened was the start of something he could not stop . . .

THE TAKE

Families should stick together, but behind closed doors, jealousy and betrayal fester. For the Jacksons, loyalty cannot win out. In their world everyone is on the take.

CLOSE

Patrick Brodie and Lily Diamond are determined their children will have everything they didn't. But when the unthinkable happens, Lily is left on her own in a world where you can trust no one and where your sins will find you out . . .

FACES

Danny Cadogan's ruthlessness doesn't stop at his front door. He rules his wife Mary and his children, with an iron will – and his fists. But for a Face at the top of his game, there's only one way to go. Down . . .

THE BUSINESS

When Mary Dooley's husband is killed, she watches her daughter Imelda's life spiral into a vicious cycle of drugs and prostitution, whilst her adored grandchildren fight for survival – against the odds.

HARD GIRLS

When a prostitute's body is found lifeless, mutilated and brutally raped, DCI Annie Carr and retired DCI Kate Burrows are determined to put the killer behind bars. But the killer is just warming up . . .

THE FAMILY

Phillip Murphy loves his wife Christine with a vengeance. To Phillip, family is everything. But he has rules, and he expects loyalty. Once you're in the family, you're in it for life.

THE FAITHLESS

To the outside world, Cynthia Tailor is someone to envy. But behind closed doors, her family see her for the cruel woman she really is . . . and, for her children, the pain she causes them will stay with them for ever.

THE LIFE

Lena Bailey is desperate to shield her daughter Tania from the Life. But when you're married to one of the East End's most powerful gangsters, protecting your young isn't so easy.

THRILLING.
COMPULSIVE.
DANGEROUS.
THE NEW NOVEL FROM
THE NO. 1 BESTSELLER
MARTINA
COLE
REVENGE